Engaged Emancipation

Cover illustration. Vasiṣṭha kneels in front of his hermit cave on a skin with water vessels and a text beside him struck with awe as he is approached by Śiva and Pārvatī. Attributed to Kesu Das. Library folio 230r.

Hindu Tradition Series

The Hindu Tradition Series aims to bring together books of the highest academic standard that critically interrogate Hindu tradition in the widest sense. Its focus is on cultural and religious history, including relevant political and social developments. The interaction with other traditions, whether originally from inside or outside the Indian subcontinent, will figure prominently among its volumes.

5

Engaged Emancipation

Mind, Morals, and Make-Believe in the *Mokṣopāya (Yogavāsiṣṭha)*

Edited by

Christopher Key Chapple

Arindam Chakrabarti

MOTILAL BANARSIDASS PUBLISHERS
PRIVATE LIMITED • DELHI

First Indian Edition : Delhi, 2017
Published in arrangement with
State University of New York Press, Albany, NY
www.sunypress.edu

ISBN: 978-81-208-4093-5

Available at
MOTILAL BANARSIDASS
41 U.A. Bungalow Road, Jawahar Nagar, Delhi 110 007
8 Mahalaxmi Chamber, 22 Bhulabhai Desai Road, Mumbai 400 026
203 Royapettah High Road, Mylapore, Chennai 600 004
236, 9th Main III Block, Jayanagar, Bengaluru 560 011
8 Camac Street, Kolkata 700 017
Ashok Rajpath, Patna 800 004
Chowk, Varanasi 221 001

Library of Congress Cataloging-in-Publication Data

Engaged Emancipation : Mind, Morals, and Make-believe in the Moksopaya (Yogavasistha)/Edited by Christopher Key Chapple and Arindam Chakrabarti.
pages cm
Includes bibliographical references and index.
ISBN : 978-81-208-4093-5
1. Moksopaya 2. Moksa 3. Hindu Philosophy. I. Chapple, Christopher Key, 1954—editor. II. Chakrabarti, Arindam, editor.
B132.M64E65 2015
181145—dc23 2014049309

Published by
Motilal Banarsidass Publishers Private Limited
www.mlbd.com • *mlbd@mlbd.com*
Printed by Replika Press Pvt. Ltd.

Contents

Foreword by the General Editor

Major developments have taken place during the last few decades in the study of the Yogavāsiṣṭha. Walter Slaje and his collaborators have shown that this texts "hides" another one, the Mokṣopāya, and have been making attempts to distinguish between the two. Beside this important historical/philological work, there is a growing interest in the contents of this unique work. The present book is a testimony of this renewed interest. The Mokṣopāya/Yogvāsiṣṭha deserves wide interest, and it is most fortunate that an Indian reprint of the present volume is now available in the Hindu Tradition Series.

Johannes Bronkhorst

Introduction

The *Mokṣopāya* or *Yogavāsiṣṭha,* a text that developed for many centuries before reaching its present form about a millennium ago, gives practical advice for living the philosophical life. This wisdom, imparted by the sage Vasiṣṭha to his young protégé Lord Rāma, defies the outward forms of seriousness. Vasiṣṭha teaches not by admonishment but through the telling of a good story—not one story, but no fewer than sixty-four interwoven tales.

In this collection, the authors explore a variety of themes in these stories. The first, and the one for which the text is most famous, is the tenuous relationship between dream and reality (*svapna/satya*). Can there be such a thing as objectivity? Can the public be trusted as holding the world in its truth? Numerous stories told by Vasiṣṭha suggest that the world of appearance can be a place of great mystery. In particular, in the story of Lavaṇa, a king comes under the spell of a court jester, lives an alternate life within a poor tribal community, regains consciousness, and then finds out that his supposed "dream" was in fact confirmed when he visited his former "imagined" realm and discovered that his alternate family was real. This raises a fascinating question. Must there be a stopping place or ultimate frame of reference in the receding frame of dreams within dreams which is supposed to be this world?

Another important discussion in the *Mokṣopāya/Yogavāsiṣṭha* centers on space (*ākāśa*). Space, in addition to the term *ākāśa,* is referred to as *nabha, vyoma, viyat, gagana, kha,* and *ambara.* In its various uses, it can refer to a gap, a hole, a slit in a physical sense. It also refers to the field of possibilities, serving as the locus of all things. According to the Sāṃkhya schematization of reality, space contains all sound and is especially related to the capacities of the human ear and the sense of hearing. As such, it is the first cosmic mutation. Space has no limit. It is eternal. It has no parts. It is subtle, colorless, and objectless. It is that which is mistaken for the world. The word *ākāśa* consists of two parts: *ā*, which indicates that which is all around, and *kāśa*, which stands for light and illumination. One translation for *ākāśa* might be the "circum-illuminator."

This leads us to a related term that finds frequent mention in conjunction with space: consciousness or *cit*. In the *Nirvāṇa Prakaraṇa*, many verses refer to the *cid-ākāśa*, the space of consciousness that Vasiṣṭha identifies with freedom. By moving through the stuff of thoughts and materiality to the space of pure consciousness, various protagonists in Vasiṣṭha's tales, including the "sage from outer space," exemplify the liberated being. This particular yogi proclaims "in truth, all this is pure void and all these are only notions that arise in the mind" (CYV 409).

Vasiṣṭha discusses the concept of the individual in interesting ways. On the one hand, he ascribes agency to individual souls (*jīva*), asserting that they create their own situations due to their will (*pauruṣa*) and their effort (*yatna*). He also claims that because of the efficacy of karma, all souls tend toward correct action or dharma. Precisely because all worldly pursuits are dream-like and fiction-like, the human soul must first come to an experience of nondualistic, mind-only metaphysics, and then, after attaining this wisdom, promote moral activism.

Given the dream-like quality of reality, and the numerous stories within stories told by Vasiṣṭha, the *Mokṣopāya/Yogavāsiṣṭha* seems to advance a theory of infinite worlds within an apparently finite physical space. The story of the two Līlās, the story of Lavaṇa, and various tales that seem to indicate that past lives overlap into our current experience suggest a plurality of worlds with various explanations. These worlds might just be an individual's mental constructions, experienced with amazing clarity. They might also be versions of the same material world, experienced from differing perspectives. Or, perhaps, they may constitute simultaneous parallel universes, an idea that might be plausible in quantum physics.

The vector of these various philosophies, and the narrative arc of the collection of stories, leads eventually to a description of Vasiṣṭha's own experience of liberation, both in his own story and in the stories that he tells of sojourners on the path. Given that his task, like that of Kṛṣna in the *Bhagavad Gītā*, is to encourage his young prince to engage in warfare, this enlightened experience cannot mean utter retreat from the world and its attendant responsibilities. Vasiṣṭha addresses the following question: How can continued embodiment and conduct of responsible social life be compatible with loss of ego and loss of a sense of the "hardness" of the world? This leads to a state of dispassion and a pacification of desire (*vairāgya/śāntarasa*). As in Abhinavagupta, tranquility constitutes the paramount aesthetic sentiment that sets one free. In a sense, the pedestrian disgust for the world that Rāma expresses at the beginning of the text ultimately leads to a state of peace that transforms his melancholy and angst into a state of spiritual equipoise.

We have grouped these essays in a manner that addresses three central themes. The first theme examines the flimsy fixity of the world, yielding a fluid approach to reality, an approach that begins to loosen Rāma from his various attachments. Matthew MacKenzie's essay addresses the core story of Rāma's dilemma, with emphasis on the centrality of the "felt body" in the philosophical quest. Through practices of Yoga, Rāma's body loses its hard distinctions between subject and object, just as Rudra sees the universe with all its component elements within his own flesh. Bruno Lo Turco's chapter examines the story of Līlā as undermining how one generally understands the reality of the world. He writes that "the confines of these worlds . . . are totally permeable," leading to an expanded sense of consciousness. Sthaneshwar Timalsina's chapter on appearance (*ābhāsa*) cites several instances from the stories that seem to indicate that the world of appearance cannot be separated from the shining truth of the ultimate reality. He points out that the term *ābhāsa* is used in two opposite senses, indicating self-luminosity and false appearance. By conjoining these meanings, one can be tricked, perhaps, into seeing that the apparent is none other than the real. As Timalsina stated at his presentation of this chapter, how can the waves not be the ocean? The last three chapters in this section address the theme of expanded subjectivity from philosophical and physical perspectives. Arindam Chakrabarti discusses the philosophical possibilities that arise when dreams are taken seriously. Garth Bregman introduces an interpretation of quantum mechanics that actively entertains the possibility that multiple worlds exist simultaneously. In his second chapter in this section, Timalsina draws parallels between the magical realisms of Borges and the *Yogavāsiṣṭha.*

The second theme taken up in this volume deals with issues of human agency. Pranati Ghosal's chapter shows the important role of human endeavor in determining the worlds that one inhabits. Free will shapes the decisions that alter one's place; Vasiṣṭha emphatically states that all persons have agency and control over their destiny, that the gods are merely a fiction. Roddam Narasimha shows how the faces of the *Yogavāsiṣṭha* reveal the power of the mind. Christopher Key Chapple's chapter on ethics and psychology demonstrates how Vasiṣṭha's didactic tales in the *Upaśama Prakaraṇa* inspire Rāma to overcome his selfish desires and take up the three virtues of knowledge, restraint, and dispassion. Menaha Ganesathasan's chapter on dreams and fiction demonstrates how various allegories in the text result in previously repugnant characters seeing the error of their ways and choosing to follow the morally correct path. Arindam Chakrabarti examines the relationship of self, will, and body.

The last theme examined in this book is embodied or living liberation, referred in the book title as engaged emancipation (*jīvanmukti*). Andrew Fort examines the strange twins of detachment and worldly action; Vasiṣṭha advocates that both be practiced simultaneously. Christopher Key Chapple's chapter in this section profiles the role of nature in the description of Vasiṣṭha's own enlightenment and revisits sections quoted by MacKenzie in the first chapter. By examining Vasiṣṭha's own body-felt experience through the practices of Yoga, the reader can sense the exuberance of nonduality.

This volume is the result of several gatherings in Hawaii, Los Angeles, and Bhubaneshwar. Rajiv Malhotra of the Infinity Foundation helped facilitate a series of lectures at the University of Hawaii (1997) and a conference at Loyola Marymount University (1999), cosponsored by the Southern California Seminar on South Asia of the Southern California Consortium for International Studies. The scholars included in this volume also met and shared their ideas and research at the Society for Asian and Comparative Philosophy Meeting in India (1999) and the South Asian Studies Conference in Los Angeles (2007).

The *Mokṣopāya/Yogavāsiṣṭha* project at the University of Halle, the recipient of a major grant from the European Union, will carry forward the critical edition and complete the English translation of this important text under the supervision of Professor Walter Slaje.

All the authors are indebted to the early scholars of this important text, including B. L. Atreya, Swami Venkatesananda, T. G. Mainkar and Vihari Lal Mitra. Ana Funes, Nicole de Picciotto, Jodi Shaw, Hunter Joslin, and Kija Manharé devoted long hours to the preparation of this book, for which we are deeply grateful. For many years, Arindam Chakrabarti heard the stories of the *Yogavāsiṣṭha* whispered late into the night in the ashram where he resided near Rishikesh. We hope that this work inspires readers to explore the

Yogavāsiṣṭha, and learn about both the real and the unreal from its fascinating, layered, and complex fables.

Christopher Key Chapple
Loyola Marymount University

Arindam Chakrabarti
University of Hawaii

Note: The *Oxford English Dictionary,* consulted by the copyeditors, now includes several words as English words that originate from the Sanskrit language. These include atman/*ātman,* brahma/*brahmā,* samsara/*saṃsāra,* sutra/*sūtra,* karma/*karma,* dharma/*dharma,* yogin/*yogin,* and so forth. Because they are now deemed to be part of the English lexicon, no diacritics or italics are used.

Abbreviations

BG	*Bhagavad Gītā*
BSBh	*Brahmasūtra*
BU	*Bṛhadāraṇyaka Upaniṣad*
CYV	*The Concise Yoga Vāsiṣṭha*
JMV	*Jīvanmuktiviveka*
LAS	*Laṅkāvatārasūtra*
MB	*Mahābhārata*
MK	*Māṇḍūkya Kārikā*
MWI	Many-Worlds Interpretation
MSA	*Mahāyānasūtrālaṅkāra*
MP	*Mārkaṇḍeya Purāṇa*
MṬ/ed.	*Mokṣopāyaṭikā*
MU	*Mokṣopāya*
NL	*Nyāyalīlāvatī*
SK	*Sāṃkhya Kārikā*
US	*Upadeśasāhasrī*
YS	*Yoga Sūtra*
YV	*Yogavāsiṣṭha*
YV/ed.	*Yogavāsiṣṭha*

I

Flimsy Fixity

Reality Shifts

1

Radical Transformation in the Yogavāsiṣṭha

A Phenomenological Interpretation

Matthew MacKenzie

> After thus contemplating the infinite consciousness for some time I suddenly realized that all this creation was within myself, my own body, just as the tree is in the seed.
>
> —*Yogavāsiṣṭha*

> My body is made of the same flesh as the world . . . [T]his flesh of my body is shared by the world, the world reflects it, encroaches upon it and it encroaches upon the world. They are in a relationship of transgression or of overlapping.
>
> —Maurice Merleau-Ponty

The *Yogavāsiṣṭha* (YV) is a text that, primarily through narrative, conveys a transformative philosophy. By transformative philosophy I mean, following John Taber, a system that is both philosophical and soteriological, the proper reception of which is meant to effect "a total transformation of consciousness, the basic relationship between knower and the things he knows."[1]

There are four criteria of a transformative philosophy: (1) experience—a higher level of consciousness which is a precondition for the intelligibility of the system; (2) praxis—a method for cultivating this higher consciousness; (3) knowledge—a body of the doctrine which constitutes the main topic of the system and articulates the experiential component; and finally (4) transformation—a dramatic and thorough rebirth resulting from this insight.[2]

The present study will take up the relations among these aspects of the *Yogavāsiṣṭha*'s transformative philosophy, particularly focusing on the relation between experience and practice.

Specifically, this chapter has three related objectives. First, I will show that the YV aims to evoke a radical transformation of, not just the prepared receiver's worldview or philosophical outlook, but her concrete lived experience, her existential orientation in and to the world. Second, I will introduce the phenomenological notion of the "horizon of interiority" in order to interpret certain yogic practices described in the text. I will call the experiences these practices evoke "expansion experiences" and outline four marks of such experiences. Third, I will show how, within the context of the YV, the expansion experience provides the ontological framework for the liberated reengagement with samsara.

Rāma's Dispassion

The overarching narrative structure of the YV is a dialogue between young prince Rāma and the great sage Vasiṣṭha, in which the latter provides liberating spiritual instruction to the former. Within this structure a dizzying array of stories, characters, and dialogues interweave and fold in on themselves; Rāma hears of worlds within worlds, dreamers dreamt, and paradoxes upon paradoxes—all the while being instructed in the right path for the attainment of liberation. However, for my purposes, it is not the mind-bending, paradoxical tales of the YV that are of primary interest, but the purpose of the instruction, namely, to bring about Rāma's liberation from samsara and his reengagement with the world. And to understand these, we must look to Rāma's condition at the beginning of the tale.

One first encounters Rāma in a state of extreme dispassion and despair, bordering on nihilism. Having recently returned from a pilgrimage, Rāma has lost his taste for the riches of the palace and for his duties as prince. As the chamberlain reports:

> Even when offered charming and pleasing objects, he looks at them with sad eyes, uninterested. He spurns the palace dancers, regarding them as tormentors! He goes through

> the motions of eating, walking, resting, bathing, and sitting like an automaton, like one who is deaf and dumb. Often he mutters to himself . . . 'What is the use of adversity?' All this is unreal. (YV I:10.8)[3]

Rāma is paralyzed by his newfound belief in the illusory nature of the world. Upon realizing that what most find to be of greatest value (i.e., wealth, power, even life itself) can only lead to suffering and ignorance upon ignorance, Rāma can no longer find the will to participate in the seemingly useless charade. And why should he? It seems that nothing is of any real, eternal value. Thus, Rāma rejects the world in disgust.

Yet despite his existential crisis, Rāma has been called upon by his father and by the great sage Viśvāmitra to defeat a hoard of demons harassing the sage in his forest retreat. But upon being called to court to be ordered to defeat the demons, Rāma instead pours forth a long discourse on the illusory nature of the world and the endless cycle of suffering. At the end of the monologue, Rāma asks, "Who are those heroes who have freed themselves from delusion? And what methods did they adopt to free themselves? If you consider that I am neither fit nor capable of understanding this, I shall fast unto death" (YV I:31). Rāma, it seems, is quite serious.

It is at this point that the first aspect of transformative philosophy must be recalled: the higher level of consciousness that is a precondition for the intelligibility of the system. Rāma's pilgrimage has led him to deep insights into the nature of reality, and these insights provide the precondition for his embarking on the path to liberation. Moreover, it is not just Rāma's philosophical insights, but his existential condition that is to be addressed by the great sage Vasiṣṭha. The change to be effected must be of Rāma's concrete lived experience, his engagement with the world.

After Rāma's eloquent if despairing monologue, the entire court, including the great sages and celestial beings, is awed by the depth of his insight. The sages immediately recognize both his insight and the particular existential situation from which it is presented. Vālmīki remarks, "Surely no one but Rāma, who was full of dispassion, could have uttered the words he gave expression to, not even the preceptor of the gods could" (YV I:32, 33). And with regards to his insight, Viśvāmitra lauds, "O Rāma, you are indeed foremost among the wise, and there is really nothing further for you to know" (YV II:1). We see, then, that Rāma's insight is identified as the truth by his great teachers, even at the beginning of his journey toward liberation. Hence, the truth of Rāma's worldview, his philosophical outlook, is not enough. The young prince's worldview must be, as Viśvāmitra says, "confirmed," and he must be taught the path to "the peace that passeth understanding" (YV II:1).

Thus the next five chapters of the YV confirm and strengthen Rāma's insights, while also teaching him to dissolve the ego, attain liberation, and reengage the world in order to fulfill his duties as prince and warrior. In order to complete his teaching, and in order that he may reengage the world, the teachings of Vasiṣṭha must effect a radical transformation of Rāma's whole being, his entire orientation in and to the world. The transformative philosophy of the YV must, therefore, go beyond the abstract, philosophical level and reach down to the core of Rāma's concrete lived experience.

We find here a mutuality between the teachings and the student in the YV. The stories and dialogues of the YV cannot themselves effect a radical transformation of the hearer (or reader). The system presented requires the receiver to be prepared—both intellectually and existentially—to receive the teachings. Indeed, Rāma himself, as part of the YV, can be viewed as the system's model receiver. Further, through presenting the model receiver, one who meets the preconditions for further instruction leading to liberation, the YV becomes more intelligible to the less than model receiver. One may trace the starting point of the student through the praxis and to the final goal, thereby coming to understand the purpose and particular character of the philosophy. However, it must be pointed out that, as a transformative philosophy, the intellectual and existential state of the model receiver is a precondition for the process of radical transformation. Again, while the YV incorporates abstract philosophical reflection and reasoning, it moves beyond that level and reaches down to radically alter the concrete experience of the prepared receiver. Hence, it is to the nature of this transformation and its effect on concrete experience that I will turn in the next section.

Concrete Lived Experience

In the first section it was argued that the teachings of the YV should be viewed as a transformative philosophy that aims to lead the prepared receiver to a radical alteration of her concrete lived experience. In this section I will articulate what is meant by concrete experience, as well as introduce the notion of the "horizon of interiority."

By lived experience I mean experience within the context of the interactions of an embodied subject with other subjects and with and in a world. Hence, this quite broad notion includes both abstract, discursive practices (such as writing philosophy) and more fundamental aspects of our being, such as sensory interaction, eating, moving, and so forth. Lived experience, then, to borrow terms from phenomenology, is just our being in and vis-à-vis the life-world. For my purposes, I shall focus attention on the concrete end of the abstract-concrete continuum, the further exploration of which will follow.

The notion of lived experience used here is not intended to presuppose a particular metaphysical status for the subject or the subject's world. The phenomenological description of lived experience and of the life-world at this level cannot tell us about the ultimate existence of the self or the world. This is important because, as we have seen, the YV presents the view that the world and the particular self are ultimately unreal. Yet, like Śaṅkara's version of the Advaita Vedānta, the YV allows for the description and elucidation of the structures of illusory, samsaric experience. Thus, in the context of the YV, the notion of lived experience retains its value but must always be understood as samsaric experience. In the YV view, we are not only engaged with the world, but those who are not liberated are also entangled in and deluded by the (illusory) world. Indeed, our ignorance is not merely conceptual or philosophical—that is, simply having the false belief that the world is real—but reaches down and constitutes even the most prereflective, concrete aspects of our being-in-the-world. Therefore, it is due to the depths of ignorance elucidated by the YV system that we must examine concrete experience and its radical transformation in attaining *mokṣa*.

What, then, are the aspects of the concrete lived experience with which we are concerned? As mentioned above, the concrete end of our lived experience includes the prereflective, the nondiscursive, the sensory, and the bodily. One's perceptual horizon, for example, in part constitutes one's concrete lived experience. The perceptual horizon includes one's present visual field and also involves the range of possible perception. That humans are only able to perceive certain parts of the spectrum, or can only hear a certain range of sounds, is part of the deep structure of lived experience.

In addition, as embodied subjects our motility structures our being in the world—even if, as the YV contends, we are in truth radically separate from our bodies. Our bodily interactions with the world are integral to our ability to individuate and understand the objects with which we are presented in the world; the kinesthetic horizon, along with the perceptual horizon, allows us to create a topology of the life-world. Furthermore, it is in great part through our bodies that we come to understand, in a very concrete way, the otherness of the world. The experience of weight, resistance, and solidity, the very hardness of the world, is first and foremost experienced through the body. Indeed, the resistance, the hardness of the world to us, provides the ground for the experience of the world existing over and above (or over and against) the subject.

Next, the notion of concrete lived experience includes the body-subject, that is, the experience of being a subject interacting with the world in and through a body. We do not simply have bodies like we have cups and books and the like; our bodies are, as Maurice Merleau-Ponty put it, "the vehicle of our being in the world."[4] Further, the notion of the body-subject includes the notion of the felt-body, which is what our bodies feel like, as it were, from the inside. But more than that, having a body is, for a living creature, "to be intervolved in a definite environment, to identify oneself with certain projects and to be continually committed to them."[5]

At the level of concrete experience we are, through the fact of our embodiment and the projects with which we identify, always already caught up in the world. Moreover, the kinds of projects to which the subject is committed are extremely varied. The notion of a project involves purposive actions like walking across the room, reaching for an object, and so on, as well as more refined and learned behavior like driving or typing. As subject-bodies, then, we are intervolved with the environment or life-world at multiple levels of being, from the most basic physical projects to the most abstract.

Finally, the phenomenological structure of our experience can be described in terms of the subject-object, inner-outer distinctions. The relations between these phenomenological structures are varied and complex. However, in this context I will only treat them in broad outline. We may say that the subjective pole of experience is the locus of that experience; it is the point of view around which our experience of the life-world is centered. The subject pole is the site of our perceptions, thoughts, and desires. Here we also find that the subject is fundamentally tied to the "inner." By the "inner" I mean the experience of our own private thoughts and sensations, including the felt-body. (As Merleau-Ponty puts it, "I am always on the same side of my body."[6]) In contrast, the object pole of our experience is the world with which we are confronted with tables, chairs, and so forth. The object pole is that which is external to us, the outer. The outer, then, is the objective order in which we act and on which we have a point of view. We have now the general view of the subject with its interiority confronting or being intervolved with a world of objects (and other subjects) that are experienced as exterior or outer. This is, of course, an extremely simplistic sketch of a complex set of phenomenological structures, but it provides sufficient background for the elucidation of the notion of the horizon of interiority.

As has been shown in our brief sketch of certain features of concrete lived experience, the subject, at the level of appearances at least, is embedded in and involved with the world on several levels simultaneously. Further, the outer world, the objective order, is both what we act in and what we act on in the various projects to which we are committed. It is this relation between subject and world, in part through the body, which Merleau-Ponty meant by our being "intervolved" with the world. Moreover, it is in exploring this notion of intervolvement that the horizon of interiority becomes important. For, while we have asserted that the inner-outer distinction is a phenomenological structure of our experience, the relation between poles cannot be understood in terms of a radical break. Although the inner is the realm of one's private thoughts and feelings as well as the felt-body, the notion of the interior can be expanded even to include other objects. In other words, we may push the inner along its line of continuum toward the outer, and it is this intermediate range that I term the horizon of interiority.

Three notions help us to understand the expansion of interiority: habituation, intimacy, and control. Through our various projects in the world we come into contact with a wide range of objects experienced as other than us; the objects transcend our subjectivity and are certainly not interior to us. However, through the course of being intervolved with certain objects and environments, we become habituated to them. In the case of basic objects, we may think of the painter's brush, the gardener's spade, or the blind person's cane. We become habituated to the use and manipulation of these tools, and, in virtue of their application in our projects, they become extensions of our subjectivity. "The blind man's stick," Merleau-Ponty observes, "has ceased to be an object for him, and is no longer perceived for itself; its point has become an area of sensitivity, extending the scope and active radius of touch, and providing a parallel to sight."[7]

In the case of environments, we become habituated to the interaction with and navigation through them; one need look no further than one's home or neighborhood for an example of this level of habituation. Through habituation one builds a sense of rapport with the outer, to the point that its otherness becomes less apparent. In other words, the otherness of the world is mediated through habituation. This habituation to certain parts or features of the world, in turn, leads to the development of intimacy.

Our rapport with objects and our habituation to their use (or look, feel, etc.) brings them "closer to us." If we may exploit this ordinary expression, the objects with which we are intimately familiar are closer to us in a field of interiority, with its accompanying horizon. The spatial metaphor reflects the level of intimacy, the depth of association with our own subjectivity. As a rather mundane example of such an intimately familiar object, which our horizon of interiority has expanded to include, take a trusty pair of eyeglasses. This object can be understood phenomenologically as an extension of one's bodily perceptual being in the world. The intimacy of one's eyeglasses arises, then, from the fact that they are involved directly or indirectly in a great number of our projects and because they extend something so fundamental to our concrete being in the world.

Further, it is important to recognize the personalized character of objects within our horizon of interiority. The glasses are my glasses, and not just because I bought them and they have the proper prescription. I invest them with a significance, perhaps through aesthetic considerations, and others associate them with me. The frames of my glasses might have been my father's, or might, within my cultural milieu, represent education or sophistication. And with regard to places, the layers of significance may increase greatly. Furthermore, objects and places within my horizon of interiority are invested with significance on a variety of levels. One's childhood home, for instance, may be almost disconcertingly intimate. Indeed, the process of habituation leading to intimacy lays bare how the notion of the horizon of interiority is associated with rootedness, place, and being at home in the world.

Last, the notion of control has a complex relation to the horizon of interiority. At a fundamental level the ability to control parts of the environment, to some extent, undergirds the process of habituation and the development of intimacy. To be able to control a tool is a precondition for the possibility of it coming within one's horizon of interiority as a tool. More generally, one's intervolvement with the world rests on one's ability to cope with and to some extent control the environment through one's projects. Moreover, on the level of significance, the horizon of interiority in its connection to the sense of at-homeness is in turn connected to safety, predictability, and control.

The intrusion into the life-world of forces beyond one's expectation or control can reinstate the otherness of the world beyond the immediate, inward subjectivity. Yet, these intrusions occur with great frequency, making any simple association of interiority with control somewhat problematic.

Let me, then, sum up the notion of the horizon of interiority. The horizon of interiority demarcates a space within the larger phenomenological field in which our projects are carried out. Through becoming habituated to parts or features of our life-world (from objects to places to other subjects) we associate them closely with our own subjectivity; that is, we become intimate with them. This may occur on several levels, for instance, kinesthetic, emotional, or symbolic. Parts of the life-world, one could say, become to some degree parts of us. The horizon of interiority then mediates the otherness of the world (its resistance, its hardness and intractability) by bringing certain features or parts of the world closer to subjectivity by way of intervolvement and the bestowal of meaning.

All well and good, but, one might ask, what does any of this have to do with young prince Rāma? Recall that we are out to understand how the teachings of the YV are able to radically transform Rāma. I am claiming that Rāma is transformed down to the level of his concrete lived experience, his most basic experience of the world. Thus, Rāma comes, not just to know, but to experience the world as an illusion. And as I will discuss in detail below, it is through certain forms of yogic practice that one is able to change one's most basic experience of the world. Furthermore, I am proposing the notion of the horizon of interiority as a tool for understanding the connection between these yogic practices and concrete lived experience. Hence, with the notions of concrete lived experience and the horizon of interiority in place, we may again return to the YV and the path of Rāma's liberation.

The Transformation

So far I have argued that one can interpret the YV as the presentation of a transformative philosophy, a philosophy that radically alters not only one's worldview, but also one's concrete experience. I have turned to Western phenomenology in order to spell out certain features of concrete lived experience, the most important of which in this context is the notion of the horizon of interiority. In this section

I shall attempt to put the insights from the first two sections to work in order to give a phenomenological interpretation of what I term "expansion experiences." These experiences are evoked through yogic practices and are fundamental to Rāma's liberation and reengagement with the world. They constitute the praxis through which the radical transformation of Rāma's being is affected.

Such a radical transformation of one's existential orientation to the world requires that even the deepest ontic structures are to be altered or, rather, revealed to be false. Not just our view of the world, but our very being in the world must be transformed. Hence, the system presented in the YV must work on several levels of being concurrently, allowing the student an experience of reality that destroys old structures. On the one hand, at the more abstract level, the teachings of the YV must attack our usual metaphysical presuppositions. On the other hand, the teachings of the YV must allow the student to experience reality in a way that explodes her most fundamental ontic structures.

At the abstract, philosophical level, as Wendy Doniger points out, the YV wreaks havoc on some of our most deeply held philosophical distinctions.[8] The tales of the YV continually undercut our assumptions about the nature of reality, turning our usual sense of the real inside out. Indeed, fundamental to Doniger's reading of the text is that it is an attack on hard distinctions. The text problematizes the lines between dreaming and waking, the real and the unreal, the dreamer and the dream, the self and the other. In the tales of the YV, all of our supposedly hard distinctions are undercut, softened until they eventually disappear. Vasiṣṭha teaches Rāma: "Birth, death, *Māyā*, delusion, . . . bondage, liberation, good and evil, knowledge and ignorance, embodied and disembodied states, . . . you and I and the other, truth and falsehood, . . . all these are pure consciousness" (YV II:18). The result, particularly for the uninitiated, is a kind of metaphysical vertigo in which all sense of reality is lost. Yet, there is a method to the madness. As Vasiṣṭha remarks to Rāma, "Such illustrations have been used in this scripture with a definite purpose and a limited intention. They are not to be taken literally, nor is their significance to be stretched beyond the intention . . . Parables have only one purpose: to enable the listener to arrive at the truth" (YV II:18–19). What is the truth to be conveyed through the stories? First, the world is an illusion. Second, the Self (atman) and Reality (Brahman) are one. And yet, as we have seen, truth here is to be understood as direct experience of the truth. The student must not only have her intellectual distinctions softened, but also experience the world as an illusion, without the hard lines between self and other, inner and outer. The reality of the world must be experienced as soft and pliable.

Yet, as has been pointed out, Rāma already knows that the world is illusory, and this insight has given rise to a deep, paralyzing dispassion. What then reaches down to bring about the direct, concrete experience of the truth leading to reengagement with the world? What is it that explodes the ontic structure of ignorance? It is the realization of the unity of the Self and Reality while remaining in samsara that allows Rāma to reengage the world. Moreover this realization affects every level of his being, from the spiritual to the most concrete, prereflective structures of his being in the world. At the ultimate level, Rāma realizes that the existence of his true Self just *is* the existence of Brahman. Creation, from the ultimate point of view, is merely a division in consciousness. And while he also knows that this has been true all along, the experience of unity is of a merging of existences—Rāma's being merges with the absolute.

At the phenomenological level, that of his concrete lived experience, Rāma experiences an existential opening to the world. The world is no longer the other which stands over against his subjectivity. The realization of the ultimate unity of Self and Reality, then, allows the expansion of Rāma's horizon of interiority to include the entire world. His being has opened to the world, and he experiences the world as not fundamentally separate from himself. We thus have a picture of transformation in which realization at the ultimate level of being grounds a radical transformation of another, more limited level of being.

I still have not answered how the YV evokes this radical transformation in Rāma's being. The direct experience of the unity of Self and Brahman is accomplished through the yogic practices described in the text. Through concentration on the inner reaches of the self, and through the manipulation of *prāṇa* (life-force), the practitioner is able to go beyond the ontic structures that limit his samsaric being in the world. In particular, through practice, one may radically transcend the inner-outer distinction, which divides the self from the world. Through the cultivation of these yogic practices, then, Rāma can achieve the kind of expansion of interiority required for his liberated reengagement with samsara. Here an examination of two accounts of experiences arising from yogic practice will help to flesh out the notion of the expansion of interiority.

The World within the Rock

In this section Vasiṣṭha recounts to Rāma two expansion experiences (YV V:2.59–92). First, we encounter Rudra, who stood observing the division in consciousness known as the creation: "In a moment he swallowed the division as it were. Then Rudra stood alone, one with the space as if he himself were space. In a few minutes, he became as light as a cloud and his size was fast shrinking. I saw . . . that he had become smaller than an atom. In a moment he had become invisible. He had become supreme peace. He had become one with the absolute *Brahman*" (YV V:2.86). Here we find three important elements. First, Rudra, while contemplating the nature of the world in relation to consciousness, is able to transgress the inner-outer limit. We may look at the expression "swallowed the division" in at least two ways. On one hand, creation just is the division. Hence Rudra swallows the entire universe during his contemplation. The universe is encompassed by Rudra's consciousness, the swallowing being, on my reading, a metaphor for the realization that the existence of the phenomenal world is not different from the existence of the self. On the other hand, the division that is creation is a (false) division of consciousness. The illusion of the universe arises from the subject-object distinction. The YV, in several places, teaches that, through a process of objectification of aspects of consciousness, the world becomes falsely divided into subject and object. Thus, we may also see swallowing of the division as the radical dissolution or transgression of the inner-outer, subject-object structure of samsaric being. These two readings, we will see, complement one another.

The second important element of this account arises from the second line. Having swallowed or internalized the universe, Rudra actually experienced what it was like to be the creation. He became one with space as if he himself were space. Rudra's expansion experience is more than the realization that the universe is an illusory projection of pure consciousness. The interiorizing of the creation allowed Rudra to experience the creation as if he himself were space. The subject is no longer merely presented with the world, illusory or not. Now the subject pervades the world to such an extent that the structures of the creation, like space, are also the structures of the subject's being. So just as one experiences one's body from the inside (the felt-body), Rudra is able to the experience the creation from the inside (the felt-universe).

The third important element to be gleaned from this passage is the interrelation between the ultimate, metaphysical level and the phenomenological level. The contemplation of creation by Rudra leads him to the realization that ultimately both the individual self and the world are merely divisions in Brahman. Thus, the swallowing of the world is the realization of the ultimate falsity of the division. Yet, at the level of Rudra's individual being, the experience described allows him to break out of the ontic structures which falsely limit him and to experience the world from the world's point of view. Hence, the ultimate need not negate the phenomenological level, but may only restructure it. The expansion experience, then, operates on more than one level simultaneously. It should also be pointed out, however, that in the case of Rudra, the phenomenological level is eventually negated, and he becomes one with the absolute Brahman.

The second expansion experience recounted to Rāma is Vasiṣṭha's own. Through the cultivation of a yogic practice connected to the elements of the universe (earth, air, water, wind, etc.), Vasiṣṭha is able to expand his horizon of interiority to include the world. Yet, unlike Rudra, Vasiṣṭha's yogic exercise allows him to become one with each element in turn, experiencing the creation through that element. His practice begins with the contemplation of consciousness leading to the expansion of interiority. As Vasiṣṭha recounts to Rāma:

> After thus contemplating the infinite consciousness for some time I suddenly realized that all this creation was within myself, my own body, just as the tree is in the seed. When one closes his eyes to sleep, he enters into an inner world created by his inner vision; when sleep comes to an end, one wakes up and his vision enters the world of one's waking state. In the same way creation is experienced by one's entering into it with his own heart. (YV V:2.87)

Once the sage has entered into the creation, he experiences it from the perspective of space.

> When I experienced space, I knew what earth was. I became earth. In that earth I experienced the existence of countless universes, without ever abandoning the awareness that I am the infinite consciousness. I saw the most amazing earthly phenomena and events within that earth (within me). In fact, I experienced even the farmer ploughing me (the earth), and I experienced the burning heat of the sun and the cool flow of rainwater. I became the fearful space in which the Lokāloka Mountains (the boundaries of the

> world) exist, and I explored the actions and movements of countless beings . . . I experienced the weeping and wailing of those who had lost their dear and near ones, here I experienced the joy of dancing girls; there were cries of the hungry, the joy of the affluent, drought and earthquake, war and destruction, beautiful birds and lakes, suffering worms, flourishing forests, meditating sages. O Rāma, in this earth-body of mine all these took place. (YV V:2.87, 88)

In this rich account of Vasiṣṭha's experience we find four important aspects. First, as with Rudra, the creation is internalized by Vasiṣṭha through contemplation. Vasiṣṭha's horizon of interiority is coextensive with the entire creation. His consciousness pervades the world, and it is only a part of him. Second, while he merges with creation, Vasiṣṭha does not simply become further immersed in the illusion of samsara. Indeed, in the second sentence we find that he merges with the world "without ever abandoning the awareness that [he is] the infinite consciousness." Hence, as with Rudra's experience, the expansion of interiority at the phenomenological level is grounded in the realization of ultimate unity. The ultimate unity grounds the phenomenological expansion. The third aspect found in this account is the vicarious knowledge gained through the expansion experience. Vasiṣṭha not only realizes that he is not different from the earth, but he also learns what it is to be earth. Just as Rudra felt as if he were space, so Vasiṣṭha, through yogic practice, learns what it is to be creation from the point of view of each of its elements. Yet, Vasiṣṭha's experience exceeds Rudra's in an important respect. Vasiṣṭha's vicarious knowledge leads him to experience not just the structures of the world like space, but also to experience the joys and sorrows, pleasures and pains of the earth and its creatures. Hence, the fourth aspect of this experience, which is not present in Rudra's expansion, is empathy. The existential opening achieved by Vasiṣṭha through his yoga allows him to truly empathize with the joy and suffering of the entire creation, while remaining always rooted in the awareness of its illusory nature. Moreover, it is this fourth aspect that is of utmost importance for Rāma's reengagement.

However, before turning to the subject of liberated engagement with samsara, we should examine an interesting question asked by Rāma. Upon hearing the incredible account of Vasiṣṭha's various expansion experiences, Rāma asks, "When you were engaged in the contemplation of the earth (*pārthiva-dhāraṇā*), was the earth real or only mental?" (YV V:2.88).

The question cuts to the heart of the matter. In the expansion experience, what is it that is really experienced? Does the yogic practitioner simply imagine that she is the world and can empathize with it? Has the inner-outer distinction been dissolved at the level of one's fundamental being, or is the expansion experience just phenomenological delusion? To Rāma's question Vasiṣṭha responds: "Truly, this was mental and I had myself become the earth; equally truly, this was not mental nor did I actually become the earth. Apart from the mind, there is no earth. Whether you consider something as real or unreal it is but mental action. I am but pure infinite consciousness; . . . [I]t is the earth, it is the world, it is the creator; this world appears in space . . . just as a fancied city exists in the sky" (YV V:2.88, 89). Vasiṣṭha's answer, then, is both and neither. While Rāma's puzzlement seems perfectly reasonable to us, it is in this context the wrong question. For, in the YV system, the world is nothing more than an emanation from pure consciousness. Hence, ultimately, there can be no distinction between what is real and what is "only" mental. Yet, this metaphysical unity is at a deeper level than that of the samsaric ego. Hence, Vasiṣṭha did in fact experience the world, the only world to be experienced at all. In the YV, the expansion experience is neither a mere trick of imagination which leaves the fundamental structures of one's being intact, nor an escape from the realm of consciousness into a separate world. The "only mental" is more real than the "real earth." This doubt of Rāma's having been dispelled, we can now turn to the subject of reengagement.

The Reengagement

In the last section I identified four aspects of the expansion of interiority: (1) the world is brought within the horizon of interiority; (2) the existential opening is grounded in the ultimate unity of Self and Reality; (3) the experience leads to vicarious knowledge of creation; and (4) the vicarious knowledge leads to a deep empathy with all of creation. In this section I will examine how the expansion of interiority allows Rāma to overcome his paralyzing dispassion and reengage with the world.

As we have seen, the horizon of interiority mediates the otherness of the world, providing the subject with a certain feeling of intimacy and control over her environment. The life-world (the samsaric plane in the YV) is imbued with meaning and so is less radically other. The subject achieves a certain rootedness and is more or less at home in the world. And yet, the division between subject and object remains. Hence, in the YV view, the subject is still ignorant and entangled in the cycle of birth and death. Indeed, the mediation of the otherness of the world that imbues it with meaning actually contributes to the maintenance of ignorance, of samsara. First, by imbuing the world with meaning and by associating it with oneself, the ignorant person takes the world to be real. Second, the limited self, the ego, believes that it can possess a certain amount of this real world.

However, if, like Rāma, one realizes the illusory, changing nature of the world, then the experience of creation is radically altered. What once seemed meaningful and real becomes delusion and suffering. Moreover, the world that one had become at home in is once again set over and against the subject, this time as a terrible delusion. As we see in the case of Rāma, the initial reaction is an utter rejection of samsara as false, evil, and other. At this stage, there can be no motivation to be engaged with the world. The best course, it seems, is to simply wither and die.

Yet, through the practice of yoga on the path to liberation, one's orientation toward the creation again changes. Rāma's attitude of rejection is realized to be incomplete. For, if the world is mere illusion, what is to be rejected?

To view saṃsara as the enemy is still to objectify it, to give it undue reality. If one remains identified with the limited ego, but rejects the world, the division of subject and object only increases. Hence, the expansion experience serves to dissolve even this division. Grounded in the realization that ultimately the world and the ego are unreal, the false boundaries of the ego are dissolved and a merging with creation occurs. The practitioner's concrete lived experience expands to include creation, yet all the while she realizes its ultimate unreality.

The expansion experience radically transforms the subject and her existence in and toward the world. The creation is neither rejected nor reified. Instead the transformed person is existentially open to creation while understanding its illusoriness. She is engaged, but not bound. The world becomes radically her world, but in a double sense of the genitive. First, at the existential level, the process of interiorizing and empathizing with all of creation explodes the ontic structures that close off the subject from the creation. Once a person has transgressed the limits of the ego and felt the joys and sorrows of the earth, even the worms, she can no longer feel the world as radically other. Intimacy is expanded until one is truly at home in creation. The world that was once hard and alien has softened and become pliable.

However, the experience of the world as her world cannot be the feeling of possessing it, for possession is a function of the limited ego, which desires to possess and control that which is other. But for the liberated person, there is nothing to possess and no one to possess it. This is the balance of dispassion and intimacy that allows the living liberated (*jīvanmukta*) to engage with the world without being ensnared or entangled by it. Further, this balance, in the YV system, is only possible through the understanding of the second sense of the genitive. At the ultimate level, the world is her world because the Self and Brahman are one. Hence, she is both creator and creation. The metaphysical underpinning allows the liberated person to continue to exist in the world, never forgetting its illusory nature.

Rāma, then, through his practice of yoga and his eventual liberation, is able to overcome his paralyzing rejection of the world and accept his role in it. The world and the duties of state are to be embraced without the assumption that they are ultimately real. As Vasiṣṭha says of the liberated:

> They were free from psychological predisposition and hence they did not seek nor reject either life or death. They remained unshaken in their direct experience . . . Yet, they roamed the forests, islands and cities . . . They conquered their enemies and they ruled as emperors. They engaged themselves in diverse activities in accordance with scriptural injunctions as they realized that such was appropriate conduct . . . They even engaged themselves in great wars. They retained their equanimity . . . [They were] utterly free from delusion, from egoistic notion (I do this) and from desire for achievement or the rewards of their actions. They did not indulge in vain exultation when they defeated their enemies nor did they give way to despair and grief when they were defeated. They were engaged in natural activities, allowing all actions to proceed from them non-volitionally. (YV VIa:12–13)

Moreover, the actions of the *jīvanmukta* are repeatedly described as free and spontaneous—the source of the action is not the ego, with its cravings and aversions, but pure consciousness. Hence, according to the text, one who rests in the self, that is acts from beyond the ego, does not accrue karma. The expansion of interiority to include the world, then, allows the *jīvanmukta* to act unfettered by the constraints of egotistical drives and the false separation of self and world, inner and outer. The existential opening to creation, grounded in the realization of the ultimate unity of atman and Brahman, provides the ontological framework for Rāma's liberated reengagement.

Conclusion

By a somewhat indirect route through phenomenology, we seem to have gained some insight into Rāma's liberation and reengagement. Rāma begins the YV with an insight into the nature of samsara. He finds that the world is an illusion, that what is often valued in the world leads only to suffering, and he wants no part of it. But his rejection of the world is an incomplete response. He understands, on an abstract level, the idea that the world is illusory. However, his experience of the world, his existential orientation, is still limited. The structure of his being-in-the-world, from which he interprets and acts in the world, is still one of subject and object. In order for Rāma to be truly free, he can neither reify nor reject (itself a reification) the world. He must embrace it, but from a radically different existential orientation. That orientation is one in which the world is neither seen nor experienced as other. Instead, based on the realization of the ultimate unity of atman and Brahman, Rāma must embrace the world and his dharma. This is achieved in part through yogic practices that lead to expansion experiences—the expansion of the horizon of interiority leading to empathic union with creation. Further, this union restructures Rāma's being-in-the-world by dissolving the illusory division between subject and object, leaving him free of the divisive ego that closes him off from creation. And it is within this radical new mode of being that Rāma can become an enlightened hero and ruler.

Notes

1. John Taber, *Transformative Philosophy: A Study of Śankara, Fichte, and Heidegger* (Honolulu: University of Hawaii Press, 1983), 2.

2. Ibid., 95.

3. All quotations are taken from Swami Venkatesananda, *The Concise Yogavāsiṣṭha* (Albany: State University of New York Press, 1984).

4. Maurice Merleau-Ponty, *The Phenomenology of Perception*, trans. Colin Smith (London: Routledge Press, 1962), 151.

5. Ibid.

6. Maurice Merleau-Ponty, *The Visible and the Invisible,* trans. A. Lingis (Evanston, IL: Northwestern University Press, 1968), 148.

7. Merleau-Ponty, *Phenomenology,* 143.

8. Wendy Doniger-O'Flaherty, *Dreams, Illusions, and Other Realities* (Chicago: University of Chicago Press, 1984), 3–13.

2

Ākāśa and Jīva in the Story of Līlā

Bruno Lo Turco

The *Līlopākhyāna* (Story of Līlā), or *Maṇḍapākhyāna* (Tale of the Pavilion), the longest tale of all those included in the *Yogavāsiṣṭha* (YV) (ed. III:15–68) or *Mokṣopāya* (MU),[1] is very interesting as regards its treatment of the various states of consciousness and levels of existence. This story is a rather complex one. According to what is stated, it is being told first and foremost so that the listener should abandon the notion of the world. As Vasiṣṭha says:

> atredaṃ maṇḍapākhyānaṃ śṛṇu śravaṇabhūṣaṇam |
> niḥsandehaṃ[2] yathāiṣo 'rthaś citte viśrāntim eti te[3] ||
>
> In this connection, listen to this Tale of the Pavilion, ear ornament, so that this meaning [of the word 'world'] ceases in your mind.
> (MU III:15.17)

According to Rāma this story has the power to increase right understanding (*sadbodha*):

> sadbodhavṛddhaye brahman samāsena vadāśu me |
> maṇḍapākhyānam akhilaṃ yena bodho vivardhate ||
>
> Tell me at once, O Brahmin, concisely, so that my right understanding is increased, the whole Tale of the Pavilion,

Figure 1. A vision of Queen Līlā's past life floats in a swirl of blue clouds above a village. Attributed to Haribans. Library folio 47r. © The Trustees of the Chester Beatty Library, Dublin.

> the one through which understanding increases.
> (MU III:15.18)

Hence, the notion of the world is the opposite of right understanding. But what is right understanding with regard to the world? The reply of the MU is, as is repeated countless times, that there is not any world. In order to clarify what the nature of the world is, the work resorts to metaphors that express an impalpability taken to the extreme. Let us take, for example, something evanescent like a cloud. Then let us take its imaginary counterpart, in other words, an imagined cloud. While we can attribute some degree of reality to the former, the latter certainly has no reality whatsoever. The relation between these two is useful for illustrating the relation between space and the world. While space has a certain degree of reality, the same cannot be said of the world. The world of shared experience is even more impalpable than space; it is even more intangible than an imaginary world:

> idaṃ tv acetyacinmātraṃ bhānor[4] bhānaṃ nabhaḥ prati |
> tathā sūkṣmaṃ yathā meghaṃ prati saṅkalpavāridaḥ ||
> yathā svapnapuraṃ svacchaṃ jāgratpuravaraṃ[5] prati |
> tathā jagad idaṃ svacchaṃ saṅkalpitajagat prati ||
>
> This [world], manifestation of splendour, which is nothing but consciousness devoid of objects, in comparison to space is as subtle as an imaginary cloud in comparison to a [real] cloud.
>
> As a dreamed city is impalpable in comparison to a big city seen in the wakeful state, so this world is impalpable in comparison to an imaginary world.
> (MU III:15.11–12)

But how can we know this? The argument adopted is that any perception of concreteness (*piṇḍagraha*) is logically impossible. In other words, we never have a real perception of matter, of what is supposed to be the real counterpart of what is manifested to us as knowledge. In fact, we cannot take a step outside the circle of knowledge, in order to observe, so to speak, the process from the outside, to observe a subject who, through knowledge, grasps the knowable or in order to verify the reality of the knowable. This alleged reality is something that no one has ever seen, exactly like the horn of a hare. The object of knowledge is not an alleged concrete entity beyond knowledge.

The object of knowledge is knowledge itself. This argument probably comes to the MU from the *Vijñānavāda*, which maintains that an object and its cognition are not different, because they are never perceived separately.

Objectivity, therefore, is a pure impression, a subjective construct, a mirage; all the magnificence of the world is merely a projection in space. The magnificence that is manifested to us is not the reflection in the mirror of consciousness of alleged external entities, but it is the luminous aura that accompanies that very consciousness:

> piṇḍagrāhaḥ[6] sad ity asmin vijñānākāśarūpiṇi |
> marunadyāṃ jalam iva na sambhavati kutracit ||
> svapnādriṇeva jagatā tulādeśau[7] na kaucana |
> pūritau kalanonmuktā dṛśyaśrīr vyoma kevalam ||
>
> In this [world], which has the nature of the space of consciousness, it is never possible to find the perception of a concrete body, namely the perception that one has when one thinks that something exists, as water in a desert.
>
> Neither of the scale-pans is shifted by the world, as [it would not be shifted] by a dreamed mountain; the glory of all is perceivable, freed from the projective activity, is pure space. (MU III:15.7, 9)

Precisely because there is nothing outside consciousness, the world is not founded on anything; it is devoid of a material basis. In other words, it has no external referent. If we admit that the world is the fruit of a projection, there is nothing on which it is projected, no real basis, whatever it might be. The world is not like a fresco, or rather, the representation of something unreal on a material base. Its basis is consciousness. The world is naturally inherent in consciousness, and it cannot be thought of separately from this:

> taikṣṇyaṃ yathā maricabījakaṇe sthitaṃ svaṃ
> stambhe 'tha vā racitaputrakajālam[8] antaḥ |
> dṛśyaṃ tv ananyad idam evam aje 'sti śāntaṃ
> kasyāsti bandhanavimokṣadṛśaḥ[9] kutaḥ kāḥ ||
>
> As spiciness is inherent in peppercorns or, rather, as there is a multitude of carved figures on a pillar, so the perceiv-

> able, which is one, quiescent, resides in the not-born; [thus] what is the use of the doctrines about the liberation from the bond?
> (MU III:20.53)

If the world could be placed on a scale pan, its weight would not be counterbalanced by the weight of an atom placed on the other scale pan:

> jagad eva mahākāśaṃ cidākāśam abhittimat[10] |
> tad deśasyāṇumātrasya tulāyāś cāprapūrakam[11] ||

> The world, which is the universal space, the space of consciousness, devoid of supports, cannot counterbalance the weight of only one atom on a scale pan.
> (MU III:15.15)

The problem of the relationship between world and consciousness, on a rougher level, can also be seen, according to the MU, from a temporal perspective. From such a point of view consciousness is imagined as something which has the capability to crystallize and melt. The liquid state corresponds to the manifestation of the universe. The universes, the eggs of Brahma, are bubbles appearing on the surface of the melted consciousness:

> mahākāśamahāmbodhau mahāśūnyatvavāriṇi[12] |
> mahāciddravabhāvotthān budbudhān[13] arbudapramān[14] ||

> In the ocean of the universal space, the water of which is the universal emptiness, [one could see] immeasurably huge bubbles appearing on the surface from the state of melting of the universal consciousness.
> (MU III:30.4)

Therefore, it is reaffirmed that the only reality is consciousness and that the world is but a state of this very consciousness.

It is almost superfluous to emphasize how much the doctrine of the nonexistence of the world which is characteristic of the MU is reminiscent of the *Vijñānavāda*. Just like the MU, the *Vijñānavāda* compares the universe either to a dream, to a mirage, to a magic illusion, to a bubble of water, or to a cloud.

svapnasambhramasaṅkalpasvānubhūtiparamparāḥ |
pramāṇāny atra mukhyāni sambodhāya pradīpavat ||

The series [of perceptions] in the individual experience of dream, illusion, imagination are here the principal means of knowledge, like lamps, for the purpose of clear comprehension.
(MU III:20.21)

This statement appears to be in complete agreement with what the *vijñānavādins* maintain: all our knowledge is made up of series of transient perceptions devoid of an objective counterpart. This is strikingly evident in the case of dreams, in which we have images separate from an alleged external reality.

This is not enough. Right understanding can be deepened. In fact,"world" and "space," are empty (*śūnya*) in the final analysis, or rather, they do not express any reality. We do not attain reality through these words. They are founded on the only true reality, which is consciousness. They come from reality, but they do not seize reality:

tasmād acetyacidrūpaṃ jagad vyomaiva kevalam |
śūnyau vyomajagacchabdau paryāyau viddhi cinmayau ||

Thus, the world, which consists in consciousness devoid of objects, is pure space; know that the words 'space' and 'world' are empty, equivalent, made of consciousness.
(MU III:15.13)

Yet again, we cannot leave the circle of consciousness. Consciousness imposes itself on us as the absolute. The MU considers the best metaphor for the absolute that of space. Just as everything dwells in space, and space receives everything without becoming exhausted and without its all-pervasive nature being diminished, so every object is manifested in the depths of consciousness.

Līlā, the protagonist of the story, is the wife of an extraordinarily virtuous king, Padma. She is very devoted to the sovereign. Her greatest wish is that he may live forever. She therefore questions the wisest Brahmans on how to attain immortality. They reply that it is impossible to attain. Not being able to prevent the king's death, Līlā determines at least to prevent his soul from abandoning their private apartment, the *maṇḍapa*. To this end she decides to propitiate her favorite divinity, Sarasvatī, who promises to grant her wish. Moreover, the goddess concedes to appear to Līlā every time she should request it. Some time later Padma dies in battle. Līlā becomes extremely depressed. However, Sarasvatī's voice reminds her of the promise that her husband would stay by her side, and his body would not decay. That very night, in solitude, Līlā evokes the goddess and asks her to lead her into her husband's presence. The queen's consciousness is thus allowed to enter her husband's new world, a world which, mysteriously, is to be found in the *maṇḍapa* itself. Padma appears to her as a young sovereign who reigns over a powerful empire. The people she used to know, and others she has never seen, also appear before her. This makes her fear that her fellow citizens, finding themselves in that kind of intermediate existence, are all dead. However, when she returns to her ordinary world, she finds everything as it was before. So Līlā asks the goddess which of the two worlds is real, and which is illusory. The goddess replies that they are both fictitious, based on reminiscences. How then from the reminiscence of one world has the other world arisen? The goddess tells a story. In a mountain village, in another world, there lived a Brahman, Vasiṣṭha, with his wife, Arundhatī. Arundhatī too had been granted the wish that her dead husband's soul should remain close to her. One day the Brahman watched a great king and his retinue pass by. This made him want to become a great sovereign too. The years passed, and the Brahman died. He remained in the residence and became a splendid king. Arundhatī also died and joined her husband in his new world. All this, says the goddess, happened eight days previously. The Brahman and his wife were Padma and Līlā in their former lives. Since Līlā does not believe the story, Sarasvatī leads her into the Brahman's world and allows her to talk with the couple's son. Then Sarasvatī reminds her of all her previous lives. Then the two of them return to the world of the king, whose name is now Vidūratha. Many decades have passed since the first vision. He now has a consort, whose name is also Līlā. The goddess and the first Līlā appear to the king in his apartment. This makes him remember his previous life as Padma. He therefore wishes to go back to being Padma. The second Līlā asks in turn a favor from the goddess: to be Vidūratha's wife again in the next life. Soon King Vidūratha is killed in battle. His soul, which has never left the *maṇḍapa*, now takes possession of Padma's body. Padma comes back to life, and when he regains consciousness he finds before him the two Līlās, with whom he will live happily for many years.

When Līlā asks what has happened to her husband:

> kva mamāmba sthito bhartā kiṃ karoty atha kīdṛśaḥ |
> samīpaṃ[15] naya māṃ tasya naikā śaknomi jīvitum |
>
> Where is my husband, O mother? What is he doing? In what state is he? Take me into his presence. I cannot live alone.
> (MU III:17.9)

While his lifeless body is lying covered with flowers in the *maṇḍapa*, the goddess Sarasvatī replies by stating one of the capital doctrines of the MU: the doctrine of the three spaces. There are three spaces: the space of universal consciousness (*cidākāśa*), the thinnest of all, that is absolutely empty; the space of the individual mind (*cittākāśa*); and the space properly called *ākāśa*:

> cittākāśaṃ cidākāśam ākaśaṃ ca tṛtīyakam |
> tebhyaḥ śūnyatamaṃ[16] viddhi cidākāśaṃ varānane ||
>
> Know the space of mind, the space of consciousness and, third, the [material] space; the space of consciousness is the emptiest of all, O you, whose face is beautiful.
> (MU III:17.10)

The whole world resides in the space of consciousness and shares its condition of void; only the space of consciousness is real in the true sense of the word. The multiplicity of subjects implicit in the concept of the "space of the individual mind," is free from substantiality:

> śūnyam evedam akhilaṃ jagat tatra vyavasthitam |
> ahaṃ tvam iti dṛśyātmanānātā caiva[17] nirvapuḥ ||
>
> This entire world, which is empty, resides in that [principle]; the multiplicity consisting in the knowable, [which implies a separation between] 'you' and 'I,' is devoid of substantiality.
> (MU III:17.11)

The world is devoid of material support; it is the fruit of the imagination (*kalpanā*); its nature exists in the light of perception (*jñaptibhā*) and is free from any concreteness:

abhittimayam evedaṃ kalpanārūpitaṃ jagat |
jñaptibhāmātrakaṃ deśatulāpūraṇavarjitam ||

This world, which is devoid of support, consisting of imagination, made only of the light of perception, cannot shift a scale-pan.
(MU III:17.12)

In the *Līlopākhyāna* the intermediate existence between death and rebirth is also described. This also constitutes a reflection on the nature of the 'space of the mind.' Līlā is, in fact, allowed to observe her husband, who in the ordinary world is lying dead in the *maṇḍapa,* in that world that is manifested to the deceased himself immediately after his death.

She discovers that a vision of a world not dissimilar from the one in which he lived unfolds in the deceased's *cittākāśa* and that it appears as solid and real as that world (cf. MU III:17.19 ff.). In this other world there appear the same customs and people that accompanied the royal couple in the previous world: the same ministers, the same scholars, the same jesters and servants. How can they all be there? Are they perhaps all dead? We soon discover in the course of the story that nothing has changed in the world where the sovereign is lying dead. On the other hand, however, the princess also observes new characters and new customs (cf. MU III:17.36 ff.).

Līlā is astounded at the concrete appearance of the other world, and she is no longer sure which is the real one (cf. MU III:18.6 ff.). However, she believes that the visions manifested to the deceased are based on his memory of his previous life:

smṛtiḥ sā Devī madbhartus tathā sphāratvam āgatā |
smṛteś ca kāraṇaṃ vedmi sargo 'yam iti niścayaḥ ||

O goddess, it is the memory of my husband which unfolded in this way; and I am certain that this world is the cause of memory.
(MU III:18.24)

But more precisely, what the story up to this point has intended to exemplify is that the world that unfolds in the deceased's *cittākāśa* is only partially based on memories of the previous world. In fact, it also seems to contain new elements that cannot be explained on the basis of memory, namely apparently random constructs. In other words, there is not a deterministic relation between the two worlds.

Nonetheless, the new world possesses its own inner consistency, so that it appears surprisingly concrete even to an outside observer such as Līlā.

Līlā acknowledges that the actual world, the world of shared experience, is already an example of an illusory world, the nature of which is the space of memory; Sarasvatī confirms that the nature of both worlds is space; they do not differ substantially:

> smṛtyākāśamayaḥ sargo yathā bhartur mamoditaḥ |
> tathaivemam ahaṃ manye sa sargo 'tra nidarśanam ||
> evam etad asatsargo bhartus te bhāti bhāsvaraḥ |
> tathāivāyam ihābhāti paśyāmy etad ahaṃ sute ||
>
> As the world of my husband manifested itself to me, made of the space of memory, so I believe that this manifests itself; in this respect that world is the example.
>
> Thus the unreal bright world of your husband appears to you, just in the same way this [world] appears here; I see that, O daughter.
> (MU III:18.26–27)

It is space that sustains the *jīva*, the individual soul, and it is also space that substantiates the memory of that soul; and what the soul projects on the basis of its reminiscences is still space:

> smṛtir ākāśarūpaiva yathā tajjas tathaiva te |
> bhartṛsargo 'nubhūto hi sa kham eva tathābale ||
> bhrāntimātrakam ākāśam eva[18] jīvasvarūpadhṛt ||
>
> As memory consists of space, so what arises for you from that [memory]; therefore your husband's world, which you have perceived, is space, O woman.
>
> It is only delusion, which is nothing but space, to support the essential nature of the individual soul.
> (MU III:18.25; 20.3cd)

Let us take, for example, Līlā's world. The goddess reveals to Līlā that what the princess considers to be the ordinary, real world is to be found in the space of a Brahmin's house. This Brahmin once decided to become a sovereign. This wish made him, in effect, become reborn as a king. The sovereign is King Padma; the wife of the Brahmin is Līlā. Padma and Līlā were thus reborn in a world contained within the space of one room. Now, however, Padma is dead and has been reborn once again in a world contained within one room. Hence, there are worlds within worlds.

This story illustrates that what we mistake for the ordinary world is unreal, since it is no different from the world that is manifested in the *cittākāśa* of a deceased person. The activity proper to the *cittākāśa* is the manifestation of worlds; these cease to arise only when the mind has achieved an unobstructed and unlimited understanding:

> bhramād asmāc cidādarśe bhramo 'yam pratibimbitaḥ |
> asatya eva cāsatyād bhavati[19] bhavabhaṅgadaḥ ||
> tasmād bhrāntimayaḥ kaḥ syāt[20] ko vā bhrāntyujjhito
> bhavet |
> sargo nirargalānantabodhān nānyad[21] vijṛmbhate ||
>
> From this delusion only this very delusion is reflected in the mirror of consciousness; from the unreal only the unreal arises, which denies phenomenic reality.
>
> Thus which [world] is made of delusion, or which is free from delusion? From a consciousness that is devoid of hindrances a world [that is supposed to be] something different [from that consciousness] does not unfold.
> (MU III:20.4–5)

The confines of these worlds, the fruit of the activity of various individual *citta*, are totally permeable. In the story Līlā is reborn in her husband's world. Hence these worlds are a collective projection, though it would seem that some subjects have a greater power to project than others.

The activity proper to consciousness, whatever the plane of reality where the consciousness arises, consists in the projection of a fictitious objectivity. This projection is only partially based on the subject's reminiscences. The essence of the activity of projecting is the unfolding of the seeds of the *vāsanās*[22] with which the soul is imbued. Just as the essence of memory is space, so space is the essence of the projected worlds, the basis of what we mistake for objectivity. The universe is inherent in consciousness. According to the MU:

asatyaiveyam ābhāti satyeva ghanasargatā |
tasyāsatyāvabhāsasya cidvyomnaḥ kośakoṭare ||

This Earth, unreal, appears as if it was a solid creation in the hollow of the receptacle of that space of consciousness, which is endowed of unreal manifestations.
(MU III:20.18)

Vasubandhu, founder of the *Vijñānavāda*, says, just at the beginning of his *Viṃśatikā*, something rather similar: the whole world, as it appears to us, is nothing beyond the perception we have of it, for it is but consciousness to manifest itself taking the form of objects devoid of existence.

Furthermore, according to the *Līlopākhyāna*, the visionary world that unfolds during the intermediate existence is similar to the dream state. In both only the *vāsanās* are manifested. It is the person who dreams who invests what appears to him with objectivity.

But how is it possible for an entire world to exist within the space of one room? And how is it possible for there to be worlds within worlds?

It is by virtue of the fact that their nature is space that entire worlds dwell in the interstices of other worlds. Worlds exist even in every atom (*paramāṇu*):

paramāṇau paramāṇau santi vatse cidātmani |
antar antar jagantīti kenaitan nāma saṅkhyate ||

Who can doubt, my dear, that [whole] worlds exist inside each atom, the nature of which is consciousness?
(MU III:20.25)

In the depths of the space of consciousness, the spatial extension (*deśadairghya*), like the temporal extension (*kāladairghya*), is fictitious; it is merely appearance and nothing other than this:

deśadairghyaṃ yathā nāsti kāladairghyaṃ tathaivaca |
nāsty eveti yathānyāyaṃ kathyamānaṃ mayā[23] śṛṇu ||
yathaitat pratibhāmātraṃ jagatsargāvabhāsanam |
tathaitat pratibhāmātraṃ kṣaṇakalpāvabhāsanam ||

Listen! I am going to explain appropriately to you that neither spatial extension nor temporal extension exists.

> As this unfolding of creation is made only of images, so made only of images is this unfolding of instants and eras. (MU III:20.27–28)

The fact that temporal extension is the product of the imagination also implies that the true dimension of consciousness is nontemporality. The temporal confines, like the spatial confines, can therefore be violated in any direction. Worlds exist one inside the other, regardless of their apparent size, and times exist contemporaneously; thus, time does not pass inevitably in one direction, except in the subjects' imagination.

We have already noted how in the MU the manifestation of the world is directly inherent in consciousness. It is possible to describe the mechanism of this manifestation in greater depth.

Immediately after having experienced the illusory death of the body, the subject, whose nature is space, finds himself in space:

> anubhūya kṣaṇaṃ jīvo mithyāmaraṇamūrchanam[24] |
> tadaivonmeṣamātreṇa vyomny eva[25] vyomarūpy api ||

> A soul, having experienced the illusory numbness due to death, [finds itself] in that very moment, in the twinkling of an eye, in space, [that soul itself being] made of space. (MU III:20.30)

For a second it is as though the soul returns to its true nature. However, it immediately imagines it is something that can be contained within a container, namely, a soul within a body. Immediately it experiences certain personal events: it sees a certain father, a certain house, certain friends. This event also seems to involve other subjects: they project it and are simultaneously hypnotized by it:

> ādheyo 'ham ihādhāre sthito 'ham iti cetati |
> hastapādādimān deho mamāyam iti paśyati || 31
> yadaiva cetati vapus tadaivedaṃ[26] sa cetati |
> etasyāhaṃ[27] pituḥ putro varṣāṇy etāni santi me || 32
> ime me bāndhavā ramyā mamedaṃ ramyam āspadam |
> jāto 'ham abhavaṃ bālo vṛddhiṃ yāto 'ham īdṛśaḥ || 33
> bāndhavāś cāsya me sarve tathaiva viharanty api |
> cidākāśaghanaikyatvāt svātmany api bhavanti[28] te || 34
> nimeṣeṇaiva jīvasya mṛtimohād anantaram |
> trijagatsargadṛśyaśrīḥ pratibhām upagacchati || 43

yathādeśaṃ yathākālaṃ yathārambhaṃ yathākramam |
yathotpādaṃ yathāmātṛ yathāpitṛ yathaurasam || 44
yathāvayo yathāsaṃvid yathāsthānaṃ yathehitam |
yathābandhu yathābhṛtyaṃ yathehāstamayodayam || 45
ajātam eva jāto 'ham iti paśyati cidvapuḥ |
deśakālakriyādravyamanobuddhīndriyāṇi ca || 46
jhagity eva mṛter ante vapuḥ paśyati yauvanam |
eṣā mātā pitā tv eṣa bālo 'bhūvam ahaṃ tv iti || 47

He thinks: 'I am what is contained herein, I lie in this container.' He sees that he has a body with hands, feet etc. When he perceives a body, then he perceives that he is the son of a certain father, at a certain age.

Here are my lovely friends, here is my lovely house; I was born, I became a boy, I grew with such-and-such characteristics.

And in this way my friends part from one another. And still they lie in their own self, because the space of consciousness is a single compact mass.

In the twinkling of an eye, immediately after illusory death, the glory of that object of perception which is the triple world manifests itself to the soul, in accordance with appropriate space and time, due beginning and order, in accordance with appropriate [characteristics and events]: birth, father and mother, firstborn, age, intellect, place, job, relatives and servants, and the joys and sorrows of life.

The body [made] of consciousness, not born, perceives that it was born and perceives space, time, action, substance, *manas, buddhi* and the senses.

Immediately after death this body [made of consciousness] sees [again] his own youth. It thinks: 'This was my mother; this was my father; I was this boy.'
(MU III:20.31–34, 43–47)

This complex and articulate vision is projected in the space of consciousness; its essence remains space, and it does not change the nature of space. For example, let us take a dream: here it is evident that the object of knowledge consists of consciousness; it is no different from the consciousness of the dreamer. Hence there is no separation between the knower, the process of knowledge, and the object known. Now, the soul's creation of a world during a dream is no different from what occurs in the intermediate state. In its turn the world created in the intermediate state is no different from this. The nature of the manifestation, which is consciousness, remains identical in all cases. And since the world remains in the depths of consciousness, and in itself it is nothing, it does not exist. It is always consciousness that plays the role of the object, but in so doing it does not have to become anything different from what it is, since the manifestation is inherent in it, it is an inseparable part of its nature:

evaṃ nāmodite 'py asyāś citeḥ[29] saṃsāraṣaṇḍake |
na kiñcid apy abhyuditaṃ sthitaṃ vyomaiva nirmalam ||
svapne draṣṭari yadvac cit tadvad dṛśye cid eva sā |
sarvadaikatayā tasmāt sā svapne[30] draṣṭṛdarśanam ||
yathā svapne tathodeti paraloke 'pi sā[31] citiḥ |
paraloke yathodeti tathaivehābhyudeti sā ||
tat svapnaparalokehalokānām asatāṃ satām |
na manāg api bhedo 'sti vīcīnām iva vāriṇi ||
ato 'jātam idaṃ viśvam ajātatvād anāśi ca |
kharūpatvāc ca nāsty eva yaś ca bhāti cid eva sā ||
yathaiṣā cetyanirhīṇā paramavyomarūpiṇī |
sacetyāpi tathaivaiṣā paramavyomarūpiṇī[32] ||
yasmāc cetyam ato nānyad vīcitvād iva vāritā |
vīcitvaṃ ca na caivāsti śaśaśṛṅgavad eva hi ||
saiva cetyam ivāpannā svabhāvād acyutāpy alam |
tasmān nāsty eva dṛśyo 'rthaḥ kuto 'to draṣṭṛdṛśyadhīḥ ||

Even if the forest of saṃsāra arises this way from this mind, nothing [really] arises; only spotless space exists.

When one is dreaming, as consciousness resides in the perceiver, so that very consciousness resides in the object of perception; therefore, when one is dreaming, it is always that [consciousness], since it is unitary, which is the vision of the subject.

As in a dream, so consciousness manifests itself in the other world; as it manifests itself in another world, so too it manifests itself in this one.

> Thus there is no difference, as among waves in water, among the dream, the other world and this one, all of which are inexistent entities.
>
> Therefore this whole universe was never born, and since it was never born, it is not subject to destruction, and since it has the nature of space, it does not exist at all; what unfolds is nothing but consciousness.
>
> As it [= consciousness], devoid of perceivable objects, has the nature of supreme space, so, even if it is [seemingly] provided with perceivable objects, it has the nature of supreme space.
>
> In fact, the object of perception is no different from that [consciousness], just as being a wave is no different from being water; and the condition of wave does not exist, just like the horn of a hare.
>
> It [= consciousness] has somehow become the perceivable object, even if it never loses its own essence; therefore there is no perceivable object at all; thus, what is the use of the concept of perceiver and object of perception?
> (MU III:20.35–42)

Is it possible to determine a criterion whereby the soul projects the illusory appearance of a samsara? According to the MU the projection is based on the memory of the previous life; hence the new life tends to be similar to that one (cf. above MU III:20.47).

Now, the cause of the creation and manifestation of eras is indeed the memory (*smṛti*) of souls, but this is not necessarily based on something that has effectively been experienced. Memory is not a collection of objective data, but an accumulation of impressions. Various examples are used in order to explain this. Memory is inconsistent like the sense of time of someone in love: when he is separated from his beloved a day seems a year. Memory is inconsistent like a dream: you dream of dying or of having different parents. Moreover, when memory projects this new world, it is like the memory of a drunken man, who remembers things he has never experienced or transforms the things he has experienced into something completely different. Therefore, the new world becomes a kind of parody of the world we have lived in, like a dream is a parody of real life. Certainly it is based on memory, but the impressions it accumulates are only a distorted reflection of what has been actually experienced:

> nimeṣeṇaiva sa kālo[33] gata ity anubhūyate |
> rātrir dvādaśavarṣāṇi hariścandre[34] tathāpy abhūt ||
> kāntāvirahiṇām ekaṃ vāsaraṃ[35] vatsarāyate |
> mṛto jāto 'ham anyo me piteti svapnadhāmni ca ||
> abhuktasyaiva bhogyasya bhuktadhīr upajāyate |
> bhukte cābhuktadhīr dṛṣṭam ity alaṃ kitavādiṣu ||
> śūnyam ākīrṇatām eti tulyaṃ vyasanam utsavaiḥ |
> vipralambho 'pi lābhaś ca madasvapnādisaṃvidi ||
>
> [A long] time is perceived as going by in a moment; in fact for Hariścandra a night lasted twelve years.
>
> A day seems a year to those who are separated from their loved ones; and in the sleeping state, one dreams of dying, being born, having a different father.
>
> The thought arises of having experienced something that was never experienced; and, regarding something which was experienced, the thought arises of having never experienced it, just as happens to the drunken.
>
> What is empty becomes full, disgrace becomes equal to festivity, and also separation becomes union, when the state of consciousness peculiar to drunkenness, a dream, etc. is present.
> (MU III:20.49–52)

Therefore, after death, a mnemonic process (*smṛtimayaḥ kramaḥ*) begins in the soul. The subject remembers his previous life. However, it is not necessary for the object of the memory to have been effectively experienced (*anubhūta*). The subject may also have memories of events that never happened. The soul projects worlds that can be based on both his former memories and random occurrances. Some souls live in a world actually based on the memory of passed perceptions; others project worlds without the contribution of memory.

While on the one hand memory is unreliable; on the other hand its alleged objective counterpart is also unreal. The cause of the projection of worlds while being in the intermediate state is not the memory of a real world in which we have formerly lived. In fact, no objective world exists, since there is nothing outside the space of consciousness. Even the present world consists of memory. In the final analysis, knowledge, whether experienced or not experienced, arises freely from causes and is merely consciousness:

> nānubhūtānubhūtā ca jñaptir itthaṃ dvirūpiṇī |
> pūrvakāraṇariktaiva[36] cidrūpaiva pravartate ||
>
> Therefore perception, whether it has not been experienced or already experienced, in twofold shape, arises free from previous causes, made of consciousness.
> (MU III:21.6)

In the cosmos, as described in the MU, there is no determinism, nor is the process of the karma real. An effect that derives from a single cause must be identical to that cause. In fact, we can only have a real effect from a concomitance of causes:

> kāraṇānām abhāve yad udeti[37] sahakāriṇām |
> tat pūrvakāraṇān nānyat sarveṇety anubhūyate ||
>
> What arises in the absence of concomitant causes is no different at all from the cause which precedes it.
> (MU III:18.23)

Therefore, the world, having consciousness as its only cause, cannot enjoy the status of a real effect: it does not have a separate existence; in itself it is purely inexistent:

> saṃsāraś cāyam ābhogī param eveti niścayaḥ |
> kāraṇābhāvato bhāti yad ihābhāvam eti tat ||
>
> It is certain that this world of enjoyment is the supreme principle itself; what appears in the absence of causes is non-existent for us.
> (MU III:21.15)

Freedom consists in the profound understanding that neither subjectivity nor the world ever arise and in forgetting the existence of an objectivity. Once objectivity is forgotten, at death the mnemonic process ceases, and no new world arises. In order for there to be true freedom, the word "world" must become meaningless for the *yogin*.

A momentary pacification of the world, for example, via a state of *samādhi* is not sufficient; at the end of such a state the world would arise again. It is like those who believe in ghosts; until they stop believing in them, even if for some reason a ghost disappears, another will reappear sooner or later:

> ardhaśānto na śānto 'sau samety anyatayā punaḥ |
> udety ekapiśacānte piśāco 'nyo 'py adhīmataḥ[38] ||
>
> Something that is half appeased is not appeased [at all]; it remains the same, even if it arises again taking another form; for a fool, after a *piśāca* [ghost] another one arises.
> (MU III:21.14)

At this point we could ask ourselves, as Līlā does, where memory comes from, since, while imaginary worlds are projected on the basis of memory, an objective world that was its original source has never existed:

> brāhmaṇabrāhmaṇīrūpe sarge yā[39] kāranaṃ smṛtiḥ |
> katham abhyuditā sā syāt smaraṇīyam idaṃ vinā ||
>
> How has the memory which is the cause of the creation having the nature of the Brahmin and his wife arisen, without this object of memory?
> (MU III:21.16)

Worlds are forged on the basis of reminiscences of worlds, which in their turn are forged on the basis of reminiscences, and so on. What starts this process, if a concrete world that may be the object of memory has never existed?

The *vijñānavādins* had to face a similar problem. Where does the impregnation of the *ālayavijñāna* come from? There is not any proper answer. The impregnation exists *ab aeterno*; it has not any beginning, although it might have an end, at least in the individual series of perceptions.

The MU has a parallel answer. The original repository of all reminiscences is the memory of Brahma, which does not depend on the past. Brahma, in fact, is free from previous births:

> pitāmahasmṛtis tatra kāraṇaṃ tasya ca[40] smṛtiḥ |
> pūrvaṃ na sambhavaty eva muktatvāt pūrvajanmanaḥ |

> The cause of that is Brahma's memory, and his memory does not arise at all previously [= from previous experiences], since he is free from previous births.
> (YV/ed. III:21.17)

Brahma is nothing but an individual soul that has assumed this function by chance. When this soul imagines a world from nothing, without the basis of pre-existent impressions, then it is Brahma:

> pratibhāsata evedaṃ keṣāṃcit smaraṇam vinā |
> cidaṇūnāṃ prajeśatvaṃ kākatālīyavad[41] yataḥ ||

> To some the world manifests itself without [the contribution of] memory, since the function of lord of the creatures is taken by individual souls by chance.
> (MU III:21.10)

In the *Vijñānavāda*, the individuals and the universe emerge as subjective representations from the *ālayavijñāna*. In a similar way, according to the MU, the individuals and the universe surface from Brahma's mind as mere appearances, Brahma himself being mere appearance. According to both doctrines, the individuals, in their turn, nourish such bases, *ālayavijñāna* and Brahma's mind, through their own *vāsanās*.

Thus it is insisted that the memory, whether it reflects or does not reflect previous experiences, is not based on anything objective, but arises spontaneously, and that its cause is only the space of consciousness (for Brahma himself has no real existence):

> dvividhāyāḥ smṛter asyāḥ kāraṇaṃ paramaṃ padam |
> kāryakāraṇabhāvo 'sāv ekam eva cidambaram ||

> The supreme plane of this [consciousness] is the cause of the twofold memory. That causality is just the space of consciousness, which is one.
> (MU III:21.21)

But stating that the space of consciousness is the cause of every phenomenon does not fully grasp the point. Yet again, we can only have an effect in the presence of concomitant causes. An effect does not really derive from a single cause, since the effect would be the cause. Hence every manifestation is inherent in consciousness—it is inseparable from it—and we can only speak of causality on a conventional plane. Causality too is projected by memory:

> kāryakāraṇayoḥ sattā kāraṇaiḥ sahakāribhiḥ |
> kāryakāraṇayor aikyaṃ tadabhāvāc ca[42] śāmyati ||
> mahācidrūpam evedaṃ smaraṇād viddhi vedanam |
> kāryakāraṇabhāvo 'tra tena śābdo[43] no vāstavaḥ ||
>
> The existence of the cause-effect relationship is due to the concomitant causes; and the cause-effect relationship ceases, since the concomitant causes do not exist.
>
> Know that this perception, the nature of which is the universal consciousness itself, comes from memory; therefore causality is verbal, it is not effective.
> (MU III:21.22–23)

The condition of the world (*jagattva*) does not really and truly exist on the plane of consciousness (*citpada*). Worlds are perceived as being structured (*mūrtiman*) only because of an obstinate inclination (*āgraha*) of the mind:

> jagantīmāny[44] amūrtāni mūrtimanti mudhāgrahāt |
> bhavadbhir avabuddhāni hemanīvormikā dhiyā ||
> hemny ūrmikārūpadhare 'py[45] ūrmikātvaṃ na vidyate |
> yathā tathā jagadrūpe jagattvaṃ nāsti citpade ||
>
> These formless worlds erroneously are perceived by your noble person as having a material form because of an obstinate inclination, as mind perceives a ring in [what is but] gold.
>
> As in gold, even if it has taken the shape of a ring, the nature of ring does not exist, so on the plane of consciousness, which has the shape of world, the nature of world does not exist.
> (MU III:21.32–33)

The essence of freedom is the defeat of this inclination. In fact, when the idea of objectivity ceases, the subject no longer accumulates the seeds of the *vāsanās*. The state of liberation occurs when the subject is free from these seeds, of the impressions accumulated in memory:

prakṣīṇavāsanā yeha jīvatāṃ jīvitasthitiḥ |
amuktair aparijñātā sā jīvanmuktir ucyate ||

The condition of life of the living beings in which the vāsanās have been destroyed, unknown to the non-liberated ones, is named 'liberation while living.'
(MU III:22.8)

Those who do not abandon their idea of being something separate do not recognize the world as Brahman. The bodies of those who are liberated are similar to the body of an imaginary city. Those who are liberated recognize that their bodies consist of space, of consciousness, and with those bodies they see the plane of the consciousness of the Brahman. The bodies of the liberated consist of pure knowledge. In the final analysis, the liberated person recognizes the Brahman, the atman, the world as his own body:

jagad ākāśam evedaṃ brahmaiva na tu dṛśyatā |
dṛśyate kācid apy atra dhūlir ambunidhāv iva ||
brahmaiva paśyati brahma nābrahma brahma paśyati |
sargādināmnā prathitaḥ svabhāvo 'syaivam īdṛśaḥ ||
na brahmajagator asti kāryakāraṇatodayaḥ |
kāraṇānām abhāvena sarveṣāṃ sahakāriṇām ||
yāvad abhyāsayogena na[46] śāntā bhedadhīs tava |
nūnaṃ tāvad atadrūpā na brahma paripaśyasi ||
tatra rūḍhim upāyātā ime ye tv asmadādayaḥ |
abhyāsād brahmasamvitteḥ paśyāmas te hi tat padam ||
saṅkalpanagarasyeva mamākāśamayaṃ vapuḥ |
brahmaiva vātaḥ paśyāmi dehenānena tat padam ||
viśuddhajñānadehā 'haṃ[47] yathāite padmajādayaḥ |
brahmātmajagadādīdam aṅgam asmākam aṅgane ||

This world is space, the Brahman itself; there is no objectivity, as there is no dust on the sea.

Only the Brahman perceives the Brahman; the non-Brahman does not perceive the Brahman; thus its own essence is named 'world.'

In the Brahman and the world the manifestation of the cause-effect relationship does not exist because of the non-existence of all the concomitant causes.

Until your notion of separation is not appeased by virtue of a constant application, until then, you, not being identical to Brahman, will not see it.

But, in such circumstances, we etc., who came to maturity by virtue of a constant application, see the plane of the consciousness of the Brahman.

My body, made of space, like the one of an imaginary city, is the Brahman itself; with this very body of mine I see that plane [of the consciousness of the Brahman].

Brahma and the other gods, like me, have bodies made of pure knowing; our body, O beautiful one, is Brahman, atman, the world etc.
(MU III:21.34–40)

By contrast, the bodies of the nonliberated are characterized by a perception of concreteness. Only by virtue of the consummation (*tānava*) of the *vāsanās* and the application to understanding do these bodies achieve the thin state (*ātivāhikatā*):

śuddhasattvānupatitaṃ cetaḥ prodbhinnavāsanam[48] |
ātivāhikatām[49] eti himaṃ tāpād ivāmbutām[50] ||
avabodhaghanābhyāsād dehasyāsyaiva jāyate |
saṃsāravāsanākārśye[51] nūnaṃ cittaśarīratā[52] ||

Mind, when it is conformable to the purified sattva, when its vāsanās are shattered, becomes subtle, as snow, because of heat, becomes water.

The condition of mental body comes, exactly for this very body, from the firm application to understanding, once the wordly *vāsanās* have been dissolved.
(MU III:22.9, 17)

Then the material body is revealed to be inexistent, like a body dreamed of after the dream is over. In reality it neither lives nor dies. As in the case of a body that is dreamed of, it makes no sense to speak of life or death:

yathā svapnaparijñānāt svapnadeho na vāstavaḥ |
anubhūto[53] 'py ayaṃ tadvad vāsanātānavād asan || 1
yathā svapnaparijñānāt svapnadehaḥ praśāmyati |
vāsanātānavāt[54] tadvaj jāgraddeho 'pi śāmyati || 2
dehas tv ayaṃ na mriyate na tu jīvati kiñcana |
ke kila svapnasaṅkalpabhrānter maraṇajīvite || 19
jīvitaṃ maraṇaṃ caitat saṅkalpapuruṣe yathā |
asatyam eva bhāty etad asmin putri śarīrake || 20

As a dreamed body does not seem concrete anymore, after one has understood that one was dreaming, so this body, even if one has experienced it, shows itself to be non-existent by virtue of a weakening of the vāsanās.

As a dreamed body dissolves after [the dreamer] has understood that he was dreaming, so also the body that we have in the state of wakefulness dissolves by virtue of a weakening of the *vāsanās*.

This body does not live, nor does it die at all; what are life and death to that delusion [= imaginary body] which is the outcome of dream or imagination?
(MU III:22.1–2, 19–20)

As life and death fictitiously appear in an imaginary man, O daughter, so also appear life and death in this body. The minds and bodies of the liberated become one, even if they are in different creations and rebirths:

ātivāhikatāṃ[55] yātaṃ buddhaṃ cittāntarair manaḥ |
sargajanmāntaragataiḥ siddhair milati netarat ||

Only the awoken mind, which has achieved the subtle state, merges into the other accomplished minds which reside in other creations and rebirths.
(MU III:22.10)

In order to lessen the idea of the world a constant application (*abhyāsa*)[56] to the *brahman* is necessary:

yad eva[57] kriyate kiñcid yena yena yadā yadā |
vinābhyāsena tan neha siddhim eti kadācana ||

taccintanaṃ tatkathanam anyonyaṃ[58] tatprabodhanam |
tadgataprāṇamananaṃ brahmābhyāsaṃ vidur budhāḥ ||

All that each one undertakes is never carried out without constant application.

Sages consider the constant application to the brahman to be the reflection upon it, the discussion of it, the awakening of each other to it, a reflection upon the vital principles inherent in it.
(MU III:22.23–24)

The *tapas* (ascesis) consists in the consummation of the *vāsanās* by means of an ever-increasing understanding of the inexistence of the knowable:

dṛśyāsambhavabodhena rāgadveṣāditānavam |
tapa ity ucyate loke dṛṣyadoṣas tu duḥkhakṛt[59] ||

The dissolution of greed, haṭred etc., which occurs by means of the understanding of the non-existence of the knowable, is named *tapas;* while in this world the evil represented by the knowable is known as the 'maker of grief.'
(MU III:22.32)

In conclusion, the story of Līlā increases correct understanding in the sense that Līlā's world provides a paradigm for the understanding of the conventional world, namely the world of ordinary experience. The latter, despite its apparent consistency, does not imply any degree of reality. It is an imaginary world, which is to be found within other imaginary worlds, and in its turn, it contains other worlds. These worlds are the fruit of desires, memories, and so on. In the final analysis they do not belong to anyone. Since even the multiplicity of subjects is fictitious, Līlā's world arises together with various worlds within the categories of space, time, and matter.

Hence it is the imagination (*kalpanā*) that creates what is mistaken for objectivity. In affirming this we are, however, still on the plane of conventional truth. In the depths of the space of consciousness, the imagination, that is the source of objectivity, like objectivity itself, is not real. The space of consciousness, the supreme, is quiescent (*śānta*) by definition:

kaṭakatvaṃ yathā hemni taraṅgatvaṃ yathāmbhasi |
satyatvaṃ ca yathā svapnasaṅkalpanagarādiṣu ||
nāsty eva satyānubhave tathā nāsty eva citpade |
kalpanaṃ vyatiriktātma tatsvabhāvād anāmayāt ||
yathā nāsty ambare pāṃsuḥ pare nāsti tathā kalā |
akalākalanaṃ śāntam idam ekam ajaṃ tataḥ ||

As the nature of a bracelet in gold, as the nature of a wave in the sea, as reality in a city arisen from imagination or a dream, do not exist at all, so on the plane of consciousness, the experience of which is real, the imagination that consists in separate objects does not exist, because of its [consciousness's] own pure intimate nature.

As there is no dust in the sky, so there are no parts in the supreme plane; therefore it is devoid of the projection of parts, quiescent, one, not born.
(MU III:21.64–66)

In the final analysis, only the vast, pure, empty space of consciousness can be found.

Concordance

MU, quoted stanzas	YV/ed.
III:15	
7	7
9	9
11	11
12	12
13	13
15	15
17	17
18	18
III.17	
9	9
10	10
11	—
12	—
III:18	
23	23
24	24
25	25
26	26
27	27

III:20	
3	3
4	4
5	5
18	19
21	22
25	26
27	28
28	29
30	31ab–32ab
31	32cd–33ab
32	33cd–34ab
33	34cd–35ab
34	35cd–36ab
35	36cd–37ab
36	37cd–38ab
37	38cd–39ab
38	39cd–40ab
39	40cd–41ab
40	41cd–42ab
41	42cd–43ab
42	43cd–44ab
43	44cd–45ab
44	45cd–46ab
45	46cd–47ab
46	47cd–48ab
47	48cd–49ab
49	50cd–51ab
50	51cd–52ab
51	52cd–53ab
52	53cd–53ef
53	54
III:21	
6	6
10	10
14	14
15	15
16	16
—	17
21	21
22	—
22cd	
23	23
32	32
33	33
34	34
35	36
36	37

37 38 39 40 63 64 65	38 39 40 41 64 65 66
III:22	
1 2 8 9 10 17 19 20 23 24 32	1 2 8 9 10 17 19 20 23 24 30cd
III:30	
4	4

Notes

1. Scholars have long thought it evident that the title of the oldest nucleus of what was to become the YV must have been MU (cf. Bhattacharya 1948: 203). Moreover, the stratification of the text has been evident since the forerunners of the research (cf. Divanji 1935). However, the fact that only the printed edition (cf. Śāstrī Paṇsīkar 1918), questionable in many respects, was taken into consideration has prevented a grasp of the full extent of the work's heterogeneity. Only Slaje (1994), having examined the Kashmiri Śāradā manuscript tradition, relatively free from reworkings in favor of orthodox Brahmanism and late Vedāntic influences, has been able to make glaringly obvious the difference between what can be taken as the "original" text of the YV, which probably did not present the framework of the dialogue between Rāma and Vasiṣṭha, and the printed edition. Slaje (1994: 65) notes that the latter has done research on the YV a very bad turn, precisely because it reflects late Vedāntic influences. As regards the manuscript tradition, Slaje (1994: 63–64) has distinguished two currents: the above-mentioned Śāradā tradition and the Devanāgarī tradition, reflected in the printed edition. The first is evidence of an earlier version of the text, while the second modifies the text to tone down its anti-orthodox tendencies. As the printed edition of the YV is not reliable

and shows a late phase of the text, I shall base my exposition on (and draw my quotes from) the Śāradā manuscript tradition (with a few exceptions). I shall refer to the Śāradā YV as the "MU." I have made use, together with MṬ/ed. (which breaks off at III.16.41), of three Śāradā manuscripts (on the extant manuscripts of the YV/MU see Slaje 1994: 31–48; 1996; 2000; 2005; Hanneder 2005: 139–140; Stephan and Stinner 2005):

Ś1: reproduced by Lokesh Chandra (see Chandra 1984);

Ś3: Sri Pratap Singh Library of Śrīnagar No. 8771; microfilm: Bibliothek des Indologischen Seminars, Bonn Di804; F66. This manuscript seems to give the best readings. I express my gratitude to Roland Steiner, who transcribed for me part of the microfilm.

Ś9: Staatsbibliothek zu Berlin—Preussischer Kulturbesitz, Orientalabteilungms Hs.or. 12511.

2. *niḥsandehaṃ : niḥsandeho* Ś9 MṬ/ed.

3. *eti te : eṣyati* MṬ/ed.

4. *acetyacinmātraṃ bhānor* YV/ed. : acetyacinmātrabhānor Ś1 Ś3 Ś9 MṬ/ed.

5. *jāgrat° : jagat°* Ś1.

6. *piṇḍagrāhaḥ : piṇḍagrahe* Ś1 Ś3 Ś9.

7. *tulādeśau : tulākāśau* Ś1.

8. *°putraka° : °putrika°* Ś3.

9. *°dṛśaḥ: °dṛśāḥ* Ś1.

10. *abhittimat : abhittikam* Ś3.

11. *cāprapūrakam : ca prapūrakam* Ś9.

12. *°vāriṇi : °dhāriṇi* Ś1 Ś9.

13. *budbudhān : budbudān* Ś9.

14. *arbudapramān : arbudhakramān* Ś1, *arbudakramān* Ś3.

15. *samīpaṃ : samapaṃ* Ś1.

16. *śūnyatamaṃ : śūnyam imaṃ* Ś1.

17. *dṛśyātmanānātā caiva*, conjectural emendation : *dṛśyātmanānānānaiva* Ś1 Ś3 Ś9.

18. *eva : evaṃ* Ś1.

19. *bhavati*, conjectural emendation : *bhavato* Ś1, *bhavator* Ś3 Ś9.

20. *kaḥ syāt : ka syāt* Ś1.

21. *nirargalānantabodhān nānyad : nirargalānālpabodhān nanyad* Ś1, *nirargalānalpabodhān nānyad* Ś3.

22. I preferred not to translate the term *vāsanā*, which could be approximately rendered as "subconscious sensations," because of its wealth of meaning in the history of Indian philosophy. It is hardly necessary to recall how pivotal the concept of *vāsanā* is, for example, in the *Yoga Sūtra* and in the literature that accompanies it: there the *vāsanās*, arising from the memory, indefinitely nourish the *cittavṛtti*. The latter are actualized in *karman*. But this in its turn sows the seeds of new *vāsanās*. The control of these is therefore fundamental for attaining the *kaivalya*, the *jīvanmuktatā*. Also in the YV the exhaustion of the *vāsanās* is fundamental: it is they, in fact, who give form to the samsara. Likewise, the concept of *vāsanā* is central to the *Vijñānavāda*.

The accumulation of *vāsanās*, left by the memories of past perceptions, forms the *ālayavijñāna*, or the store consciousness, which is the base of the universal manifestation.

23. *kathyamānaṃ mayā : kathyamānam idaṃ* Ś9.
24. *mūrchanam : mūrchanām* Ś1, Ś3.
25. *vyomny eva : vyomneva* Ś1.
26. *tadaivedaṃ : tathaivedaṃ* Ś1.
27. *etasyāhaṃ : jātasyāhaṃ* Ś1.
28. *api bhavanti : abhibhavanti* Ś1.
29. *citeḥ : citte* Ś1.
30. *sā svapne : sasvapne* Ś1 Ś9.
31. *paraloke 'pi sā*, conjectural emendation : *paralokadṛśā* Ś1 Ś9 Ś3.
32. Hemistich omitted in Ś1.
33. *kālo*, conjectural emendation : *kalo* Ś1 Ś3 Ś9.
34. *hariścandre : haricandre* Ś1.
35. *ekaṃ vāsaraṃ : ekavāsaraṃ* Ś1.
36. *pūrvakāraṇariktaiva : pūrvaṃ kāraṇarikteva* Ś9.
37. *yad udeti*, conjectural emendation : *'pi yadeti* Ś1 Ś3 Ś9.
38. *'py adhīmataḥ : hi dhīmataḥ* Ś1.
39. *sarge yā : sargo yaḥ* Ś1.
40. *ca*, conjectural emendation : *na* Ś1 Ś3 Ś9.
41. *prajeśatvaṃ kāka° : prajeśatvakāka°* Ś1.
42. *°abhāvāc ca*, conjectural emendation : *°abhāvān na* Ś1 Ś3 Ś9.
43. *śābdo : śabdo* Ś1. Ś9 and Ś3 have *śabdo* corrected to *śābdo*.
44. *jagantīmāny : jaganty amūny* Ś9.
45. *°dhare 'py : °vane 'py Ś1, °vany apy* Ś9.
46. *na* omitted in Ś1.
47. *dehā 'haṃ : dehārhaṃ* Ś9.
48. *prodbhinna° : prabhinna°* Ś9.
49. *ātivāhikatām : ātivāhakatām* Ś1.
50. *ivāmbutām : ivāplutam* Ś1 Ś9.
51. *°kārśye : °kārśyaṃ* Ś1 Ś9.
52. *°śarīratā : °śarīrataḥ* Ś1.
53. *anubhūto : anudbhūto* Ś1.
54. *°tānavāt : °tānave* Ś1.
55. *ātivāhikatāṃ : ātivāhakatāṃ* Ś1.
56. Of course this term is pivotal not only in the MU, but also in many Yoga (in a broad sense) treatises like, for example, the *Yoga Sūtra* (I:12), the BG (VI:35), the *Śivasaṃhitā* (IV:9–11).
57. *yad eva : yadaiva* Ś1.
58. *°kathanam anyonyaṃ : °kathanaṃ tv anyonyaṃ* Ś9.
59. *duḥkhakṛt : duḥkhabhāk* Ś1.

3

The Concept of Ābhāsa in the Yogavāsiṣṭha

Sthaneshwar Timalsina

Introduction

Studying classical Indian philosophy poses multiple challenges. One of them is the shift in the meaning of terms at different times, and another is the application of the same term with a different intent in different schools of philosophy. It is not easy to recover the meaning of each and every term used in all different contexts to resolve this crisis. In the midst of applications, what is meant becomes blurred. Textual interpretation becomes impossible, if it is argued that terms have the potency to denote every possible meaning. Understanding a text, therefore, is a negotiation among potential meanings. One can see this fluidity particularly vibrantly in the case of the technical terms having different meanings when they are applied in different philosophical contexts. The term and the concept for discussion in this chapter is *ābhāsa,* often translated as appearance.

The term *ābhāsa* appears in Madhyamaka and Yogācāra Buddhism, the Advaita of Śaṅkara, Trika Śaiva philosophy, and the text *Mokṣopāyaśāstra* (MU) or its redaction, the *Yogavāsiṣṭha* (YV).[1] The centrality of this term in discussions on Indian philosophy becomes even more crucial with two of the aforementioned schools, Trika Śaivism and the Advaita of Śaṅkara, having a specific doctrine based on the formulation of the term. Within Śaṅkara's school of Advaita, the stream of the philosophy identified with *ābhāsa* is attributed to

Sureśvara, the disciple of Śaṅkara. Somānanda and Utpala are credited for the monistic *ābhāsa* doctrine of Śaivism.

The objective of this chapter is not to compare all these schools of philosophy. However, one point is crucial to initiate this conversation. The Buddhist models of both Madhyamaka and Yogācāra utilize the term *ābhāsa*, explicitly saying that duality is nonexistent and compared with illusion, mirage, or perceptual error. Trika Śaivism defends its monistic stance by propounding that duality is the play of consciousness or an expansion of the intrinsic powers of the singular reality. Advaita Vedānta defends its nondualism by rejecting duality while confirming the substrate of the perception of duality as the Brahman. Both the Buddhist and Upaniṣadic philosophical schools utilize examples like dream, the snake perceived in rope, mirage, perception of a bundle of hair in front of the eyes, a shell perceived as silver, and so on. They interpret it either with the confirmation of the substrate through negation or with an application of the negative terms in order to simply negate. The application of *ābhāsa* found in all these contexts cannot be reduced to a single meaning. A broader historical context becomes one of the most essential parts of the hermeneutic exercise for unraveling the hidden sense of language.

Deriving meaning applicable to one specific school of philosophy is not as complicated as understanding texts that have gone through multiple redactions and multiple shifts of the paradigm itself. The context here is the MU/YV (These almost identical texts come with two different titles, the *Mokṣopāyaśāstra* and the *Yogavāsiṣṭha*); it has been edited and rewritten to include *Laghu Yogavāsiṣṭha* and other versions of concise rewriting. This is an epic with profoundly aesthetic compositions as well as a philosophical text. During the period of its composition, the text embodied most of the monistic and nondualistic ideas and texts available at that time, including the Upaniṣadic literature, the epic compositions of Kālidāsa, linguistic philosophical treatises such as *Vākyapadīya*, the Buddhist Madhyamaka or Yogācāra literature, and texts of the school of Trika Śaivism. Reducing meaning to one single nuance for a word that is an anthology of broadly ranging concepts in its own historical context is therefore inappropriate. This being the case, the best approach is to discern the variations, analyze them separately, find the supporting philosophy for deriving such meaning, and endeavor to find an overarching philosophy if the text so provides. Without reducing various meanings to one sense, this approach allows the author/authors to define meaning within the boundary of specific understanding without a superimposition of inapplicable meaning.

The Scholastic Advaita Concept of *Ābhāsa*

The Advaita of Śaṅkara predates both Trika Śaiva doctrine and the MU/YV. Although there are unmistakable imprints of Buddhist texts in the application of *ābhāsa* in the Advaita of Śaṅkara, the meaning shaped in this school plays a vital role in determining its application in subsequent Hindu literature. Before identifying the instances of *ābhāsa* found in the MU/YV, it is therefore essential to introduce key concepts found in the *abhāsa* school of Advaita Vedānta to the discourse. Select applications in the school of Śaṅkara that are crucial to the current discussion on *ābhāsa* are:

1. Following the application of *anābhāsa* in the commentary upon *Māṇḍūkyopaniṣad* attributed to Śaṅkara, the term *ābhāsa* refers to an appearance of imagined objects.[2]
2. Śaṅkara repeatedly uses this term in *Upadeśasāhasrī* (US) with the understanding that *ābhāsa* is "false" (US XVIII:115; XVIII:88).
3. The application of *ābhāsa* in US parallels another term (US XVIII:88, 114). In this identification, *ābhāsa* is the counter-image of "seeing" or consciousness (US XII:6). In the later scholastic Advaita of Śaṅkara, *pratibimba* and *ābhāsa* doctrines are sometimes recognized as identical and at other times are seen as contradictory. The parallel found in these instances opens up the possibility of bridging these two models of Advaita. This identification facilitates a comparison of *ābhāsa* with an example given by Sureśvara, where he compares the destruction of *ābhāsa* with the destruction of the substrate, such as the counter-image of the sun seen in a pot full of water.[3]
4. Sureśvara is credited with propounding the *ābhāsa* doctrine of Advaita. He is consistent in using the term *ābhāsa* to refer to entities that are distinct from pure consciousness.[4]
5. Contrary to these instances, Ānandagiri uses the term *ābhāsa* to refer to the subject of awareness, with an etymological interpretation of the term, '*ābhimukhyenāhamityāparokṣyeṇa bhāsata ity ābhāsaḥ*"(*ābhāsa* is that which manifests directly [in the form of] I-sense).[5]

6. The application of the term *avabhāsa* in Śaṅkara's commentary upon *Brahmasūtra* (BSBh) and its interpretation by Vācaspati[6] comes closer to the understanding of *ābhāsa*, in which the term refers to a falsely appearing entity that is sublated with the rise of true knowledge.
7. Sometimes the application of *ābhāsa* gives an Advaita understanding of cosmology, with *ābhāsa* being both cause and effect. Adopting this hierarchy, the consciousness manifesting in the form of subject is the "cause ābhāsa"and the consciousness appearing in the form of the objects of cognition are identified as "effect ābhāsa."[7]
8. Within Śaṅkara's school of Advaita, whenever the terms *ābhāsa* and *pratibimba* are contrasted, the term *pratibimba*, referring to counter-image, is identified with bimba (image) and is therefore real, whereas the term *ābhāsa* is described as *anirvacanīya* and compared with the substrate of illusion and therefore is identified as "false."[8]
9. A clear distinction can be made between *pratibimba* and *ābhāsa* on the basis that *avidyā* is often identified as *ābhāsa* but never as *pratibimba*. This again confirms that *ābhāsa* refers only to the substrate (*upādhi*), which is not the case with *pratibimba*.[9]

Many of these applications, including that of the fluid interchangeability between *pratibimba* and *ābhāsa,* predate the Advaita literature of Śaṅkara and predominantly follow the applications found in the Yogācāra literature. It is therefore contextual to analyze select applications of the term *ābhāsa* found in Buddhist literature.

Ābhāsa in Buddhist Literature

The application of *ābhāsa* in Buddhist literature ranges from that found in the Madhyamaka texts to the Yogācāra literature. While "emptiness" (*śūnyatā*) remains at the core of both doctrines, Madhyamaka emphasizes the negation of phenomena by application of the term *ābhāsa* in order to confirm *śūnyatā*. In the case of Yogācāra, *ābhāsa* is applied in order to establish that external entities are merely the *pariṇāma* of *vijñāna*. For the Yogācāra understanding of the term, Schmithausen explains it as: "corporeal matter and the external world, as the object of *ālayavijñāna* . . . mental images in *ālayavijñāna*."[10]

The instances found in the *Mahāyānasūtrālaṅkāra* (MSA) of Asaṅga and the *Laṅkāvatārasūtra* (LAS) are crucial to an understanding of the early Yogācāra application of *ābhāsa*. In MSA, the term can mean something falsely appearing and nonsubstantial. It frequently appears as *dvayābhāsa,* or the *ābhāsa* of the dyad of subject and object.[11] In the examples found in these texts, *ābhāsa* is explained as the nonbeing of the substance to which the term *ābhāsa* is referring.[12] The substrate for the rise of the dyad is the storehouse consciousness, and it is caused by *avidyā*.[13] The application of the term *advayābhāsa* in MSA does not confirm the appearance of *advaya,* but rather, it is applied in order to negate the appearance of the dyad of subject and object (*dvayābhāsa*).[14]

In response to what this *dvayābhāsa* is, MSA explains that it is mind or *citta* alone that is acknowledged in terms of *grāhya* (object of cognition) and *grāhaka* (subject of cognition). In absence of mind (*citta*), there is no causal constituent such as passion, and in absence of the causal complex, there is no rise of subject and object.[15] This is the appearance of passion or aversion or the appearance of the properties of the other that give rise to the duality of the form of subject and object.[16] The application of *ābhāsa* in MSA appears to be synonymous to the term *pratibhāsa*.[17]

MSA elaborates upon the ontology of *ābhāsa,* with *ābhāsa* in the form of subject and object giving rise to their own sets of triads: three categories emerging from the appearance of subject, and another three, from the object. The first triad, the appearance of word (*padābhāsa*), meaning (*arthābhāsa*), and body (*dehābhāsa*), is considered as the triad belonging to the subject of perception (*grāhaka*). The next triad, the appearance of mind (*manas*), fivefold sensation (*udgraha*), and mental modification (*vikalpa*), is considered to belong to the object of cognition (*grāhya*).[18] This categorization falls under *paratantra,* or the interdependent character among the three essential natures discussed in Yogācāra literature.[19]

Explicitly, all instances identified in this discussion fit with a general application of the term *ābhāsa* as false appearance and attributed to ignorance. Both of these categories are applicable to the scholastic Advaita of Śaṅkara whenever the term *ābhāsa* has been applied. This understanding is also consistent with some applications of the term in the MU/YV.

It has been previously addressed that the application of the term *ābhāsa* in Buddhist literature aligns with both the Madhyamaka and Yogācāra positions. In order to elaborate upon the Yogācāra application of the term *ābhāsa,* the *Laṅkāvatārasūtra* (LAS) is crucial. This text describes *ābhāsa* in terms of the appearance of external entities, with "false appearance" describing external entities that stand for confirmation of essential *vijñāna* nature. The concept of inside and out, *vijñāna* and *artha*, or other dyads, serves the same purpose. This application does not contradict that found in the scholastic Advaita of Śaṅkara. In this particular case, Yogācāra terminology has apparently shaped the Upaniṣadic discourse of Advaita. LAS considers the appearance of entities due to the union of *ābhāsa* and *bīja* (LAS X:495). Apparently, the seed (*bīja*) here refers to ignorance (*avidyā*) and mental imprints (*vāsanā*), as found in MSA. The application of "the appearance of false entities" (*mithyābhāsa*) (LAS X:147) further confirms the argument that this *ābhāsa* is false. In the context of Yogācāra application, this confirmation of falsity leads to the final confirmation of emptiness (*śūnyatā*), which remains the foundational concept for both Madhyamaka and Yogācāra doctrines.

In agreement with the application of *ābhāsa* as false appearance, variants of this term are often associated with *artha* or *bhāva*, referring to entities outside of the mind. The appearance of these entities (*arthābhāsa*) is compared with the improbable rabbit horn (LAS X:571), which simply applies to something that does not exist. It is not the case that something else is being mistaken for the horns of a rabbit. This example may have been borrowed from the Madhyamaka usage. The objective of Yogācāra in providing for the illusory nature of entities is not to reject their false appearance. The examples such as shell silver, or rope snake demonstrate the illusory nature of the entities that appear, without rejecting their substrate.

In the instances where *arthābhāsa* is used in LAS, it explicitly refers to something that appears but does not exist (LAS X:571–73). The appearance of entities is caused due to not knowing one's own mind (LAS X:273). When the mind is stimulated by impressions, entities appear (*bhāvābhāsa*, LAS II:158).[20] The illustrations applied in these contexts need to be read in light of the overarching philosophy, and in this case, examples such as rabbit horn confirm the Yogācāra doctrine of mind only (*cittamātra*).

While the appearance of entities is due to the mind manifesting external entities because of mental impressions, the true nature of mind is devoid of appearance. This reality is often identified by the term *nirābhāsa*. This *nirābhāsa*, devoid of appearance, gives rise to eight-fold cognition (*aṣṭadhā vijñāna*) (LAS X:354, 644).[21] In another depiction, a yogin perceives the great path (Mahāyāna) by abiding in *nirābhāsa* (LAS X:235, 257). It is *prajñā* or wisdom that leads to attainment of this state of *nirābhāsa* (LAS II:180; X:285).[22] In this state of *nirābhāsa*, the mind is free from objects, and there is no sequence because there are no entities (LAS X:206–7). One can achieve this *nirābhāsa* by surpassing mind-only (*cittamātra*) (LAS X:110). In agreement with the Yogācāra ontology of the eightfold analysis of mind, *citta* is explained as having seven grounds, with *nirābhāsa* considered to be the eighth (LAS IV:2). This enlightened state of mind not only frees a yogin from the external entities of appearance, but also from defilements that cause the mind to appear in the form of the dyad of subject and object.

Ābhāsa in the *Mokṣopāyaśāstra/Yogavāsiṣṭha*[23]

The illusory nature of *ābhāsa* is consistently found in both Buddhist sources and Advaita literature, where the term refers to a product of ignorance which is caused due to one's mental impressions. The main distinction between the Madhyamaka application of *ābhāsa* and the use of *ābhāsa* in the YV is that in the case of the first, there is no substrate for *ābhāsa*, whereas in the second, there is *cid* or consciousness that is appearing otherwise.[24] This brings the meaning of *ābhāsa* comparatively closer to the Yogācāra application. However, the difference in overarching philosophy determines the difference in the application of these terms. The Madhyamaka application of *ābhāsa* is not identical to its application in the YV in the sense that this term, in the case of the Madhyamaka usage, describes what is nonexistent and confirms negation, whereas in the case of the YV, even when the term is describing illusory appearance, it is not used in simple negation but rather as confirmation of the substrate. For instance, the example of mirage in the YV confirms the existence of sunlight.[25] Select examples to establish this argument follow:[26]

> yathā saṅkalpanagaraṃ saṅkalpān naiva bhidyate |
> tathāyaṃ jagadābhāsaḥ paramārthān na bhidyate ||
>
> [Just] as the city [constructed] of intention does not differ from the intention (*saṅkalpa*) [itself], so also does the appearance of the world not differ from the supreme reality.
> (YV VIb:42.20)
>
> yad idaṃ jagadābhāsaṃ śuddhaṃ cinmātravedanam |
> kātraikatā dvitā kā vā nirvāṇam alam āsyatām ||

> The appearance [in the form of] this world is pure [and of the character of] the awareness of consciousness only. In here, what is singularity or duality? Abide in the state of enlightenment. This is all (*alam*).
> (YV VIb:43.12)

For comparative understanding, this chapter explores, first, the instances of the application of *ābhāsa* in the MU/YV that align with the Buddhist understanding of the term and, second, the instances in which the meaning differs. It is expected that congruence in the application of the term and the concept of *ābhāsa* exists, at least within this text itself. Jurgen Hanneder points out that "to appear" (*bhā*) is "to be perceived erroneously," citing a verse from the MU which explains that the perception of duality is not rooted in cause, and what appears is not really there.[27] This rejection of substantiality of appearance tallies with the previous instances which assign appearance to ignorance, because what appears due to ignorance is not present in reality. Hanneder cites other instances where *ā+bhā* is explained in terms of false appearance, like a bundle of hair due to eye disease. He compares these instances with the widely cited first verse from Vasubandhu's *Viṃśikā*.[28] Explicitly, there is a parallel between Yogācāra and Advaita literature where both explain *ābhāsa* and *avabhāsa* synonymously.

Illustrated with numerous examples and explained repeatedly, the central concept of *ābhāsa* describes the nonsubstantial nature of the world that is perceived. The application of *ābhāsa* is in order to reject any origination.[29] Both perceiver (*draṣṭṛ*) and perceived (*dṛśya*), following the Ābhāsa terminology, are merely appearing and of the character of error.[30] Within this setting, both the external entities (*bhāsa*) and their appearance (*vibhāsana*) are understood by the terms derived of the verbal root √*bhās*.[31] The concept that something fundamentally real exists, with false appearances taken to be reality, is a concept that gives rise to the notion of two degrees of truth, as found in both Mahāyāna Buddhist literature and scholastic Advaita. Although this is not the only way the Advaita tradition interprets the phenomenal world while establishing nondual Brahman, the doctrine of Ābhāsa fundamentally relies on this twofold reality. To confirm this understanding, the MUŚ applies *ābhāsa* in the sense that it is real in its appearance, and not real otherwise. This is compared with the reality of bubble in the sense of bubble and not real otherwise. "Body" is real in the sense of the body and not real in any other sense.[32]

When *ābhāsa* is applied to reject illusory appearance, it is often used to stress the nonexistent (*asat*) aspect of what appears. This nonexistent nature of illusory appearance comes from the understanding that ignorance (*avidyā*) is in fact nonexistent. In this understanding, error and ignorance are identical, and nonexisting ignorance gives the appearance of something having existence.[33] Within this setting, *ābhāsa* rejects the phenomenal being of the world in any mode of time, without rejecting the substrate in which the world appears, consciousness itself.[34] Following this, the world that is perceived is an error (*bhrama*) because it is *ābhāsamātra*, or appearance alone.[35] This application of *ābhāsa* rejects origination as such. That which appears as if existing, following this description, is never originated and there is therefore no cause of origination.[36] This *ābhāsa* is compared with dream, and consciousness that is compared to the void is alone the witness of the apparent forms.[37] This identification of the appearance with dream is not intended to reject appearance as such, but rather, this analogy is applied to confirm that appearance is in truth *ābhānamātra*, of the character only of awareness.[38] Explicitly, the application of dream in this interpretation of Advaita is not to negate entities by confirming their parallel to dream, but rather, it is to affirm their essential nature of awareness-only.

The interpretation of *ābhāsa* as an appearance of something else (*anyathā bhāsa*) in another form does not allow for the ontological aspect of that which appears in the state of illusion. The only meaning that can be established on the basis of this interpretation is the nonexisting nature of the falsely appearing entities. However, there are other instances where the application of *ābhāsa* coincides with the scholastic Advaita understanding of *avidyā* as indeterminable of either existing or nonexisting. Following this application, either the reality is confirmed as *cinmātra* and all that appears is due to *ābhāsa* and nothing is either real or false,[39] or with an application of *ābhāsamātra*, all that appears is merely appearance alone.[40]

The MU often describes the rise of the notion of the self in pure consciousness as the first step in the process of the emanation of the world. This metaphysical stance differs from the one that considers the rise of the notions of the self and other, and subject and object, as simultaneous. Following the first order, when the consciousness becomes conscious (*cetati*), it gives rise to the notion of the self, identified here as *cidābhāsa*.[41] In this sequence, the self, having I-sense (*aham ātmā*), is found in the triadic form of subject, object, and cognition.[42] It is noteworthy that the Advaita understanding, in which subject and object arise parallel to each other, aligns with the Buddhist concept wherein the rise of *dvaya* of the form of *grāhaka* and *grāhya* is simultaneous.

A stark difference between the Mahāyāna and Advaita applications of *ābhāsa* can be found in the application of the term *cidābhāsa* in the case of the second. This Advaita usage confirms consciousness, considered as changeless, to be foundational. However, the general application of *cidābhāsa* found in Advaita literature refers to either *jīva* or the subject of consciousness. In agreement with this understanding, the MU describes the rise of *jīvahood* by comparing it with the ignition of lamps from one single lamp. In this metaphor, Prajāpati is compared to the first lamp that ignites others.[43] Following this description, it is due to the *ābhāsa* of Prajāpati that individual selves arise.[44] The commonly found term *jīva* is interpreted, following the *ābhāsa* terminology, as *cidābhāsa,* with consciousness coming into contact with (literally, facing towards") the entities of awareness (*cetyonmukha*).[45]

However, in the case of the MU/ YV, one can not only find the application of *cidābhāsa* to address *jīva* as the appearance of pure consciousness, but also to explain the appearance of the world as all that appears, to be the very *ābhāsa* of consciousness. Furthermore, this application confirms Brahman, rather than negating the world.[46] This position takes for granted that there is no distinction between the object erroneously conceived and its substrate, the real object. The experience of the self in the body, when using *ābhāsa,* is explained in terms of *cittadoṣa* or "defilement of mind" and is distinguished from *cidābhāsa,* where *cidābhāsa* describes the experience of the self in other than the body.[47] Following this understanding, it is sensation that gives rise to the notion of reality outside of consciousness. The MU compares this sensation to the vibration (*spanda*) caused by wind.[48] This rise of duality occurs when consciousness appears projected onto itself as if other (*pṛthag ivāvbhāsa*). The appearance of the other is of the character of determination (*saṅkalpa*) and imagination (*kalanā*). In this process, mind itself assumes form and appears in the form of the world.[49] Unlike the Mahāyāna application of *ābhāsa* as fundamentally false, and in alignment with the scholastic Advaita understanding of *avidyā* in which ignorance is not simply not knowing but rather the cosmic force that gives rise to the world, in some instances found in the MU/YV, this is the very *ābhāsa* that appears in various forms (*ākāra*). In this sense external entities are compared to the entities of dream, where mind projects the form of dream entities.[50] When *cidābhāsa* is identified with the objects of perception, it is often distinguished from the atman, which appears in the form of the appearance of consciousness (*cidābhāsa*) that gives rise to the notion of objects. This manifestation of plurality is pertinent to the very self, due to itself, and manifesting upon its own substrate.[51] Whether applied only to refer to the subject of awareness or to both the subject and object of awareness, the application of *cidābhāsa* is definitely a development in the meaning found in early Mahāyāna literature.

Congruent with Mahāyāna literature, some instances in the MU/YV confirm the positive being of mind in the absence of all entities of appearance. The MU/YV frequently utilizes the terms *anābhāsa* and *samasamābhāsa*, both referring to pure consciousness, free from modifications, and devoid of all the external images.[52] Parallel to the application of *nirābhāsa* in LAS to refer to the highest state or the eighth consciousness (*vijñāna*) in which sevenfold consciousness arises, the MU describes *anābhāsa* as the true nature of Brahman, the foundation for the rise of external objects.[53] This absence of external entities is also referred to with the identical term, *nirābhāsa* in a rare instance in the MU/YV that makes further comparison possible:

> ekam eva nirābhāsam acittvam ajaḍaṃ samam |
> na san nāsan na khaṃ nākham idam advayam avyayam ||
>
> [There exists] only one that is free from all appearances. [This one is] indifferent, neither conscious nor unconscious, neither existing nor non-existing, neither empty nor not empty. This [is] nondual (advaya), and indestructible. (YV VIb:33.34)[54]

Instead of identifying this *nirābhāsa* state as ultimately existing (*sat*), this passage describes it as neither existing nor nonexisting (*na san nāsan*), the terminology in scholastic Advaita that consistently refers to *avidyā*. This is also described as neither conscious nor unconscious. Although Brahman is not the subject of consciousness, scholastic Advaita consistently describes it as having the character of awareness. This apparent discrepancy can be resolved by the Advaita proclamation that Brahman is confirmed as existing only to reject nonexistence, and the identification of awareness as its essential character is only in order to reject the absence of consciousness. The MU identifies this *nirābhāsa* as the state of a yogin's mind compared to deep sleep (*suṣupta*), which, although is *nirābhāsa* or devoid of the instances of appearance, is the origin of all appearances.[55]

Ābhāsa as Pure Consciousness

The above description establishes that, depending upon the context, the concept of *ābhāsa* confirms subjective illusionism, nondual awareness, the monistic perspective of consciousness alone, or the nonsubstantial nature of all the entities that appear. Common to all these understandings is the notion that *ābhāsa* stands for something that is not real. This, however, is not the only application in which the term *ābhāsa* has been used. There are several instances where *ābhāsa* is used as synonymous to consciousness (*cid*). This position confirms the monistic perspective that illusion in form of subject and object or in form of the world has never occurred.

A general agreement among the schools applying the term *ābhāsa* is that it is *māyā* or *avidyā* that gives rise to duality. This, however, is not always the case, as shown by other instances of its occurrence in the MU. In some, *ābhāsa* is not caused due to ignorance, but it is consciousness (*cid*) itself and without any external cause.[56] Following this understanding, the world in the form of time, space, and so on is compared to the momentary appearance of lightning, affirming that consciousness itself is momentarily appearing in the form of the external world.[57] Along these lines, it is this "shining" (*bhās*) and not "false appearance" of the very solitary awareness free from beginning and end that gives rise to the concept of plurality.[58] The examples that agree with this specific understanding, wherein the objects of perception are considered as *ābhāsa*, as well as cognition or the absence of cognition, are identified with the same term, *ābhāsa*.[59] In these instances, the application of *ābhāsa* is in order to confirm the existence of Brahman alone.

The apparent discrepancy in Advaita literature, where the world is identified at the same time with ignorance as well as Brahman, needs to be explored in order to demonstrate how the MU reconciles this contradiction. If the world is identical to Brahman, then, *ābhāsa* does not explain illusory nature, as there is no illusion as such. However, the world cannot be the very Brahman shining, if the world is a false projection of illusion. The text demonstrates awareness of this contradiction. The MU distinguishes these two positions and confirms that the first position, the negation of the world identified with error, functions as a pedagogical strategy to confirm the higher position that there exists only Brahman.[60]

When *ābhāsa* is understood as "shining," or "illumination," the world is perceived as identical to Brahman. This concept rejects any origination and establishes *ekasattā*, the Advaitic stance that establishes a single degree of reality. Although rare in application, this specific position contrasts with the general agreement between the applications of the term *ābhāsa* found in Mahāyānic Advaya and Upaniṣadic Advaita. Following this position, the world and Brahman do not posit two different degrees of reality, and *ābhāsamātra* in this context does not refer to the falsity of the world but rather to the self-aware nature of the Brahman:

> ananyac chāntam ābhāsamātram ākāśanirmalam |
> brahmaiva jagad ity etat sarvaṃ sattvāvabodhataḥ ||
>
> With the knowledge of the reality (*sattva*), the world (*jagat*) is the very Brahman, [and] thus all of this [is] identical [to Brahman], in its essential form, of the character of consciousness only (*ābhāsamātra*) and free from impurities, such as the [clear] sky.[61]
> (YV III:9.30)[62]

The application of the term *ābhāsamātra* in the above example is noteworthy, as this understanding is congruent with other instances where *cinmātra* or *dṛṣṭimātra* is instead applied. The interpretation of the term *ābhāsamātra* as "consciousness only" is also supported by the commentary of Ānandabodhendra.[63] This understanding is found elsewhere, as in the following application of the term where it is used in the sense of pure awareness:

> anādicinmātranabho yat tat kāraṇakāraṇam |
> anantaṃ śāntam ābhāsamātram avyayam ātatam ||
>
> The sky of the character of awareness only, free from beginning, is the cause of all the causes. This is endless, free from functionings, appearance only (*ābhāsamātra*), free from destruction, and all-pervading.
> (YV VIb:82.4)
>
> evam ābhāsamātrasya kacato "niśam avyayam |
> sargādimadhyāntadṛśo mudhaivātroditāḥ sthitāḥ ||
>
> In this way, of this "appearance only" (*ābhāsamātra*), which is forever shining and indestructible, the perceptions of the beginning, middle, and end of creation are falsely arising or existing in this [essential nature].
> (YV VIa:94.63)

> bhittimātraṃ yathā citrajagad ālokamātrakam |
> citi cidvyomamātrātma tathaivābhāsamātrakam ||
>
> As the world in a painting is merely the canvas alone, [comprised of] perception (*āloka*) only, in the same way, [the world is] only *ābhāsa,* of the character of the void of consciousness in consciousness [alone].
> (YV VIb:168.6)

Further strengthening the aforementioned understanding of *ābhāsa* as pure consciousness with the self-aware nature of consciousness, the MUŚ/YV uses this term as identical to the witnessing self (*sākṣin*), and it is considered as the foundation for the functions that gives rise to the notion of duality. As explained:

> sākṣiṇi sphāra ābhāse dhruve dīpa iva kriyāḥ |
> sati yasmin pravartante cittehāḥ spandapūrvikāḥ ||
>
> As in the existence of a lamp, actions [are revealed], in the existence of the unbound and witnessing awareness, the activities of mind manifest subsequent to the pulsation [of mind].
> (YV III:9.68)[64]

Remarkably, the witnessing self in this verse is identified as *ābhāsa,* in whose existence the functions of various forms occur. The metaphor of lamp given in this verse requires explanation. The verb "to illuminate" (*pra+√kāś*) is applied to describe the function of lamp. However, a lamp cannot be an agent of the action of illumination. The *ābhāsa* or shining of the witnessing self is considered to be the same. With this example of lamp, luminosity is explicitly of the character of awareness. This shining, or the active engagement of being aware of something, does not constitute duality of the self. The appearance of the world is what appears in this awareness itself, when *ābhāsa* is used to describe the world. In fact, *ābhāsa* is not the outward appearance, but the character of consciousness.[65] Along the lines of this interpretation, *nirābhāsa,* a state of mind free from agitation, denotes the state of *ābhāsa,* or the flashing of the character of the self.[66]

This *ābhāsa* or illumination is considered as action only relative to the entity that it manifests. In one example where the concept of *ābhāsa* and *pratibimba* tally, this notion explicitly considers that something appears in the relative sense:

mukure cāmalābhāse pratibimbaṃ pravartate |

Counter-image occurs in the shining mirror free from dust (*amala*).
(YV VIa:36.11)

Explicitly, it is the nature of mirror to reflect what is in front of its surface. This, however, does not mean that the mirror, "reflecting" objects, is an agent of action that does certain activities. Congruent with this understanding, *ābhāsa* and *cit* are described as property and substance. Following one example found in the MU, just as gems have their radiance, so also is awareness endowed with worlds.[67] Creation, following this understanding, is identical to Brahman. This identity can be found described in terms of waves and the ocean, where the waves are, although considered to be different from and originated of the ocean, not separate from ocean itself.[68] This understanding of "as identical to Brahman" helps explain verses like:

dikkālādyanavacchinnarūpatvād ativistṛtam |
tad anādyantam ābhāsaṃ bhāsanīyavivarjitam ||

The Brahman (*tat*) is beginningless and endless and omnipresent (*ativistṛta*) because it is free from the limitations of space, time, and so on. [It is] *ābhāsa*,[69] devoid of entities to be illuminated.
(YV III:10.33)

This *ābhāsa* is described in terms of the supreme (*para*), one (*eka*), and unmade (*akṛtṛma*).[70] Also described as *sadābhāsa* and identified with *sat*, a synonym of the Brahman, it explains the awareness pertinent to liberated beings who have freed their minds from the entities of perception.[71] Three terms, *sat*, *cid*, and *ābhāsa* describe this nondual awareness that is free from modifications. This *ābhāsa*, identical to *sat*, is the foundation where *kalā* arises, which in turn gives rise to functionings. This nondual *ābhāsa* and the rise of *kalā* are compared to water and the waves.[72]

Congruent with the understanding of *ābhāsa* as awareness, this *ābhāsamātra* is *amala* or free from defilements and is conscious of all sentient beings. This is Brahman, identical to awareness (*cid*).[73] *Cinmātra* or consciousness only as the highest principle, identical to *ābhāsa*, is explained in terms of self-awareness (*svānubhūti*) and described as the immediate awareness in all instances.[74] These instances only verify that the application of *ābhāsa* in Advaita literature does not always confirm the illusory nature of entities that are described in terms of *ābhāsa*. These descriptions further function to portray the self-luminous nature of awareness, which in other instances is depicted in terms of *prakāśa* or *svaprakāśa*.[75]

This *ābhāsa*, described as the essential nature, is undoubtedly the very Brahman, with the passage applying the term *ābhāsa* parallel to terms such as essence (*sāra*), unborn (*aja*), free from beginning and end (*ādyantaśūnya*), and one (*eka*).[76] This understanding of *ābhāsa* differs from the one that stands for illusory appearance in the sense that it is pure and is of the character of the self, free from mental modifications.[77] If this *ābhāsa* is understood as other than the awareness of the character of the self, it will be difficult to comprehend instances such as the following:

> yat saṃvedyavinirmuktaṃ saṃvedanam anirmitam |
> cetyamuktaṃ cidābhāsaṃ tad viddhi paramaṃ padam ||
>
> You should know the awareness that is free from the object of consciousness [and which is] not constructed, the *ābhāsa* of consciousness that is free from objects of consciousness as the highest stage (*pada*).
> (YV VIa:6.4)

As in the instance above, *cidābhāsa* describes the very awareness itself with its inherent nature of shining. This *cidābhāsa* is free from mental modifications (*nirvikalpa*),[78] which further confirms that the meaning of *cidābhāsa* in this instance is different from the application of this term in scholastic Advaita.

As it has been pointed out, the term *ābhāsa* is used in two opposite senses: in the sense of pure awareness and to describe its self-luminous nature, and in the sense of false appearance. This understanding further complicates the reductive sense of meaning that can be derived from the MUŚ/YV, where *ābhāsa* follows the scholastic Advaita understanding of false appearance. Particularly, one cannot escape from the influence of mainstream Advaita while reading commentaries on the MUŚ/YV.[79] With this new understanding of *ābhāsa*, the necessity for an overarching philosophy that can resolve the contradictions within the single text becomes apparent. Arguably, the early Bhedābheda doctrine can resolve this apparent inconsistency. The foundation for this understanding is that duality and singularity are similar to the waves and the ocean: waves do not exist independent of the ocean, and the duality seen in the perception of waves does not constitute duality when perceived as water.

Cinmātra and *Ābhāsa* in Light of the Concept of *Bhedābheda*

The biggest hermeneutical challenge posed by the MU/YV is to resolve the contradiction occurring with the application of terminology in which the same language sometimes refers to something nonsubstantial, essentially false, and illusory, or at other times refers to the highest reality, the only reality that exists. Textual interpretation of *ābhāsa* could take any direction, without one philosophical position that allows for multiple understandings. In particular, the understanding of *ābhāsa* as pure consciousness itself does not even seem possible if the *ābhāsa* model of the scholastic Advaita of Śaṅkara is followed.

This problem of textual interpretation can be resolved more easily if a different philosophical model is adopted as the foundation for the concept that permeates the MU/YV. The doctrine of Bhedābheda, assigned to Bhartṛprapañca, an Advaitin earlier than Śaṅkara, arguably, gives an easier philosophical model for the hermeneutical challenge the text poses. Following this model, *bheda* (difference) and *abheda* (the absence of difference) are not inherently contradictory. These are two modes of the same reality. Along these lines, *prapañca* (verbal construction) is what constitutes duality, and *vilaya* (dissolution of such verbal construction) rejects the notion of duality.

This understanding also recognizes the Brahman's powers (*śakti*) to manifest in the form of the world, just as the ocean can take the shape of waves. This position does not reject the essential monistic position of the state in which there is no creation, that of pure Brahman itself. This position can be easily reconciled with the position of Maṇḍana which utilizes *prasaṅkhyāna* or mental reflection to resolve the difference that gives rise to the notion of duality. More appropriately, this position allows the active life to be a part of realization, as in the case of Janaka or Rāma, both kings and central characters in the philosophical epic the MU/YV.

In order to confirm that, while adopting the concept of *ābhāsa* in the YV, there are nonetheless instances that support the notion of *bhedābheda*, it is contextual to analyze some passages. The application of *ābhāsa* to describe luminosity serves as a model to describe the world as an inherent nature of Brahman:

> yathā dravatvaṃ salilaṃ spandatvaṃ pavano yathā |
> yathā prakāśa ābhāso brahmaiva trijagat tathā ||
>
> As the fluidity of water, the undulation (*spandana*) of wind, the luminosity (*ābhāsa*) of light, so is the world of Brahman.
> (YV III:11.19)

Following this understanding, there is no actual dissolution of the world, as the world is the property of Brahman, just as luminosity inheres to light. For liberation, then, the individual recognizes its own essential nature. Here, *ābhāsa* is the nature of Brahman, like the light of the sun. The world is not once more assigned to ignorance. Again, explaining origination as verbal construction, the text compares the rise of the world in pure awareness to the "shining of the sun" that permeates the sky. For the sun is light itself and is not shining or illuminating.[80]

This description suggests that there is actually no origination, but not because what appears is illusion in its phenomenal sense, but because what is considered as originated and different from its cause is not different in reality. For instance:

> yathāmbhasataraṅgādi yathā hemno 'ṅgadādi ca |
> tad evātad ivābhāsaṃ tathāhambhāvabhāvitaḥ ||
>
> As the waves etc. of water and as bracelets etc. of gold, the very [substance] appears as if not that. The same [is the case with] something imagined by I-sense.
> (YV VIa:112.6)

The rejection of entities with an application of the term *ābhāsa* needs to be read in light of this stance, where negation functions only to reject duality due to linguistic construction.[81] This understanding of *ābhāsa* aligns with the *ekasattā* doctrine that there exists only a single reality.[82] In this context, the question then is, what is *ābhāsa*? The MU explains *ābhāsa* in terms of "*pṛthak cetanam ābhāsa*" (appearance is to be aware differently).[83]

And what is the liberated state in which there is no duality and no bondage? It is apparent that, in this understanding, having the world or not having the world is not what causes bondage. Rather, it is the false perception of difference. This, however, does not reject the nondual state. Following the example of waves and water, just as there is calm water in the absence of waves, so also is there the essential consciousness only in which the world is dissolved.[84]

Following the example of the waves caused by the wind, the world is described in terms of *dṛśyābhāsa* (appearance of the objects of perception).[85] To illuminate is the inherent nature of pure consciousness, and its shining is explained in terms of the worlds of waking or dreaming.[86] Duality in the form of the world and awareness in its essential nature are two aspects that are always present: the world appears when perceived in terms of world, and there is never the world but only consciousness when perceived in those terms.[87] Bondage and liberation are two perceptions: the one who perceives bondage is bound, and the one who perceives liberation, is liberated. There is no phenomenal change, but only the change in perception, because it is merely a verbal construction that creates duality in terms of the subject of experience, other subjects, and the world of experience.[88]

Conclusion

Clearly, from the above description, select terminology is shared by different and sometimes contradictory philosophical positions. It cannot be argued that a term's meaning is found in its earliest historical occurrence, thus ruling out other possibilities. The case of *ābhāsa* explicitly compels multiple understandings of the same term. This again is directly antithetical to the argument that meaning can be reduced to a single understanding of a term found in one philosophy or one text, particularly the YV. Although identified as one single text, the YV displays multiple nuances of concepts, and the terms used preserve multiple meanings. However, it is not the intent of this chapter to leave the meaning open-ended, for textual interpretation is possible only when certain terms provide certain meaning. The quest for an overarching philosophy that can allow apparent contradiction, in this case resolved by the concept of Bhedābheda, is an approach for deciphering textual meaning which can be established by peeling away the layers of history built up as texts accrue multiple understandings and embody apparent contradiction. The reduction of textual meaning to one single sense is not possible, as this analysis demonstrates, wherein the authors of texts employ crucial technical terms in their fluid sense and in that way, are not exact in their application of terms, metaphors, or examples. It is therefore not reasonable to interpret or translate texts in a reductive fashion without considering the overarching philosophy of the text, as the terms found in the text have to be congruent with the foundational thought the text provides. Just as the example of dream does not confirm the same philosophy, although it is found equally in Madhyamaka, Yogācāra, and Advaita texts, so also is the case with the term *ābhāsa*. It is also explicit that a single text does not always use a term with the same meaning. Whether or not the term *ābhāsa* refers to false appearance, what is consistent in the case of the YV is that the term is congruent with the philosophy of *cinmātra*, where the nondual awareness in itself is free from the discourse of affirmation or negation.

Notes

1. For references on the YV, see Vasudeva Laxmana Sharma Pansikar, ed., *Yogavāsiṣṭha, with the Tātparyaprakāśa commentary* (Delhi: Motilal Banarsidass, 1984 [1918]).

2. anābhāsam na kenacit kalpitena viṣayeṇāvabhāsate | Māṇḍūkyopaniṣad-bhāṣya 3.4.

3. buddhyādikāryasamhāre pratyakcaitanyarūpiṇaḥ | cidbimbasyāpi samhāro jalārkapravilāpavat || Bṛhadāraṇyakopaniṣad-Bhāṣya-Vārttika (BĀUBhVā) 4.3.1174.

4. BĀUBhVā 2.3.191; 2.1.4; 4.3.73.

5. *Chāndogyopaniṣadbhāṣya-Ṭīkā* 6.3.2.

6. avasanno 'vamato vā bhāso 'vabhāsaḥ (Bhāmati 18.7, Joshi ed.).

7. Satyadeva Misra, "*Śāṅkarādvaitasammata ābhāsavada*" *Ṛtam* 1–1 (Lucknow: Akhila Bharatiya Sanskrit Parishad, 1969), 29–39.

8. Ibid., 34.

9. Ibid.

10. Schmithausen 1987, 203. See, *Ālayavijñāna: On the Origin and the Early Development of a Central Concept of Yogācāra Philosophy.* Part I: Text, Part II: Notes, Bibliography and Indices. Studia Philologica Buddhica Monograph Series IVa. and IVb. (Tokyo: The International Institute for Buddhist Studies, 1987).

11. dvayābhāsā iti grāhyagrāhakābhāsāḥ | MSA 11.32.

12. dvayābhāsatāsti dvayabhāvaś ca nāsti | MSA 11.21; dvayābhāsatāyā bhāvaḥ sa eva dvayasyābhāva iti | MSA 11.22.

13. svadhātuto dvayābhāsāḥ sāvidyākleśavṛttayaḥ | MSA 11.32.

14. MSA 11.33.

15. MSA 11.34.

16. MSA 11.35.

17. MSA 11.35.

18. MSA 11.40. For the first triad, see also MSA 11.44.

19. For treatment on three characters (*svabhāva*), see *Trisvabhāvanirdeśa* of Vasubandhu.

20. This is also addressed as *viṣayābhāsa* LAS 10.217.

21. See also LAS 2.99, 123, 128.

22. The application of *anābhāsa* is synonymous to *nirābhāsa*. See LAS 10.94.

23. I am thankful to Jurgen Hanneder for providing valuable references on the *Mokṣopāyaśāstra*.

24. For instance, see: cidākāśam eva bhāti jagattayā | (YV VIa:29.142).

25. brahmaiva jagadābhāsaṃ marutāpo yathā jalam | brahmaikālokanāc chuddhaṃ bhavaty ambu yathātapaḥ || (YV VIb:47.22–23).

26. In addition to the examples discussed above, following are significant to confirm this concept:

sad evāsambhavaddvitvaṃ mahācinmātrakaṃ tu yat || viśvābhāsaṃ tad evedaṃ na viśvaṃ san na viśvatā || (YV VIb:42.16)

eka evaiṣa ābhāsaḥ sabāhyābhyantarātmakaḥ | ā samudraṃ nadīvāhaśatasaṅghamayātmakam || (YV VIb:43.38)

cidvyomaśūnyatārūpamātra ābhāsa ātataḥ | idam apratighaṃ śāntaṃ jagad ity eva bhāsate || (YV VIb:161.14)

ābhāsamātraṃ dṛśyātma cinmātraṃ śāntam avyayam | sthitam āsthāḥ kim etasmin svabhāve sve vicāryate || (YV VIb:163.31).

27. nirmūlam eva bhātīdam abhātam api bhātavat | tasmād yad bhāsuram idaṃ tat tad eva padaṃ viduḥ || (YV VIb:163.28).

"Although without a cause, this [world] appears; although [it has] not appeared, it is as if [it had] appeared. For this reason, what is appearance is this [world] (*idam tat*), the same (*tad eva*) is known as supreme (*para*)." Translation by Jurgen Hanneder, *Studies on the Mokṣopāya*. Wiesbaden: Harrassowitz, 2006, 145–46.

28. Hanneder 2006, 146–47. The verses from the MUŚ cited by Hanneder in this context are MU 6.284.4; 6.284.2; 6.262.14.

29. YV VIb:106.34.

30. YV VIb:106.35.

31. mānasī kalanā yena yena bhāsāṃ vibhāsanam | (MUŚ III:9.75) and Bhāskarakaṇṭha's commentary there as: yena bhāsāṃ ghaṭādijñānānāṃ | vibhāsanaṃ sphuraṇaṃ | bhavati |.

32. pratibhāsavidhau dehaḥ sann asaṃś cānyadā smṛtaḥ || ābhāsamātram evedam itthaṃ samprati bhāsate | (YV VIa:28.18) MUŚ reads *saṃpratibhāsate* as a single word.

33. ā viriñcāt pravṛttena bhrameṇājñānarūpiṇā || asad eva sadābhāsam idam ālakṣyate 'nagha | (YV VIa:29. 10–11).

34. na viśvam asti naivāsīn na ca nāma bhaviṣyati | idam ābhāsate śāntaṃ cidvyoma paramātmani || (MUŚ VIa:260.79); See also (MU VIa:262.41).

jagat svapnabhramābhāsaṃ mṛgatṛṣṇāmbuvat sthitam | asad evedam ābhāti satyapratyayakāry api || (YV VIb:189.8).

35. ābhāsamātram evāyaṃ tathā dṛśyātmako bhramaḥ | cakracāpe yathā bhānti nānāvarṇā nabho 'ṇavaḥ || (MUŚ VIa:282.65). For similar reference, see also (YV VIb:28.13).

36. ādito yad anutpannaṃ na sambhavati karhicit | asadrūpam anābhāsaṃ kathaṃ tad anubhūyate || asad eva sadābhāsam anutpannam akāraṇaṃ | jāgrat svapnavad udbhūtam arthakṛc cānubhūyate || (YV VIb:190.74–75).

37. tena svapnavad ābhāsam idaṃ paśyati cinnabhaḥ | svarūpamātrakacanam ākāravad ivākulam || (YV VIb:205.6).

38. bhānaṃ bhāmātram ātmatvaṃ nijaṃ yat tac cidātmanaḥ | nabhasā svapnaśabdena kathyate jagadākṛti || (YV VIb:205.7).

39. For instance, see: cinmātraṃ sarvam evedam itthaṃ ābhāsatāṃ gataṃ | neha satyam asatyaṃ vā kvacid asti na kiñcana || YV, Nirvāṇa 12.23; na gṛhṇāti malaṃ bhūyas tāmratām iva kāñcanam | ābhāsamātram evedaṃ na san nāsaj jagattrayam || (YV VIa:28.46).

sarvaṃ svābhāsam eveti samyagālokanaṃ viduḥ | sadasanmayasaṃsāre yathābhūtārthadarśanāt || (YV VIa:28.49).

40. ābhāsamātram evedam ittham evāvabhāsate | dvicandravibhramākāraṃ sad asac ca vyavasthitam || (YV VIa:28.13).

41. taṃ cetati cidābhāsaṃ pūrvam ātmā svam ātmanā | tatra tanmayatāṃ dhatte tena tanmayarūpiṇīm || (MU VIa:177.11). The term *cidābhāsa* is not found in the parallel reading in (YV VIb:20.11).

42. aham ātmā trikoṇatvam upagacchati kalpanam | asad eva sadābhāsaṃ manyate cetanād vapuḥ || (YV VIb:22.32).

43. asmād udeti jīvālī dīpālī dīpakād iva || eṣa sa eva pūrvoktaḥ prajāpatir eva | sarveṣāṃ padārthānāṃ praticchandaḥ samaṣṭirūpaḥ ābhāsaḥ | bhavati | sarveṣām ābhāsānām etatsvarūpatvāt | (MUŚ III 14.10) and the commentary of Bhāskara thereon.

44. asmād eva praticchandāj jīvāḥ samprasaranty amī | asmāt prajāpatināmnaḥ | praticchandāt ābhāsāt | amī pratyaksaṃ sphuramāṇāḥ | jīvāḥ | samprasaranti sañcāraṃ yānti | (MU III 14.12) and Bhāskara's commentary thereon.

45. evaṃvidham tat kalanam ātmano 'ṅgam akṛtrimam | cetyonmukhacidābhāsaṃ jīvaśabdena kathyate || (YV VIb:188.2).

46. bhedo na bhedas tatrāyaṃ bhedo 'yaṃ yanmayaḥ kila | tad brahmaiva cidābhāsaṃ cidrūpaiva hi bhinnatā || (YV VIb:129.18).

47. deho 'haṃ cittadoṣo 'yaṃ kim anyat paridīvyate | dehāc ced anya evāhaṃ cidābhāsas tad aṅga he || YV, Nirvāṇa 29.59.

48. MU VIa:98.50.

49. tadā pṛthag ivābhāsaṃ saṅkalpakalanāmayam | mano bhavati viśvātmā bhāvayan svākṛtiṃ svayam || (YV VIa:114.16).

50. ākārarāśirūpeṇa bhūribhāvavikāriṇā | ābhāsa eva sphurati svapna eva mano nṛpa || (MU III 124.29).

51. sargasyādau tathaivedam ātmaiva svātmanātmani | vyomātmaiva cidābhāsaṃ dṛśyam ity avabhāsate || (YV VIa:171.9).

52. See for instance MU III:43.6; 44.3; 63.43; 100.26; 101.4; 124.31; 137.50; 161.30; 354.52.

For use of *samasamābhāsa*, see MU III:N2.24; 37.31; 46.17; 127.18; 354.26.

53. For instance: anākāram anādyantam anābhāsam anāmayam | śāntaṃ cinmātraṃ sanmātraṃ brahmaivedaṃ jagadvapuḥ || (MUŚ, III:297.34); sarvam apratighaṃ śāntaṃ jagad ekaṃ cidambaram | aniṅganam anābhāsam ātmany evātmanāsyatām || (MUŚ III:301.78).

54. (MU III 190.34) For the use of *nirābhāsa*, see also: na cānādinirābhāsaṃ nirākāraṃ cidambaram | dṛśaḥ kāraṇam anyasyāh kvacid bhavitum arhati || (YV III:364.32).

55. tena yogī suṣuptātmā vyavahāry api śāntadhīḥ | āste brahma nirābhāsaṃ sarvābhāsasamudgakaḥ || (YV III:10.26). See also: kāṣṭhamaunadaśābhāsaṃ sansāram avaśiṣyate | (YV VIb:42.25).

56. YV VIb:195.45.

57. janayaty accham ābhāsaṃ bhaṅguraṃ sphuraṇāt svataḥ | jagadrūpaṃ niśāvidyud iva cit kālakhādi ca || (MU VIa:134.2).

58. evam ādyantarahitam ekam evedam ātatam | ittham ābhāsate bhāsā svayā nānyāsti kalpanā || MU, Nirvāṇa 136.12.

59. ābhāsamātram evedaṃ dṛśyam ity avabudhyate . . . bhedo 'tra vāci na tv arthe tasmān nāsty eva bhinnatā || (YV VIb:103.14–16).

60. bhrāntir eveyam ābhāti jagadābhāsarūpiṇī | bhrāntir evāpi vā naiva brahmasattaiva kevalā || MU, Nirvāṇa 350.2.

61. The commentary of Bhāskara on the *Mokṣopāya* thereon is also significant: anena prasaṅgena jagadbrahmaṇoḥ aikyam eva punaḥ punaḥ kathayati [ananyac . . . |32|] jagat kartṛ | ananyat sarvarūpatvena sthitatvāt svavyatiriktavasturahitaṃ | śāntaṃ svarūpe viśrāntam | ābhāsa-mātra-kam ābhāsamātrasvarūpam | ākāśanirmalam ākāśavat svaccham | brahma eva bhavati | ity eva etad eva | satyāvabodhinaḥ satyajñānayuktasya | satyaṃ bhavati || The commentary of Bhāskara on (MU III:9.32). For the commentary of Bhāskara on the Utpatti section of the MU, see Walter Slaje, *Bhāskarakaṇṭhas Mokṣopāya-Ṭīkā: Die Fragmente des 3. (Utpatti-) Prakaraṇa*. Graz: EWS-Fachverlag, 1995.

62. MU reads this verse as: . . . ity eva satyaṃ satyāvabodhinaḥ || (MUŚ III 9.32).

63. *ābhāsamātram cinmātram* . . . Tātparyaprakāśa commentary on (YV III:9.30).

64. Bhāskara's commentary in this verse helps to clarify the metaphor of the lamp and the concept of witnessing self: sākṣiṇi sarvāsāṃ staimityaspandāvasthānāṃ grāhakatvena sākṣibhūte | sphāre vyāpake | ābhāse sphurattaikasāre | dhruve udāsīne | yasmin sati sannidhimātraṃ bhajati sati | citrehāḥ nānāvidhāḥ manovyāpārāḥ | kathambhūtāḥ | spandapūrvikāḥ śarīraceṣṭāḥ | pravartante | tatsahitā ity arthaḥ | asati āntare kasmin cittattve vikalpānāṃ śarīraceṣṭānāṃ cotthānaṃ yuktaṃ na syād iti bhāvaḥ | kā iva | kriyā iva lokakriyā iva | yathā dīpe sannidhimātraṃ bhajati lokakriyā svayam eva pravartante | tathety arthaḥ || Bhāskara on (MU III:9.70).

65. nūnaṃ bodhe 'virūḍhasya nāhantā na jagatsthitiḥ || bhāsate paramābhāsarūpiṇaḥ kāpy avasthitiḥ | (YV VIb:45.59–60).

66. yaḥ prabuddho nirābhāsaṃ param ābhāsam āgataḥ | svacchāntaḥkaraṇaḥ śāntas taṃ svabhāvaṃ sa paśyati || (YV VIb:52.38).

67. kā nāma vimalābhāsās tasmin paramacinmaṇau | na kacanti vicinvanti vicitrāṇi jaganti yāḥ || (YV, Nirvāṇa 37.2).

68. For instance, see (MU III:9.71) and the commentary of Bhāskara thereon.

69. For explanation of Bhāskara: . . . bhāsanīyavivarjitam ābhāsajñeyarahitajñānasvarūpam ity arthaḥ || (MUŚ III:10:33).

70. sampannaḥ śāntam ābhāsaṃ param ekam akṛtrimam | kvāstam etu kva vodetu kīdṛgvapur asāv iti || (MU VIa:155.11).

71. dṛśyād yo viratiṃ yāta ātmārāmaḥ śamaṃ gataḥ | sa sann eva sadābhāsaḥ paritīrṇabhavārṇavaḥ || (YV VIb:38.31).

72. saṃvedyenāparāmṛṣṭaṃ śāntaṃ sarvātmakaṃ ca yat | tat saccidābhāsamayam astīha kalanojjhitam || samudeti tatas tasmāt kalā kalanarūpiṇī | (YV VIa:, 9.2–3).

73. ābhāsamātram amalaṃ sarvabhūtāvabodhakam || sarvatrāvasthitaṃ śāntaṃ cidbrahmety anubhūyate | (YV, Nirvāṇa I, 11.67–68).

74. cinmātram amalābhāsaṃ kalākalanakalpanam | pratyakṣadṛśyaṃ sarvatra svānubhūtimayātmakam || (YV VIa:39. 18).

75. This reading of *ābhāsa* can be further confirmed by the application of *ābhāsvara*:

bhuvanāḍambarādarśe cidā [tmānam upāsmahe] | aciraskahakārāntam ābhāsvaram akhaṇḍitam || (MU VIa:11.122).

76. ajam asaram anādyaṃ buddham ādyantaśuddhaṃ śivam amalam ajalpaṃ sarvagaṃ śāntam ekam | bahir abahir apīśaṃ jñaṃ vinirmāṇam agryaṃ kam api tam upagamyaṃ sāram ābhāsam āhuḥ || (MU VIa:155.37).

77. pratyakcetanam ābhāsaṃ śuddhaṃ saṅkalpavarjitam | agamyam enam ātmānaṃ viddhi duṣṭadṛśam iha || (MU III:62.5).

78. tasmāt sāratarāt sāraḥ kiñcid anyan na vidyate | nirvikalpacidābhāsa eva sarvatra kāraṇam || (MU VIa:135.25).

79. The application of *ābhāsa* in the following verse where *sadābhāsa* is identical to *vyomātman* can be interpreted in the first sense, pure awareness. However the commentary of Bhāskara explains *ābhāsa* explicitly in the sense of illusory appearance: ardhonmīlitadṛgbhrūbhūmadhyatārakavaj jagat | vyomātmaiva sadābhāsaṃ svarūpaṃ yo 'bhipaśyati || . . . sadābhāsaṃ sad ivābhāsata iti sadābhāsam | paramārthato na sad ity arthaḥ || (MU III:9.56).

It contradicts with the following application of sadābhasa, if the meaning of this term is derived only following the lines of Bhāskara: etat tat sadābhāsam etat prāpya na śocyate | puṣpasyāntar ivāmodaṃ prāṇasyāntar avasthitam || (MU VIa:26.56).

80. idaṃ tv acetyacinmātrabhānor bhānaṃ nabhaḥ prati | tathā sūkṣmaṃ yathā meghaṃ prati saṅkalpavāridaḥ || tu viśeṣe | acetyacinmātrabhānoḥ cetyādūṣitacitsūryasya | bhānam ābhāsaḥ | idaṃ jagat | MU Utpatti 15.11 and the commentary of Bhāskara. This metaphor of sun is found elsewhere as well: taraṅgabhaṅgurāṇy antar bahiś cāvṛttimanti ca | ābhāsamātrarūpāṇi tejasy ātmavivasvataḥ || (YV VIb:59.56).

81. The verse in the sequence of gold and ornaments where the existence of the other is rejected is: tasmād anyan na tatrāsti yad asti ca sa eva tat | yac cānyat tattadābhāsaṃ na ca paśyati durmatiḥ || (YV VIa:112.18).

82. There is an explicit reference of *ekasattā* in the MUŚ that tallies with this the examples discussed here: bṛṃhitā bharitākārā sattaikā pāramārthikī | ābhāsaiḥ prasphuraty evam abdhir ūrmyādibhir yathā || (MU VIb:124.45).

83. pṛthak cetanam ābhāsaḥ saṃvid astīti niścaye | bhāvānām avikārāṇāṃ bhrāntijānām abhāvanāt || (MU Via:127.11).

84. spandātmatāyāṃ śāntāyāṃ yathāspandaṃ jaladravaḥ | na vetti jagadābhāsaṃ citaḥ prasaraṇaṃ tathā || (MU Via:169.2).

85. spandaśaktis tadicchedaṃ dṛśyābhāsaṃ tanoti sā | sākārasya narasyecchā yathā vā kalpanāpuram || (MU Via:241.6).

86. śuddhā saṃvit svabhāvasthā yat svayaṃ bhāti bhāsvarā | tasyā bhānasya tasyāsya jāgratsvapnābhidhāḥ kṛtāḥ || (YV VIb:143.16).

87. idaṃ tribhuvanābhāsam īdṛśaṃ bhāti sarvadā | śāntaṃ rāma samaṃ brahma neha nānāsti kiñcana || (YV VIb:212.15).

88. tvam ahaṃ jagad ityādi śabdārthaiḥ brahma brahmaṇi | śāntaṃ samasamābhāsaṃ sthitam asthitam eva sat || (YV VIb:54.2).

4

Is This a Dream?

A Critique of *Mokṣopāya*'s Take on Experience, Objecthood, and the "External" World

Arindam Chakrabarti

The Ineliminable Possibility That the Current Experience Is a Dream

"What evidence could be appealed to, supposing we were asked at this very moment whether we are asleep or awake,—dreaming. . . . or talking to one another in the waking state?," Socrates asked Theaetetus. "Indeed, Socrates," answered Theaetetus, "I do not see by what evidence it is to be proved; for the two conditions correspond in every circumstance like exact counterparts" (*Theaetetus*, 158c–e). Theaetetus was a clever young man. Perhaps what he anticipated was the following difficulty. Even if one found a set of decisive criteria (call it "W") consisting of, say, coherence, continuity, clearness, vividness, or uncanceled contents, which marks off waking life from dreaming, one could never be sure, on any particular occasion of applying those criteria W whether or not one was just *dreaming that* the current experience satisfies W.

Since then many stones have been kicked by the Dr. Johnsons, many hands have been raised and displayed by the G. E. Moore, and many proofs of the external world have been offered by the Udayanācāryas and Vyāsatīrthas. But the dream possibility keeps cropping up and haunting philosophers. And when the fragility, absurdity, disjointness, and agonies of this world become unbearable to a reflective person, one cannot but hope to wake up one day from this nightmare of the so-called waking life. Texts such as Gauḍapāda's *Māndūkyakārikā,* Vasubandhu's *Vijñaptimātratāsiddhi,* and the *Yogavāsiṣṭha* / *Mokṣopāya* (YV / MU) take this ineliminable skeptical possibility to its mystical idealistic culmination. More or less following the line of Gaudapāda, the MU first shows that the conventional distinction between dreamt content and wakefully perceived content is drawn in terms of inner versus outer, being enclosed or limited (*samvṛta*) within the sleepy mind of a single person versus being open to the public, being unstable versus being stable, being canceled versus remaining uncanceled, and so on. Generalizing from these hallmarks of a dream or a sustained illusion, Gaudapāda had formulated his favorite dictum: "*ādau ante ca yat nāsti, vartamāne api tat tathā*" (MK 2/6), That which was not there in the beginning will not be there at the end, and must be nonexistent even at present (when it appears to be existent). Vasiṣṭha produces numerous stories to shake our externalist realist conviction that the common world where we think we are all awake, alive, and kicking is stable, uncanceled, continuous, unenclosed, and safely reidentifiable across time.

So-called waking life is connected by stable, temporally continuous pieces of cognition. Dream experience is fickle and discontinuous. But if one notices how ephemeral and momentary the objects of wakeful perceptions are, and if one can have the same or a continuous dream even at other times, then waking life would become dream, and dream life, because of its continuity, would become waking.

Thus, the impermanence thesis about the external world boils down to the dream thesis. At this point, one vital difference must be pointed out between the Yogācāra Buddhist deployment of the impermanence-to-subjectivity argument and Vasiṣṭha's use of the dream-world equation. While "imagination" and "language" are regarded by the Buddhist as fictional conceptual proliferations "distorting" the real flow of consciousness and mental states, the "sparks of speech," the beginningless Vedic Logos—giving us the blueprint of the creative imagination of the playful First Mind—are valued positively by Vasiṣṭha. The world-dream of the Absolute is rendered possible by primordial speech, which is the root of the plural public world as well as of our moral obligations. The *Yogavāsiṣṭha* (YV) unites the Mīmāṃsā idea of unuttered Vedic sentences as the foundational source of ethical obligation with the Tantric idea of listening to one's own body to hear the cosmic sounds. A mysterious verse in the last Canto of the YV states:

aveda-śāstreṇa jagatyaśeṣair bhūtaih svadehālaya bhitti-
bhāgāt |
etad vidheyam na vidheyam etad dhvanih svatah ṣrūyata
eva nityam ||
(YV VIb:131.49)

The statement "This has to be done, that should not be done" refers to sound that is audible constantly and spontaneously arising from the foundation stone of the house which is one's own body, constituted by those innumerable material elements, through this sonorous body which is itself an "unknowing disciplining text."

Utpattiprakaraṇa—the chapter on origin—starts with this pregnant verse:

Vag bhābhir brahmavid brahma bhāti svapna ivātmani |
Yad idam tat svaśabdothhair yo yad vetti sa vettu tat ||
(YV III:1.1)

With the sparks of speech, within Its own self, Brahman—Absolute subjective consciousness—who alone knows Brahman, appears as this world, as it were in a dream. Whoever knows whatever expressed through pronouns such as "what," "this," "that," "itself" comes to know that same consciousness.

The underlying fusion of a Bhartṛhari-type speech cosmogony and accommodation of an impersonal intrinsic validation of Vedic injunctions within a broadly idealistic dream-world-identification is unique to the MU and cannot, by any means, be called Buddhist. This entirely syncretic, yet predominantly Upaniṣadic, origin story is given in subtle details in a dense passage of *Utpattiprakaraṇa,* chapter 12, verses 6–15.

There are further arguments which show dream and waking to be *counterparts* of one another; almost like mirror images, except that there is no telling which one is the original and which one is the mirror image. Elsewhere Vasiṣṭha puts this succinctly, not with the usual Buddhist double-moon example, but with a double-sun example:

yathā dvau sadṛśau sūryau yathā dvau sadṛśau narau |
jāgrat-svapnau tathaivaitau manāgapyatra nānyatā ||
(YV VIb:105.18)

Like two isomorphic suns or two identical persons, waking and dream are identical; there is not an iota of distinction between them. This claim is defended against Rāma's realist qualms regarding sublation (the overriding cancellation of a previous state by a subsequent more real state): Doesn't waking up break or annul a dream, whereas nothing seems to annul waking life? Why should not this be the crucial dissimilarity between them? Vasiṣṭha says: "No, just as the span of the dream is enclosed by two periods of wakefulness, the span of each segment of waking life is flanked by two periods of sleep. If the dream person dies as he wakes up, the waking person also dies as he falls asleep." Dead here in a dream, he is said to be alive and woken up elsewhere; then dying there, he is back and born again in another dream—living thus from one dream to another. Both the periods—the sleep life and the waking life—have their own narrative histories equally convincing internal stories to tell, and thus they become analogues of one another.

> itihāsmayau eva jāgrat-svapnau ubhāv api |
> parasparam gatāvetau upamānopameyatām ||
>
> Both wakefulness and dream are made of histories, and they have become reference-points for comparison for each other.
> (YV VIb:105.20–31)

What is happening in the YV is more than mere analytical argumentation or throwing of a skeptical challenge. A series of phenomenological analogies or points of resemblance between dream and waking are being deepened through the literary and meditative devices of imaginary narratives. The stories are very similar to bizarre science fiction thought experiments in contemporary Western philosophy. They craftily interweave multiple dreams and deaths within dreams and multiple waking-up experiences within a dream, until the possibility that one is passing from one dream to another when one seems to be waking up and the possibility that while falling asleep one is just waking up into another equally real—or, what is the same thing, equally ephemeral—world comes alive. Such vividly imagined possibilities open the way to an objectless nonintentional pure empty consciousness to shine forth without this flimsy ontological hierarchy of objective and subjective worlds.

To illustrate the narrative-meditative-imaginative method of the YV, take the following story from *Nirvāṇa* (VIa) chapter 62. In the story, there is a man, suggestively called "Jīvata"—the living fellow—who, like any average person, wants to be a learned scholar. So he becomes a learned scholar, but he becomes frustrated. Very soon, he has a different ambition. Envying the powerful rulers of the region, he says, "I want to be re-born as a local chieftain, as a tribal lord or a powerful king." So, in this mind-only world where to recurrently imagine is to re-incarnate, he becomes a tribal chief. But, as a local chieftain, he is always tortured by the monarch of the larger state to which this hunter community belongs, so he becomes the king of this country. As the country's king, he is constantly thinking about a celestial beauty, a fairy queen (an *apsaras*), because powerful kings are always besotted by heavenly females. Obsession leads to identification, so he actually becomes a celestial female. Then, the celestial female is jealous of a pet doe who has eyes more beautiful than hers. She becomes the doe. Constantly thinking about a particularly succulent creeping vine, now the doe becomes the vine. The vine falls in love with a bee and becomes a bee. The bee is, of course, so fond of the honey in the lotus that it becomes a lotus. Fear can lead to obsession too! The lotus one day is nervous about a huge elephant which always moves about near it. Afraid of being trampled and crushed by it, the lotus keeps thinking of the elephant as a prospective aggressor. The thinker transforms into the object of thought, and the lotus becomes the elephant. The elephant somehow, through a series of changes, manages to become a bee, and the bee this time makes friends with the swan—which happens to be the swan of Brahma—and then friendship congeals into identification, and he becomes the swan of the Creator God. And as the swan of Brahma he accompanies him on some of his social visits. Brahma often visits Rudra: Creator meets Destroyer. Now, Jīvata, who is this swan, thinks to himself, "This is my chance of a lifetime. I should meditate and fixate one-pointedly about this Rudra and become a Rudra." And he does. Once he becomes a Rudra, he thinks of his previous hundred incarnations as a bee, as an elephant, as a creeping vine, as a lotus, as a doe, as hundreds of beings, and he makes himself all these hundred things. Thus emerges the myth and reality of the hundred Rudras in dream world (*svapna-śatarudrīya*).

This imaginative deepening of a logical possibility is a spiritual meditative exercise. Philosophical argumentation, vivified by imaginary identity-rupturing narratives, congeals into meditation. Spiritual experience is expected to dawn through simultaneously fictional, poetic, and analytically argumentative discourse in the YV. The underlying reasoning behind this spiritual exercise has been formulated very succinctly in several classical Indian philosophical texts as follows:

> Waking experiences are with external basis / object.
> Because they are experience

Just as dream experiences are
(jāgrat-pratyayaḥ nirālambanaḥ, pratyayatvāt,
svapna-pratyaya-vat)

To spell it out in the form of a set of initially plausible premises leading to an idealistic conclusion:

1. Dreams are devoid of external objects.
2. The so-called correct experiences of external objects during our waking life are phenomenologically indistinguishable from dreams.
3. If two experiences are indistinguishable in their felt quality, then, if one of them is known surely to be false or devoid of external objects, the other must be so too.

Therefore, the so-called correct experiences of waking life are also false or devoid of external objects.

In the rest of this chapter, I try to make the strongest case *against* this general dream idealism, following the classical Indian realist line of argument. But in the conclusion of the chapter, I *return to the phenomenological plausibility of "disillusionment"* or a spiritual awakening experience which may make this "solidly objective external world" melt away like a richly textured, many-layered dream.

The refuter of idealism—Mīmāṃsāka, Naiyāyika, or a Western realist such as Thomas Reid, G. E. Moore, or Bertrand Russell—would attack the argument spelled out above by either questioning one or more of its premises or questioning the panillusionist philosopher's right to draw inferences at all, that is, pointing out a self-refutation in the idealists' claim to have proved anything at all during what he is telling us is his own dream. Accordingly, the refuter of idealism has the following four avenues of attack.

A. Premise 1 is false. Dreams *do have* external objects. As Kant puts it, no inner experience is possible without outer experience, and especially without a correct location of the perceiver's body in the objective spatiotemporal framework. If one explains illusory experiences in general and dream experiences in particular in terms of the *anyathākhyāti* (otherwise-presentation) theory of error, then every individual bit of dream experience borrows its object from the external world given to wak-

> ing life. After all, it is memories of waking life which get recombined and presented, "otherwise," in the wrong order, in dream. In so far as dreams have physiological causes such as indigestion or the stimulation of the sensory centers in the brain during R.E.M. sleep, those physical causes of a dream could be called its objective supports (*ālambana-s*) anyway. When, after a heavy and spicy dinner accompanied by heavy drinking at a restaurant, a philosopher dreams that he is having a conversation with an attractive woman never seen before, what he could politely tell the woman within his dream is: "Madam, it was nice meeting you, but I know you are nothing but that undigested piece of Tandoori chicken I ate last night." Both as mere causes as well as recognizable appearing objects with names and descriptions that we have learned in waking life for them, external objects support dream experiences, since the only objects available to us are external after all.

Adopting a very strong realist line, Madhvāchārya challenges the equation of reality and externality as follows: "Even in dreams, a truly real world subsisting in the mind in the form of wishful-impressions is seen as if it is externally existing" (*Viṣṇu-tattva-vinirṇaya,* 345). The point seems to be that as far as the reality of the objects is concerned, dream objects are just as real as waking objects. It is only a mistake to take them as public external objects. In one sense therefore there is nothing inherently "false" about a dream.

B. Premise 2 is false. Dreams and waking experiences are not indistinguishable. This is the line of attack I want to flesh out in the next section using the *Nyāyalīlāvatī* (NL) of Vallabha. There is a modern, Western way of questioning this premise which is interesting and has no parallel at all in Indian philosophy. This line, taken by Norman Malcolm, holds that there are no *dream-cognitions,* properly labeled. If we are dreaming, then we are asleep. If we are asleep, then we cannot be thinking or judging. There cannot be any cognitions, correct or erroneous, without thinking or judging. Therefore, there are no experiences or judgments in a dream even to be contrasted, let alone compared with waking experiences, waking judgments. All we have is a language game of talking about one's dreams *after one has woken up*, but that can be explained without assuming that some experiences were going on in the mind of the dreamer during the dream. I shall not spend time on this provocative view on which there is a substantial amount of critical literature (see, for example. Margaret Macdonald's paper "Dreaming and Waking" *in Mind* [72] 1953).

C. Premise 3 is false or counterproductive. From inside the content of the experience, the experience of looking at a lifelike statue, like a Madame Tussaud wax image, or an illusionistic painting of the sky, may be exactly similar to the experience of looking at a man or through the window at the sky outside. But *ex hypothesi* the two experiences do not have the same kind of objective support. As Śaṅkarācārya has clichéd the issue in his refutation of Vijñānavāda under "*vaidharmyāt na ca svapnādivat*" (BSBh II:2.29)—in spite or indeed because of the felt similarity with the awareness of things outside us—we say about dreams: *yad antarjñeya rūpam tat bahirvat avabhāsate*" (That which is merely inside appears as if it is outside). Now, if any "outside" does not exist at all, if the very notion of things without the mind is as incoherent as the son of a barren woman, then how can we even say "*bahir-vat*" because nothing can even appear to be *like* the son of a barren woman?

Finally, the tables could be turned against the idealist precisely on the basis of this premise: if the two experiences are exactly similar, and waking experiences are known to have real external objects, then by the same logic, dream experiences also should have real external objects. This could also, technically, take the form of a counterargument proving the opposite conclusion: dream experiences have external objects because they are experiences, just as waking experiences do!

D. The entire argument and, for that matter, any argument, is unavailable to the idealist who believes that she is and we are constantly dreaming. One can get intellectual inspiration from dreams, but if a logical argument is given only during a dream, then one has merely

> *dreamed* that the conclusion follows from the premises but has *not proved* that they actually do. The whole dream argument is operationally self-refuting because if it is valid and sound, then it is as valueless as sleep talk. Of course, there can be some controversy whether a deductive inference drawn entirely within a dream can be claimed to be valid, but, for sure, the material (outside the dream) truth of a conclusion cannot be claimed from an allegedly sound inference entirely drawn within a dream!

Nyāyalīlāvatī on the Similarity and Dissimilarity between Dream and Waking

Svapna (dreaming) is listed as a case of "nonknowledge" (*avidyā*) in the standard Vaiśeṣika taxonomy along with doubt, error, and non-ascertaiment. On behalf of a skeptical opponent, Vallabha asks: "But why is dream a case of nonknowledge, since it does not differ in nature at all from knowledge?"

The state of dream and the state of wakeful knowledge appear to be exact counterparts of each other like the appearances of the left and the right breasts of a woman. (The point of this odd analogy seems to be: if you trust one, you have to trust the other as real! Not a terribly strong argument). Suppose it is said that dreams are, after all, canceled, broken, superseded. The skeptic's response would be, "What does cancellation amount to here?" The experiential content or object is not taken away, neither is the (scary or erotic or agitating) effect of the dream on the person nullified, by the so-called annulment of the dream. All it amounts to is that there is another subsequent conflicting experience, which is true even of waking life, when it is followed by a conflicting dream. Your dream that you are swimming in an ocean "cancels and supersedes" your waking experience that you are in your bedroom, but your experience that you were on your bed in your own house was originally canceled and superseded by your dream that you were swimming in the ocean! You cannot hope to establish that waking life is posterior hence truer because one never knows how often, in a beginningless series, an apparently "final" waking up period has been followed (hence "canceled") by a subsequent dream period. If we try to use some sort of a coherence criterion to distinguish the two states, we would have to say something like the following, as indeed Udayana did at the end of his *Ātmatattvaviveka* chapter on the refutation of the idealist Buddhist. During the waking state, an internally coherent mutually corroborating set of experiences is the rule, and incongruence and mutual cancellation is the exception (with occasional errors and disagreements between the verdicts of different senses etc.), whereas during the dream state, incoherence seems to be the rule, and an accidental (like the crow sitting on the palm tree and the ripe fruit falling at the same time by fluke!) occasional consistency is the exception. When dreams corroborate each other, this happens just by fluke. But this distinction between accidental and regular concordance is ultimately arbitrary. Even within the so-called fortuitous fitting together of the vivid, credible, and coherent experiences of a dream, the correct re-identification of an item (a room or a friend) encountered earlier is as common as in a waking experience. Within our waking life, on the other hand, the apparently coherent re-identification of the continuous flame of a candle as "the same" is rejected, upon scrutiny, as erroneous. Surely, just the larger and fewer number of corroborating factors or the longer or shorter duration of the uncanceled experiences cannot be the deciding factors for the objectivity of one and the mistakenness of the other. As Socrates remarked against such a quantitative evaluation: "We now, are we going to fix the limits of truth by the clock?" (Theaetetus, 156e).

And Vallabha's imaginary skeptic refers to the same counterevidence here. "Not only is there occasional cancellation of our perceptions during the waking states. If we consider the 'waking world' of a madman it will most probably have larger number and longer duration of a chaos of mutually incongruous cancellable elements than many of our dream-worlds" (NL:454–57). So, just by a larger number of incoherences or cancellations within their contents, one cannot demarcate dreams from wakeful states.

Let us now concentrate on *Nyāyalīlāvatī*'s own examination of the skeptical no-distinction claim: the claim that dream and waking are indistinguishable. There could be three senses in which dream and waking could be exactly on a par, as the skeptic above has claimed. First, both of them are veridical experience (*pramāṇatvena aviśeṣa*).

Second, both of them are erroneous (*apramāṇatvena aviśeṣa*); dream as dream and waking as waking are equivalent because dreamhood is the same as wakinghood.

Now, the first option is hopeless because the distinction between veridical and nonveridical experience is publicly established, and it is the very basis for the concepts of waking and dream. When I dream that I am swimming and experience soon after wakefully that I am and was not swimming, both the verdicts cannot be equally true or veridical since p and not-p cannot be true together. It is veridical wakeful experience which can ascertain when one has really woken up, and once the waking up moment is ascertained, it is impossible to call the previous and the subsequent states equally veridical (unless one is ready to say that it is the same man who is a tribal chief in a jungle and at the same time a king in a palace in a faraway city).

The second option—that both dream judgments and wakeful judgments are equally false—would lead to the rejection of the skeptic's or idealist's thesis. The belief of the pan-illusionist and his contention that dream and waking are indistinguishable, in so far as it is a wakeful judgment, would also have to be false. Therefore its opposite must be true, and therefore, the two states must be actually distinguishable.

The third option is directly controverted by our immediate experience. Dreams have a quite different status, especially after they have been distinguished from the status of waking. What if this immediate experience of ours that testifies to the distinction between the two states is itself false? What if, as philosophers, we need to correct or reject the commonsense idea that dreaming is one thing, and waking is another?

Here Vallabha makes a masterly move. What about this special philosophical corrective awareness which tells us that our immediate experience of dream reality distinction is false? Is that falsity-revealing awareness itself true or false? If it is itself false, then our natural commonsensical experience is correct, and the distinction stands. If the corrective awareness is true, and waking and dreaming are nondistinct after all, then as a waking awareness it has to be nondistinct from all immediate experiences and thus will have to be true and false at the same time.

Finally Vallabha says that even if fail to offer watertight definitions of what it is to be awake and what it is to dream, the distinction between them is as patently evident as the distinction between pain and pleasure. Just as if someone, faced with some difficult cases where a painful experience is inextricably mixed with a pleasurable one, perversely claims that pain and pleasure are qualitatively the same feeling or that their distinction is not intelligible by analysis, we can only appeal to our own experience—here too the general and radical distinction between dream and waking is to be accepted on the basis of direct experience.

It is slightly ironic that Vallabha uses the parallel example of the antithetical couple pain and pleasure, because in explaining why

Udyotakara lists "*sukha*" as one of the twenty-one kinds of "*duḥkha*," Vācaspati says explicitly in the *Tatpāryaṭīkā* that even *sukha* is *duḥkha* because it is always connected with and indistinguishable from the latter.

In their debate with the "All is suffering" thesis of the Buddhist, the Nyāya philosophers of life emerge with the following subtle stand. Pleasures do exist in human experience, pleasures, distinct from, although felt alongside, pains. But if one has to be liberated from all existential suffering, *one ought to look upon even those rare and unstable pleasures as pains.* What if one applies the same wisdom to the dream-waking distinction? Yes, there is a real distinction. We are not dreaming all the time. Sometimes we are genuinely awake and in touch with a real external world. But our so-called wakeful life is also so mixed up with errors and illusions and tiny bits of dreams and misjudgments that if one wants to attain "*tattva-jñāna*" (knowledge of the true nature of things), one should *strategically* look upon even waking life as a kind of coherent protracted dream.

I know that this is not what any classical Nyāya-Vaiśeṣika philosopher would come out and say. But Udayana's conjecture that the Advaita philosophers, in their urgency to get liberated, find this world to be of "little use" (*manda-prayojantvāt)* is perhaps a gesture towards a compromise like the above.

The Alleged Unintelligibility of Objecthood

My own hunch is that the hidden insight of the pan-illusionist finds an underlying link between intentionality of any sort and "falsity," in the sense of rational unintelligibility. In so far as all our wakeful cognitive acts are directed towards an object other than themselves, they involve a mixture of dreamlike conceptual linguistic imagination, and to that extent they are equivalent to dreams. Not only are our dreams, illusions, and false beliefs products of ignorance, but to perceive or cognize anything outside of consciousness itself, with the natural claim that what is perceived or accessed can and does exist unperceived or unknown, is to cognize an object of our ignorance. An object of ignorance is seen as also partly unseen; what is known as knowledge-independent and partly unknown, is grasped as escaping our grasp. That is why normal object-directed awarenesses are constituted by ignorance, just as our dreams are. Notice how the claim of falsity (or ignorance-generatedness) is not based upon subjectivity (that our subject mental states have constructed these contents), but based precisely upon the claim of the objectivity of the content. For, to be objective or external is to be such that while knowing such content we can simultaneously remain somewhat ignorant about the content as well. This known-unknown nature is one of the incoherences inherent in our notions of the world that manifests itself to our waking consciousness. We reject dreams as illusions because they are incoherent. While undeniably "presented," dreams must be "nonreal" because they are subsequently annulled and superseded. The idealists' point is that any object-directed cognitive state is incoherent in the same sense as dreams are: what appears in it is undeniably presented, but it is equally vulnerable to subsequent annulment and equally incoherent because it is known as unknown to us.

Later Advaitins (such as Madhusūdana Sarasvatī) have examined all (how can one prove this completeness-claim?) offered definitions or analyses of the relation between an awareness and its object. This relation is broadly called cognitive intentionality in the West and "*viṣayatā*" or "*viṣaya-viṣayī-bhāva*" in Indian epistemology. What is that relation or relational property in virtue of which something counts as an object of an awareness or cognition? If it can be shown that no coherent answer can be given to this question, then the very claim that a cognition latches on to something other than itself in the external world will be unintelligible, and thus the world will be proved to be "false" or dreamlike simply because it is presented to have such an incoherent property as "objecthood."

Nine such alternative definitions were considered by the dualist realist Vyāsatīrtha (of the Madhva lineage). They are as follows:

Objecthood of the cognition (C) is:

Def 1: The property of being the locus/bearer of the effect/outcome of cognition C (*jñāna-janya-phaladharatvam*)

Def 2: The property of being the target of attitudes of rejection, welcoming or indifference resulting from cognition C (*jñāna-janya-hanādi-buddhi-gocaratvam*)

Def 3: The property of being the accusative of cognition C (*jñāna-karmatvam*)

Def 4: Being that which endows its own form onto the cognition C (*jñānakarārpitatvam*)

Def 5: Being that which, while appearing as such, endows its own form onto the cognition C (*dṛśyamāṇatve sati jñānakarārpitatvam*)

Def 6: Being fit to be mentioned by the use of linguistic expression immediately prompted by the cognition C (*jñāna-janya-vyavāhara-yogyatvam*)

Def 7: Being that entity as a result of the cognitive instrument's proximity to which a cognition C of that very entity arises (*yat-sannikṛṣṭa-karṇena yajjñānam utpadyate tattvam*)

Def 8: The property of being illuminated by or reflected in the particular modification of cognition C (*saṃvidi bhāsamantavam*)

Def 9: Being that which demarcates cognition C from other cognitions without being dependent on any other relationship with the cognition (*saṃbandhantaram antara jñānavacchedakatvam*)

The details of the refutation of each of these definitions are mind-bogglingly difficult, and none of them has gone unanswered by the opponent Madhva defenders of objecthood as a perfectly intelligible feature of external entites of the real world, so we shall not consider the Advaita attack here in detail. But the general spirit of the attack against objecthood is well summarized by Madhusūdana himself: "Objecthood belongs only to the known object, intentionality or object-grasping character only belongs to the grasping awareness, yet the so-called 'relationship' is supposed to subsist at the same time in both object and the awareness that it relates, since relations ought to be in both the relata. Yet no such two-place predicate of objecthood can be clearly formulated." Underneath this attack lies, I think, a general suspicion of all relations. In the case of "being about" or intentionality, that general suspicion becomes acute since it has proved extremely difficult to spell out (*durnirūpyatvāt ca*) without circularity what makes my thought of a tree *of a tree* or what exactly is the link that connects someone's perception of a cup to that cup.

Difficult, but not impossible. That is what a realist such as Udayana or Vyāsatīrtha would say. Just as each of the premises of the general dream argument has been rebutted, the concept of objecthood has been very intricately and sensitively analyzed by such great Navya

Nyāya stalwarts as Gadadhara Bhattacharya. (See *Gadadhara's Theory of Objectivity,* in two volumes by Sibajiban Bhattacharya, [ICPR, Motilal Banarsidass, 1990]). The objecthood property or relation has been construed as a self-linking relation (*svarūpa saṃbandha*) either as reducible to the cognition itself, or as reducible to the object itself, or as a third entity.

In the final analysis, the original remarks of Vyāsatīrtha (in *Nyāyamṛta*) make a whole lot of sense: "Just because one cannot analytically articulate what constitutes 'objecthood,' it does not follow that objects are illusory or false. We cannot articulate what makes a grasping consciousness or cognition a cognition either (by the same token)." Yet we cannot honestly or consistently deny that right now a cognition of something is occurring. If the reality of awareness remains undeniable even when an intentional awareness cannot be defined easily, why should the reality of the grasped objects be denied because the definitions of objecthood are hard to defend?

Conclusion: Disillusionment

There is one haunting problem with the alleged philosophical-mystical experience of waking up from the world dream, or the process of correction of the world error. How can the philosopher-mystic be certain, once having used the skeptical ladder to climb up to this antirealist height, that this waking up is not itself another kind of dream awaiting a further disillusionment? What if our knowledge of Brahman as one nondual subjective universal timeless consciousness itself is subject to further correction? The official Advaita answer to this worry is: there is no content at all, no intentional object, of this dawning nondual knowledge which cancels and supersedes the world illusion. Hence there is nothing left to be annulled. But that answer complicates matters. A normal waking experience, when it corrects a dream experience, replaces it with another set of conflicting contents. Can a contentless "experience" even have the power to "break" or "cancel" a dream? In so far as pure Brahman consciousness is not contradicted by anything, it seems impotent to even contradict anything!

Leaving aside such well-known problems, I want to end this chapter by drawing attention to one striking feature of the Advaita theory of correction of sustained error or disillusionment. Sibajiban Bhattacharya (in his editor's introduction to Advaita Siddhi, a partial English translation by Karuna Bhattacharya, ICPR 1991) has remarked: "Our awareness of appearance gets cancelled by subsequent knowledge. *This involves backward causation.* Here we have a cause with retrospective effect" (my emphasis).

Bhattacharya illustrates this with a poignant dialogue from Henrick Ibsen's famous play *A Doll's House:* When after a long married life, Nora expresses her 'disillusionment' with her relationship with her husband, he says, appealing to the past good times: "How unreasonable and how ungrateful you are, Nora! Have you not been happy here?"

Sticking to her guns, and revising her own past opinion and nullifying by a later act of interpretation all previous experience, Nora replies: "No, I have never been happy. I thought I was, but it has never been really so."[1]

If it is correct that such radical disillusionment claims to change one's assessment of the past by a present or future canceling judgment, then, to the extent backward causation is unintelligible or incoherent (of course, not every philosopher of time thinks so), the Advaita insistence on a future spiritual awakening proving for us that our past life experiences have been as insubstantial as a dream would also be unintelligible. The best we could say would be that this external world causes me pain, it is not of much use or interest to me any more, but it would be existentially "ungrateful" for us to say that this world of externality, materiality, plurality, and pain never actually was even seen or known by us. After all, it is from this very external world and its object-directed intentional awarenesses that we gleaned all the wisdom of our ancestors and revealed traditions, and it is here that we learned all the philosophical techniques that enabled us to question its ultimate ontological value or worth. Like a broken relationship, even a broken world dream cannot be nullified as "never having been there at all." Disillusionment must be compatible with living amicably with the empirical world and paying one's moral and social debts to it, just for old time's sake, as it were! If, as K. C. Bhattacharya had said in a creative reconstruction of the spiritual significance of Advaita, our experience of waking up from the world error is as deeply liberating as a sense of incredulous repentance at a past misdeed of our own, in the feeling:

> "How could I have done that, was that really me?" The full phenomenological content of such profound disillusionment requires that I still recognize, even when enlightened, that I did indeed experience the world as external to myself and that the transactional world was all that I ever

> *knew.* I cannot afford to forget or deny my life of worldly vicissitudes and differences even when I have got the new eyes to see through change and beyond differences.[2]

To dismiss the external world altogether from a nondualistic metaphysical high ground would be risky even for the nondualists' enlightenment project, in so far as that requires good patient reasoning and proper moral conduct.

The flimsy fixity of the world as presented in the YV serves dual purposes. It loosens attachment to the notion that the changes within awareness hold substantial, enduring meaning. Everything changes. And yet, precisely because everything changes, and we know nothing other than change, the world, even in its fragility and evanescence, must be taken seriously, albeit in a playful, wry manner. Once we even consider the possibility that the real is not necessarily what we might have considered it to be, then we must take up the responsibility to apply good, patient reasoning and proper moral conduct; both are needed to advance human freedom.

Notes

1. Henrik Ibsen, *A Doll's House and Two Other Plays* (London: J. M. Dent and Sons, 1910), 80.
2. K. C. Bhattacharya, "Advaita and Its Spiritual Significance," *Studies in Philosophy*, ed. Gopinath Bhattacharya Delhi: Motilal Banarsidass, 1983), 113–26.

5

The Existence of an Endless Number of Worlds

Jagadānantya in *Mokṣopāya* and the Many-Worlds Interpretation of Quantum Mechanics

GARTH BREGMAN

In the classical Indian text *Mokṣopāya* (popularly known as *Yogavāsiṣṭha*), which is essentially a dialogue between the great sage Vasiṣṭha and the young Lord Rāma, Vasiṣṭha combines elaborate and intricate stories with philosophical discourse in order to help the dispassionate Rāma attain *mokṣa*. In several of these stories he speaks of the simultaneous existence of an endless number of worlds. The Sanskrit term for this is *jagadānantya*. It is a genitive *tadpuruṣa* compound of *jagatām,* the genitive plural of *jagat,* which means the "world" or "universe," and *ānantya,* an abstract noun meaning "an endlessness," which is derived from the adjective *ananta,* or "endless." The simplest translation of *jagadānantya* then is "endlessness of worlds." The actual term occurs in a colophon in section 3 of book 4 of the *Mokṣopāya* (MU), yet the idea of an "endlessness of worlds" pervades the entire text.

In the 1950s, Hugh Everett III, a physicist at Princeton University, unhappy with the pervading Copenhagen interpretation of quantum theory, developed his "relative state" formulation. He published his thesis in 1957. Although it was not well received at the time, it gradually gained support, particularly in the late 1960s due to the effort of Bryce DeWitt,[1] who popularized it as the "many-worlds interpretation" (MWI).

In an unofficial poll of seventy-two "leading cosmologists and other quantum field theorists," conducted by researcher L. David Raub, 58 percent said they thought MWI is true against 18 percent who thought it is false.[2] The remaining 24 percent were undecided. Among those who support MWI were Stephen Hawking and Nobel Laureates Murray Gell-Mann and Richard Feynman. Max Tegmark also writes that a "(highly unscientific) poll taken at the 1997 UMBC quantum mechanics workshop gave the once all dominant Copenhagen interpretation less than half of the votes. The MWI scored second, comfortably ahead of the consistent histories and Bohm interpretations."[3]

Clearly MWI has entered mainstream quantum theory and may very well become the dominant interpretation of quantum theory, assuming it has not already usurped this position from the Copenhagen interpretation. MWI,[4] as expounded by Deutch, the "leading champion of the many worlds interpretation today,"[5] posits the existence of a single multiverse made up of a [potentially] infinite number of universes. Exactly what this means should become clear during the course of this chapter.

There have been many recent attempts to show how various tenets of Eastern mysticism and theoretical physics support each other.[6] This chapter is not one of them. Rather it is exploratory, the goal of which is to gain a better understanding of the metaphysics and epistemology of both MU and MWI by comparing and contrasting the parallel universes of MWI with *jagadānantya* in MU. I will argue that *jagadānantya* and MWI are focused on very different issues and are not responses to the same questions.

Why then compare them in the first place? One of the initial reasons for writing this chapter was to do justice to the metaphysics and epistemologies of both MU and MWI. Many comparisons of "Eastern mysticism" and "the new physics" include numerous equivocations and other shoddy reasoning, often with the goal of justifying the mystical tradition by giving it scientific credibility through association with quantum physics. The fact that the blanket term "Eastern mysticism" encompasses all Eastern mystical tradition should be a first warning sign. After all, how could one possibly hope to make the same metaphysical or epistemological claims about the hundreds of variants of Buddhism and Brahmanism (let alone numerous non-Indian philosophies in other parts of Asia) when the primary distinctions between them are often metaphysical or epistemological. Anyone making such mistakes would be advised to read Said's *Orientalism*.

However, this chapter is more of a preemptive response to those trying to demonstrate how a specific branch of Eastern philosophy and quantum theory might be strongly connected. Often the person attempting to connect the two has a solid background in only one of the disciplines and is unaware of the philosophical difficulties involved in such an enterprise. The result is often a caricature of quantum theory or of the mystical tradition or of both. In attempting to separate MWI and *jagadānantya* I am not underestimating the importance of the latter. Rather, I want to do both MWI and *jagadānantya* justice through a careful comparison and by avoiding the equivocations that often plague such comparisons.

I will start off with an analysis of *jagadānantya* by examining two stories from MU. This analysis should provide a basic understanding of the ontological commitments required for taking *jagadānantya* seriously. I will then examine MWI: what it interprets, what it explains, and the ontological commitments it entails. While laying out how "multiple-world" models feature in both theoretical physics and classical Indian metaphysics, I will also discuss their respective treatments of interaction between worlds, views on space and time, and the role played by the human mind.

Jagadānantya in *Mokṣopāya*

Before I commence with *jagadānantya,* however, I must introduce that syncretic Indian cosmology which is expounded in MU. "Know that the universe has arisen from Brahman and it is Brahman alone."[7] This one quote reaches the essence of Vasiṣṭha's teachings and seems also to accord with Advaita Vedānta. Advaitins are nondualists, concerned with showing the illusory nature of all distinctions. Yet this is not to say that they posit only one kind of primary substance, one kind of objective being, which would lead to a monism, which Śaṅkara goes to great pains to distinguish from nondualism. Perhaps the best way to understand the distinction between nondualism and monism is to bear in mind that Śaṅkara is a realist with regards to the transactional level of the empirical world, not a subjective idealist, as many monists tend to be. Obviously then, this "realism" of the external world is a different "realism" to the *ultimate* reality, the pure consciousness of "Brahman." "For Advaita, 'oneness' holds only on the level of Brahman-experience and must never be confounded with the world of multiplicity."[8]

Yet the text is so diverse that it has been claimed as an important text by schools as distant from Advaita Vedānta as Kashmir Śaivism. Doniger's description of the text as a "blend of abstract, classical Indian philosophy, and vivid detailed Indian folklore"[9] helps explain this phenomenon. The text has mass appeal and was to classical India what Shakespeare was to Elizabethan England. Yet as well as providing pure entertainment, one of its major strengths is its ability to explain *māyā,* or illusion, to the nonphilosopher. Yet together with the artistic license taken in its exposition of *māyā* come certain complications. It clearly diverges from Śaṅkara's Advaita realism with regard to the empirical world. The MU is in fact notorious for its elusiveness in terms of an identifiable school of philosophy. It comes closest to a mixture of Yogācāra mind-only Buddhism and a special Kashmir school of Vedic interpretation directly linked to Gaudapāda's *Māndūkya Kārika.*

The existence of a first cosmological event and the constant talk of Brahman clearly have more in common with Vedānta than Yogācāra. The "first event" is an inexplicable ripple in the pure consciousness of Brahman. Rāma asks Vasiṣṭha how or why this first ripple occurred:

> R MA: Lord, how could there be even an intention
> to diversify in the infinite consciousness?
>
> VASI HA: O Rāma, you will see the beauty of the truth
> in my statements when you attain the vision of truth.[10]

Rāma is to believe that a mystical vision or insight will make everything fall into place. Yet MU is not alone in struggling to explain a cosmological first cause for the material universe. Cosmologists have the same problem. After all, even if one accepts the Big Bang as the first event, there seems no way to determine why it "banged" as it did or why it even banged at all. To talk of causation before the first space-time event is meaningless. And since "mystical experiences" are not generally regarded as having any epistemic value by scientists, it seems unlikely that cosmologists could ever be completely satisfied. Here then we have an important common concern: both MU and contemporary cosmology are at a loss to rationally and satisfactorily explain the beginning of the universe.

Out of this ripple in Brahman emerges the cosmic mind of the creator, Brahma. Brahman must be understood as the impersonal space of pure consciousness, whereas Brahma is the first intending individual arising from this pure consciousness. And as soon as there is mind, there is thought. Brahma creates with thought, and the more Brahma creates, the more the mind diversifies, which leads to more thoughts, creations, and many diverse creatures (*jīva*). Yet all these thoughts and creations are not different from Brahman: all the diversification is illusion, *māyā*. Brahma, like all the most powerful Gods, is aware that even he himself is illusory. Human beings too are part of *māyā* as we are just creations of mind.

Brahman is coupled with *ātman*, "that pure, undifferentiated self-shining consciousness, timeless, spaceless, and unthinkable, that is not-different from Brahman and that underlies and supports the individual human person."[11] Therefore *mokṣa* (liberation or self-realization), which is Rāma's goal, is equivalent to *ātman*-realization, and *ātman*-realization is Brahman-realization. Thus attaining self-realisation means that one has realized the nonduality of reality. This process is captured in the Upaniṣadic saying *tat tvam asi*—"thou art that." Such sayings are not, for the Advaitin, mere tautologies: they are the concrete representation of a movement of thought from one ontological level (of particularity) through another (of universality) to yet another (of unity) wherein the attainment of the latter negates the distinctions between the former. One begins with individual consciousness (*tvam*), passes on to universal consciousness (*tat*), and arrives at the pure consciousness that overcomes the separative reality of both the individual and the universal and that constitutes their ground.[12]

This wonderful mixture of Vedic interpretation, mind-only Yogācāra, and various folk tales both enriches the text and makes it more difficult to extract from it a single set of ontological commitments. As Atreya points out in *The Philosophy of the Yoga-Vāsiṣṭha*, "the answer of Vasiṣṭha [as to the cause of the original ripple in consciousness] differs from the views of almost all other schools of Indian thought including even that of Śaṅkara."[13] Despite these difficulties, I will now examine *jagadānantya*.

In "The Story of the Sons of Indu," Vasiṣṭha relates how Brahma, who created our universe, learned that his creation was not the only universe. He discovered that the ten brilliant sons of a holy man, Indu, having discussed the most desirable goal, decided that it was not merely to be a king or even a god, but rather to attain Brahmahood and each create his own universe. They meditated for a "long,

long time . . .till an epoch came to a close"[14] on the mantra "I am Brahman, seated on the full-blown lotus."[15] Although their physical bodies died, they continued to meditate in disembodied form.

When the cycle of the universe ended and there was a new "cosmic night," an infinite void, each son became the creator of his own universe. Brahma realizes, "The ten sons of the holy man were able to achieve Brahma-hood by their mental effort: even I could not prevent it."[16] And at the same time Brahma is aware that these ten sons are also his creations. And now that they have been created, what function need Brahma perform? The sun, in response to this question, answers: "Lord, in your own consciousness create the world as you like. In truth, the infinite consciousness, the mind (one's own consciousness) and the infinite space are all of one substance, pervaded by the infinite consciousness. Therefore regardless of what the young men have created, you can create as many worlds as you like!"[17]

This story illustrates the nondual nature of Brahman by emphasizing the illusion of the universe—that it is nothing but thoughts in a cosmic mind which is itself not independent of Brahman. Vāsiṣṭha provides an excellent summary of the interrelationships. The last paragraphs, of particular relevance, are:

> Rāma, space is three fold—the infinite space of undivided consciousness, the finite space of divided consciousness and the physical space in which the material world exists.
>
> The infinite space of undivided consciousness (*cid ākāśa*) is that which exists in all, inside and outside, as the pure witness of that which is real and of that which appears to be. The finite space of divided consciousness (*citta ākāśa*) is that which creates the divisions of time, which pervaded all things. The physical space is that in which the other elements (air, etc.) exists. The latter two are not independent of the first. In fact the others do not exist.[18]

As far as *jagadānantya* is concerned, there is no limit to the number of possible universes. Space and time are divisions which occur in *citta ākāśa*, and so are themselves illusory, even nonexistent in relation to Brahman. The physical space of our universe is even more crude, even less real than that of divided consciousness. The influence of mind-only idealism is clearly evident here.

Whereas Brahma is liberated, aware of the nonduality of all things, it is unclear whether the ten sons are liberated or whether they are rather so entrapped by *māyā* that they believe that being a creator is better than enlightenment. The MU is full of just such stories, where individuals long for material success, martial victory, and the like, and because of the strength of their mental will, they attain their desires. Yet these *jīvā* still work within the framework of *citta ākāśa* and the physical universe, so they are still caught up in the veil of *māyā*. Within *māyā*, there is no limit to the number of universes that can exist simultaneously, because there is no limit to the cosmic mind's ability to diversify.

This brings me to a further story, that of "The World within the Rock." Here Vasiṣṭha gives an account of how he entered the state of *samādhi*, seeking out the source of a sound he had heard. In this state of infinite consciousness he saw "countless universes, which were diverse in composition and time-space structure . . . There is infinite diversity . . . in accordance with the notions that arise in consciousness."[19]

Vasiṣṭha discovers that the source of the sound is a woman. She has sought him out because of his reputation as a great sage. Both she and her husband yearn for *mokṣa*. She explains that she is from another universe, and that she lives within a rock. In this rock her husband is the Creator of an entire world. She herself is a creation of her husband's mind. Vasiṣṭha accompanies her to this rock. At first Vasiṣṭha sees only a rock, not the world within the rock. But by repeatedly affirming the existence of this world within the rock, Vasiṣṭha begins to experience it. He meets the Creator, and the three of them begin to meditate.

Vasiṣṭha describes it to Rāma: "[I]f one sees the rock with the physical eye as if it lies at a distance, only the rock is seen. In every part of the rock I saw this creation, sustenance and dissolution take place. I saw the universe in the past, present and future."[20]

Vasiṣṭha continues to meditate on the infinite and suddenly realizes that the rock, the world within the rock, the woman, her husband, his universe and all the universes are in his mind. From this we are to understand that it is the same with every one of us. We each create a universe, and part of creation is other minds, which in turn create their own universes.

> In the infinite play of the infinite there are infinite minds with infinite worlds in them. In every one of them there are continents and mountains, villages and cities inhabited by people who have their own time-space scale and life-span. When these *jīvā*, reach the end of their life-span, if they are not enlightened, they continue to exist in infinite

> space, creating their own dream-worlds. Within them are other people within whom are minds; within those minds are worlds in which there are more beings, ad infinitum.[21]

The richness of this description boggles the mind. Now we can see that even if there is only one unenlightened *jīva* on this planet, this *jīva*'s mind will automatically dream up a universe, thus creating other *jīva*s, which will lead to a potentially infinite number of universes. In fact the only way to stop this potentially infinite expansion of the number of universes along any one of its potentially infinite number of branches is for the *jīva* at the end of each branch to attain *mokṣa*. Once this is done, and provided the unenlightened *jīva*s do not think up more *jīva*s, it is only a matter of time before all the *jīva*s are enlightened. When all *jīva*s have achieved *mokṣa* and are one with Brahman, we have a Cosmic Dissolution, and just as dreams end, leaving one in deep sleep, so does the Cosmic Cycle end, leaving behind only Absolute Consciousness. And then the process of creation starts all over again, with a vibration in Absolute Consciousness ushering in a new epoch.

Vasiṣṭha says, "In relation to a mountain a subatomic particle is small; in relation to the infinite the entire universe is a subatomic particle."[22] Yet even such an analogy fails to capture the illusory nature of the universe. The analogy uses a scale of physical and numerical magnitude to show the insignificance of the universe in relation to Brahman. Yet magnitude itself must be understood as part of the *māyā* and is hence not part of infinite consciousness (*cid ākāśa*). Therefore when MU talks of the infinite consciousness, this must be distinguished from the possibility of an infinite number of worlds. In the first sense "infinite" is used figuratively to suggest the all-encompassing nature of Brahman, and in the second sense "infinite" is used literally to refer to the actual number of worlds. Worlds or universes arise out of infinite consciousness, but the creation and dissolution of worlds have no affect at all on the infinite consciousness. The important point is that even though infinite consciousness is always infinite, the number of worlds is only potentially infinite. All it takes is one ripple in infinite consciousness, and from having no worlds we immediately have a potentially infinite number of worlds.

The Many-Worlds Interpretation of Quantum Mechanics

And now for a change of tempo, I will leave *jagadānantya* and proceed to the many-worlds interpretation of quantum mechanics. Let me start by explaining the relationship between theories and interpretations. Following Nagel, in *The Structure of Science*, I will distinguish between

> (1) an abstract calculus that is the logical skeleton of the explanatory system . . . ; (2) a set of rules that in effect assign an empirical content to the abstract calculus by relating it to the concrete materials of observation and experiment; and (3) an *interpretation* or model for the abstract calculus, which supplies some flesh for the skeletal structure in terms of more or less familiar conceptual or visualizable materials.[23]

In this chapter we are concerned with quantum theory and interpretations of quantum theory. It is important to realize that theories are about specific systems, not about the world in general. Hence social theories, for example, which are about social systems or environments, would have no relationship to quantum systems. The abstract calculus of the quantum system is that which provides us with the basic building blocks for theories about the quantum system. Such an abstract would introduce us to terms such as "electron," "particle," and "wave-function." This abstract calculus is useless without a set of rules that sets out the relationship between these various building blocks, and most importantly, how we can test such rules through experimentation and observation.

Interpretations, which accompany all steps in this process, are further developed after the rules have been confirmed by experiments. If one accepts that the rules govern the system, what further extrapolations can be made? In quantum theory one finds many interpretations of the same rules, of which MWI is just one. All these interpretations are attempts to extrapolate from microscopic quantum systems to achieve a better understanding of the "big picture." What is perhaps most important in understanding the relationship between theories and interpretations is that these various interpretations are not testable. It is the theories' rules that are tested.

All interpretations, of which the Copenhagen and MWI are the most popular, make exactly the same predictions for the outcome of experiments in quantum systems, since they all adopt the same abstract calculus and rules. There is no experiment that could verify or falsify any of these interpretations.[24]

In physics, as in philosophy, one finds both realists and pragmatists. In quantum theory and its interpretations, these two approaches are clearly visible. The realists believe that the rules governing the quantum systems can be said to be "true" or "false" in that they really map onto aspects of the world. The realists who believe that these rules governing quantum physics are true wish to determine the metaphysical consequences of accepting them as true. They are the interpreters, the speculative metaphysicians interested in "how things really are." The pragmatists would rather avoid any talk of "true" and "false" and are concerned only with the usefulness of the mathematical formulations of quantum mechanics to predict the outcomes of experiments involving quantum systems.[25]

Nobel laureate Richard Feynman, mentioned earlier as a supporter of MWI, writes: "I think it is safe to say that no one understands quantum mechanics. . . . Do not keep saying to yourself, if you can possibly avoid it, 'But how can it be like that?' because you will get 'down the drain' into a blind alley from which nobody has yet escaped. Nobody knows how it can be like that."[26]

The various interpretations accept "that it is like that," not asking why it is "like that," but rather concerned with the metaphysical consequences of its being as it is. One of their major concerns is to better understand the workings of the "wave function," which underlies most mathematical formulations of quantum mechanics. The wave function "encapsulates everything knowable about a quantum system and evolves according to the Schrödinger equation. The most remarkable prediction of the equation is that quantum measurements may have no definite outcome."[27]

This leads to "Schrödinger's cat," which I will use to demonstrate the major difference between the Copenhagen interpretation and the MWI. "Schrödinger's cat" refers to a thought experiment in which a cat is placed in a sealed box together with a lethal dose of cyanide gas. The gas is released if a certain radioactive decay is detected. The radioactive decay represents the microscopic quantum system. The cat's dead state or alive state is each a macroscopic possibility dependent on whether or not the decay is detected. For the thought experiment to work, one has to allow for a superposition of these two macroscopic events—the cat living and the cat dying—so that we can have a wave function for the entire system. In this situation, the wave function carries all possible outcomes concerning not only the quantum system, but also the corresponding macro phenomena.[28]

According to the Copenhagen interpretation, one, and only one, of the possible outcomes carried by the wave function is actualized when, and only when, an observation of the quantum system is made. So there is a "collapse" of the wave function only when someone looks inside the box. Until this collapse takes place, there is no fact of the matter as to whether the cat is dead or alive. It is not the case that "we don't know whether the cat is dead or alive," as this wording suggests that there is a fact of the matter, a state of affairs which we do not know about. Rather, there actually is no state of affairs until an observer collapses the wave function. From the observer's point of view, "the cat was neither alive nor dead until the box was opened."[29] Since, from our intuitive point of view, the cat must be either dead or alive, we have a paradox if we accept the Copenhagen interpretation.

This paradox is overcome by the MWI. According to MWI, the universe splits into two universes whenever there are "measurement-like actions associated with thermodynamically irreversible processes."[30] In other (i.e., simpler) words, whenever an interaction within a microscopic quantum system results in a nonreversible event (such as the decaying of a radioactive isotope) there is a split.[31] Although these events are measurable, there is no requirement of an observer for a split to occur, unlike in the Copenhagen interpretation which requires an observer to collapse the wave function.

So as far as Schrödinger's cat is concerned, we still allow that the wave function carries all the information about the quantum system, but rather than claim that one of two states is actualized when an observation collapses the wave function, we allow that as the decay occurs, the universe splits into two parallel universes, one in which the decay occurs, and one in which it does not. Thus, when the box is opened there is no collapse of the wave function, but rather just a glance to see in which of the possible universes we have ended. So the split in MWI takes place before the collapse of the wave function would take place in accordance with the Copenhagen interpretation.

Having set out the bare basics of MWI, I must acknowledge that I am not going to discuss the many arguments for and against MWI for two reasons: because that is not the focus of the chapter, and more importantly because I would need a Ph.D. in quantum physics to do such a discussion justice. Rather, if I accept MWI, I want to ask, "Are the universes all equally real, how can they interact, and what is the role of the human mind in such a 'multiverse'?" Whether I can answer these questions (without having the aforementioned Ph.D.) is also questionable. Nonetheless, I am going to make an attempt.

But first, a quote which I will use to put MWI and *jagadānantya* into a mutual context. It is taken from a review in *New Scientist* of Max Tegmark's essay entitled "The Interpretation of Quantum Mechanics: Many Worlds or Many Words?"

> Practical-minded experimentalists, who have traditionally adopted the "shut-up-and-calculate interpretation,"

> typically show little interest in whether cozy classical concepts are in fact real in some untestable metaphysical sense or merely the way we subjectively perceive a mathematically simpler world where the Schrödinger equation describes everything—and that they are therefore becoming less bothered by a profusion of worlds than by a profusion of words.[32]

This in a sense also sums up the earlier distinction between the pragmatists and realists. There seems to be a parallel here with the different approaches of Indian schools of thought such as Advaita and Yogācāra, which place strong emphasis on rigorous metaphysical speculation, and certain Buddhist schools, which reject such metaphysical talk as unedifying and avoid it. Although the Advaita and Yogācāra vehemently argue for their positions, they would not deny that practitioners of another system can attain enlightenment (just as an MWI's advocate would not deny that a Copenhagen supporter can get exactly the same experimental results). Acceptance of a specific ontology is not a prerequisite for liberation. Vasiṣṭha expounds a mind-only Brahmanic view; Śaṅkara is a realist; Yogācāra supports an idealist, mind-only Buddhism. Yet these philosophies are almost never exclusive. Gurus in these respective systems, aware of the veil of *māyā,* cannot be exclusivists. Each can only argue that adopting his approach is more conducive to attaining *mokṣa* (or *nirvāṇa*) than any other approach.

Nonetheless, this comparison is a little misleading, as those schools which value the intellect and rational argument view such activities as themselves edifying and an essential part of any enlightenment process. After all, Vasiṣṭha is telling Rāma the various stories and discussing the related ontology in order to help him attain *mokṣa.* Thus the metaphysical discourse serves a practical function. According to Nagel's definition of a theory, interpretation plays an important role. Yet in quantum theory, interpretation seems to fulfill no practical function at all (as it does not aid us in any predictions), unless of course a "good explanation" is in itself functional, which is another issue altogether. Yet clearly those physicists who avoid interpretations and adopt the "shut up and calculate" approach would not be in agreement with Nagel in this particular case.

My next question is, "What interaction[33] is possible between the parallel universes according to MWI?" Well, the short answer is, "Very little." The only interaction occurs at the quantum level, and it manifests experimentally as interference phenomena such as those popularized by twin-slit experiments, in which photons interact with "invisible" entities, which turn out to be photons in the hypothesized parallel universes.

In fact the only universes with which our universe interferes are those universes with which our universe splits at the moment of "measurement-like actions associated with thermodynamically irreversible processes." As soon as this process of *decoherence* has taken place, the universes are completely separate. So no macroscopic event in one universe can affect another universe, because the split between the universes would have occurred long before this macroscopic event occurs. Thus, it is impossible to communicate in any way with the other universes. For practical purposes, the other universes may as well not exist after decoherence has occurred.

This brings me to quantum computing, which rests on the possibility of simultaneous calculations taking place in parallel universes. Answers would be instantaneous. In an online debate between Deutsch and Lloyd (both supporters of MWI) concerning whether the other universes are "equally real," Lloyd, who argues against the equal reality of all parallel universes, claims that if the computer works, it would show that decoherence has not actually taken place and that we are not actually separate from the other universes, which might seem to cause serious difficulties for MWI. Deutsch then introduces the idea of the "multiverse," which he discusses in *The Fabric of Reality*. In response to Lloyd, Deutsch answers:

> You also say: "The very fact that the quantum computer gives us an answer that depends on all the branches at once means that the universe has not really split: Those branches were part of our world, not of other worlds! The universe splits if and only if its branches decohere." I entirely agree! Reality consists of a multiverse, an enormous entity which, on a gross scale, has a structure that resembles many copies of the universe of classical physics, but which is, on a sufficiently fine scale, a single, unified system. In an absolute sense, there are never any splits at all.[34]

Here Deutsch writes that there are "many" universes. Well, how many exactly are there? Let us return to Schrödinger's Cat. The decay of the radioactive isotope that triggers the release of the cyanide gas can occur at any moment, and as discussed before, this will lead to a split into two universes. At every moment, the universe must split into two universes, one in which the isotope decayed in the previous moment, and one in which it did not. In that universe in which it did not decay, another split must occur in the next moment, one in which the decay occurs and one in which it does not. In other words, the universe in which the decay has not occurred continues to split at every moment, whether the isotope is in the box with the cat or after we have opened up the box and found the cat still alive. Let us isolate the number of universes to those that result from the occurrence or non-occurrence of the decay in a one second period. We will be able to specify the number of decohered universes only by specifying how many moments occur in one second. Is there a discrete number of moments (with duration) per second or is time continuous, allowing us to slice up a second into an infinite number of moments. Anyone familiar with Zeno's paradoxes will be aware of the problems which face any atomistic talk of moments.

Nonetheless, I would argue that there are a discrete number of moments per second in our present case and use Planck time as the duration of each moment. Planck time refers to the "'quantum of time,' the smallest measurement of time that has any meaning, and is equal to 10^{-43} of a second. No smaller division of time has any meaning."[35] If we adopt this approach, then we would have a maximum of 10^{43} splits after one second, and thus we would have a finite number of parallel universes.

If we take into account that quantum systems have been around since the beginning of the universe (i.e., from the time when the universe was 10^{-43} seconds old), we must acknowledge that the number of universes grows exponentially as each universe continues to split into further universes. Nonetheless, the maximum potential number of splits per second for any particular quantum system remains 10^{43}, and this limits the total number of universes to a finite number at any time.

Yet what happens when we view this "Block" universe in its nonrelativistic four-dimensional space-time structure? According to the most popular pervading classical paradigm, the universe has been expanding ever since the Big Bang. There are two possible alternatives for the future of the universe. Either the universe will continue to expand (either asymptotically towards a finite limit or unbounded by such a limit), or it could reach a critical point when the gravitational pull between the center and the periphery is so great that expansion stops, and the universe starts contracting. This latter state of affairs is called the Big Crunch. Once this contraction starts, it will only end when the entire universe has been crushed back into a singularity such as that out of which it first "Banged."

If we examine the multiverse, view time as merely one dimension, and admit the possibility that the universe might never stop expanding, we would have a potentially infinite number of universes, as there would be no upper bound to the number of splits such as that imposed by the occurrence of a Big Crunch. In MWI then, providing that at least one universe is still expanding (i.e., not all of them have "crunched") we will have a multiverse with a potentially infinite (or more technically: "nondenumerably infinite") number of universes.

Where Are These Other Worlds or Universes?

Where do these parallel universes exist? According to the quantum field theory of MWI, they occupy the same space-time as our universe. How should we interpret this claim? Perhaps as certain popular accounts suggest, they branch off into other dimensions of this space-time. Clearly then the term "parallel" must be understood metaphorically as meaning that the universes exist at the same time, yet once they have split, just like parallel lines, they never meet.[36] Of course this still leaves a great deal unexplained. There seems no comprehensible answer as to where these parallel universes exist that can fully satisfy us human beings functioning in classical three-dimensional space and classical time. We cannot interact with these other branches, and "For all intents and purposes the other branches and their corresponding 'worlds' do not exist [for us in our universe to which we have privileged access]."[37]

As far as MU is concerned, we, in this world, are firmly grounded in our existence and are not in a position to communicate with beings in other universes or to experience their worlds. This is my reading of the text, yet I know that there are passages which could be used to contradict this reading. It is therefore impossible after all to extract any commitment of any sort from MU which is not contradicted in other verses. If I believe that I have actually broken through the barrier of my universe into another, I have not really done so, as the universe into which I believe I have broken is still a creation of my mind, and hence still part of my illusory universe. This point can be seen clearly in Vasiṣṭha's own realization in "The World within the Rock." We have to use dream analogies to understand the existence of other universes, and this is the closest we can get.[38] The MU is made up of stories with exceptional characters who are able to travel from one universe to the other. Yet like Rāma, we are to understand that we ourselves are not in a position to put out our thumbs and hitch a ride with one of those beings who hops from universe to universe. This view, like any mind-only view, could be seen to lead to solipsism.

The only way to break out of this universe is to attain *mokṣa*. This could be seen as an interesting parallel to the thesis of Big Bang followed by Big Crunch, followed by Big Bang . . .[39]

As far as a comparison goes, we have, according to MWI, a single mulitiverse made up of a potentially infinite number of parallel universes, and in MU we have the infinite Brahman, pure consciousness, out of which a potentially infinite number of universes arise. Yet in *jagadānantya,* the universes are not necessarily parallel in the same way as the universes in MWI. In some sense, the universes of the sons of Indu are parallel, in that they were all created at the same time. Yet the world within the rock shows how parallelism fails to capture the essence of *jagadānantya*. There is an entire world within a rock, a potentially infinite number of universes created by my mind at this very instant. As soon as I think up a universe, every other person I dream up also thinks. Each one of these persons creates her own universe, and so on. There is no time delay. The first ripple in Brahman occurs concurrently with my typing on this keyboard. In the greater scheme of things, I have no past, I am not typing now, time is illusory, and I have never been separated from Brahman. In fact there is no "I" and no ripple in Brahman.[40]

Mental Force and Free Will

This leads me to my final distinction, the importance of mental force, particularly free will, in MWI and MU. Of all points of comparison, this, I feel, is where *jagadānantya* and MWI diverge most significantly. It is clear that in MU, the mind is all important in that the universe arises out of mind, and mental effort is required both to understand the nonduality of the universe intellectually and to realize the nonduality "spiritually" through meditation and other related practices. Everything, including this chapter, my notion of Brahman, is an entrapment of *māyā*. It takes hard work to liberate oneself from such a powerful veil of illusion and realize that there is in fact no *māyā,* no *avidyā*, no karma, no chapter which I am writing or which you are reading.

One advantage such a philosophy has over every other philosophy is that it is an all-encompassing, inclusivist philosophy. It can allow for gods, no gods, materialism, idealism, in fact any possible worldview, as it allows that everyone creates her own universe. Irreconcilability does not even come into question.

To argue that classical determinism is incompatible with the ontology of MU misses the point which Śaṅkara makes in defense of his realism, namely that "'oneness' holds only on the level of Brahman-experience and must never be confounded with the world of multiplicity." I hope I have emphasized the "depth" and all-encompassing nature of the philosophy of MU. Of course this all-encompassing nature of Brahman also makes such a notion of Brahman indefeasible. It is, by definition not falsifiable. And to verify it, if possible at all, requires many lifetimes of very hard work! It seems too that the various interpretations of quantum mechanics are also indefeasible, as they are after all, interpretations, and hence not verifiable or falsifiable. Here then we do have a common feature—indefeasibility.[41]

Mental force only comes into the MWI indirectly through a free-will-versus-determinism debate. Can Deutsch be correct in his claim that the multiverse is compatible with free will (which DeWitt, in his critical review, mentions but does not evaluate)? Deutsch only spends a couple of pages on it, glossing over the issue as if it is obvious that the multiverse allows free will back into the scientific picture. Yet his line of argument is purely statistical. For example,

> After careful thought I chose to do X [translates into] After careful thought some copies of me including the one speaking, chose to do X . . .
>
> It was the right decision [translates into] Representation of the moral or aesthetic values that are reflected in my choice of option X are repeated much more widely in the multiverse than representations of rival values.[42]

There is something very wrong here. One of the most important reasons for the success and popularity of MWI is that it takes human observers out of the picture by doing away with the collapse of the wave function. Yet now Deutsch is bringing human action back into the picture. The fact that my deliberation over eating an apple may be followed by my eating an apple in some universes and not eating an apple in other universes has absolutely nothing to do with free will. I can say, "It turns out that I am in the universe in which I am eating the apple," but all this proves is that "It turns out that in this universe I am eating the apple," not that I made a free choice (i.e., a choice not completely determined by classical physics and quantum physics (including random quantum events).

In support of my argument, I will quote an alternative MWI response to the question, "Is many worlds a deterministic theory?"

> Yes, many-worlds is a deterministic theory, since the wave function obeys a deterministic wave equation at all times. All possible outcomes of a measurement or interaction . . . are embedded within the universal wave function although each observer, split by each observation, is only aware of single outcomes due to the linearity of the wave equation. The world appears indeterministic, with the usual probabilistic collapse of the wave function, but at the objective level, which includes all outcomes, determinism is restored.[43]

The determinism referred to here is of the "determinism versus randomness" type, not the "determinism versus free will" type. The objective determinism necessitates that every possible outcome superimposed on the wave function *will* occur in at least one universe. If I am in a universe in which I eat the apple, then on the level of the big-multiverse picture, my action is determined, yet on a personal-universe level, it is completely random that I ended up in a universe in which I eat the apple. That I may end up eating and enjoying the apple in 70 percent of the universes and then thinking, "It was a good idea to eat the apple," has nothing to do with free will and everything to do with wave functions and probability.

In fact, in the same FAQ document, when asked, "Does many worlds allow free-will?," Price follows Deutsch (though far less enthusiastically) and concludes: "Our actions, as expressions of our free will, correlate with the weights associated with worlds. This of course, matches our subjective experience of being able to exercise our will, form moral judgements and be held responsible for our actions."[44]

But most deterministic classical accounts of mind also accept that we have a "subjective experience of being able to exercise our will." Yet this is what the illusion of free will is all about. There is no free will, merely a completely determined subjective experience. I fail to see how equating "I made a good choice" with "In the majority of the universes I ate the apple and enjoyed it" shows the existence of free will. It seems plain to me that the free-will-versus-determinism debate cannot even be smuggled into MWI's multiverse picture.

Conclusion

To sum up, there is little common ground for a comparison between quantum physics and classical Indian metaphysics. Yet when physicists engage in metaphysical speculation, there arises a temptation to show that perhaps cutting-edge physics and age-old mysticism are in fact describing the same big picture, but in different ways. I hope I have shown, though, that the metaphysical frameworks associated with MU and MWI provide very different pictures, not just different angles of the same picture.[45]

I have not in any way shown the irreconcilability of MU and MWI. However, I hope it is now apparent that they are asking very different questions, which lead to very different pictures. Whereas *jagadānantya* is important in showing the illusoriness of all distinctions, and thus helping the seeker realize the nonduality of Brahman, MWI is interested in developing a metaphysical framework which follows from certain experimental results in quantum systems.

Jagadānantya forces us to ponder what I would call "soteriological cosmology"—the source of our universe, why it is as it is, and how we can return to the source. MWI is not primarily interested in cosmology or explaining why the wave function is as it is. It is concerned with what the behavior of quantum systems means on a metaphysical level. The conclusion is that there must exist a potentially infinite number of parallel universes unified into a single potentially infinitely large multiverse. This multiverse exists in four-dimensional, nonrelativistic space-time with a potentially infinite number of dimensions to accommodate the splitting universes. And this multiverse exists independent of the human mind, which, to repeat, does away with the problematic collapse of the wave function associated with the Copenhagen interpretation.

On no level are these parallel universes illusory in the way in which the universes of *jagadānantya* are illusory. And in no way does mind play a part in the creation of these MWI parallel universes. This is in contrast to the total mind dependence of the universes of MU.

Yet because the questions being asked are different, one could viably accept MU philosophy and MWI together, but only if one believed the nonduality of Brahman to be a deeper, more encompassing reality than the multiverse. Rather than being the "deepest," most explanatory of all possible theories, MWI would be describing an illusion, like any other scientific or religious theory (including those theories which make claims about Brahman such as those in MU) and so would have no special status. One could agree with Śaṅkara's realism, accepting that the MWI applies in this multiverse in which we find ourselves. Yet the magnitude of this multiverse would still be insignificant in comparison with the nonduality of Brahman.

Notes

1. Bryce DeWitt was a professor at the Center for Relativity, Department of Physics, University of Texas at Austin.

2. This poll is discussed in Q2 of Price's "The Everett FAQ." This list of frequently asked questions is one of the most frequently referenced discussions of MWI available on the Internet and provides an accessible introduction to MWI.

3. M. Tegmark, "The Interpretation of Quantum Mechanics: Many Worlds or Many Words?" (proceedings of UMBC workshop "*Fundamental Problems in Quantum Theory,*" ed. M. H. Rubin and Y. H. Shih, 1997).

4. D. Deutsch, *The Fabric of Reality* (New York: Penguin, 1997).

5. J. Gribbon, *Q is for Quantum* (New York: The Free Press, 1998), 223.

6. Capra's *The Tao of Physics* is a prime example.

7. Swami Venkatesananda, *The Concise Yoga Vāsiṣṭha* (Albany: SUNY Press, 1984), 86–87.

8. Deutsch, *Advaita Vedānta* (Honolulu: University of Hawaii Press, 1969), 95.

9. Doniger, *Dreams, Illusions and Other Realities* (Chicago: University of Chicago Press, 1984), 132.

10. *The Concise Yoga Vāsiṣṭha,* 145.

11. Deutsch, *Advaita Vedānta,* 48.

12. Ibid., 49.

13. B. L. Atreya, *The Philosophy of the Yoga-Vāsiṣṭha* (Adyar, Madras, 1936), 300.

14. *The Concise Yoga Vāsiṣṭha* 87.

15. Ibid.

16. Ibid., 93.

17. Ibid., 91.

18. Ibid., 97.

19. Ibid., 401.

This quote provides an excellent example of the potential for confusion. The translator has used the English phrase "time-space structure" in his translation. In English such a phrase could not reasonably be separated from relativity theory. A reader searching for connections between contemporary physics and classical Indian mysticism might mistakenly claim the eleventh-century authors of the *Mokṣopāya* were familiar with the ideas behind relativity theory a millennium before Einstein was born. In a quote later in this chapter, the same translator uses the phrase "subatomic particle" to translate a Sanskrit term that does indeed refer to the smallest element of matter. Yet once again classical Indian notions of the structure of physical matter differ greatly from those of modern physics, and confounding the two must lead to questionable conclusions.

20. *The Concise Yoga Vāsiṣṭha,* 407.

21. Ibid., 401–2.

22. Ibid., 404.

23. E. Nagel, *The Structure of Science* (Hackett, Indianapolis, 1979), 90 (italics added for emphasis).

24. One of the most important issues in quantum theory is whether quantum theory is complete or incomplete. The issue revolves around the question of whether there are any unknown variables or constants at play that have not yet made it into the abstract calculus or rules discussed above. The belief that quantum mechanics is complete or incomplete can dramatically impact one's interpretation or whether one can have an interpretation at all. I will not go into this further, save to say that MWI is an interpretation resting on the premise that quantum mechanics is complete.

25. There are admittedly numerous views on what it means to be an instrumentalist, pragmatist, or realist. Here I have chosen a simple distinguishing factor.

26. Feynman, *The Character of Physical Law* (Cambridge: MIT Press, 1967), 129, quoted in J. Cramer, "The Transactional Interpretation of Quantum Mechanics," *Reviews of Modern Physics* 58 (1986).

27. M. Chown, "Dying to Know," *New Scientist* 20 (December 1997); 50.

28. The ease with which certain scientists have included this superposition of macroscopic states on the microscopic wave function is problematic and has rightfully received criticism. Nonetheless it makes for a very useful (and colorful) thought experiment.

29. Price, "FAQ" (1995) http://www.quantum-mechanics.com/ Q.8.

30. Ibid., Q.7.

31. One should note that one of the major difficulties faced by defenders of MWI is in explaining how time symmetrical microscopic quantum phenomena can "cause" time irreversible macroscopic phenomena.

32. Chown, "Dying to Know."

33. I am not using "interaction" here in its technical, quantum mechanical sense, but rather in its ordinary usage.

34. D. Deutsch and S. Lloyd, "Are Parallel Universes Equally Real?" *HotWired* (1997). The strong nonrelativistic nature of MWI is clearly emphasized by Deutsch's last sentence, and this should serve as a warning to anyone interested in popular science who sees quantum theory as it presently stands as the be all and end all of scientific theories.

35. Gribbin, *Q is for Quantum*, 287. Similarly, Planck length provides an atomistic measure of the smallest meaningful measurement of length. It is linked to Planck time in an equation involving the speed of light and the gravitational constant. Thus Planck length and time provide us with the smallest elements of space-time as understood by classical physics. Smaller values of time and distance are meaningless because "classical ideas about gravity and spacetime cease to be valid" (Gribbin, 286).

36. For the sake of simplicity, I will ignore the case of parallel lines theoretically meeting at infinity.

37. Lloyd, "Are parallel Universes Equally Real?"

38. See Atreya, *The Philosophy of the Yoga-Vāsiṣṭha,* 178–183, for a more detailed discussion of this.

39. After the Big Crunch, there is no reason why there could not be a second Big Bang. Whether this Big Bang will expand from the same singularity into which the previous universe was crushed or out of a new singularity is unclear. This in turn could be followed billions of years later by another Big Crunch . . . ad infinitum. Of course this "Bouncing-Ball" hypothesis stretches the limits of speculation, as talking of a second Big Bang after the previous Big Crunch requires a temporal ordering. Since physics has nothing to say about the "gap" between the two universes, it is questionable whether such talk is even meaningful.

40. In recent years the growth in virtual reality technology and its popular appeal have contributed to a number of successful films, such as *The Matrix,* in which there exist different levels of reality. Some commentators might feel inclined to claim that such movies provide analogies for the multiple worlds of *jagadānantya.* Such movies do indeed encourage us to ponder what is real and whether one is dreaming or awake. But philosophically speaking, movies such as *The Matrix* are little more than complicated brain-in-a-vat scenarios. In fact in *The Matrix* we even see this vat, although in this case there is an entire body in the vat, not just a brain. And, as in brain-in-a-vat scenarios, in *The Matrix* there is a very clear distinction between what is reality (the Real World, in which human rebels are battling *digital beings* possessing artificial intelligence) and what is virtual reality (the Matrix). It is clear that whereas the Real World can physically exist without the Matrix, the reverse is not true. This is fundamentally different from the worlds of *jagadānantya,* in which every world is equally real (or illusory, depending on one's point of view).

41. As mentioned earlier, the issue of the completeness or incompleteness of quantum theory is a big debate among physicists. If it is incomplete, then perhaps future discoveries will give rise to new evidence and/or arguments which could force scientists to dismiss some of the currently held interpretations.

42. Deutsch, *The Fabric of Reality,* 339.

43. Price, "FAQ" Q.13

44. Ibid., Q.24

45. I have to date not seen any successful arguments establishing that contemporary theoretical physics and the mystical writings of major mystical traditions are in fact describing the same picture.

6

Vasiṣṭha and Borges

In Quest of Postmodern Enlightenment

STHANESHWAR TIMALSINA

Invoking Borges and Vasiṣṭha in the same breath demands a serious consideration of the idealistic thoughts of India and the West. As the narratives of Vasiṣṭha synthesize Advaita, Yogācāra, and other parallel thoughts in India, Borges draws upon a wide range of philosophical and literary sources throughout the world. Rather than time and space posing a divide between the esoteric worlds of Borges and Vasiṣṭha, they are quite close, one could even say identical. Their writings are grounded on theology and mysticism, composed by creative writers of fiction who rigorously argue through their metaphors. Just as Borges often questions his subjective identity or casts the identified Borges as a fiction, Vasiṣṭha is a fictional character borrowed from Vedic myths, invoked by the author of *Yogavāsiṣṭha* (YV), who himself appears to be a fictional Vālmīki. Searching for the personal history of the author is meaningless in either case. This deconstruction of subjectivity is pivotal in addressing any writing that may establish parallels between the thoughts of these two writers. Following the formalist claims, they both least care for "writer as subject matter" as a topic worthy of inquiry: our concern is the work itself and not the authors' lives. While Borges explicitly makes this claim in *The Nothingness of Personality,* both the character Vasiṣṭha identified as the author of the YV and the YV's rejection of the reality of subjectivity bring these authors parallel to each other. Just as we can find multiple references to "the other" in Borges" writing, Vasiṣṭha appears again and again as a fictional character in his own writing, with the narrator and the imposed character often colliding in their world of virtual reality. We cannot reduce these authors to their historical time and space, categories for which they both care little.

The fictionality of time and that of history allows these two writers to shatter the permeable membrane separating "sacred" and "profane." The narratives of Vasiṣṭha and those of Borges cannot be categorized either as "sacred" or "profane." The sacred relates to truth claims; the profane deconstructs it. The same content found in fiction and in sacred texts aims in two opposite directions: while the first cherishes its fictionality, the second tends to support its reality. The philosophical argument and mythical statements incline to make a truth claim, whereas allegorical narratives or poetic depictions refer to reality without asserting their inherent reality. However, one cannot survive without the other. In the absence of truth claims, their demise and the subsequent carnivals are not possible, and in the absence of the imaginary, truth claims cannot emerge. The boundary between absolutes and imaginary realms collapses in the stories of Vasiṣṭha and Borges, as they both defy these claims. Vasiṣṭha, a Vedic seer, supposed by one Vālmīki to be the narrator of the stories, is a spiritual master, a mystic of the Upaniṣadic tradition, who is describing the nature of reality to prince Rāma. The use of narratives as an instrument to depict reality, a strategy applied in the YV, parallels the underlying philosophy, wherein all that is cognized is merely the pulsation of consciousness, comparable to dreams, and the duality perceived in the world is parallel to the plurality of counter-images found in mirrors. Confirming the statement of Saint-Marine that "all mystics speak the same language, for they come from the same country,"[1] Borges utilizes the craft of storytelling to describe his philosophy. Just as the stories like *Tlon, Uqbar,* and *Orbis Tertius* are incomprehensible without engaging their philosophical parameters, so also are the narratives of Līlā, Gādhi, and Cūḍālā found in the YV. As historical and fictional are interwoven in the stories of Borges, so also is the case in the stories of Vasiṣṭha, explicitly in the story of *Dāma, Vyāla, and Kaṭa,* where the fictional monsters and real kings and ministers inhabit the same realm. The interchangeability of the fictional and the real, common to both the writings of Borges and the narratives of Vasiṣṭha, facilitates the claim that the binary of the sacred and profane is nothing more than imagination, yet another fiction, to both of these visionaries.

Interestingly, both Borges and Vasiṣṭha place themselves in their narratives. The tension, co-creation, momentariness, and illusive nature of the I-sense and the socially constructed and phenomenal self are evident in *Borges and I,* wherein the author causes events to happen to the phenomenal Borges, who falsifies and magnifies "things" in the process of being Borges. This meta-Borges who created Borges is now shadowed and defined by the fictional Borges. This meta-Borges is creative and is fond of the game of time and eternity, which now is taken over by the Borges of social construction. This metanarrator within Borges laments that everything belongs to this other Borges, one of his creations.

In the story of *The Sage From Outer Space,* Vasiṣṭha creates a hermitage in the most solitary realm by the power of his imagination and returns to it after visiting the world within a rock, to find in turn that the hermitage created out of his dream is now occupied by another hermit, and his body is decomposing. As soon as he no longer desires to live there, this hermitage of his fancy collapses, and Vasiṣṭha finds himself alongside the other hermit on earth. Now, Vasiṣṭha has the body only of mind. With this mental body, Vasiṣṭha wants to be seen, perceived by gods, and he finds his corporeality. At this point, Vasiṣṭha says that the corporeal Vasiṣṭha is the creation of his mind, the mental Vasiṣṭha. Likewise, in the story of Līlā, Vasiṣṭha fancies himself to be a king and immediately finds himself as King Padma, who in turn finds himself to be king Vidūratha.

For both Vasiṣṭha and Borges, the self is the foundation for the rise of subjectivity in which the cognition of externality or objectivity arises. For both Vasiṣṭha and Borges, there is a metadreamer. Though they both are creators of their own fictional world, they both find themselves often occurring within another dream, which Vasiṣṭha calls "the golden embryo" (*Hiraṇyagarbha*), or the "self-manifest" (*Svayambhū*), and Borges identifies as God, or the dreamer.

As the subjects of narration, they are both absent; neither do they have their independent existence. The identified authors, or the narrators of the fictions are, for both of them, external projections, manipulated by the metasubjects. As Borges demonstrates a slight discomfort towards this projected ego-self, Vasiṣṭha narrates in his story of *Dāma, Vyāla, and Kaṭa* that these demons, imagined by the metademon Saṃvara to defeat the gods, conquer paradise and the gods, and the metagods alike are unable to defeat the demons due to their lack of ego-sense. Gods hide and wait till the rise of ego among these demons, and victory and fame eventually give rise to the demons' ego-sense, and they fall prey to gluttony and self-glorification. Finally, they are introduced to fear, and they are easily defeated with the rise of fear.

In the stories of Vasiṣṭha, the imagined selves crumble with the recognition of the dreamer, the state that Vasiṣṭha calls enlightenment. Nevertheless, there can be lower or limited awakenings, wherein one wakes from one dream only to find oneself in another dream, not emerging from dreams in totality. For example, in the story of one hundred Rudras, Jīvaṭa moves from one dream to another, finding his self-identity in various animals and plants and finally returning to the awareness of the metadreamer. Along the lines of the Upaniṣadic dictum of "Thou Art That," the subjects in the narratives of Vasiṣṭha attain enlightenment through recognition of the imagined character of the various self-identities. This peculiarity of superimposed identities can be found frequently in Borges's stories as well. The recurrence of multiple, dreaming subjects is explicit in *The Circular Ruines,* wherein the dreamer recognizes himself as a dream creature, existing in the mind of fire. The recognition of Tadeo Isidoro Cruz in his fight against Martin Fierro and the experience of Senora de Borges when confronted by the Indian English girl are typical examples wherein there is a sudden recognition and the dissolution of distinctness in which subjective boundaries collapse.

In these depictions of the self, the implicit philosophy found in the narratives of Vasiṣṭha range from Advaita Vedānta, Trika Śaivism, to Mahāyāna Buddhism. While the traces of multiple forms of mysticism are found in the writings of Borges, significant to this discussion are the influences of Buddhism and Schopenhauer's philosophy. The influence of Advaita Vedānta in the writings of Schopenhauer is evident, so even if Borges did not have particular expertise on Advaita, he is conversant with this philosophy through its Western iterations.[2] One of the concepts commonly shared by Schopenhauer and Borges is that the world is a vast oneness, and individuality found in the world is merely an illusion.[3] Vasiṣṭha's philosophy, which can be identified in Western terms as subjective illusionism, relies on the same assumption, that the empirical self that is the foundation of all imaginations that consequently lead to suffering, in itself is nothing more than fiction, parallel to dream or illusion.

In many of the stories of Vasiṣṭha and Borges, the protagonists endeavor to escape from unsatisfactory circumstances only to find themselves ultimately in the same situation. In the story of Śikhidhvaja and Cūḍālā, Śikhidhvaja retires from kingship and goes into seclusion to meditate by controlling his senses. Like Siddhārtha, this king abandons his beautiful wife to find himself finally in her lap, being enlightened by her instructions. Both Janaka and Rāma seek retirement from kingship only to find themselves better rulers. In these narratives, their role is as if predestined, and in this reading we can find these two writers quite close. While predestination is a topic shared by both, Vasiṣṭha often deviates from it, saying that these predestined roles are the dreams of the metadreamer, which, nevertheless, are convertible and changeable. Although the roles assumed by the characters, including the roles of Vasiṣṭha and Borges as storytellers, are products of their own action (*karma*), nonetheless, they remain in the hands of the dreamer. The tension between predestined fate and independent action comes to a climax in the story of the sons of Indu, who, recognizing that the creation of God is predestined to dissolve, assume the role of better creators, starting their own creation. In this depiction, individuals are not only capable of reversing predestined roles or roles given by the metadreamer; they can reconfigure the dream itself or become their own "programmers."

Behind the Screen of Metaphors

One needs to gaze behind the screen of metaphors to find the logic inherent in the writings of Vasiṣṭha and Borges. Neither hesitates to alter his metaphors time and again. Just as the reader may identify "magical realism" in metaphors such as the mirror, labyrinth, dream, aleph, and the fictional nature of cognition itself found in the writings of Borges,[4] the narratives of Vasiṣṭha present metaphoric logic "in the sense that instead of producing inferences within an already known language game or paradigm, it heralds a new language game or a new paradigm."[5] As Borges guides us through his essays to understand his mind, Vasiṣṭha often philosophizes upon the narratives and deconstructs narratives to initiate his argument. For example, in the story of the *Great Forest*, Vasiṣṭha describes a man with one thousand arms who beats himself, as he runs through a forest dense with thorny brush. Vasiṣṭha believes that the person with one thousand arms is the mind with countless manifestations, a well and banana grove represent hell and heaven, and the dense forest with thorny brush is the life of a worldly man. In *Nonexistent Princes*, Vasiṣṭha parallels the world that is conceived as real with a nanny's tale of nonexistent princes who quench their thirst in nonexistent rivers and enter nonexistent cities. In the case of either writer, the underlying philosophy is explicit, with their fictional and logical writings overlapping in the juncture of imaginary time and space.

Foremost among the metaphors found in Vasiṣṭha's description of reality is that of dream. The dreams of Vasiṣṭha often refute reality as conceived by Vālmīki, and they also confront it. Here, dreams not only describe the illusory nature of what is perceived but also demonstrate a creative nature of the self and by that, establish as parallel any other reality which does not bear a higher degree of reality than anything conceived by the self.

In the writings of Borges, *The Circular Ruins* and *The God's Script* are prominent in their exploration of dream. The protagonist of the first story is committed to dream a man and insert him into reality. In this, which one may say is the process of lucid dreaming, the protagonist first learns to dream properly and in due time brings his dream creation forward, complete in minute detail. Now this creator does not want his son or his dream creation to find out that he is merely a phantom. This fear comes to an end with the recognition by the protagonist that he himself is dreamt by another, as fire does not burn him but only caresses when he is engulfed in flames. In *The Other,* Borges brings to the surface a dilemma of two dreamers, one Borges, and the other, Borges. In this, the first Borges finds himself as a dream character of another Borges. The theme of creating something phenomenally real in the process of lucid dreaming is consistent in the story of *Dreamtigers* as well, wherein Borges fails to dream, or in another sense, to give life to his dream object.

The narratives of Vasiṣṭha remind us again and again of the parallel between the phenomenal and the dream world. A typical example is the story of Gādhi. Gādhi longs to know the magical power of Viṣṇu, renowned for his illusive power to project both subjective and objective realities. With this magical power, Gādhi faints briefly when bathing in a river, and awakes to find himself surrounded by his grief-stricken relatives mourning his death. He experiences his rebirth as the tribesman Kaṭañja, who one day finds himself appointed as king, renamed Gavala. Gādhi wakes up from his swoon when Gavala decides to kill himself and jumps into fire. To make the story even more interesting, Gādhi visits the place that he experienced in his dream only to confirm that it really exists and there indeed was a king Gavala. At the depth of these narratives is the shift in subjective identities. The multiple identities experienced by the subject in the story of Gādhi are equal, whether considered to be real or false.

The next significant metaphor in the stories of Borges is that of mirror. The profanity and illusiveness of mirror is explicit in Borges' stories such as *Tlon, Uqbar, Orbis Tertius*. In this story, he cites from an imaginary reference that "mirrors and fatherhood are abominable because they multiply and disseminate that universe."[6] This mirror is again hanging in the *Library of Babel,* wherein one finds it in the hallway after passing a spiral stairway. Borges describes this mirror as faithfully duplicating all appearances, suggesting that the "Library" itself is finite, pointing out the duplication produced by mirrors. In the same paragraph, Borges claims that he prefers a mirror to the "dream that its polished surfaces represent and promise the infinite."[7] A mirror is also the central theme of *The Draped Mirrors.*[8] In this story, he describes the horror of mirrors that he felt as a child with their "spectral duplication or multiplication of reality."[9] The story ends with Julia draping mirrors to avoid seeing the face of Borges, one of his former faces. Although not explicitly mentioned as "mirror image" in the stories such as *Borges and I* or in the poem *The Borges,* the conflict between real and projected self-identities is clear. These examples, while denying the reality of appearance and of plurality, nevertheless do confirm something foundational which is singular in essence.

Mirroring or multiplication of a singular reality to varied forms is the core of the philosophy of Vasiṣṭha. Commonly found in Mahāyāna Buddhism, Advaita Vedānta, and Trika Śaivism, this process of the duplication of reality into multiple forms is described in terms of counterimage (*pratibimba*), with the explicit example of a mirror (*darpaṇa*). Although the depiction of a mirror, mirror images, or reflection in these philosophies is not couched in the language of horror, these metaphors nevertheless are identified as the root of suffering, of bondage, and of death, caused by ignorance of the singularity of the reality beneath all these reflections. Both Advaita Vedānta and Trika Śaivism propound a school of thought identified as "the doctrine of the mirror-image (*pratibimbavāda*). A sentence that can represent both of these philosophies is: "The world is within the self, comparable to the city being seen in a mirror." This is being seen as if outside due to illusion like in a dream.[10] With the unmistakable imprint of Yogācāra Buddhism, the depiction of the phenomenal in the YV is often described as "appearance" with ample reference to the erroneous cognition of the "hair net" perceived due to ophthalmic disorder.

This self-duplication is at the core of the story of Līlā. When Vasiṣṭha fancies himself to be a king, he finds himself as the king Padma without leaving his earlier form of Vasiṣṭha. In order to accompany the king, Vasiṣṭha fancies his wife, Arundhatī, who manifests as Līlā, to be his queen. This Līlā, in turn, finds herself duplicated in another realm that she enters through the process of abandoning her I-sense. She is actually able to bring her mirror-image Līlā to the realm of the first Līlā with the counterimage of Padma, this time as Vidūratha. The first Līlā recognizes her true essence with instruction by the goddess of wisdom, while the second Līlā remains in her realm to please the king. Vasiṣṭha, the awakened one, is apparently also the king, the bound one, fancied by the enlightened one. At the end, the notions of the self, bondage, and even enlightenment get jumbled together, for Vasiṣṭha as Vasiṣṭha-who-does-not-have-the-ego-sense-of-Vasiṣṭha is the enlightened one, and the very Vasiṣṭha who fancies himself as the king is bound and is accompanied by his wife, who in her essence is liberated although still bound as Līlā.

In Vasiṣṭha's worldview, there is no essential being of the plurality of individualities. This allows for something that exists, or in essence experiences its being, to self-replicate and assume multiple subjectivities. This power, often associated with Viṣṇu, is also inherited by Saṃvara, a demon in the narrative of Vasiṣṭha. Correctly identified as the "concealer," this demon projects himself in the form of Dāma, Vyāla, and Kaṭa, who are free from ego sense and also emanates in the form of another set of demons—Bhīma, Bhāsa, and Dṛḍha—who are endowed with self-knowledge. In light of these stories, Vasiṣṭha describes the nature of creation as something conceived by the self within itself. Comparable to the waves of the ocean, when the self is somehow stirred with emotions, it manifests itself in the forms of subject and object. In the ground where these dualities appear, there is neither perceiver nor perception. This ground, considered to be the "Creator" is supposed to be free from delusions in relation to its creation. This creator is also equated to mind, and his body, to mental body. Comparing the ornaments of gold and gold itself, the duality in the philosophy of Vasiṣṭha exists in the mind of the creator. While all appearances are precluded from having their own being in the absence of the mind of the dreamer, the ground of dream is changeless in these depictions. Borges also does not reject the ground of all appearances. The acceptance of the ground of the appearances as real and the rejection of the absolute nature even of that foundation are the points that distinguish Advaita Vedānta from Mahāyāna Buddhism. For Nāgārjuna and along the same lines as other Madhyamaka thinkers, appearance and the foundation of appearance are both equally false. Although momentary self-identities and their falsity are explicit in Borges's *The Draped Mirrors*, other stories such as *Library of Babel, Tlon, Uqbar,* and *Orbis Tertius* allow for the possibility of something existing beneath appearance. The philosophy found in the YV can otherwise be deciphered following the philosophy of Yogācāra Buddhism, but this changeless awareness as the ground of multiple appearances is one core element that does not allow it to be completely identified with Buddhist philosophy. This could also be the reason for Borges to state that he does not consider himself a Buddhist, although his fascination with Buddhism is evident.[11]

Borges is curious about magic. He says that as a child he failed to actualize a tiger in his dream, demonstrating a lack of magical power. This longing for magical power appears fulfilled in *The God's Script*, where he finds himself in a shell as Tzinacán, the "magician of the pyramid of Qaholom."[12] As a magician he is endowed with the power to materialize his dream, and he eventually fills the prison cell with the sand of his imagination. The dreamer in *The Circular Ruins* is often identified as a magician, with his application of dream parallel with magic. Either as a dreamer or as a magician, he maintains his distance from the characters of his fiction, although he often questions the reality of one or the other.

The story of Lavaṇa is the masterpiece of Vasiṣṭha that demonstrates subjective illusion with the application of magic. In this story, a magician causes the king to swoon, and the king finds himself in a desolate forest where he is rescued by a woman leather worker, whom he marries and with whom he has a number of children. Because of his inability to feed his children during a famine, he jumps into a fire and wakes up as Lavaṇa with a lapse of just a moment. In the same way, the magical power of Viṣṇu is explicit in the story of Gādhi, described above. In these narratives, "magic" (*māyā*) is the often-repeated term for describing the phenomenal, the cause that gives rise to plurality in terms of subject and object. Just as magic as found in the narratives of Vasiṣṭha is interchangeable with dream, so also with mirror images in the writings of Borges. In his *Fauna of Mirrors*, Borges describes two worlds—the world of mirrors and the world of men—wherein one could go through one world to the other through mirrors. When the mirror people invaded the earth, the Yellow Emperor, with his magical power, imprisoned them in the mirrors. The magic spell of the Yellow Emperor is described as reducing mirror people to "mere slavish reflections."[13]

The possibility of mirroring inside the mirror image, dreaming within the dream, and the circularity of time are themes that interweave the texts of Borges and the stories of Vasiṣṭha within other stories. Both Vasiṣṭha and Borges depict themselves as characters within the story. Borges is notorious for providing fanciful references and describing texts within texts. This genre is commonly found in Indian literature, including the major epics *Rāmāyaṇa* and Mahābhārata. The narratives of Vasiṣṭha and Rāma appear in the conversation between

Sutīkṣṇa and Agastya, found in turn in the conversation between Kāruṇya and Agniveśya, which in turn is found in the conversation of Vālmīki and Ariṣṭanemi. This fabrication of the setting with layered narrators depicts confronting philosophies, as is explicit in the most external layer of the conversation the tension between action and knowledge, reproduced from the crucial dialogue between Lord Kṛṣṇa and Arjuna in the *Bhagavad Gītā*. Interweaving of philosophies in the process of metatextuality and metanarratives, in the case of Borges, is exemplary in *Tlon, Uqbar,* and *Orbis Tertius.* The conflict of realism and idealism, with contrasting models of philosophy, is apparent in the tension among the characters of this narrative.

The Labyrinth of Time and Space

Neither Vasiṣṭha nor Borges believes in linear time. Time, in their depiction, does not occur when things happen, nor is it the foundation of reality. Instead, the conscious gaze is reality, wherein time can be found and is grounded. As this awareness is found in the present mode, all that exists is the present. Memory of the past and anticipation of the future both occur in the present. Borges draws the concept of eternity from Greek sources, and this concept is equally prevalent in India. In *A New Refutation of Time,* Borges relies on Buddhist sources as well, particularly the conversation of the Bactrian king Meander with Nāgasena. His deviation from linear and singular time allows him to introduce subjective time and the concept of cyclical time in his writings. This affirmation of subjective time is explicit in many of his writings. For example, in *The Other Death,* Pedro Damian dies a cowardly death only in turn to have it overturned. The subjective aspect of time prominently appears in *The Secret Miracle,* wherein Borges injects his own philosophical arguments while describing the death of Hladic. In this story, he is also explicit about the unity of time, space, and action.[14] Hladic experiences one year's events within some fifteen minutes of phenomenal time, so compelling an adventure that he begged God to complete his drama.

Borges adopts some model of cyclical time, not in the literal sense where the same events keep recurring, but when similar events repeat in a generic sense, as the library he describes is unlimited and cyclical. He argues that "in an infinite amount of time the number of possible permutations must be reached, and the universe will have to repeat itself."[15] The most explicit depiction can be found in his essay *Circular Time,* where he "seeks to define three fundamental versions of the doctrine of the eternal return."[16] This circularity is explicit in *The Circular Ruins* and *The Golem*. It is actually this understanding of time that underlies his philosophy of history. The series of metanarratives interwoven in the Chinese doll-within-doll style found in *The Garden of Forking Paths* brings the same notion of time with certain particularities. A sentence found in this story, "the future already exists," exactly presents the Buddhist Sarvāstivāda position that all three modes of time, past, present, and future, exist at the same present moment.

The consideration of the doctrine of cause and effect and future events as the consequence of past events leads Borges to adopt a type of predeterminism. The subjects of his narrative face the predestined fate that is determined at the very moment of the first action. This is explicit in *The Garden of the Forking Paths,* where Borges states that "the author of an atrocious undertaking ought to imagine that he has already accomplished it, ought to impose upon himself a future as irrevocable as the past."[17] As this suggestion may appear to countenance a single predestined future, Borges clarifies his philosophy in depth in the last section of the story, where he states, "He believed in infinite series of times, in a growing, dazzling net of divergent, convergent, and parallel times. This network in times which approached one another, forked, broke off, or were unaware of one another for centuries, embrace all possibilities of time. We do not exist in a majority of these times; in some you exist and not I; in others I, and not you; in others, both of us."[18]

Both the cyclical and subjective aspects of time are at the core of the stories of Vasiṣṭha. Several of the stories demonstrate the illusory nature of time as a pedagogical tool for enlightenment. As found in the story of Gādhi, Vasiṣṭha instructs Rāma to "live in the present," saying that "when the mind stops linking itself to the past and to the future it becomes no-mind."[19] This "no-mind" is the enlightened state of Vasiṣṭha, as it is the mind which is identified as the hub around which the vicious cycle of rebirth revolves. Playing with the double meaning of the term *kāla* as time and death in Sanskrit, the YV depicts time in three different ways. The first is the time in which events occur. When describing this time as the creator and destroyer of everything, the statements depict a vivid image of time as magician, and mighty like a lion, rooted in the absolute Brahman. The second type of time depicted in the YV is as the God of death. This depiction of time grants it more subjective freedom than the previous concept of time. The third aspect of time, identified as *kṛtānta* or the end of action, is the inevitable result of action. This mode of time is similar to the concept of predestination found in the writings of Borges.

The stories of Lavaṇa and Gādhi are the best examples demonstrating the subjective nature of time. In a single moment, Lavaṇa experiences more than a decade of time. Even longer than that, Gādhi experiences in the same amount of time his death and rebirth as a tribesman and his appointment as a king and the death of that king. As is the time described, a magician appears in the palace of Lavaṇa to bring him to this nightmarish experience. The stunning similarity with the time experienced by Hladic in the story of Borges is explicit. The magical nature of time is somehow related to God, as is demonstrated when Gādhi requests proof of the magic of God and Lord Viṣṇu gives Gādhi a vision of his death and afterlife. The same occurs for Hladic.

The story of Līlā, complex in its depiction, can be compared to *The Garden of Forking Paths*. Here, there is not one predestined future, as a double of Līlā concurrently appears. The multiple manifestations of Līlā and the transmigration of Padma as Vidūratha depict different layers of time experienced by these two subjects, while all of these modes are predestined with a single desire of Vasiṣṭha to find himself as king. It can be said that all the events in the future, if there really is that, are predestined at the very moment the sage desires to be a king. As he is the one endowed with desire, his desire creates the double of his wife Arundhatī, who in one form of Līlā attains enlightenment but remains ignorant in another form. The complexity of time and the concept of predestination resurface in the story of Bhuṣūṇḍa, where the bird-sage experiences many cycles of creation in his single lifetime.

The stunning similarities in the depiction of time, the role of predestination, and the recurrence of time found in the narratives of Vasiṣṭha and Borges can be attributed to an idealism shared by both authors. The philosophical concept of Bishop Berkeley, *esse est perceipie*, and one of the understandings of the concept of *dṛṣṭisṛṣṭi* found in the YV are identical, leading to the denial of entities out of the domain of experience. Time has been a crucial point in this discussion, as it is frequently described in common conversation as relative. Borges appears to be less emphatic about the unreality of space compared to Vasiṣṭha, than he is about time. In either case, the nonsubstantial nature of time and space, or of timespace as a singular entity, relates to the concept of the illusory manifestation, magical appearance, or multiple replications of reality. As we find fictitiousness of time and space in the stories of both Borges and Vasiṣṭha, this raises another question: Is the subject that experiences modifications of time real, or is this the foundation for all other appearances?

The Dreamer: In Quest of the Real Self

Borges consistently presents the self with counterparts or multiple images, as found in *Borges and I* as well as *The Draped Mirrors,* where he reminds the reader of his multiple faces, and he treats himself, the individual, as a type. The first concept parallels the Buddhist concept of person, in which what is conceived to be self is nothing but a series of concepts simultaneously arising and dependent upon their cause. This cause-and-effect relationship is depicted as the twelvefold wheel of existence, demonstrating the circularity of the chain of events. In the second concept, Borges advocates some type of *avatar*, explained with a plethora of examples of mirrors with the underlying concept of infinity. A subtle distinction requires exploration, as circular causality of nonsubstantial entities is explicit in the first model, whereas the concept of *avatar* is similar to the example of mirror where the essential being of one entity is a requirement for duplication.

Borges appears bewitched by the concept of infinity, to the extent that he finds this concept to corrupt and perplex all other concepts.[20] According to Borges, "infinity" affects our perception of the world, specifically of time. For him, infinity completely envelops eternity and the concept of space and is interlinked with his understanding of the circularity of time. His metaphor of the labyrinth is somehow related to this encircling, not leading to one single point.[21] The self, in this argument, is eternally circling around the same patterns of behavior, of ideas, and eventually of the concepts of the phenomenal world that are archetypal in nature and essentially devoid of their own self-nature. He concludes the series of entertaining arguments in the *Avatars of the Tortoise* by citing Novalis: "[T]he greatest sorcerer would be he who bewitched himself to the point of taking his own phantasmagorias for autonomous apparitions."[22] Invoking an idealistic claim that the world is hallucinatory, he concludes that the world as we conceive of it is what we have dreamed it to be. This conclusion allows us to interpret the concept of the self in the writings of Borges as endowed with replication and forgetfulness so that forgetfulness of its own other manifestations ensues.

The other side of this discussion is enlightenment, in light of changing shifting personalities and the archetypal nature of the person under consideration. Borges claims that "the idea that a man may be many men is, of course, a literary commonplace . . ."[23] If we apply this statement to cosmology, it leads to the worldview with a singular center of experience, the source, or primal cause that gives rise to infinite counterimages. It is explicit in his *God's Script,* where Tzinacán's moment of highest rapture can be compared to religious ecstasy, with the essence described as "the apprehension of an ultimate nonsensuous unity in all things, a oneness or a One to which neither the senses nor the reason can penetrate."[24] The description is first unitary, as Borges describes Tzinacán having union with the divine. But he immediately relates that Tzinacán also experiences union with the universe. The perception of the wheel, which again suggests circularity and infinity, the disc of Lord Viṣṇu, and the Buddhist symbol of dharma which is described in negative terms by Nāgārjuna and here by Borges, is immediately followed by the all-confirming experience occurring at "every place at one time." The final mode of rapture comes with the statement, "I, Tzinacán, would rule the lands Moctezuma ruled. But I know I shall never say those words, because I no longer remember Tzinacán."[25] The experience of Tzinacán embodies seemingly contradictory elements such as fire and water; it harnesses opposites in nature; and there is the obliteration of time. Bell-Villa parallels the description of Tzinacán in terms of repeated "I saw" with the description of Arjuna's encounter with the divinity in the *Bhagavad Gītā*.[26] This affirmative description of the mystical experience of Tzinacán reminds Bell-Villa of the Upaniṣadic description of the unity with all that exists, found in the discussion of Śvetaketu and Āruṇī and confirmed by sentences such as "Thou art That.'[27]

This mystical encounter of Tzinacán in his *Avatars of the Tortoise* gives a glimpse of the reality as Borges conceives of it: "It is hazardous to think that a coordination of words could resemble the universe. It is also hazardous to think that of those illustrious coordinations." He concludes this discussion by invoking Schopenhauer for the statement that the world is a factory of will, in which Borges says that he has "glimpsed some trace of the universe." In this gaze where the cosmic and individual merge, and distinctions of the subject and object dissolve, the remnants of difference in the phenomenal are no more real than those of imagination, and in this world, the fictional parallels the external. Although Borges may himself be in the dream of someone else—perhaps that someone is God—he nonetheless has the same power to dream, create characters and give them life, and breathe through them, as they are also nothing but avatars, avatars of Borges, or may be, to entertain the formalist claim, in the mind of the reader, in myriad forms.

The *Yoga Sūtra* of Patañjali at one point describes that a yogin in his highest state of creativity, gained through prolonged meditation, can generate himself as multiple persons and experience different karmas simultaneously as a way of attaining a shortcut to salvation.[28] Following the *Ekajīva* model of Advaita, there indeed is a single mind conceiving plurality in the form of both subject and object. Vasiṣṭha prefers this single mind to be the primordial mind, the first ripple of "being only" or "consciousness only" that is identified as Brahman, although this naming is not really describing the thing in itself but only satisfies our need of language for dialogue. This mind, for Vasiṣṭha, is Hiraṇyagarbha or Svayambhū, the cosmic embryo or the self-manifest. Pertinent here is the Upaniṣadic depiction of Hiraṇyagarbha as the archetypal mind that collectively refers to all individual minds in their dreaming state.[29] In this picture, what we may call God is actually the collective dreamer, or the first dreamer, who dreams to become many, and multiple subjects consequently arise. One may call this cosmic projection self-emanation or *avatāras*.

This very power of the self to create its mirror image allows Vasiṣṭha to manifest as King Padma in the story of Līlā without abandoning his previous form or leaving the possibility to retrace his previous identity. This allows Līlā to not only meet her counterpart, but also to recognize that all identities are equally fictitious, including that of Arundhatī. The doctrine of *pratibimba* or counterimage not only describes the potency of the self to be many; it further confirms this self-emanation and depicts this as somehow haunting and hallucinating, binding and mesmerizing, tormenting and trembling.

In *The God's Script,* Tzinacán experiences mystical oneness with everything and then says that now he can be the king, but he also says that he is no longer Tzinacán. In Vasiṣṭha's narratives, king Janaka faces the same situation, for he is king but no longer has the ego sense of Janaka. The earlier Janaka is suffering and bound with ego sense, whereas the latter Janaka is free, endowed with self-experience, which one may call a mystical state of unity with totality. The very discourse of Vasiṣṭha with Rāma is grounded upon the same platform, with Rāma depressed because of the dissatisfactory world that culminates in suffering no matter what we do. The intention of the text itself, through the instructions of Vasiṣṭha, is to awaken Rāma to the experience of totality or to enter into the mind of the primordial dreamer. It is not to create individual dreams and be haunted by their creatures. At the end, Rāma wakes up to reality and says, "There is nothing that I should or should not do. However, your words should always be honored" (CYV, 420).

The experience of Tzinacán and that of the magician in *The Circular Ruins* resemble the narrative of Bhuśuṇḍa. In the opening of the story, Vasiṣṭha describes his own genesis, that in the infinite and invisible consciousness there is a mirage-like appearance of the world in a corner, if it exists, where the Creator dwells. Vasiṣṭha says that he is the mind-born son of this Creator. Vasiṣṭha describes that creation arose out of the notion of creation that causes division between light and world, where light refers to consciousness and the world, to matter. The circularity of time and events is confirmed through the experience of Bhuśuṇḍa, who is an everlasting enlightened crow. This immortal crow claims in this narrative that whatever is happening in the present creation has happened in exactly the same order in three previous creations. He claims to have the memory of the events of ten previous creations. While describing the cyclical nature of events and time, this also suggests a noncyclical aspect as well: creations sometimes do recur, and other times, do not. Bhuśuṇda, the hybrid of a crow born of the goddesses' lustful orgy, claims to have witnessed multiple creations wherein different gods, human beings, or demons initiate creation. The focus of this bird is only in the present moment, as he claims to not contemplate past or future. He also claims to have no consideration for being or nonbeing. The existence or the eternity of being experienced by Bhuśuṇḍa coincides with his freedom from the concept of time and of death. There actually is no death to be experienced if the subject of one's gaze is focused only in the present, the moment that is immediately given. In this pure awareness, or the awareness of being or the being of awareness, time is not cognized but felt, and since death is not felt, it does not exist.

This bird instructs Vasiṣṭha to realize this world as a long dream or a long-standing mass hallucination. Bhuśuṇḍa, confirming the experience mentioned by Vasiṣṭha, further claims that he is born of the mind of the creator. He also says that the world arises in the mind as a notion. But what is significant in this discussion is the claim Bhuśuṇḍa makes, that the Creator is but a notion in the cosmic mind, just as the world appearance is. This depiction is found earlier in this text, particularly in the section on creation, where Vasiṣṭha describes that, just as many forms are latent in gold, to be molded in the forms of various items of jewelry, so also are the creations conceived of in the mind of the creator. This mind of the creator is identified with the infinite self. The world appears in this mind, just as a mirage appears in the form of a real river. This creator, the mind, is free from the notions of subject and object, but nevertheless these concepts arise in the process of creation. These are the thoughts that pulsate in the mind of the creator, giving rise to duality. Although this primordial mind is considered to be free from delusions, this mind nonetheless dreams. The explicit reference found in this section confirms that the creator is the mind, with mind being his body. Just as thoughts are inherent to the mind, so also are the worlds in reality merely thoughts in this mind.

This demonstrates circularity and the way Vasiṣṭha resolves it is by imagining the cosmic mind as singular, as the substrate of imagination or dream. In this depiction, dreaming appears to be the mind's inherent nature, as no reason could justify the purpose of dreaming in this endless cycle. This circularity is further depicted in the metaphor of consciousness as a vine that sprouts with the sprinkling of latent tendencies and is endowed with the buds of desire wherein past creations are described as filaments. The concept of cause and effect, or that of karma and rebirth, as found in the discussion of the *Avatārs of the Tortoise* in the story of Borges, likewise has the consequence of circularity. His argument of infinity appears to surround this consequence of circularity. The inward flash, or the experience of the dreamer, if that happens, gives the awareness that the subject is in hallucination, and the appearance of the world becomes parallel to a dream in this esoteric experience.

This "self" is realized by Vasiṣṭha when he claims that he himself is a mere fiction of the Creator and by Bhuśuṇḍa, the crow who gives two different accounts of genesis (he is the mind-born of Go; he is born of the orgy of the goddesses engaged in beastiality). Although Bhuśuṇḍa does not describe his other dreams, he nevertheless maintains a dialogue with another dream-creature, Vasiṣṭha. Somehow the exchange of language is maintained in this metahallucination. This realization of the self, exchanged in conversation, confirms that the self is not the identity of either of the selves; neither is this the dilemma in which a particular identity is perceived as real. It is the realization that none of the faces is real, as Borges describes in the story of the draped mirrors.

After king Lavaṇa awakens from the swoon, he goes out on an expedition, only to find out that what he dreamt was in fact real. When Gādhi wakes up from the magical slumber, he confirms the same paradox, that he was simultaneously Gādhi and the tribesman. But was there Gādhi when there was an absence of Gādhi-consciousness? The Gādhi of the flesh cannot confirm its inherent being, and the self that finds its identity did not confirm the existence of the form of Gādhi. As in the story of Tadeo Isidoro Cruz in his fight against Martin Fierro, Gādhi does not maintain double identities. In the case of Señora de Borges, she finds self-identity when confronted by the Indian English girl.

The circularity of creation is evident in the story of the sons of Indu. In this paradigm, the ability to dream vividly creates worlds.

In the metafiction of the Creator, the characters, the sons of Indu, create their own fictions. Are the sons of Indu able only to dream of creation, placing themselves parallel to the Creator, or are they able to imagine the Creator who can carry out creation? Vasiṣṭha escapes from this circularity by maintaining the singularity of the primordial dreamer, although there is nothing mentioned about the limit or the scope of dream.

Unlike the stories of Borges when the realization of oneself as fictional dramatically ends the story, Vasiṣṭha's stories do not end that way. Knowing that it is a dream does not end the dream; it merely provides self-realization, whatever that realization may be. The god or the first dreamer, as maintained by Vasiṣṭha, is endowed with the knowledge of the self, which does not stop him from dreaming, although sometimes this Creator appears to have the arrogance of Creatorhood, and when confronted by parallel creators, is found tormented. This god is once enlightened by the Sun, in the story of the sons of Indu, who instructs the Creator to not imagine himself as anything more than someone whose nature is to keep creating. As the sun says, to be sun implies to shine, to give light. The sun cannot be the sun and not be shining. With this maxim, the sun instructs the Creator to keep creating, although cautioning the Creator to have no self-pride in doing something that one cannot do otherwise. This depiction also indicates that enlightenment is not some only once-in-a-lifetime type of experience, nor is the case of falling into a dream. Dreaming and waking up from a dream are the eternal processes of consciousness that cannot do otherwise.

While maintaining the hallucinatory nature of the world that appears, Borges tends to accept the fictionality of the phenomenal as that of fiction, whereas, in the case of Vasiṣṭha, the focus appears to be to maintain the reality of fiction, of imagined space and time. The stories of Lavaṇa and Gādhi do not appear to reject commonsense experience, but rather they confirm the experience of hallucination. This, however, does not make a categorical distinction between the two writers, as both accept the nonsubstantiality of there being either Borges or Vasiṣṭha.

Notes

I am grateful to Bill Nariccio, Arindam Chakrabarti, and Christopher Chapple for their inspiration and insight in writing this chapter.

1. Evelyn Underhill, *Mysticism* (New York: E. P. Dutton, 1961), 80.

2. Borges's development of thought can be found in the essays "Forms of a Legend," "What Is Buddhism" written with Alicia Jurado, and "Bud-

dhism," in *The Seven Nights*. He discusses Sāṃkhya and Vedānta as antecedents to Buddhism.

3. Gene H. Bell-Villada, *Borges and His Fictions: A Guide to His Mind and Art* (Austin: University of Texas Press, 1999), 38.

4. See Lois Parkinson Zamora, "The Visualizing Capacity of Magical Realism: Objects and Expressions in the Work of Jorge Luis Borges," *Janus Head* (Fall 2002): 21–37.

5. Bruno Lo Turko, "The Metaphorical Logic of the *Mokṣopāya*," in *The Mokṣopāya, Yogavāsiṣṭha and Related Texts*, ed. Jürgen Hanneder (Aachen, 2005), 138.

6. George Luis Borges, *Labyrinth: Selected Stories and Other Writings* (New York: New Directions Books, 2007), 4.

7. Ibid., 51.

8. George Luis Borges, *Dreamtigers* (Austin: University of Texas Press, 1964), 27–28.

9. Ibid., 27.

10. *Dakṣiṇāmūrttistava* 1.

11. *Seven Nights,* cited by W. H. Bossart, *Borges and Philosophy: Self, Time and Metaphysics* (New York: Peter Lang, 2003).

12. Borges, *Labyrinth*, 169.

13. For discussion on magical realism, see Zamora 2002.

14. See Borges, *Labyrinth*, 91.

15. In "The Doctrine of the Cycles," cited in Bossart, *Borges and Philosophy*, 104.

16. Bossart, *Borges and Philosophy*, 105.

17. Borges, *Labyrinth*, 22.

18. Ibid., 28.

19. Swami Venkatesananda, *The Concise Yoga Vāsiṣṭha* (New York: The State University of New York Press, 1984), 208.

20. *Avatārs of the Tortoise*, para 1.

21. For interrelatedness of circularity and infinity, see "The Garden of Forking Paths," by Jorge Luis Borges.

22. *Avatārs of the Tortoise*, last paragraph.

23. In *The Approach to al-Mu'tasim*. Cited in Bossart, *Borges and Philosophy*, 143.

24. W. T. Stace, *Teachings of the Mystics* (New York: New American Library, 1960), 14. For discussion on Tzinacan's experience, see Bell-Villada, *Gene H. Borges and His Fiction: A Guide to his Mind and Art* (Austin: University of Texas Press, 1999), 211–19.

25. Borges, *Labyrinth*, 173.

26. Bell-Villada, *Borges and His Fictions*, 213–14.

27. Ibid., 214–15.

28. *Nirmāṇacittāny asmitāmātrāt*|.

29. See *Māṇḍūkyopaniṣad. And the Kārikās of Gauḍapāda* for further discussion.

II

Human Agency and World Creation

7

Attitude of the Yogavāsiṣṭha toward Human Endeavor

PRANATI GHOSAL

> The human will stands beyond all circumstances. Before it—the strong, gigantic, infinite will and freedom in man—all the powers, even of nature must bow down, succumb and become its servants.
>
> —Swami Vivekananda[1]

The *Yogavāsiṣṭha* (YV) is a very popular, long poem diffuse in extent, puranic in character, and theologic and mystic in import. Though based on what is believed to be an incident of Śrī Rāmacandra's life, the real purpose of the composition is to handle the tenets of Advaita Vedānta in its own way.

The aim of the present chapter is to determine the attitude of the YV towards the doctrine of self-endeavor, that is, the problem of to what extent one can become the architect of one's own fate and how far one's activities in this world are preordained by some external agencies like *daiva* or destiny.

The Mahābhārata[2] also has dealt with the contribution of self-effort and destiny in human life. Some stray remarks on the same have been traced in the *Pañcatantra*[3] as well as the *Hitopadeśa*.[4] But the basic differences between these texts and the YV are that the former have attached equal importance to both fate and self-enterprise, whereas the latter has stepped a little further to declare that human endeavor is the only way to achieve any type of success, and the YV asserts that effort (*karman*) is the sole determining factor, while *daiva* or fate is merely a consolatory contrivance.[5] Whereas the *Bhagavad Gītā*[6] has admitted *daiva* as a factor in the accomplishment of action, the YV is an uncompromising champion of self-determination. The view that it upholds is rather unique and progressive in Indian literature, especially at the date which is roughly estimated for our text (ca. 10th to 11th century CE). I may venture to say here that a nineteenth-century scholar, Swami Vivekananda[7] also was apparently influenced by the stress of *pauruṣa* echoed in the YV, in many of his discourses where he upholds the supremacy of human endeavor above anything else. The stories of the YV were well known and often told by Swami Vivekananda's guru, Sri Ramakrishna.[8]

The YV places special emphasis on human endeavor and its immense possibilities. It has defined *pauruṣa* as personal endeavor at mental and physical activities in accordance with proper guidance of the *śāstras* stating that only such actions can succeed.[9] In other passages it explains *pauruṣa* as sincere and keen effort to attain the desired result, approved by scriptural injunctions.[10]

This *pauruṣa,* also known as *puruṣārtha* manifests itself in three forms: (1) movement of a specific thought (*saṃvit spanda*), (2) movement of the mind (*manaḥ spanda*), and (3) movement of the senses (*aindriya spanda*). When thought movement is followed by the movement of the mind, the body moves accordingly, and then there is a corresponding enjoyment or suffering.[11]

Self-determination (*pauruṣa*) may be classified in pairs in various ways. From the standpoint of time it may be divided in two parts: *aihika* (current) and *prāktana* (past) which are always in conflict. Whichever one is weaker is overpowered.[12] In most cases *aihika,* "the current one," since it is present and visible, gets more scope to conquer the past.[13] S. N. Dasgupta,[14] in his discourse "Energy of Free Will" has remarked that "the efforts of one's past life are certainly not stronger than the visible efforts of the moment." Furthermore, efforts of individuals (i.e., own or *ātmīya*) may be in conflict with the opposing endeavor of others (*anyadīya*) of which the stronger one wins.[15]

The propriety and impropriety of actions may be classified into two sections: (1) that which is approved by scriptures (*śāstrīya*) and (2) that which is contrary to it (*ucchāstra*). All effort has to be made in accordance with the instructions of scriptures as a precondition for success; if effort is employed incorrectly, it causes evil.[16]

Regarding the efficacy of *pauruṣa* in attaining success, the YV[17] declares that human endeavor (*puruṣa-spanda*), if employed with an unperturbed mind, is sure to win. On this point, H. G. Narahari[18] has stated that "there is nothing under the sun, which this endeavor cannot accomplish." Even the great gods like Indra, Brahma, Viṣṇu, and Maheśvara all owe their success to their own endeavor.[19] The YV[20] elucidates that even an expedition to the polar region can be successful with the aid of firm resolution and persistent endeavor.[21] It is only by self-determination and enthusiasm that the demons could drive away gods from heaven and conquer them; and by a counter employment of self-enterprise (i.e., sharp intelligence and competent technique) it was possible for the gods to restore it.[22] Not only that, Bṛhaspati and Śukra, who became lords of gods and demons, secured their position by exercising successful *pauruṣa*.[23] While describing the immense potential of endeavor, the YV[24] again explains that by the employment of self-enterprise not only can a person avoid dangers and difficulties, but by successful application of *puruṣārtha* she may also be heightened to the status of divinities. Even the attainment of supreme bliss is possible with the aid of human effort and enthusiasm.[25]

From this discussion, it becomes clear that motivation towards action is the source of success.[26] If a person desires anything and works accordingly in the proper way, he is certain to attain it, as long as he does not turn back midway.[27] Cherishing lofty ideals without accomplishing any concrete work is of no use; fleeting satisfactions cannot help one in achieving the desired object.[28] With reference to this context, we may quote the *Hitopadeśa*'s[29] advice: "[W]orks are done by industry and not by idle wishes." B. L. Atreya stated that "there is hardly anything in existence which is not attainable through right and earnest exertion."[30] One gets only what one strives for; nothing is ever achieved by lethargy.[31] It is an established fact that hunger is satisfied by eating only; speech is effected by personal effort.[32]

Now, a question arises regarding the scope of *pauruṣa*. Is it unlimited? The YV[33] has answered that there is a limit. One must remember that not all efforts are productive of a particular result. People do waste their time and energy pursuing wrong efforts. In spite of working hard, it is wrong to expect jewels from a heap of ashes.[34] Dasgupta writes, "There is of course a limit beyond which human endeavor is not possible and therefore it is necessary that proper economy should be observed . . . since mere random endeavor or endeavor on a wrong line cannot be expected to produce a good result."[35] Almost the same remark has been traced in Narahari's article, where he says, "To rush headlong indiscriminately is to court tragic disaster."[36] Sometimes the employment of endeavor causes trouble when the opposing endeavor is more powerful (YV II:5.7). In such cases, one must have grit to hold the stronger opposition at bay and carry out one's own will.[37] In spite of employing endeavor properly, loss may be incurred. In the course of our journey, danger or failure may come, but frustration or lamentation is not the way out;[38] firmness and courage are the weapons to overcome these failures. One should exercise will force with stronger determination in order to remove the evil effect of prior deeds (YV II:5.9). Sometimes accomplished works can be ruined; in that case it is clear that destructive power is stronger.[39] As a solution to these problems, Swami Vivekananda's instructions are helpful: "[W]hen you find yourself suffering, blame yourself and try to do better."[40]

With all the force at our command, the idea must be put away that we are mere puppets at the hand of some external agency like *daiva* that prompts us to act against our will.[41] In fact, good or bad results are the outcome of our own endeavor. Only fools think that destiny must lead them on and consequently do not strive properly to overcome their own evil.[42] The YV[43] has expressed its contemptuous attitude toward the determinists by saying that the person who does not try to overcome misfortune is like an animal at the mercy of God or destiny which may take one to heaven or hell. Our attempts to lay blame on God, making Him the punisher or rewarder, are only foolish. He neither punishes nor rewards (YV II:6.27). In continuation of his discourse on "Vedantism," Swamiji declares, "We, we and none else is responsible for what we suffer. Each of us is the maker of our destiny."[44] The object of endeavor is to destroy the power of so-called destiny and to exert oneself to the utmost to attain the supreme end of life.[45] In order to get released from the fetter of this world, one must force oneself out, just as a lion comes out of the cage (YV II:5.15). Only dullards are convinced in the supremacy of fate.[46] Swamiji, in "The Freedom of Soul," has advised modern India to become self-reliant and to depend on self-effort and strength.[47] Strength is the one thing that is needed. Strength is the medicine for this world disease (cf. YV II:6.43).

Now, how to employ *pauruṣa*? To this question, the YV[48] has advised that it is not proper to start recklessly; in that case failure may stare at us. In order to achieve success in life, all the efforts should be made in accordance with proper methods as prescribed in the scriptures. With firm resolution, constant effort, intellect, and enthusiasm a person may face any type of adversary and become successful (YV II:4.18). Because human endeavor is not possible beyond certain limits, it is necessary to resort to ideals of the *śāstras*, follow noble company and adhere to right conduct,[49] because these things instigate a rousing vibration in one's thought, mind, and sense faculties respectively.[50] Further, employment of endeavor sharpened by constant cultivation of scripture and good friends leads a person to the attainment of his desired success.[51] These things have been marked as the source of success also. The YV[52] elucidates that *siddhi* comes by one's own effort (*svataḥ*), through the culture of scriptures (*śāstrataḥ*) and the favor and blessings of teachers (*gurutaḥ*). Fortune embraces a person, whose level of intellect and vibratory action have been heightened and sanctified by these means.[53] By the gateway of these means it is possible to shatter the cycle of eternal rebirth just as a disease is remedied forever by the application of an infallible medicine.[54]

Intellect plays an important role in the process. The YV[55] has shown an interrelation between scripture and intellect, each of which complements the other by constant practice. The intellect moves on toward the attainment of liberation. Lethargy must be shaken off, and one must put forth the best efforts towards the attainment of the things of the temporal world as well as emancipation.[56] Had there been no lethargy in this world, everyone could become magnificent and renowned.[57] It is necessary to contemplate daily what is expedient at the present and to take up good practices which will effect release from the fetter of this world.[58] Self-introspection is necessary; it is a sheer folly to remain engrossed totally in sensual life.[59]

Now a question arises: Has *daiva* or fate anything to contribute here? The YV answers in the negative. In every case it has been proven that personal endeavor is entirely responsible, whether it produces good or evil.[60] In that case it must be admitted that we are the architects of our own fate. In *The Aesop's Fables* we find, "As you sow, so you reap" (cf. the biblical parable of the sower, the Old Testament). The Mahābhārata[61] says that "man himself is his own friend or enemy." If one does not save himself or herself nobody else can do it. If I set the wheel in motion, I am responsible for its result. Success always comes through effort and enthusiasm; that is the way of intelligent people.[62] Everywhere it is seen that intelligent, industrious, or brave people never await *daiva*; they exert themselves, which is invariably followed by success.[63] King Viśvāmitra knew it; he did not bother with thoughts of fate or *daiva*, and he achieved the status of Brahman by exercising his strong will, force, and continuous effort.[64] There is actually nothing like destiny making us miserable or unhappy. It is absolutely unreal. Whether good or bad, whatever a person does is rewarded accordingly[65] (cf. MBh XIII:5.9). The fatalists, being lost in the fancy of fate, ignore human effort, which is handy and visible; thus they destroy merit, wealth, and enjoyment, and they become their own enemy.[66]

While describing the immense potential of *pauruṣa,* the YV states that not only can endeavor overrule *daiva,* but it even eradicates it by calling it a mere consolatory contrivance of overwhelmed people.[67] If this view is considered to be correct, then it must be said that *daiva* is a nonentity. Properly speaking, *daiva,* or fate, cannot be categorized either as form (*ākṛti*), or as action (*karman*), or vibration (*spanda*) or force (*parākrama*).[68] It is not anything like mind (*manas*) or intellect (*buddhi*).[69] Because all vibratory actions have a concrete shape, *daiva* cannot be accepted as a coordinating factor of any *karman* (YV II:8.9). No concrete form can come in contact with this formless *daiva*. Nor can it be supported as one of the various accessories of *karman* (YV II:8.10). In short it cannot withstand any logical proof. By all the *pramāṇas* at our disposal, it is proved that nothing is effected by *daiva*. Had *daiva* been accepted as the controlling power, then all the human activities would be reduced to futility.[70] Wherever there is success, it is achieved, nurtured, and accomplished alone by continuous strenuous effort and enthusiasm.[71] *Daiva* does nothing. What passes as *daiva* is only a concoction of dullard people.[72] Visible efforts are all tangible and open to immediate perception (YV II:7.16; II:7.22–23), but none has experienced *daiva*. It cannot be perceived by any senses.[73] Thus *daiva* has been totally nullified.

But Śri Rāma was not satisfied with this explanation, arguing that *daiva* is fairly accepted. If it is totally a nil concept, then how did it come to be accepted (YV II:9.1)? Vasiṣṭha answered that whenever any effort comes to fruition and produces any good or bad result, people attribute it to *daiva.*[74] Actually there is no *daiva;* it can neither help nor obstruct anything.[75] At the time of any undertaking, every person has a particular resolution, and there may be success or failure as a result of the operation; but the commoners explain the whole thing as a contribution of *daiva.*[76] In fact *daiva* is a mere vacuity like *ākāśa (daivam ākāśarūpaṃ hi karoti na karoti ca*—YV II:9.7).

According to this definition, fate can be overpowered by our present activities as easily as a child is overpowered by a grown man.[77] Just as the wrong acts of yesterday can be rectified by good conduct today, the evil effect of fate can be removed in the same process.[78] Therefore *daiva* cannot stand as a separate entity. Everything arrives as an inevitable consequence of our already accomplished efforts.[79] Just as a disease of yesterday can be healed today by proper treatment, so also it is possible to wipe out the evil intent of *daiva* by the exercise of proper conduct today.[80] Volition and strength have important roles to play here.

Vasiṣṭha explains that desire (*vāsanā*) is the root cause of everything.[81] The instinctive root inclination of a prior state turns itself into karma. In fact karma is the concrete result of prior inclination. Everyone acts in accordance with these desires (*vāsanā)* and thereby gets the desired object.[82] Therefore *vāsanā* and karma are more or less the same thing. According to the YV (II:9.16–18), *daiva* is nothing but another name for karma performed with earnest longing for the result; karma is the same as *vāsanā,* which cannot be separated from *manas,* nor *manas* from *pauruṣa*. Thus *daiva* cannot exist as a concept totally separate from *pauruṣa.*

In each individual, there is a twofold circle of *vāsanā,* juxtaposing good and evil.[83] Anyone inclined to tread on good, following the pure stream, is sure to win Bliss. But vile instincts can carry one away into peril. Now it is our duty to nourish the good against the vile tendencies so that they may be overpowered.[84] The stream of desire runs in double course; one is pure, and the other is impure. The function of the human enterprise is to restrict the mind to its pure inclinations.[85] The mind already engrossed in evil intents can be corrected by force. It is like a beast that requires force to keep it under control. But it should be processed slowly, just as a child should be disciplined in a slow process.[86] It is very much possible to rouse pure inclinations in the mind by constant practice; and thus in this life we can shape and form our future (YV II:9.35–36). If it is true that my work yesterday has fixed my enjoyment or suffering today, then it must be true that today I can fix my tomorrow and move it toward enjoyment. On this point also we find an echoing statement in Swami Vivekananda's[87] composition: "If I can bring misery, I can stop it . . . What we have done, that we can undo also."

Thus, we see that the YV is the most powerful advocate of human endeavor ever met in Indian literature. It presents the view that strong volition and constant effort are invincible. By exercising them, one can achieve any success. One can even conquer past inclinations (*prāktana pauruṣa)* just as a strong young man wins over a child. Now, during this operation, former and current endeavors may come in conflict. But we are told the human alone is blessed with the power to fight and conquer fate, thereby transcending the tendencies of the past. Ultimately one overcomes the unhealthy influences found in the cycle of rebirth and enjoys supreme bliss.

Notes

1. Swami Vivekananda, *The Complete Works*, III:125.

2. *MBh* (*Anuśāsana parvan*) (13.5.1–49). For a book-length study of this topic, including text translations of relevant sections from the Mahābhārata and the *Yogavāsiṣṭha*, see Christopher Chapple, *Karma and Creativity* (Albany: State University of New York Press, 1986).

3. *Pañcatantra* (II:5.132–137).

4. *Hitopadeśa* (I:31–36).

5. YV II:7.15; II:8.15.

6. adhiṣṭhānaṃ tathā kartā kārañca pṛthag-vidham |
vividhāśca pṛthak ceṣṭā daivaṃ caivātra pañcamam ||. (BG 18.14)

7. Swami Vivekananda, *The Complete Works*, I:320; II:201–202, 224–25, 242; III: 125; IV: 386–87.

8. Shakespeare, in his tragedy *Julius Caesar*, also proclaims the efficacy of human effort: "Men sometimes are masters of their fate. The fault dear Brutus, is not in our starts, but in ourselves, that we are underlings." Act 1, sc. 2, lines 139–141.

9. sādhūpadiṣta mārgeṇa yan manoṅga viceṣṭitam |
tat pauruṣam tat saphalam anyad unmatta ceṣṭitam ||. (YV II:4.11)

10. (i) svārtha prāpaka kāryaika prayatna paratā budhaiḥ |
proktā pauruṣa-śabdena sā siddhyai śāstra yantritā ||. (YV II:6.32)
(ii) arthaprāpaka kāryaika prayatnaparatā budhaiḥ |
proktā pauruṣa śabdena sarvam āsādyate 'nayā ||. (YV II:7.24)

11. saṃvit spanda manaḥ spanda aindriya spanda eva ca |
etāni puruṣārthasya rūpaṇi . . . ||
yathā saṃvedanaṃ cetas tathā tat spandam ṛcchati |
taitheva kāyaścalati tathaiva phalabhoktṛtā ||. (YV II:7.4–5)

12. dvau huḍāvivia yudhyete puruṣārthau samāsamau |
prāktanaścaihikaścaiva śāmyatyatrālpa vīryavān ||. (YV II:5.5)

13. dvayor adyatanasyaiva pratyakṣād balitā bhavet | (YV II:6.19).

14. S. N. Dasgupta, *A History of Indian Philosophy*, II: 253.

15. dvau huḍav iva yudhyete puruṣārthaau samāsamau |
ātmīyaścānyadīyaśca jayaty atibalas tayoḥ ||. (YV II:5.7)

16. ucchāstraṃ śāstritaṃ ceti dvividham pauruṣaṃ smṛtam |
tatrocchāstram anarthāya paramārthāya śāstritam ||. (YV II:5.4)

17. sarvadā puruṣaspandas tatrānudvegavāñjayī || (YV II:6.18).

18. H. G. Harahari, "The YV and the Doctrine of Free Will," *Brahmavidyā*, X: 50.

19. YV II:4.13–17.

20. yatnavadbhir dṛḍhābhyāsaiḥ prajñotsāha samanvitaiḥ |
meravo 'pi nigīryante kaiva prāk pauruṣe kathā || (YV II:4.18); (cf. *Pañcatantra* III.13.219).

21. prārabhyate na khalu highnabhayena nīcaiḥ, prārabhyabighnavihatā viramanti madhyāḥ |

bighnaiḥ sahasraguṇitairapi hanyamānāḥ, prārabdhamuttamaguṇā na paritya janti ||. (*Pañcatantra* III:13.219)

22. utsādya deva-saṃghātaṃ cakrustribhuvanodare |
pauruṣeṇaiva yatnena sāmrājyaṃ dānaveśvarāḥ ||
ālūnaśīrṇam ābhogi jagadājahrur ojasā |
pauruṣeṇaiva yatnena dānavebhyaḥ sureśvaraḥ ||. (YV II:8.22–23)
23. puruṣārthena devānāṃ gurur eva bṛhaspatiḥ |
śukro daityendragurutāṃ puruṣārthena cāsthitaḥ ||. (YV II:7.7)
24. pauruṣeṇa durantebhyaḥ saṅkaṭebhyaḥ subuddhayaḥ |
samuttaranti yatnena na tu moghatayānayā ||. (YV II:7.18)
dainya dāridrya duḥkhārtā apyanye puruṣottamāḥ |
pauruṣeṇaiva yatnena yātā devendratulyatām ||. (YV II:5.27)
25. YV 2.4.9; 2.7.28.
26. pravṛttir eva prathamaṃ yathāśāstra vihāriṇām |
prabheva sarva-varṇānāṃ sādhanī sarva karmaṇām ||. (YV II:5.1)
27. yo yamarthaṃ prārthayate tadarthaṃ cehate kramāt |
avaśyam sa tamāpnoti na cedardhānnivartate ||.
28. manasā vāñchyate yacca yathāśāstraṃ na karmaṇā |
sādhyate mattalīlāsau mohanī nārthasādhanī ||. (YV II:5.2); (cf YV II:5.22)
29. udyamena hi siddhyanti kāryāṇi na manorathaiḥ | Hitopadeśa 1.31.
30. Atreya, *Philosophy of Yoga-Vāsiṣṭha,* 44.
31. yo yo yathā prayatate sa sa tat tat phalaikabhāk |
na tu tūṣṇīṃ sthiteneha kenacit prāpyate phalam ||. (YV II:7.19)
32. bhoktā tṛpyati nābhoktā gantā gacchati nāgatiḥ |
vaktā vakti na cāvaktā pauruṣaṃ saphalaṃ nṛṇam ||. (YV II:7.17)
33. yathā ghaṭaḥ parimitaḥ yathā parimitaḥ paṭaḥ |
niyataḥ parimāṇasthaḥ puruṣārthas tathaiva ca ||. (YV II:5.24)
34. pauruṣaṃ ca navānantaṃ na yatnam abhivāñchyate |
na yatnenapi mahatā prāpyate ratnam aśmataḥ ||. (YV II:5.23)
35. Dasgupta, *A History of Indian Philosophy*, II:253.
36. Narahari, "The Yogavāsiṣṭa and the Doctrine of Free Will," *Brahmavidyā,* X:42.
37. paraṃ pauruṣam āśritya dantair dantān vicūrṇayan ||
śubhenāśubham udyuktaṃ prāktanaṃ pauruṣaṃ jayet ||. (YV II:5.9)
38. krameṇopārjite 'pyarthe naṣṭe kāryā na kheditā |
na balaṃ yatra me śaktaṃ tatra kā paridevanā ||. (YV II:6.21).
39. pauruṣenṇa kṛtaṃ karma daivād yad abhinaśyati |
tatra nāśayitur jñeyaṃ pauruṣam balavattaram ||. (YV II:6.7)
40. Swami Vivekananda, "Cosmos," II:225.
41. yat prayānti jagadbhāvāḥ saṃsiddhā api sam-kṣayam |
kṣayakāraka-yatnasya hyatra jñeyaṃ mahad-balam ||. (YV II:6.9)
42. tajjayāya yatante ye na lobha-lava-lampaṭāḥ |
te dīnāḥ prākṛtā mūḍhāḥ sthitā daivaparāyaṇāḥ ||. (YV II:6.6)

43. YV 2.6.26–27.
44. Vivekananda, *The Complete Works*, III: 125.
45. asad daivam adhah kṛtvā nityam udrikayā dhiyā |
saṃsārottaraṇaṃ bhūtyai yatetā "dhātum ātmani ||. (YV II:5.13)
46. tatraiva mūḍhamatibhir daivam astīti niścayaḥ | (YV II:8.3).
47. cf. Vivekananda, *The Complete Works*, II: 201.
48. YV II:5.19; II:5.4.
49. YV II:5.25; II:5.4.
50. śāstraiḥ sadācāra vijṛmbhita-deśadharmair yatkalpitaṃ phalam atīva ciraprarnūḍham |
tasmin hṛdi sphurati copanam eti cittam aṅgāvalī tadanu pauruṣam etadāhuḥ ||. (YV II:6.40)
51. YV II:6.34; II:7.28.
52. śāstrato gurutaścaiva svataśceti trisiddhayaḥ | (YV II:7.11).
53. YV II:6.33; II:7.27.
54. YV II:6.43.
55. sacchāstrādiguṇo matyā sacchāstrādiguṇaḥ matiḥ |
vivardhete mitho 'bhyāsāt sarojāv-iva kālataḥ ||. (YV II:7.29)
56. na gantavyam anudyogaiḥ sāmyaṃ puruṣa-gardabhaiḥ |
udyogastu yathāśāstraṃ lokadvitaya siddhaye ||. (YV II:5.14)
57. ālasyaṃ yadi na bhavejjagaty anarthaḥ ko na syād bahudhanako bahuśruto vā | (YV II:5.30ab).
58. YV II:5.15–16.
59. kiñcit kāntānna-pānādi kalilaṃ gṛhe |
vraṇe kīta ivāsvādya vayaḥ kāryaṃ na bhasmāsāt ||. (YV II:5.17)
60. YV II:5.3; II:6.2; II:7.14; II:7.19.
61. ātmaiva hyātmano bandhu ātmaiva ripurātmanaḥ |
ātmaiva hyātmano sākṣi kṛtasyāpyakṛtasya ca ||. (MBh 13.5.27)
62. pauruṣād dṛśyate siddhiḥ pauruṣāddhīmatāṃ kramaḥ | (YV II:7.115ab).
63. YV II:7.15; II.7.21ab; II.8.12.
64. viśvāmitreṇa muninā daivam utsṛjya dūrataḥ |
pauruṣeṇaiva samprāptaṃ brāhmaṇyam . . . ||. (YV II:8.20)
65. YV II:5.18; II:6.2; II:.7.14; II.7.20.
66. ye samudyogam utsṛjya sthitā daiva-parāyaṇāḥ |
te dharmaṃ arthaṃ kāmaṃ ca nāśayanty ātmavidviṣaḥ ||. (YV II:7.3)
67. YV II:7.15; II:8.15; II:9.11.
68. nākṛtir na karmāṇi na spando na parākramaḥ |
tanmithyā jñānavadrūḍhaṃ daivam nāma kim ucyate ||. (YV II:8.1)
69. manobuddhivadapyetad daivaṃ nehānubhūyate | (YV II:8.11).
70. YV II:8.6–7; II:8.14.
71. pauruṣeṇa siddha, pauruṣopanata and puruṣārthaikasādhana—(YV II:8.4–6).
72. mūḍhānumāna saṃsiddhaṃ daivam—(YV II:8.5).
73. YV II:7.22; II:7.25; II:8.11; II:8.11; II:8.25; II:9.3.

74. YV II:8.24–25; II:9.4–6.
75. YV II:6.3–4; II:9.7.
76. YV II:9.8–9.
77. bālaḥ pravala puṃseva tajjetum iha śakyate || (YV II:6.4cd).
78. YV II:5.12; II:6.5; II:7.37.
79. prāk svakarmetarākāraṃ daivaṃ nāma na vidyate | (YV II:6.4ab).
80. YV II:6.35; II:6.37; etc.
81. YV II:9.13.
82. YV II:9.14–15.
83. dvividho vāsanāvyūhaḥ śubhaścaivāśubhaśca te | (YV II:6.25ab).
84. śubhāśubhābhyaṃ mārgābhyāṃ vahanti vāsanā sarit |
pauruṣeṇa prayatnena yojanīyā śubhepathi ||. (YV II:9.30)
85. aśubheṣu samāviṣṭam śubheṣvavatāraya |
svaṃ manaḥ puruṣārthena balena balināṃ varaḥ ||. (YV II:9.31)
86. YV II:9.32–33.
87. Swami Vivekananda, "Soul, God and Religion," *The Complete Works*, 1: 320.

8

A Fabulous Rationality

Poetry, Reason, and Action in the *Yogavāsiṣṭha*

Roddam Narasimha

Introduction

The *Yogavāsiṣṭha* (YV)[1] is, according to the author himself, a *kāvya*—a poem (YV II:8.33).[2] The poem, however, is of epic length. At 27,687 verses (in the Nirnaya Sagar Press edition) the YV is longer than the *Rāmāyaṇa*, of which it is purported to be a part. It is in the form of nested dialogues, the chief of which is that between the young (sixteen-year-old) prince Rāma and the fabled guru of his royal Ikṣvāku clan, Vasiṣṭha. This dialogue is the prescription urged on Rāma's father, King Daśaratha, by Viśvāmitra in order to cure Rāma of the depression he is suffering from, after having been exposed to the miseries of the world during a pilgrimage to various holy places. This incident recalls the experience of another celebrated prince, Gautama (the Buddha), around the sixth century BCE.[3]

The long dialogue between guru and *śiṣya* (disciple) in the YV is remarkable in many respects. It is first of all rich, diverse, and complex, and it touches on a number of aspects of life—action, belief, and knowledge—often at length, with striking stories and analogies. Second, all of this is done in pleasant, lovely Sanskrit, not without a touch of humor; the author carries his apparently formidable learning lightly. Third, the author remains completely anonymous and, while apparently quite aware of the singular nature of his project, and its likely appeal, does not claim originality for what he says (YV VIb:103.42), although many of his views appear to be unorthodox. For example, he is full of praise for *vicāra* (enquiry, analysis, investigation) and *pauruṣa* (human effort), and he dismisses the notion of fate as the invention of fools (YV II:8.16).[4] Fourth, and what is important for the theme of the present chapter, throughout the book are scattered comments on issues that have been on the agenda of the science enterprise—some for a long time, including the present. These comments are in the spirit of the *vicāra* whose virtues are elsewhere so eloquently commended to Rāma by Vasiṣṭha. Most other aspects of the work have received extensive attention—its perception of reality (O'Flaherty[5]), its numerous and fascinating stories (Venkatesananda,[6] O'Flaherty), its philosophy (Chakrabarti,[7] Venkatesananda), its approach to yoga, its views on consciousness, and so on. A compilation by Athreya[8] presents the YV's views on many of these aspects classified subject-wise. But those related to what is generally considered to be the concern of science have (to the best of my knowledge) received little attention. This chapter attempts to collect these views and will conclude with some remarks on the strange and powerful mix of fabulous story, rational worldview, and actionist philosophy that is so uniquely characteristic of the YV.

Atoms

It is interesting from several points of view that the YV is categorically atomistic. The interest in this fact lies in the way that the concept of atoms was rejected by many philosophers, in particular by Śaṅkara,[9] on both "logical" grounds as well as the argument that the concept was *aśabda*, namely that it is not mentioned in the Vedas. This incidentally also implies that the YV does not take the Vedas as necessarily infallible—a view that is confirmed by other verses in the text to which we shall return in a later section. It thus seems that the author of the YV accepted the views of the Vaiśeṣika school on this matter and was a follower of Kaṇāda,[10] who is credited in India with proposing the concept of atoms.

The YV view about atoms—*aṇus and paramāṇus*—is expressed with characteristic force at several places in the text. It is first of all declared that atoms are inert *(jaḍāḥ)*.[11] (As it was accepted that different kinds of atoms move about and could react with each other, it must be presumed that *jaḍa* refers to biological rather than physical or chemical inertness.) The whole universe is seen as a collection of atoms (YV VIb:97.6)—in fact billions or trillions of them (*koṭi lakṣeṣu*). Consistently with the philosophy of knowledge—or the epistemology—that the YV appears to adopt, it is asserted that the idea of atoms has to be accepted if that is what experience leads us to (YV VIb:97.6)—not the scriptures. At the same time the atoms that make up the universe are not without structure. We know that the Kaṇāda concept of atoms actually included molecules, often with two or three atoms. The YV goes much further, and indeed postulates complex internal structures within the atom: each atom "is seen as an internal world / By the detached philosopher." Indeed, as atoms have to be experienced—although it is not made clear how that experience is to be acquired—the YV says that even the belly of an atom can create a splendid perception in the mind of the beholder (YV II:18.27; III:1.27). After having said all this, the YV creates a characteristically poetic and fabulous picture of Brahman (YV IV:18.6), calling it a forest:

> Whose trees are uncounted thousands
> Of worlds glued to each other
> In each and every atom!

Here is a characteristic view of the YV that makes reality take fantastic forms where time, space, and matter are spoken about in a way in which large and small numbers, sizes, and durations are projected to be part of a complex reality. Subatomic structure and the whole universe feed on each other, in the way that a serpent eats its own tail.

However, the world is not a mere collection of atoms (YV VIb:103.65), for there is life. As atoms are inert, a living system needs a special class of atoms:

> That atom, with memory endowed,
> Is what is called *jīva* [live];
> At end of life it stays to reside
> In the space of the body that's dead.
> (YV III:55.6)

Thus, the YV enthusiastically embraces an atomistic view of the world but considers that some additional quality (*vāsanā*, a residual memory that "smells" of the past) is needed for life.

Creation

Although the YV does talk about creation, suggesting that there was a moment when creation occurred (we shall see that shortly), it also declares that whatever exists is not ever destroyed (YV III:4.62). This might be a version of a principle of conservation of matter, of the kind that is familiar to us from the Sāṃkhya philosophers. The Sāṃkhya school, one of the oldest in India as it is mentioned already in the *Śvetāśvatara Upaniṣad,* held that nothing material could be produced from the nonmaterial.[12] We see here that the author of the YV is not following any single school among the six orthodox systems of Hindu thought (the *ṣaḍ-darśana*). He accepts the Kaṇāda notion of atoms and the Sāṃkhya notion of conservation of matter. In fact, another verse (YV VIb:116.27) about the same issue of creation sounds very similar to what the Sāṃkhya philosophers said: what is created can evolve, so it is not unchanging;[13] and the cause of such change or evolution cannot be what is called Īśvara. The careful way that this statement is made once again recalls the kind of dictum due to the Nirīśvara school of Sāṃkhya,[14] which held that there was no acceptance-worthy evidence for Īśvara but did not reject the idea of God—a view that is implicit in what the YV says. At another place it is also said that worlds may appear or disappear (YV VIb:116.25). It is therefore clear that such appearance and disappearance are not to be considered as creation and destruction and occur without violating conservation of mass or matter: the two are not seen as a contradiction in terms (contemporary astrophysics for example postulates large quantities of invisible dark matter in the universe).

Life

Consistent with its belief in atoms, the YV is at least in part reductionist in its philosophy; that is, everything has to be reduced to some fundamental unit or particle. In another characteristically picturesque line, the author wonders (YV VIa:47.29) about how the bizarre colors of the peacock's feathers come out of the fluid of the egg. He seems clear that the way that an organism will develop is programmed in the minutest parts of the egg out of which the organism will emerge. Although I could not see the equivalent of the word "gene" anywhere in the YV (apart from the implied word *jīva-aṇu*), it is a concept that one feels that the author would have been very comfortable with. He similarly wonders about the mind: it has no form, so it must be dead, he argues; but at the same time that dead mind can kill the world, and the author once again considers what a bizarre, foolish, vicious circle this is (YV V:13.100). How does formless, immaterial mind arise in a collection of inert atoms?

More generally, if our body is composed of atoms, and atoms are inert, but life is not, is there anything that distinguishes the atoms in a live body from the inert atoms that constitute the universe? Here the YV view (as we have already hinted) is that during life, the atoms are endowed with memory called *jīva* (life), the suggestion being that what distinguishes the living from the dead is the existence of memory (YV III:55.6). Given such views, it is not surprising that the YV easily considers that the distinction between human beings and animals is not fundamental. In this respect, however, the YV follows classical Indian thinking, which from the time of the Vedas has held that man and animal are in many ways similar, even if man should be superior. For example, John Edelman[15] describes how the *Bhāgavata* sets up a hierarchy of twenty-three levels from nonliving beings to the highest kind of human being. At the bottom of the hierarchy are nonliving beings, living beings being superior to all of them. At higher levels, bees (at level 16) are, for example, superior to fish; a Brahman who can settle doubts (at level 5) is superior to one who only knows the Vedas; at level 3 is one who has won liberation through knowledge; and at the top of the hierarchy is the egoless devotee immersed in God. According to the YV (YV III:118.22) even beasts and barbarians, once they attain certain states of knowledge, can become free (*muktāḥ*).

The wealth of living forms seen in the world is both implicitly and explicitly celebrated in the text. At the same time there is a very hard-headed appreciation of the sordidness of life and the cruelties that characterize conflict (YV III:2.10), reminding one of Alfred Tennyson's famous phrase about "nature red in tooth and claw."

Consciousness

Consciousness is seen in the YV as characterizing all life (YV VIa:10.23). Consciousness is of course central to its philosophical discourse, and references to it are numerous throughout the book. The subject has therefore been extensively discussed in the philosophical literature (e.g., Athreya 1993), so it is neither necessary nor feasible to summarize all of it in this chapter. In general, much of this would be familiar to followers of Advaitic philosophy. I shall therefore confine myself here to quoting a few verses that capture what appear to me to be somewhat unusual views, ones that may resonate with a scientific view of the world.

In the first place, the physical world, the mind, and consciousness are declared to be different spaces:

> Gracious lady, please understand:
> There is physical space, there's mental space,
> And, more tenuous than either of them,
> There is the third space of consciousness.
> (YV III:17.10)

Consistent with the author's atomism, this "space" of consciousness is also seen in atomist terms (reductionism again):

> Within the atoms of consciousness lie
> Particles of *all* experience,
> Even as in taste of honey lie
> All riches of flower, fruit and leaf.
> (YV III:81.35)

The reference to *particles* (*kaṇas*) of all experience is striking. It is almost as if the author thinks of experience as quantized, therefore, necessarily digitally stored. If he were here with us today, he might be talking about (if I may invent the word) "cognons."

How then do we explain the relation of the universe to this atomistic consciousness? The answer is suggested through analogies:

> The universe rests pervasively
> In the space of consciousness,
> Like emptiness in sky, gust in wind,
> And like fluidity in water.
> (YV VIb:103.73)

The author is getting very close here to emergent phenomena,[16] and it appears as if he would be very comfortable with this notion, as this verse indicates:

> The space of consciousness doesn't differ
> From the universe at any time;

The two are like gales and wind—
Two forms of the self-same thing.
(YV VIb:103.77)

Indeed, he suggests that consciousness and apparent understanding appear "spontaneously"—by their own nature—the same way that eddies appear in fluid motion:

From it arises, by itself,
A form of some understanding
Just as the streak of a whirlpool does
From the fluid throb of water.
(YV VIa:9.3)

The emergence of consciousness, in other words, is purely a matter of internal dynamics. There is only consciousness, and what we see are merely its vibrations:

The sole stuff of the whole universe
Is consciousness—as water is of the seas;
And it vibrates through the intellect
As water pounds through ocean-waves.
(YV VIa:101.54)

Whirlpools, eddies, and wind gusts are recurring metaphors throughout the book, as the author speaks of the beauty of vortices *salila-āvarta-sundarī* (YV IV:47.41) and the inherent restlessness of wind *spanda-aika-dharmavān vāto* (YV IV:36.21). It is hard to avoid the impression that these phenomena—so easily visible to the naked eye, so accessible to common everyday experience—fascinated the author. This is extremely significant, because it permits connecting order and organization to be seen as compatible with a belief in the (inert) atomistic nature of the universe: "[W]itness the flow of water" is his argument. Here are the beginnings of the wonder of an atomist about the emergence of order out of chaos: a phenomenon characteristic of what today would be called complex systems,[17] of which the most familiar (and to this day a very difficult) example is fluid flow—the subject of the scientific discipline known as fluid dynamics.

And this line of thinking culminates in a version of what Francis Crick (1994) called an astonishing hypothesis:

The inert is not in any way
Distinct from the intelligent;

> There is essentially no difference
> Between all of creation, all that exists.
> (YV III:55.57)

Reality

There is the age-old question about what is real and what is unreal, and the YV tackles this question in an interesting way, in part through the fantastic stories that are recounted in the book (e.g., the Story of Līlā, 3:15–59). The author warns us that the stories should not be taken literally, but are only intended to make a point (YV II:19.3). Vasiṣṭha tells Rāma that the link between fable and truth is not a serious issue, for the objective of the fable is to make sure that the meaning of great thought is grasped somehow or the other (YV II:19.3). Furthermore, an analogy that had to be precise in all respects would be no different from reality, so it would serve no useful purpose (YV II:19.1).

The YV defines what is real as whatever is there "at the beginning and end, and always"—nothing else. This point is made again and again (YV IV:45.46). However, a likeness of reality resides in our mind (YV III:3.33). Indeed the YV goes so far as to say that the universe is purely mental (*mano-mātram*) on the ground that as Brahman is not physical and must therefore be purely mental, so must (Brāhmic) creation be. So also the real and the unreal, and even what the YV calls the real-unreal (*sat*, *asat*, and *sad-asat*), all arise in imagination; therefore the concept of truth (*satyam*) is seen as difficult and also arising from imagination (YV IV:53.45). This once again goes to the heart of Indic thinking about truth. While Plato thought truth was a likely story,[18] the YV thinking considers the concept dubious (YV IV:53.45).

The mixing of the real and the unreal might at first sound rather abstract if not downright self-contradictory, but for the YV it is a matter of experience. Among the many examples given is that of erotic dreams (YV III:3.17), where the physical and the mental, the imagined and the physiological, indeed the real and the unreal are inextricably mixed. At the same time the human mind is very important, for it is the great hub around which revolves, in a maddening and confusing way, the "magical" wheel (*māyā-cakra)* (YV V:50.6) of everything in this universe. At another place in the YV, the world—the imaginary magical wheel—is said to be a dream-like delusion; it is *māyā,* of the kind so strikingly described in Līlā's story.

[A] lovely whirl-pool
On the trembling waters
Of the kingdom of mind
(YV IV:47.41)

a dance in the
three-world puppet show,
Swirls in Brāhmic water and gales in Brāhmic wind!
(YV VIb:41.11)

We see here that when it comes to the concept of reality the YV views are rather similar to those of the Advaitic school; the concepts echo those that appear in Śaṅkara's philosophy. But it is equally clear the YV does not follow one school of philosophy or one interpretation of the Vedas; it makes a synthesis of these concepts into something uniquely its own. In fact, more than once Vasiṣṭha admonishes Rāma to be full of both dual and nondual, for while Being and Real are nondual, action is not nondual (YV I:1.7). That nondualist action is only possible with *vicāra* and *pauruṣa*. Here, it seems to me, lies the core of Vasiṣṭha's advice to Rāma—the advice of the sage to the prince—combining a philosophical analysis of reality that does not ignore the demands of a world for action.

Knowledge

Knowledge, *jñāna*, plays an extremely important role in the YV. In fact very early in its long text, well before the conversation between Rāma and Vasiṣṭha begins, there is the inaugural question from Sutīkṣṇa to Agasti asking how man may perfect himself. And the answer he gets is that both knowing and doing (*jñāna* and karma) are necessary, and the two are like the two wings that are both essential for a bird to fly (YV V:78.8).

Vasiṣṭha tells Rāma that knowledge is really "right observation" (*samyag-avekṣaṇa*) (YV II:5.19). The value of observation and experience is repeatedly emphasized, often in characteristically colorful terms. At one place (YV III:55.61) it is said that the man who rejects the evidence of his eyes and follows instead some (hypothetical) argument is like one who mistakes his own arms for a pair of snakes. At another it is categorically declared (YV II:19.16) that nothing whatever is known without true experience. This is in fact what is meant by *jñāna*. As has been pointed out by Chakrabarti,[19] *jñāna* is a cognitive episode and is therefore based on experience in the Indian view. There are many other verses which make this point about the centrality of observation and experience (YV II:18.2).

This emphasis on experience also means that no testimony from *any* other source can be accepted automatically. Thus even the most sacred texts (*ārṣa*) must be rejected if they do not teach it with reason, because logical sense (*nyāyya*) is the only criterion (YV II:18.3). In fact the YV goes so far as to say that even if the words are uttered by Brahma himself, they should be "cast aside like straw" if they do not make sense. However, one should accept words of sense even if they come from a mere boy.[20]

In this respect once again the YV seems to follow Sāṃkhya thinking, which refuses to accept the Vedas as suprahuman (*apauruṣeya*) and sees them as not necessarily flawless (YV V:43.10). But it must be emphasized that neither the Sāṃkhya school nor the YV *rejected* the Vedas outright; rather they see reasoning as primary—superior even to the word of the most sacred text. The ability to reason (i.e., carry out *vicāra*) is essential: even Mādhava himself (now switching to a theist idiom!) cannot gift knowledge to one who cannot reason.[21] Thus the YV is not a protestant movement, but expounds a rationalist view within a traditional framework.

The Law

What does the YV say about universal law(s)—if there is (are) any? The word *niyati* appears in several verses. In the Upaniṣads (YV III:54.22) *niyati* is paired with *yadṛccha*: the former is law or necessity, the latter accident or chance. According to the YV, what is called the Law is what operates now as at the beginning of creation (YV VIa:37.22). The Law is thus universal and depicts or states a rule which has not changed since creation. In the fascinating dialogue between Īśvara and Vasiṣṭha, *niyati* is defined by Īśvara as all the rules (*niyamas*) which lay down "this is so" (*idam ittham*) for everything—from a blade of grass to Rudra and to Brahmic energy (YV III:54.22). Thus *niyati* is not only universal in time, but it applies to everything, every being without exception—including Brahma and Rudra themselves. Even those who know everything, even Mādhava and Hari, are powerless to deflect the Law (YV II:9.18). The YV Law is therefore inexorable and applies to the most pious people and the most powerful gods. The Law, in other words, is awesome, undiscriminating, and eternal.

But how can such a Law be consistent with contempt for fate and a demand for self-effort, *pauruṣa*? The answer appears to be that the Law imposes irrevocable constraints, but within the constraints there is still considerable freedom of action. Thus, the outcome is underdetermined by the Law; its violation is impossible, but its enforcement is insufficient to completely determine the future. This is incidentally a position entirely understandable in contemporary science. In quantum mechanics, for example, Schrödinger's equation is inviolable, but it permits (indeed it contains) the uncertainty principle of Heisenberg. In the modern theory of nonlinear dynamical systems, where the basic principles are strictly classical (i.e., not quantal), a deterministic equation or set of equations can possess multiple solutions and exhibit behavior that is "chaotic," that is, apparently random, obeying appropriate *statistical* principles.

It is not the intention here to suggest that the specific examples we can give from contemporary science were known or even suspected by the author of the YV. But it is not difficult to surmise his line of thinking based on his own copious (and often-repeated) assertions. There is first of all his firm conviction that inert atoms constitute all matter. Then there is his fascination with fluid flows—the organized motion of "beautiful vortices" (*āvarta-sundarīs*) and the chaotic motion in waves and foam and spray and gale (in water, air and their mixtures) all again constituted out of the same inert atoms of water or air. These two views force the third: chaos, order and atoms are not inconsistent with each other; the eternal, universal Law certainly permits local, transient, collective phenomena exhibiting either order or disorder or combinations of both. If you think this is not possible, says the author of the YV, there is the counterexample of how the same water flows in so many different ways. There can be little doubt that he recognizes the phenomenon that is today called "emergence." Then, by a not entirely justified philosophical extrapolation, he could argue that the inexorable Law, *niyati*, is not inconsistent with *pauruṣa*, human free will or self-effort.

God

At first sight, gods seem to appear in many of the stories in the YV; we have just made mention of Rudra, Mādhava, and Hari. Īśvara appears in the fascinating dialogue with Vasiṣṭha already mentioned, and tells him:

> God is not lotus-eyed Viṣṇu,
> God is not three-eyed Śiva! . . .

God is not a *brahmin* or a king—
And not I, nor you, O great Brahmin!
(YV VIa:29.118)

Īśvara thus appears to make a disclaimer about his godness. At first this appears to be another Vāsiṣṭha riddle, like those normally attributed to Zen monks. But the verses following *do* identify God:

God is not any divine form
Nor any configuration of the mind . . .
What is called God is Brilliance—
Uncreated, without beginning or end.
(YV VIa:29.119–121)

(The original Sanskrit word that I have translated as Brilliance is *devanam.*) God thus is a quality—the timeless, abstract quality of Brilliance.

This view is reinforced by what the *Vāsiṣṭha* says about form worship (*ākāra-arcanam*, including presumably idol worship), such a touchy and ancient subject in global religious polemic. First of all, it is categorically stated that form worship is not [true] worship, which can only be offered to God-soul (*deva-ātmā*) with (the metaphorical) flowers of serenity and knowledge (YV VIa:29.128). The common (botanical) flowers and incense, although offered with great joy and imagination (YV VIa:30.7), are meant only for use by childish, immature minds (YV VIa:30.4); but this is not ununderstandable for, says the *Vāsiṣṭha*, if somebody cannot walk a *yojana* (probably four or five miles), surely one has to find a shorter stage of a *krośa* (a quarter of a *yojana*) (YV VIa:29.124)? In any case, no worship is necessary if the senses have been conquered; but then no worship yields any gain if the senses have *not* been conquered (YV V:43.22).

There is much discussion in the YV of the related concepts of *daiva*. If *deva* is god, *daiva* can be godly or divine, and it appears to be used sometimes in this sense; for example, certain kinds of action are described as *daiva* (YV II:9.18). More often however, as is common even today, *daiva* seems to mean fate. The *Vāsiṣṭha* is severely critical of the notion of fate. It is almost the first issue to be treated by Vasiṣṭha as his dialogue with Rāma begins; two cantos, both named *daiva-nirākaraṇa* (the rejection of fate), are devoted to the subject. Vasiṣṭha says that *daiva* was invented by fools (YV II:8.16); those who are obsessed by *daiva* are enemies of their own soul, and destroy dharma, *artha*, and *kāma*—virtue, wealth, and passion (YV II:7.3). What really is (i.e., plays the role of) *daiva* (divine / fate), Vasiṣṭha tells Rāma, is self-effort (YV II:9.18).

To summarize, in the YV view God is abstract brilliance; not Viṣṇu, Śiva, and the rest, and certainly not the idols and pictures that are worshipped with flowers and incense by the childish, albeit with great enthusiasm. Late in the work (YV VIb:103.69), Vasiṣṭha tells Rāma that the creation of the world does not seem without intelligence (*na-abuddhi-purvam*), but he goes on to ask, "If intelligence is at work, who would be so mad as to toil so much in vain?" (Here the YV is probing the ancient and enduring scientific/philosophical issue of Design. As far as I can see, the YV leans towards but does not explicitly go as far as Sāṃkhya, which outright rejects the idea of Design.) It would appear that the YV adopts frequently the idiom of God to convey a point of view (recall that it is a *kāvya*), with a discreet suggestion of a Sāṃkhya-type noncommittal attitude towards traditional concepts of God always hovering in the background.

Conclusion

The YV's fabulous tales are widely known, but the accompanying streak of its rationality has attracted less attention. I have tried to describe the latter briefly in this chapter. Before concluding, let us consider a few other pointers to that rationality, based on the work's praise of *vicāra* (enquiry, investigation, analysis) and *pauruṣa* (human effort).

Vicāra is seen as a powerful instrument for success in worldly affairs, as well as for securing liberation. Thus, early on in their conversation, Vasiṣṭha tells Rāma that wealth, power, and liberation are "the fruits of that magical tree known as Reason" (YV II:14.10). A king who faces a crisis can expect to succeed only through the power of analysis (YV II:14.38). Sentimentality has no place: the man who insists on drinking water only from his grandfather's well, rejecting the pure waters of the Ganga right before him, is headed for ruin (YV II:18.4). Indeed, a man who cannot reason loses his soul (YV II:14.42), whereas reason is the only instrument that can give one great joy (*mahā-ānanda*), so it must not be forsaken even for a moment (YV II:14.2). Worldliness can also become a chronic disease, and when it does, the only cure is, once again, reason (YV II:14.45), and it is only logical thought (*nyāyena parāmarśo*) on the folly of worldliness that is true analysis (*vicāra*) (YV II:14.50).

Similarly, human (i.e., self-) effort, if thoughtfully planned, helps every person attain his object (YV II:4.8). Such effort is never wasted (YV II:5.26); and the one who strives harder (YV II:6.23), and has bold faith in his own effort (YV II:6.12), always wins. That is how the legendary Viśvāmitra won his battle for Brahmanhood (YV II:8.20)—so Vasiṣṭha tells Rāma—and he should know, for in that famous legend of Viśvāmitra's epic struggle it is Vasiṣṭha's approval that Viśvamitra desperately seeks.[22] Rāma is told:

> There arises like the moon
> A cool gladness in the heart
> When the fruit one seeks is gained
> By self-effort, and not any other way.
> (YV II:4.9)

Those incapable of such effort become victims of the bolder men (YV II:6.13); lethargy is the enemy (YV II:5.3).

Vasiṣṭha takes care to say that not *any* effort will be successful: it has to be *śāstric*—in consonance with the *śāstras* (YV II:5.3), which presumably provide the ethical constraints—otherwise it can lead to ruin.

The YV has thus several strands to it. There are the fantastic stories, not intended to be taken literally but nevertheless offered as reflections of complex reality. There are extensive discussions of yoga and consciousness. Then there is a great deal of instruction to Rāma on worldly affairs—on kings and warfare, on the importance of analysis and human effort and action. But there is also a running commentary in the background on rationality: not holding any human text as ultimate authority; respecting the opinion of even a young boy if it makes sense; not believing in fate or *daiva*; on seeing ritual form-worship as a need of weaker minds; on God not so much as Viṣṇu or Śiva but the abstract quality of eternal brilliance; on the importance of avoiding a sentimental attachment to the old or traditional; on the great value of the conquest of one's own mind; on observation, experience, and reason as the ultimate sources of knowledge; and above all on achieving perfection and liberation by combining knowledge and action.

It is a disarming mixture of poetry, fable and reason.

Notes

I take much of the discussion on consciousness from Narasimha 2003. I thank A. Chakrabarti for his comments and suggestions on the first draft of this chapter.

1. Fabulous = . . . full of fables, mythical . . . astonishing . . . (Oxford Universal Dictionary).

2. References to verses in *Yogavāsiṣṭha* are given in the *form prakaraṇa: sarga.śloka* (chapter:canto.verse). The sixth *prakaraṇa* (Nirvana) is in two parts, *pūrva-ardha* and *uttara-ardha,* respectively, the early half and the later half denoted by VIa and VIb. Translations that appear in the text without any attribution are by the author, and taken from Narasimha (2000, 2009).

3. See, e.g., Narasimha 2000.

4. See section on knowledge below.

5. Wendy Doniger O'Flaherty, *Dreams, Illusion and Other Realities* (Chicago: University of Chicago Press, 1984. Delhi: Motilal Banarsidass, 1987).

6. Swami Venkatesananda, *The Concise Yoga-Vāsiṣṭha* (New York: State University of New York Press, 1984).

7. Chakrabarti 2009.

8. Athreya 1993.

9. Because it plays such a striking and fundamental role in YV thinking, it is perhaps worthwhile to explore the rationale of Indic atomism. Although the concept of an indivisible atom was not universally accepted in India, there was widespread support for it, and it is interesting to ask why. Kaṇāda, who is acknowledged to be the original author of the proposal, is too cryptic in his *Vaiśeṣika Sūtra,* but those who followed him in support are progressively more specific. The chief explicit argument perhaps appears first in Gautama's *Nyāya Sūtras*. One sutra (4.2:25) speaks of *anavasthā*, which stands for instability in general and nonfinality of a proposition, perhaps because of an endless series of statements that the proposition entails. (All of these meanings are from Monier-Williams.)

The text of the sutra mentioned is "anavasthā-kāritvād anavasthā'nupapatteś ca apratiṣedhaḥ" which can be translated as "Because it [the concept of continuous matter] makes for instability (endless series of statements), which (i.e. such *anvasthā*) does not lead to a conclusion, no objection [can be raised to the notion of indivisible atoms]."

Gangopadhyaya (1991) offers an interesting account of the more explicit arguments of Gautama's followers. Basically, the problem with a continuous (nonatomist) theory of matter is that both the smallest and the largest objects—the mote and the mountain—would have to consist of an infinite number of parts; and there could then be no [objective] distinction between "small" and "large," and indeed therefore no objective measure of size. As Vacaspati Misra put it in an alternative metaphor, both a mustard seed and the Meru mountain (*Meru-sarśapa*) would be equivalent in some sense—indeed in the kind of sense that Georg Cantor's famous proposal on different kinds of infinity revealed. Phrased in modern terms, the Indian atomists felt the need for an absolute length scale and argued that this must come from the size of the indivisible atom. Coupled with the observed stability of properties of any substance, even on minute division (smell, taste etc.), one can see that so many Indian philosophers (including the author of the YV) became convinced of the existence of atoms. (Of course we now know (especially with the recent spectacular developments in nano-science) that matter with only a small number of atoms (hundreds or so) will have very different properties than bulk matter.)

Now Śaṅkara's objections to the atomic theory are many-fold. Some of these are rational or "logical." For example, he finds the notion of the "eternal activity" (/perpetual motion) of atoms unacceptable (*Brahma-Sūtra-Bhaṣya* [BSB] II.ii.14, Gambhirananda 1965). This is understandable; we would now say that perpetual motion (in the bulk) is thermodynamically impossible; however, this is not inconsistent with perpetual motion among the atoms, as the Vaiśeṣikas argued. Śaṅkara again argued that if atoms were eternal they could not possess color, smell, and so on, which are all impermanent; as already pointed out, even a small number of molecules would not have properties all the same as bulk matter: a hundred atoms of iron do not behave like the familiar metal iron. But Śaṅkara also said (BSB II.ii.17)

aparigrahāc ca atyantam anapekṣā

Because of lack of acceptance [by the worthy (such as Vedic scholars) there is] extreme distaste [for the atomic theory].

This argument is similar to his criticism of Sāṃkhya(I.i.5),

īkṣater na aśabdam |

[The pradhana of the Sāṃkhyas is] not [acceptable], because it is unvedic [as is clear from] inspection [of the texts?].

Our main point here, however, is that *Yogavāsiṣṭha* does not respect, and in fact is not concerned with the *aśabda* argument.

10. Kanāda's *Vaiseśika Sūtra* in Agrawal (2001).

11. *jaḍāḥ*, 6u:103.73.

12. The *Sāṃkhya Sūtra* (1.78) says:

na avastunā vastu-siddhiḥ |

Nothing material can be produced from the nonmaterial

13. An essential feature of Sāṃkhya doctrine is its theory of change or evolution, *pariṇāma-vāda*. As the doctrine postulates the effect is in the cause, the constant change observed in nature is a result of internal dynamics, governed by the three *guṇas* (*sattva, rajas, tamas*). These *guṇas* do clash with each other—resulting in pain for the intelligent according to Patanjali's *Yoga Sūtra* (2.15; guṇa-vivṛtti-nirodhāc ca duhkham eva sarvaṃ vivekinaḥ), and presumably in continuous change in the universe. Sāṃkhya ideas on evolution are succinctly and elegantly described by Hiriyanna (1956:273).

14. The Nirīśvara school of Sāṃkhya says (*Sāṃkhya-Sūtra*)

Īśvara asiddheḥ | 1,92

Because God is not demonstrated and

Pramāṇa-abhāvān na tat siddhiḥ|

It [God] is not established because of absence of [acceptable] demonstration.

15. Edelman (2009).

16. As Gell-Mann has described it, the doctrine of emergentism is that "we do not need something else in order to get something else" (Horgan 1996:213–4), and he added, interestingly, "[T]here are lots and lots of eddies

in that process," which leads to "many violations of that tendency" of the universe to wind down thermodynamically.

More specifically, emergent phenomena are those that arise in collections of individual units, e.g., atoms, showing large-scale behavior, that are not obviously or explicitly built into the laws or rules governing the behavior of the constituent units. Is life an emergent phenomenon in a collection of inert, inorganic atoms or molecules? Computer simulations in what are known as cellular automata (e.g., Wolfram, see review by Narasimha 2002) show that extremely simple rules governing the motion of residents of cells into neighboring cells can lead to extraordinarily complex patterns—highly organized as well as chaotic. See also Johnson (2001).

17. Complexity and complex systems have been discussed e.g. by Stewart (1998).

18. Plato's ideas can be briefly summarized as follows (Cornford 1997: 2ff.). The world has a cause—a maker or father, who is hard to find. His work will be good only if he fashions it after an eternal model. The world is good; therefore its model must be eternal. Finally, remembering that we are only human, it is fitting that we accept the likely story and look no further.

19. Chakrabarti, personal correspondence.

20. According to the *Sāṃkhya-Sūtra*

na nityatvam vedānām kāryatva sruteḥ | (5.45)
There is no eternality about the Vedas, for from the scriptures
[themselves there is admission that they are] human creation.

21. In the *Śvetāśvataro-'panishat*, the opening *śloka* (61) asks, "What is the cause? Whence are we born? . . . Who presides over this system in which we live, in happiness and in sorrow?" The reply is given (1.2), "Time, inherent nature; *niyati, yadṛcchā*; . . ." Radhakrishnan translates *niyati* and *yadṛcchā* as necessity and chance, respectively; the two are seen as opposites, as symbolizing deterministic law and accidental event, respectively, or even perhaps determinism and free will. Chance and necessity have been another set of ancient and enduring issues, discussed in recent times by Jacque Monod (1972) and Richard Dawkins (1986).

Recent work on what has now universally come to be called "chaos" (e.g. Gleick 1987) suggests that there are a large number of instances of dynamical systems and their associated nonlinear models where the distinction between determinism and stochasticity is difficult to sustain. As an example, consider the simple mathematical system

$$xn = 4\ xn—1(1—xn–1)$$

where we have a sequence of numbers xn whose entry (xn) at place n is determined uniquely by the previous entry xn—1. Here n is a label which takes the values 0, 1, 2, . . . ; x0 is an initial guess, which must be some number between 0 and 1. All later numbers of xn, beginning with n = 1, will remain for all n within the same limits, except that when x0 is a natural fraction the sequence will eventually terminate at 0 or 1. Now, although the law governing xn for given xn–1 is strictly deterministic, i.e., the future (/ present) entries are in principle determined entirely by the present (/past) value, the sequence so obtained looks random and would be so characterized by statistical tests. For example, the statistical correlation between successive entries is zero. Thus, the boundary between determinism (*niyati*) and chance (*yadṛcchā*) is no longer sharp, as a strictly deterministic law can yield "random" outcomes; i.e., what is seen as *yadṛcchā* can result from *niyati*. (The culprit turns out to be the exquisitely sensitive dependence of the result on initial conditions. The smallest perturbation on [say] the present value will eventually lead to an entirely different future; this is like the way in which the small change that the pointsman makes at a railway track will eventually take the train to a totally different destination. Thus, the immediate future is quite predictable, but the distant future is not. Incidentally, given the present, the past cannot be uniquely recovered; a whole class of different histories can lead to the same present.) Einstein famously said, in relation to the inherently probabilistic nature of quantum mechanics, that he did not believe that God played dice. Dice constitute a nonlinear dynamical system whose output is chaotic. So Einstein's puzzle has two resolutions: (1) even dice are deterministic, so Einstein was right to doubt that the laws of quantum mechanics are inherently probabilistic; (2) even if God relied entirely on deterministic laws, the resulting outcome will be statistical in nature if His system were appropriately nonlinear, so He is in effect acting in support of statistical systems. See Narasimha (1987), Stewart (1998) on these issues.

What is remarkable about the YV view is that it combines the "free will" that is inherent in its praise of self-effort (*pauruṣa*)—whose ultimate success in that view is assured—with the inexorably indiscriminate and ruthless operation of a universal deterministic Law, at least in some matters, such as death, for example. If there is a Law that even Hara or Mādhava cannot alter, where is the room for the free will that *pauruṣa* implies? One possible answer would be that the Law does not rule out free-will-like (in the limit chaotic) behavior. The other possibility is that the theory of chaos also permits control, generally by some external agency; for the same reason that the system is sensitive to perturbations, it is also sensitive to appropriate control inputs—such as, for example, the teaching of a guru. Indeed, the whole point of the YV is to show how Vasiṣṭha successfully restored Rāma's sense of free will after his episode of fatalistic dejection that is the starting point of the work. To repeat, the Law is a strict constraint on, but not a strict determinant of the future.

22. In the legend, Viśvāmitra is a Kṣatriya prince who aspires to Brahminhood and carries on a long fight with Vasiṣṭha, who is at one and the same time the object of envy and emulation as well as an adversary. In the end Viśvāmitra achieves his goal, becomes one of the seven great *ṛsis*, and is reconciled with Vasiṣṭha.

9

Ethics and Psychology of the Yogavāsiṣṭha in the *Upaśama Prakaraṇa*

CHRISTOPHER KEY CHAPPLE

The *Upaśama Prakaraṇa*, the fifth book of the *Yogavāsiṣṭha* (YV), consists of instructions and examples given to Rāma by Vasiṣṭha on how to pacify his mind, establish himself in a state of yogic equipoise, moving toward living liberation (*jīvanmukti*). It provides stories that illustrate how one can effectively dissolve attachment to the world through reasoned reflection and meditation. This chapter will focus on the psychology and ethics contained implicitly and explicitly in this portion of the text.

The *Upaśama Prakaraṇa* includes nine stories, all of which point Rāma toward the goal of living liberation. The stories are named after their protagonists: King Janaka; Puṇya and Pāvana; Bali; Prahlāda; Gādhi; Uddālaka; Suraghu; Bhāsa and Vilāsa; and Vītahavya. The first tells of a king famous for accomplishing all worldly goals, including the just rule of a large kingdom, with the even-mindedness of a yogin. The last story tells of a yogin who conquers all desires and the vicissitudes of physicality. In examining these narratives, I hope to show the inseparability of psychology and ethics in Vasiṣṭha's teachings and also explore how Vasiṣṭha advocates aligning purified consciousness with the exigencies of daily action.

As a mind-only text in the tradition of Yogacara Buddhism, the YV *posits* a pan-psychic world. The world utterly depends upon our construal of it as shaped by past influences (*vāsanā*). The movement

Figure 2. Puṇya and Pāvana sit in front of a thatch hut with a conical roof of leaves that is surrounded by the water of the Ganges flowing past. Attributed to Artist A. Library folio 139v. © The Trustees of the Chester Beatty Library, Dublin.

from consciousness to the realm of the five senses and the five elements depends upon the structures of the mind. Psychic constructs shape and inform our interaction within the external world. The core message of the YV entails clearly seeing this relationship. Recognizing the constructive power of the mind, one is urged to apply yogic techniques to reverse the outward flow of the mind, which habitually relies upon past conditioning and karmic accretions. This stabilization leads to the negation of compulsive entanglement with the external realm and establishes one in a state of equilibrium informed by an insight into the fleeting nature of reality. This insight into the experience of pure consciousness enlivens and empowers all things but allows one to remain unperturbed by them.

At the conclusion of the *Upaśama Prakaraṇa,* Vasiṣṭha speaks of three "virtues": knowledge of essential truths (*tattva-jñāna*), restraint of the mind (*mano-nāśa*), and abandonment of desires (*vāsanā-kṣaya*) (YV V: 92.14). Swami Venkatesananda translates these as "realization of truth, cessation of the mind, and the ending of conditioning" (CYV, 254). This triad reflects Vasiṣṭha's insistence on the psychic nature of the troublesome aspects of the human condition. Humans suffer due to desire. Desire arises within the mind and habituates individuals toward particular actions. By understanding the connection between one's psychic state and one's relationship with the world, one gains insight into mental control and eventually is able to bring about transformation of the mind. Once committed to the practices of Yoga, one can reverse the influences of past desires, purify one's mind, and bring a lighter, enlightened approach to the world.

King Janaka

The name Janaka is synonymous with wisdom in Indian tradition. The *Bṛhadāraṇyaka,* perhaps the earliest of the Upaniṣads, includes an extensive dialogue between the sage Yājñavalkya and Janaka, the emperor of Videha. Several great teachings associated with the Hindu tradition arise from this encounter, including some of the earliest teachings on karma theory and reincarnation. Janaka learns six aspects of Brahma as expressed within human experience: speech, breath (*prāṇa*), sight, hearing, mind, and heart. In each of these capacities dwells the ultimate reality. Through Yājñavalkya's teachings on "not this, not this," Janaka attains a state of fearlessness. Through the teachings on the dream state and the senses, Janaka learns about and experiences the nature of bliss. Yājñavalkya tells about how unresolved desire leads to a new birth. Reinforcing Ghosal's earlier chapter about the role of will and resolve in the YV, Janaka learns that resolve arises from desire and that one performs actions accordingly, reaping the results. Higher than all worldly endeavors, one should strive to know the soul:

> It is unseizable, for it cannot be seized.
> It is indestructible, for it cannot be destroyed.
> It is unattached, for it does not attach itself.
> It is unbound. It does not tremble. It is not injured.[1]

If one knows this soul, Yājñavalkya proclaims that one becomes "free from evil, free from impurity, free from doubt."[2]

The Janaka story in the YV, perhaps because of Janaka's renown, does not include a fancy plot or narrative; of all the stories of the YV, it is one of the most straightforwardly philosophical. The frame of the narrative starts when the king, while walking through the garden, hears a group of perfected sages chanting in the gardens that surround his palace. Their message announces that despite hearing about the omnipresence of the self, people expend their energies in pursuit of follies prompted by desire. Janaka immediately goes into seclusion, lamenting his own attachments to worldly appearance. After a self-imposed period of retreat, he experiences a breakthrough, described in Venkatesananda's translation as follows:

> Having abandoned all concepts of the desirable and the undesirable,
> freed from all psychological conditioning and intention,
> he engaged himself in spontaneous and appropriate action—
> as if in deep sleep, though wide awake.
> (YV V: 11, 2; Venkatesananda, 207)

From this point forward, King Janaka operates within the world with great zeal yet without attachment. Vasiṣṭha proclaims to Rāma that Janaka became liberated (*jīvanmukta*) from that time forward (YV V: 12, 9; Venkatesananda, 209). He exhorts Rāma to follow Janaka's example.

Puṇya and Pāvana

In the next story from the *Upaśama Prakaraṇa*, two brothers face the death of their parents. A playful cascade of poetic narrative describes the process of reincarnation. It suggests that because all humans have once been animals, insects, and even trees, we can feel empathy for each of these life forms. Through reflecting on these other existences, we can lessen our attachment to this particular precious human birth.

Puṇya, the older brother, has attained the state of liberation (*jīvanmukta*). The brothers' father, a holy man named Dīrghatapā, dies. Their mother, using yogic techniques, follows him in death. Pāvana, the younger brother, is inconsolable in his grief. Puṇya instructs him regarding the fleeting nature of the body and eventually frees his brother from his affliction, bringing him to liberation through tales of birth and rebirth. His teachings admonish Pāvana to remember his past births as a myriad of beings. By reflecting on the joys and pains of various past births, Puṇya prompts his brother to gain a new perspective on his current circumstance. Ultimately, this insight liberates Pāvana. The dialogue includes the following:

> You are a spiritual substance (*liṅga śarīra*)
> and have undergone many births.
> You have had many friends and properties in your past lives.
> Why not think of them also?
> You had many friends in the flowery plains
> where you had your pasture in your former form as a stag.
> Why not think of those deer,
> who were once your dear companions?
> Why do you not lament for your lost companions of swans,
> in the pleasant pools of lotuses, where you dove
> and swam in the form of a gander?
> Why not lament for your fellow trees in the woodlands,
> where you once stood as a stately tree among them?
> You had comrades of lions on the rugged crags of mountains.
> Why not lament for them also?
> You had many friends among the fishes
> in clean lakes adorned with lotuses.
> Why not lament your separation from them?
> You have been a monkey in the green woods of Dasārṇa.
> You have been a prince in the land of frost.
> You have been a raven in the woods of Puṇḍra.
> You have been an elephant in the land of Haihayas,
> a donkey in Trigarta, a dog in the country of Sālva,

a bird in the wood of sāl trees.
You have been a papal tree on the Vindhya Mountains,
a wood insect in a large oak,
a rooster on the Mandara Mountain,
and then you were born as a Brahmin in one of its caverns.
You were a Brahmin in Kosala, a partridge in Bengal,
a horse in the land of snows,
and a beast at the sacred grounds of Puskara.
You have been an insect in the trunk of a palm tree,
a gnat in a big tree, and a crane in the Puskara.
Now you are my younger brother.
You had been an ant for six months,
laying within the thin bark of a bhugpetera tree
in a glen of the Himalayan foothills.
You are now born as my younger brother.
You were a millipede in a dung-hill at a distant village,
where you dwelt for a year and a half.
Now you are my younger brother.
You were once the baby of a hill tribe woman
and dwelt at her breast like a honey-sucking bee . . .
You are now my younger brother.
In this manner, you were born in many other shapes
and had to wander all about this continent for years.
You are now my younger brother.
(YV V: 20:8–22, adapted from Mitra)

Under the tutelage of his older brother, Pāvana achieves liberation through reflecting on the many past lives that he has experienced. By seeing his connections with past embodiments, Pāvana gains the dispassion needed to heal his grief and engage the world through a state of equanimity. According to Vasiṣṭha, the two brothers lived for many years in the forest, perfect in their spiritual knowledge (*jñānavijñānaparagau*). Through moving himself away from self-concern, Pāvana becomes free to act again within the world without depression or fear, important lessons for the young Rāma.

Bali

The story of Bali involves a warrior figure with a pedigree that stretches back to the Upaniṣads. His father, Virocana, rejected Prajāpati's higher teachings about the Self in the *Chāndogya Upaniṣad*. The son has become famous for robbing India's wealth, dropping it into the ocean, and assisting the gods in its recovery, though they merely used this ruse as to recover the nectar of immortality (*amṛta*) from the ocean's depths. Bali, who succeeded his father as king of the Asuras, defeated the gods in battle. Bali was eventually driven from power by Vāmana, one of the incarnations of Vishnu, and was later reborn as a donkey.

In the YV, however, Bali is represented as a noble king of the netherworld who one day, like Rāma many years later, laments at the meaninglessness of power and wealth. He turns to his father, Virocana, who counsels him to seek out deeper meaning through overcoming the minister of desire that dwells within his heart and mind. Virocana states, "When the minister (*mantrin)* arises, the three worlds are manifested, even as the lotus blossoms when the sun rises. When he retires, the three worlds become dormant" (YV V: 23. 25; Venkatesananda, 227). This minister seems to be a metaphor for the intellect or *buddhi*, the repository of past impressions (*saṃskāras*) and hence the motivator for all action. In language that reflects the description of liberation in the *Sāṃkhya Kārikā*, Virocana proclaims that "once the king is seen, the minister comes completely under one's control; and when the minister is under one's control, the king is seen clearly. . . . When the king is not seen the minister plays havoc and spreads sorrow; when the minister is not conquered, the king remains unseen. Therefore, one's intelligent practice has to be simultaneously two-fold: to behold the king and subdue the minister" (YV V: 24.5–8; Venkatesananda, 228). In language that echoes Vasiṣṭha's teachings to Rāma in the *Mumukṣuprakaraṇa*, Virocana advises his son Bali to abandon reliance on the gods and "grinding one's teeth and with intense right self-exertion (*pauruṣa*), cultivate dispassion" (YV V: 24.61–62; Venkatesananda, 230).[3] Śukra, the great teacher of the Asuras, then appeared to Bali and the members of Bali's court, affirming this teaching that Bali had received from his father. Subsequently, Bali ruled from a place of nonattachment, worshipping the gods, treating his relatives with deference, and rewarding his servants amply (YV V: 29. 22–23; Venkatesananda, 234). Vasiṣṭha exhorts Rāma to become like Bali, to gain control over his impulses and to tame his mind.

Prahlāda

Keeping to his theme of demon lore, Vasiṣṭha tells Rāma about another famous Asura, Prahlāda, father of Virocana and grandfather of Bali. Prahlāda's father and brothers were killed by Narasiṃha, an incarnation of Viṣṇu. Traumatized by the loss of his family, Prahlāda decided to worship Viṣṇu, which made the pantheon of gods friendly toward Prahlāda. Lord Viṣṇu himself appears to Prahlāda and gives him knowledge of the true nature of self. Prahlāda proclaims:

> The one self . . . is therefore the experiencer in all:
> hence the self is said to have a thousand hands and eyes.
> With this beauteous body of the sun, the self which is "I"
> roams through space as also in the body of the air.
> (YV V: 34. 41–42; Venkatesananda, 240)
>
> I am woman, I am man, I am the youth, I am the senile
> old man.
> From the ground of the infinite consciousness I raise
> trees and plants,
> being present in them as their very essence.
> Even as clay in the hands of a playful child,
> this world-appearance is pervaded by me for my own
> delight.
> (YV V: 34.48–49; Venkatesananda, 241)

As Prahlāda became entranced with this understanding, he withdrew from the affairs of state to abide for more than one thousand years in this *samādhi*. This caused Viṣṇu to fear that the Asuras would lose their ferocity and ascend up the heavens and even attain liberation. He roused Prahlāda from his reverie and urged him to take up command once more of the netherworlds. Ironically, by re-establishing the resistance of the Asuras, the balance of power returned, allowing both groups to prosper, although remaining adversarial.

Viṣṇu brought Prahlāda to a deep state of spiritual understanding and bliss. He also awakened Prahlāda and prompted him to rule once again, but with dispassion, taking up the role of being liberated within and through the body (*sadeha*). Rāma pointed out to Vasiṣṭha a seeming contradiction. Did Prahlāda achieve his great insight through his own effort (*svayatna/pauruṣa*), or was the deity responsible (*daiva*)? Vasiṣṭha assures him that although Viṣṇu helped facilitate this awakening, Prahlāda's own efforts guaranteed success.

Gādhi

Gādhi was a Brahman who left his body while in a river, took birth in the womb of a tribal woman, and became king of Kīra, a prosperous city, disguising himself as high caste. He ruled Kīra for eight years before being "outed" as a lowly tribal. Out of remorse for his deception, he immolated himself along with the other leaders of Kīra to atone for his ruse. At the moment of his death, he regained consciousness as the Brahman Gādhi and learned from Viṣṇu the reality of his experiences as a tribal masquerading as a king. Eventually, after ten years of meditation, he gained liberation.

The moral of the story of Gādhi hinges on understanding the driving power of desire. Vasiṣṭha urges Rāma to go beyond desire, hope, and dharma itself. He tells him to "proceed to that dharma that is beyond all dharma (*nirdharmadharmatam vraja*, YV V: 50.40). He then states that "when one is firmly rooted in self-knowledge even the worst of poisons turns into immortalizing nectar" (YV V: 50.41). This might be hinting at tantric practices, or more innocently, it might be reflecting gratitude that one has surmounted difficulty.

Vasiṣṭha urges Rāma to strike down all thoughts to overcome avarice and craving. He urges Rāma to recognize the burden of thought and to work at overcoming desire:

> In the heart of the body,
> as in the hollow of a tree,
> multitudes of thoughts grow
> like clumps of orchids.
> Bearing the budding blossoms of hope and desire,
> they hang down with the fruits and flowers of death and disease.
> Lop off the large trunk of the poisonous tree of desire
> that has risen as high as a hill in the cavity of your heart.
> Use the sharp saw of your reason.
> Prune the leaves of desire without the least delay.
> (YV V: 50.64–65. Mitra)

With thick imagery, Vasiṣṭha locates the nexus of desire as residing deep within Rāma's body and urges him, like Gādhi, to extirpate his suffering at its source.

Uddālaka

The story of Uddālaka fits within the genre of tales of heroic meditators. From the time of his childhood on the great mountain of Gandhamadana, Uddālaka exhibited spiritual inclinations and an inquisitive mind. Although earnest in his pursuit of knowledge, he was distracted by his changing moods and myriad thoughts. While seated in a beautiful cave, he articulated his problem through five animal similes:

> Do not perish like a deer, trapped by the sound of music or bells,
> nor like an elephant lured by the touch of the female elephant,
> nor like a fish whose yearning for taste brings it to the fisherman's hook,
> nor like the moth, attracted by the sight of flame and then burnt by it,
> nor like a bee, whose sense of smell traps it deep within the flower.
> (YV V: 52.16–22)

Moving through various similar realizations, Uddālaka then engages in *prāṇāyāma*. This indicates the central relationships among breathing, *mantra* recitation, and meditation. After his first pronouncement of Om, he held the exhale breath, burning away karmic residues. After his second Om, he retained the inhale breath, such that his very (subtle?) body turned to ash and dispersed into the wind. With the third Om, his breath energy generated rays of light. From the ashes arose a four-armed form, and Uddālaka "shone like a divinity . . . seated in the lotus posture." He closed his rectum (*mūla bandha*) and "held his mind in his heart" (YV V.54). For six months he remained in this posture. The sages and gods came and paid their respects. Pārvatī, the wife of Śiva, came with a retinue of goddesses and placed her crown upon his head.

Vasiṣṭha used this story to explain to Rāma how meditation works to still the mind and deliver one from all desire and suffering. He urges Rāma to leave all conditioning behind, to renounce all notions of ego, and to see that consciousness is found in all things. Rather than following this story with a call to action, Vasiṣṭha seems to use this particular tale to emphasize the need for radical purification of mind and body.

Suraghu

Suraghu, King of the Yellow Haired Tribe (Hemajata) laments one day that the business of ruling his people causes them suffering. He presents his dilemma to the sage Māṇḍavya, who urges him to seek self-knowledge. Suraghu comes to realize that he is not his kingdom, he is not his tribe, he is not his city, he is not his body, and he is not his mind. After this profound realization, he meets up with his old friend, the Persian king Parigha, who has had a similar awakening. During their discourse, Suraghu describes the culmination of Yoga, which entails both contemplation and action:

> The enlightened ones are forever in *samādhi*
> even though they engage themselves in the affairs of the world . . .
> That is known as the state of *samādhi* in which there is eternal satisfaction,
> clear perception of what is, egolessness,
> not being subject to the pairs of opposites,
> freedom from anxiety and from the wish to acquire or reject . . .
> When nothing is worth acquiring,
> it follows that nothing is worth renouncing.
> (YV V: 63; *Vasiṣṭha's Yoga*, 285)

This philosophy of nondifference allows Suraghu to rule his kingdom justly and without remorse.

Bhāsa and Vilāsa

Bhāsa and Vilāsa, two friends, were the sons of the sages Bṛhaspati and Śukra, respectively. At around the same time, the two elders died, leaving Bhāsa and Vilāsa fatherless and bereft. In their grief, they went their separate ways, searching for meaning and wisdom. After some time, they were reunited. As they shared their insights, they attained supreme knowledge and supported one another in their discernment. Vasiṣṭha uses the example of their enlightenment to explain to Rāma that, on the one hand, his true self has no association with anything at all. On the other hand, it can be proclaimed:

> I am the space. I am the sun.
> I am the directions, above and below.
> I am the gods. I am the demons. I am all beings.
> I am darkness. I am the earth, the oceans,
> the dust, the wind the fire, and all this world.

> I am omnipresent. How can there be anything other than me?
> (YV V: 73; *Vasiṣṭha's Yoga,* 295)

This theology combines a rejection and embrace of the world. Everything is suffused with soul. The very desires and manifestations and objects that cause attachment and pain cannot be separated from the consciousness that pervades them. Hence, the world itself, and the myriad experiences it provides, becomes an occasion for spiritual insight.

Vītahavya

Vasiṣṭha tells the story of Vītahavya as an example of a Yogin who conquered all desires and attained a state of liberation:

> Repeating aloud the sacred syllable Om,
> the sage obtained internal peace,
> having gotten rid of thoughts
> and become free of desires . . .
> He drew his mind inward,
> away from internal and external organs,
> as also from gross and fine feeling
> and the sensibilities of his heart and body.
> He dismissed all things of the three worlds
> and converted all his desires to indifference . . .
> His mind was like the clear firmament . . .
> and his heart was bright,
> without the light of the sun, moon, or stars.
> His intellect was unclouded
> by the fumes, dust, and clouds of ignorance.
> His soul was as clear as the autumnal sky.
> Then, raising his voice from the ventricle
> to the top-most part of his cranium,
> his mind transcended the region of the sensations . . .
> He then beheld a flood of light in himself.
> Having attained to that state of ineffable light,
> he found his mental urges burnt down quickly . . .
> This sage stopped the course of his thought,
> as a current of wind stops its motion . . .
> He was joyous in his joylessness
> (*nirānando'pi sānanda*),

existing in nonexistence
(*saccāsaccapi*).
He became that transparent substance,
which is pure and purifying,
which is all pervasive, yet without body.
(YV V: 87:1–17, Mitra)

The text goes on to state that he became the emptiness of the Mādhyamika Buddhists, the Brahman lauded by Vedāntins, the knowledge of the Jñāna-Yogis, the Puruṣa of the Sāṃkhya philosophers, the Īśvara of the Yogins, and the Śiva of the Śaivites.

It could be argued that having attained this state of rarefied spirituality there would be no incentive to stir from that bliss to exhibit any concern about the affairs of the world. However, Vasiṣṭha states that Vītahavya entered into a state with form (*svarūpa*) through which he manifested friendliness and other such qualities (*maitrādayo guṇaḥ*). The term *svarūpa* refers in the *Yoga Sūtra* to the state that the mind attains after having achieved the cessation (*nirodha*) of thought and desire (see *Yoga Sūtra* I:3, 43; II:23, 54; III:3, 44, 47; IV:12, 34). Friendliness (*maitri*) is the first of the Brahma Vihāras, the four "immeasurables" of Buddhism that indicate the enlightened view and the modalities through which the awakened Yogin operates within the world: friendliness toward those who experience pleasure, compassion for those who suffer, happiness toward the virtuous, and equanimity toward the vicious (*Yoga Sūtra* I:33). Though the sage is "freed form the pains of repeated births," he nonetheless "has best wishes for all living beings" (YV V: 90.18). His "joy shines forth like the light of the moon" (YV V: 90.20). In terms of the *Yoga Sūtra,* he would enter into the state of *dharma megha samādhi,* wherein, according to Patañjali, there would be no impure actions (*Yoga Sūtra* IV:29–30).

The compassionate aspect of Vītahavya's accomplishment can be seen in the gratefulness expressed by him toward his former state of adversity. He proclaims that his entry into the path (*mārga*) was prompted by his suffering (*duḥkha*), and he thanks and blesses his former difficulty. He even asks forgiveness of his desires and avarice now that he has attained a state of nonattachment (*vairāgyam*) (YV V:86.39).

Conclusion

The penultimate book of the YV displays Vasiṣṭha's vast knowledge of Indian mythology, from the Upaniṣads to the Purāṇas. It demonstrates his intimate familiarity with Sāṃkhya as seen in the story of Bali, with the practices of Haṭha Yoga in the story of Uddālaka and with the particular nondual view espoused by Abhinavagupta, a view that sees God in all things and all things as not different from God. It employs straight philosophical and complex narrative, laden with rich imagery and symbolism. Particularly in the visions of Uddālaka and Gādhi, we move into a world of magical realism, not unlike that found in Borges, as discussed in the chapter by Sthaneshwar Timalsina.

The *Upaśama Prakaraṇa* employs a number of devices to convince Rāma that an enlightened awareness will allow him to move through the world without being affected by its allure or its disappointments. A verse from the Suraghu story encapsulates this message, translated first by Vihari Lal Mitra, and then by Swami Venkatesananda:

> Though the spiritual man is engaged in worldly affairs
> and is subject to *rāga* and *dveṣa*,
> yet he is unstained by them in his heart,
> as the lotus bud is unsullied by water.
> (YV 64:8, Mitra)
>
> Even if you engage yourself in the activities relating to
> your daily life
> and even if likes and dislikes arise in you,
> your inner being will never become impure.
> (*Vasiṣṭha's Yoga*, 286)

The psychology of the YV assesses the human condition in terms of karmic conditioning. If one is subject to karmic residues and attachments, then one will inevitably experience discomfort and suffering (*duḥkha*). If one takes the time to examine the root causes of desire and applies the effort (*pauruṣa/yatna*) to purify oneself through reflection, breathing, and meditation, then one can overcome attachment and attain the state of living liberation while in the body (*sadeha jīvanmukta*). Vasiṣṭha argues for the re-engagement of the world after having undergone the purification process.

Due to its emphasis on the importance of action, the YV holds a deep ethical message. The ultimate good entails the cessation of desire and the temporary withdrawal from an unthinking, unreflective involvement in worldly affairs. For Vasiṣṭha, it also requires taking up the tasks of the world following this transformative experience. In his classic work, *Varieties of Religious Experience*, William James articulated a similar dynamic:

> To be converted, to be regenerated, to receive grace, to experience religion, to gain an assurance, are so many phrases which denote the process, gradual or sudden, by which a self hitherto divided, and consciously wrong, inferior and unhappy, becomes unified and consciously right . . . the shifting of the emotional centre brings with it, first, increase of purity. . . . The cleansing of existence from brutal and sensual elements becomes imperative.[4]

According to William James, this results in an increased capacity for maintaining sobriety; the founders of Alcoholics Anonymous cited James and Carl Jung as major inspirations for their very successful movement.

Indian traditions have often been criticized, particularly by Christian missionaries, for their overemphasis on otherworldliness. David Haberman, citing the Maharaj libel case in a Bombay court in 1862, has noted that the opinion of Oriental scholar and Christian missionary John Wilson was used to define "legitimate forms of Hinduism as . . . ancient, ascetic, individualistic, transcendent, world-denying . . . [with] the singular goal of *mokṣa*."[5] The YV conforms to this notion that the world must be transcended. However, in contrast to the characterization that religion in India requires rejection of the world, it also emphasizes that one must return and embrace the world. The ultimate good entails cessation *and* action. Vasiṣṭha teaches Rāma the importance of renouncing attachment and expectation, as seen in the story of Pāvana and Puṇya. He also teaches acceptance and surrender, as in the story of Gādhi, who paradoxically moves through three radically different embodiments in the sociological continuum—priest, tribal, and king—and learns to leave each of them behind.

After one's extrication from and transcendence of attachment to the world, whether momentary or through the course of an alternate experienced lifetime or several lifetimes, Vasiṣṭha describes with vigor the nature of the action that one should take up after returning to the world. All of the rulers manifest justice, generosity, zeal, and enthusiasm when they take up their duties after their cleansing, re-ordering spiritual encounter. The ordinary, nonroyal characters of these stories take up lives of happiness and fulfillment. Whether through Yoga practice, memory of past lives, living through a parallel life, or simply emerging from a deep, transformative depression, the liberated beings of Vasiṣṭha's stories engage life to the fullest, serving as a model for others. Vasiṣṭha emphasizes doing things well, with gusto and without attachment.

The ethic of the YV requires a refined, purified psychological state, carefully cultivated through effort (*yatna*) and creativity (*pauruṣa*). This process eschews reliance on past cultural norms, though one might and probably will embody those same cultural norms after returning from the transformative experience. By clearing one's psyche and body of the cobwebs of the past, one attains a clarity that brings one a place of immediate sensory perception. Without expectation of the future or reliance on the past, the liberated person is able to act freely and set an example for others.

Many ethical systems, in India and elsewhere, present a fixed code of expected behaviors or commandments. Yoga and Jainism set forth five rules to be followed: abstention from violence, lying, stealing, sexual misadventures, and hording. Buddhism abides by the same set, but substitutes abstention from intoxicants for not hording. The Buddhists and Jainas go into even greater detail, setting out exhaustive lists of hundreds of rules to regulate the behavior of monks and even more for nuns. The Theravāda Buddhist monastic discipline lists 227 rules for monks and 311 rules for nuns. The Mahāyāna Mūlasarvastivadin Vinaya requires 253 expected behaviors of its monks and 364 for its nuns. By contrast, the YV explains a method for purifying action that focuses on one's attitude rather than fixed behaviors. By first erasing one's attachment to the world through meditation and reflective realization, one is then able to reenter and reconstruct the world from a fresh perspective.

The stories of the *Upaśama Prakaraṇa* are fairly evenly divided between tales of celebrity kings and tales of somewhat anonymous meditators. Kings Janaka, Bali, and Prahlāda are well-known figures mentioned in the Upaniṣads, the Mahābhārata, and the Purāṇas. Gādhi masquerades as a king, and Suraghu serves as a tribal king, though both appear to be more locally known figures or perhaps were invented by the storyteller. All five kings use their insight to rule their kingdoms more effectively and justly. The other characters, without the benefit of kingly status, seem more accessible, more human. The struggle of Pāvana, Bhāsa, and Vilāsa to deal with the grief they experience over the death of their parents and the sincerity of the spiritual quest of Uddālaka and Vītahavya speak to the concerns that bring many individuals to the practice of Yoga and meditation.

In summary, the *Upaśama Prakaraṇa* presents tales of kings and commoners who have suffered, persevered, and set themselves free. These stories advance Vasiṣṭha's philosophy of mind-only voluntarism. They are rich in metaphor. They urge Rāma, and consequently the reader, to overcome latent tendencies, to move into a vision of oneness, and move into freedom, while still engaging the world as appropriate.

Notes

1. *Bṛhadāraṇyaka Upaniṣad*, 4.4.23, as translated in Robert Ernest Hume, *The Thirteen Principal Upanishads* (Oxford, Oxford University Press, 1921), 143.

2. Ibid, 144.

3. For an extensive study of this proactive philosophy as found in the Mahābhārata and the *Yogavāsiṣṭha*, see Chapple, *Karma and Creativity* (Albany: State University of New York Press, 1986), 55–79.

4. Willliam James, *The Varieties of Religious Experience* (London: Collier, 1961), 160, 165, 221. This classic work was first published in 1902.

5. David L. Haberman, *River of Love in an Age of Pollution: The Yamuna River in Northern India* (Berkeley: University of California Press, 2006), 28.

10

Dreams, Fictions, and the Quest for Morality in the Yogavāsiṣṭha

MENAHA GANESATHASAN

I

The *Yogavāsiṣṭha* (YV) describes the teachings of the sage, Vasiṣṭha, to the young prince, Rāma. Rāma has everything that a sixteen year old may desire and yet has lost all taste for life. Vasiṣṭha's[1] insightful stories and philosophical discourses lead Rāma to liberation and back to shouldering the responsibilities of his kingdom. The YV has interesting implications for a paradox facing nondualist traditions: the difficulty of adequately explaining the importance of moral behavior in a world that is considered to be pure illusion.

Broadly speaking, proponents of Advaita Vedānta, the major system of nondualism in Indian philosophy, distinguish three ontic levels of being: reality, appearance, and unreality.[2] The experience of reality is described as unsublatable because it can never be replaced or revised by any other experience; appearance can be so sublated, whereas unreality is that which neither can nor cannot be sublated by other experiences. Ultimate reality is Brahman, *saccidānanda*: *sat* (being), *cit* (consciousness), *ānanda* (bliss). At the appearance level, Advaitins recognize ontological differences between the phenomenal world and "illusion." The latter category includes experiences such as hallucinations, dreams, erroneous sense perceptions, and fantasies. According to these philosophers, the world is granted a practical reality, *vyāvahārika*, because it lends itself to relative knowledge and truth. Hallucinations, dream experiences, and so on, at the illusory or *prātibhāsika* level, are sublated by the experiences of the empirical world and thus, assigned a lower level of being. When we wake up, we know that the dream was just a dream. Finally, at the level of unreality are placed objects that are logically nonexistent, such as the son of a barren woman, or physically nonexistent, such as the horns of a hare. Such entities cannot even appear.

Vasiṣṭha[3] greatly complicates matters by collapsing the distinction between the practical world at the *vyāvahārika* level and illusion at the *prātibhāsika* level. He argues that there are *no* crucial differences between the awaking, phenomenal world around us and the sleeping worlds inhabited in dreams, but he emphasizes decency in conduct. In almost every story in which kings and queens are facing personal liberation, Vasiṣṭha first mentions their virtuosity and then goes on to outline their path to liberation. Lavaṇa is called "righteous, noble, chivalrous, charitable, and in every way a worthy king" (YV III:103–104). Janaka is extolled as "a great monarch, a cornucopia to all who seek his aid, sun-like to friends, and a great benefactor to all good people" (V:8). Bhagīratha is "devoted to *dharma*" (YV VI:1.74). Even the hungry vampire "would not kill anyone. . . . unless the victim deserved such treatment" (YV VI:1.70–71). These stories indicate that integrity of character is of the utmost importance. Harm and suffering carry weight in deciding a course of action. This paradox can be formulated as follows:

1. Vasiṣṭha's concept of dharma (righteous conduct, virtue) embraces a rigorous system of morality that requires the existence of the individualized agent and the differentiated other in order to lend substance to the agent's regard for the other.

2. Vasiṣṭha considers the transactional, phenomenal universe to be just an illusion.

3. For Vasiṣṭha, notions of "I" and "Other" exist separately *only* in the phenomenal universe. In reality there is no such distinction between individuals. In reality, there is only Brahman, pure undifferentiated consciousness.

4. As individuality and multiplicity exist only in the phenomenal world and not in reality (premise 3), and as the phenomenal universe is just an illusion (premise 2),

for Vasiṣṭha, there is no individualized agent or patient, and thus there is no moral agency.

The conjoining of these postulates gives rise to a contradiction. For Vasiṣṭha, moral considerations are of paramount importance (premise 1), but his view that the phenomenal world is just illusion undercuts and makes irrelevant the moral imperative (premise 4). If the world is just an illusion, there is little one can do about it, since any action would also be imagining that one is acting. There is little anyone *should* be doing because nothing really wrong is happening that needs to be changed.

II

Vasiṣṭha's response to this dilemma is to present the ubiquitous argument based on an analogy with dream.

1. The world is nothing but a long dream.
2. Just as in the dream, the dreamer is caught up in the dream and sincerely believes that her experiences of objects and events are real, and the awoken individual is so entangled in the machinations of the world that she regards her sense experiences as constituents of reality.
3. Given the psychological impact of this phenomenological snare, particularly in the generation of pain or pleasure, it is necessary to introduce rules of moral conduct in order to reduce suffering and increase happiness.

According to Vasiṣṭha, the major criteria commonly used to distinguish dream experiences from world experiences are incoherence, evanescence, sublation, and subject-object unity. Usually, these four attributes are said to be characteristics of dream, but not phenomenal experiences. However, Vasiṣṭha argues that these features are also qualities of the world.[4] He concludes that the world is nothing but a dream. In addition, as far as Vasiṣṭha is concerned, the awoken individual is just as constrained by the world as the sleeper by her dream (YV VI:1.61). The dreamer is absorbed by the dream and has no awareness that she is dreaming. She is at the mercy of dream sufferings and dream pleasures. The awakened individual is in a similar predicament. She is also immersed in the world and cast adrift in an ocean of desires, aversions, and cravings. Thus, even in a world that is illusion, rules of conduct are required in order to reduce suffering and encourage the formation of a calm and harmonious society. Otherwise, Vasiṣṭha notes, the big fish will simply eat the little fish, and chaos will ensue (YV VI:1.69).

In offering such a response, Vasiṣṭha does not reject any of the propositions that give rise to the paradox. All the postulates are still plausible and remain intact. Vasiṣṭha's solution plays on the assumption underlying the first and second propositions of the paradox, that the differentiation between agent and patient is necessary to lend substance to the agent's regard for the other. The supposition here is that one requires the independent existence of individuals, irrespective of the mind's operations, in order for morality to make sense. However, Vasiṣṭha argues that the psychological impact of just believing the world is real, that there is individuality and multiplicity, that sense experiences generate pleasures and pains, is sufficient to lend substance to the reality of individuality and multiplicity and justifies the construction and implementation of the rules and regulations governing moral behavior.

According to Vasiṣṭha, just as the dream generates emotions such as fear and love and the desire to limit suffering and increase happiness, the entanglement with the world gives rise to these very emotions and desires and lends credence to the development and implementation of moral standards and rules. Although a viable notion of ethics must presuppose duality, and duality is nullified by the overarching infusion of Brahman as pure, undivided consciousness, the dream analogy presents an acceptable response for this paradox. After all, if a nonreal dream can trigger actual "real-life" symptoms, surely the nonreal world can trigger the appearance of diseased symptoms that have to be alleviated. The question is this: does Vasiṣṭha's psychological impact story, occurring in both dreaming and waking lives, give credence to the rigorous codes of conduct, the mores of behavior, that plague Rāma in his journey from fool to unenlightened seeker to enlightened sage,[5] or is the notion of morality just another case of the delusional activity emerging out of the machinations of diseased minds?

Vasiṣṭha's fool is the embodied *jīva* who is thoroughly embroiled in the world appearance. She is born; she is active; she hopes, suffers, enjoys, and dies. Worldly experiences, such as a cut on the body or the lack of accolades, are very real to the fool, just as the dream of being cut and burned seems very real to the dreamer. Moral injunctions and prohibitions are important because they force the fool to act in ways that avoid pain and promote pleasures for herself and others. Vasiṣṭha's seeker is more sophisticated in her dealings with the world appearance. She recognizes that pleasure is also pain, that pleasure and pain shadow one another. The seeker also requires moral rules and regulations, but for a different purpose. She begins to realize that the following of rules and regulations to the letter, so necessary for the well-being of the fool, provides little comfort to her. Even when society's excesses are restrained, and order prevails, life brings no happiness. There has to be something more to life than the life of a fool. For the seeker, codes of conduct encourage a harmonious society and provide a safe place for the important work of liberation.

Vasiṣṭha describes the sage as the *mahākartā* (the great doer of actions), who is "freed of doubts and performs appropriate actions in natural situations whether they are regarded as *dharma* or *adharma*," as the *mahābhoktā* (the great enjoyer), "who does not hate anything nor long for anything, but enjoys all natural experiences," and the *mahātyāgī* (the great renunciate), who has "banished from his mind concepts like *dharma* and *adharma*" (YV VI:1.115). This does not mean that once the dictates of mundane morality have served their purpose in leading to liberation, the sage is no longer concerned about dharma per se. Vasiṣṭha notes that those who are "*sattva* are naturally good" (YV III:94) and describes the sage, who is the *mahākartā*, *mahābhoktā*, and *mahātyāgī*, as one "who has completely abandoned from his heart the notion of world appearance" and is "without swaying by likes and dislikes, by success and failure, without ego sense or jealousy, . . . whose very nature is at peace and equilibrium or equanimity which is sustained in all situations." In the core of his being, he is "non-violent and virtuous" (YV VI:1.115).

Even after liberation and seeing the world appearance as world appearance, goodness itself is not worthless to Vasiṣṭha's sage but intrinsic to her nature. At this stage of living liberation, words such as "good" and "bad" are redundant because they have no counterparts to make them meaningful. However, goodness is a constituent of the liberated state just as eggs, flour, and sugar are the constituents of a cake. The idea that morality is just an instrumental means to liberation is not what Vasiṣṭha has in mind. The liberated one acts morally because it is second nature to her. She knows the world as "appearance," but she has not left behind morality. Vasiṣṭha requires another analogy to make sense of his emphasis on the moral character of the sage in a world that is illusion; an analogy with fiction.

III

An analogy with stories, the metaphor of fable, or even the equation of the world with a set of tales is very much compatible with the YV. The text is organized as a nesting of stories, just like the nesting of Russian dolls. The Story of Rāma and Vasiṣṭha is an inner "doll," and when that is "opened," fifty-five other stories drop out. These are Vasiṣṭha's stories to Rāma, and they, in turn, move Rāma towards enlightenment. Vasiṣṭha goes so far as to claim that a thorough investigation of the content of certain stories leads one to enlightenment (YV V:42). The reader of the YV is not exempt from the jolting impact of the stories. By persuading the reader to journey into this Russian doll-style nesting of fictional world within fictional world within fictional world, the author creates a breach in the taken-for-granted reality of the reader's own world. As the reader steps out of story within story within story and back into her own world, she is driven to questioning her own mundane reality. Is she the author of her life story, a character in someone else's story, both, or neither? Vasiṣṭha's stories present the seeds for this argument:

1. Vasiṣṭha's world-appearance is no more real than the world projected in a story.[6] It is just an idea in the mind of the "author."
2. Just as the functioning of the literary imagination in stories enhances the moral capabilities of the reader, the creative imagination in Vasiṣṭha's world appearance also enables and enriches the development of the ideal moral character.
3. Given the special function of the creative imagination, it makes sense for the sage, who knows the world is illusion, to evolve into Vasiṣṭha's ideal moral being.

In his stories and philosophical discussions, Vasiṣṭha has the material to establish this analogy in a definitive way. Each of these steps, explored below, weaves together those aspects of fiction and Vasiṣṭha's world appearance in such a manner as to situate and establish the great saying, *tat tvam asi* (that thou art), from the ethical perspective of the sage.

Step 1: The World as Story

Vasiṣṭha's first step may well have been that the world appearance is no more real than the world projected in a story. It is just an idea in the mind of the "author." There is no better place to unpack this assertion than with Vasiṣṭha's descriptions of the creation of the world. Vasiṣṭha may establish the claim that the world is just a story in two ways: by utilizing (1) a metaphysical explanation and (2) a metaphysical argument.

VASIṢṬHA'S POSSIBLE METAPHYSICAL EXPLANATION FOR THE IDENTITY OF WORLD AND STORY

In the beginning of a cycle of emergence / creation / destruction, according to Vasiṣṭha, there is nothing but Brahman, pure, undivided, infinite consciousness. However, Brahman is not inert and empty, even though the term "*śūnya*" (emptiness) is used about it. In Brahman resides every conceivable world. All powers, possibilities, and potentialities are inherent in its nature. The creative latencies of trees, birds, animals, the movement of wind, the solidity of stone, the heat in fire, the liquidity of water, the powers of joy in the cheerful and sorrow in the afflicted, as well as the potencies for decline, stagnation, and destruction are all concealed in Brahman (YV III:100). Even the bizarre and the peculiar are not excluded. "In some universes, moonlight is hot, sunlight cool, there is sight in darkness, and blindness in daylight, good is destructive whereas evil is constructive, poison promotes health and nectar kills" (YV VIb:60–61). The possibilities are endless, constrained only by imagination. Whatever notion that could possibly arise in the individual consciousness and whatever object towards which the mind flows inhere in Brahman and are available for materialization. Unfortunately, so is the individualized needy and self-serving ego. As Vasiṣṭha states, "Just as there is an image in a marble slab, even if it has not been carved, even so this notion of "I" and "the world" exists in the infinite consciousness" (YV III:61).

This is where the trouble begins. According to Vasiṣṭha, the creative power of Brahman (*spanda-śakti*) induces, as it were, a "hiccup," a spontaneous vibration in consciousness, which results in the beginnings of the breach between the knower and the knowable. This initial rupture of the unified Brahman is the emergence of "an idea concerning its form and with an inquiry concerning itself" (YV III:12). This initial idea, "Who am I?" resulting in the positing of a counterinquiry, "What is that over there?" condenses into the knower and the knowable. The knower matures and identifies itself with further forms of that-which-could-be. The creative thoughts of space, sound, and the ego are added. Once the ego gets going, there is no stopping. The faculty of discrimination and the rationalizing intellect appear, and discursive thoughts radiate in all directions. The mind thinks, "I am atomic in nature and stature," and it becomes so. Each arising thought is accompanied by desire. The desires to see, hear, touch, taste, and smell generate the eyes and other sense organs (YV III:13). The desires multiply, and eventually, in Vasiṣṭha's universe, elements combine to produce an apparent materiality. The composite of thoughts is given reality as the cosmic *jīva* (the embodied soul). It calls itself "Brahma." This "Brahma" has the desire for creation. He wonders what to do. He has visions of innumerable worlds furnished with mountains, rivers, oceans, a vast array of beings, scriptures, and so on. These images fashion the blueprint of Brahma's new universe, the next "story."

Thus, Vasiṣṭha may point out that not only is the individualized Brahma developed and nurtured by a "story" that is made up of the ideas emerging from the field of play that is Brahman, but also, most importantly, Brahma may be viewed as the first "story-teller" (YV III:93). The universe flows into existence from the creative process of Brahma in a manner similar to the production of a story by an author. However, Brahma is not the sole creator; he is not the only "story-teller." Brahma "designs" this universe and the original individual beings that will eventually propagate his world, but even after his work is done, the creative process continues in the imaginative activities of his created sentient beings.

In the story of Līlā, a highly convoluted narrative with layers upon layers of interpretation, Vasiṣṭha makes it clear that fervent, incessant thoughts materialize, even for the created beings of Brahma. Regardless of whether lives are shaped by the intercession of gods and goddesses granting boons or an individual's own efforts, it is the individual's imagination that is the primary culprit in propelling her from one distinctive lifestyle to another to another. The imaginer is the lead "character" in her imaginings, and it is the intensity of her cravings and aversions that are carried over into the next life, the next "narrative."[7]

In Līlā's Story, it is the holy man's dissatisfaction with his austere life and his desire for the opulence of a kingdom that propel him headlong into the turbulent wheel of samsara, the repetitive history of birth after birth after birth. After death, the holy man is reborn as King Padma. The holy man's wife, Arundhatī, on account of her wish that she and her husband never be parted, is born and reunited with Padma as Queen Līlā. Padma is killed in battle, but he is still caught in the snare of the luxurious life of royalty. He is reborn as Vidūratha, who is also crowned as king. The momentum of Arundhatī's wish continues unabated in Līlā. Līlā is distraught at Padma's death. With the aid of the goddess Sarasvatī, she enters into the "other" physical space in which Vidūratha resides and sees, to her astonishment, that Vidūratha is accompanied by a replica of herself, Līlā2.

However, this is not a straightforward story of incarnation after incarnation. The intense desire of Līlā1 to be bound to her husband generates her double Līlā2, who marries Vidūratha. Līlā1 is not only the "creator" of Līlā2 through the intensity of her desire, but is also the blueprint for Līlā2.[8] In a way, she is the "same" person as Līlā2. As Sarasvatī notes, "The other youthful Līlā was indeed yourself" (YV III:51, 52). Līlā2 is a bodily replica of Līlā1. Vidūratha's kingdom is a replica of Padma's kingdom. Līlā2 has all the memories and experiences of being born in Vidūratha's kingdom and living with Vidūratha, events that are uncannily similar to the experiences and memories of Līlā1.

Nonetheless, at some point the experiences and the memories begin to diverge because Līlā2 is not Līlā1 and develops different needs and desires. Līlā2 is still caught up in her desire to be with her husband and is the "creator" of the packaging for her next life of matrimony. When Vidūratha dies, by the grace of Sarasvatī, his ethereal form enters into Padma's body, which is still lying (without decomposing) in his palace. Padma has life again. Līlā2's desire is to be reunited with her husband. She follows Vidūratha to Padma's kingdom and lives with him as Padma's wife. Līlā1 proceeds in another direction. This first Līlā's initial entry into Vidūratha's world is made possible only by the intervention of Sarasvatī, but as her understanding grows, she is able to traverse time and space on her own. She realizes that she and her husband had been living ordinary, unenlightened lives, and her desires focus on liberation. Līlā1 advances towards enlightenment, while Līlā2 is still caught up in the snares of the world and the continued evolution of her own story.

VASIṢṬHA'S POSSIBLE METAPHYSICAL ARGUMENT FOR THE IDENTITY OF WORLD AND STORY

Just as in the dream analogy, Vasiṣṭha may also use a metaphysical argument in establishing his claim that the world is nothing but a story.

1. The story has the features of evanescence, sublatability, and subject-object unity.
2. These features of evanescence, sublatability, and subject-object unity are commonly used to distinguish the story from the world appearance.
3. The world appearance has the features of evanescence, sublatability, and subject-object unity.

THUS, THE WORLD APPEARANCE IS JUST A STORY

Vasiṣṭha's ontological claim that the world is illusion remains undisturbed. Story does have similarities with dream. Three of the four criteria that Vasiṣṭha uses to establish his claim that the world is a dream (evanescence, the lack of subject-object distinction, and sublatability) are also seen in the presentation of the world as a story. Stories are short. Even full-length novels of hundreds of densely printed pages can be read in a week. There is no distinction between the subject (the author) and the object (the narrative). The characters are make-believe, the products of the author's imagination. Moreover, the reality of the story world is negated by events in the waking world. Stories have a similar psychological impact on the reader as dreams have on the dreamer. The reader may be absorbed in a story but is awakened to its fictionality when she puts aside the novel.

Nevertheless, story has some advantage over dream. Vasiṣṭha's fourth criterion of dreams, incoherence, does not apply as well to fiction as it does to dreams. Stories tend to have a beginning, middle, and end. Even the most convoluted of narratives follow a structured pattern of events running in sequence. This works to Vasiṣṭha's benefit. He does not have to adopt the torturous route of providing an explanation for the incoherence of the world when common sense dictates otherwise. Worldly events do not just happen, even if they present such an appearance. They are preceded and influenced by other events. These events may be viewed as a tangled web of interrelationships that defy easy explanation, but there is some underlying order imposed by the structures of the universe. So it is not difficult to substantiate the claim that storytelling is adopted by Vasiṣṭha just because he considers his world to be a story world anyway and the unfolding of life to be as incorporeal and insubstantial as the developing activities of the characters in the story.

Thus far, there isn't much of a difference between the analogy based on dream or story. However, had Vasiṣṭha utilized the analogy with story, his justification for the "fictional" nature of the world appearance might have been reinforced by two additional criteria: (1) the creative origins of the world-appearance and story, and (2) the interdependence of author, reader, and character.

THE CREATIVE ORIGINS OF THE WORLD APPEARANCE AND STORY

Vasiṣṭha's explanation for the birth of the universe and the lives lived in it bear a strong resemblance to the creation of a novel in that the universe and the novel are both products of imagination. As far as literary works are concerned, the centrality of imagination of the author and the propulsion of her ideas and desires are not controversial matters. The author wishes to bring some realities to light and develops plots and characters to reveal these truths in an intelligent and stimulating manner. The intensity of her imagination may take the shape of some strife between characters, conflicts within the personality of a character, and so on. Storybook characters are not portrayed as just victims of external forces beyond their control, but as vibrant, dynamic agents, sometimes struggling against great odds in order to bring about some desired goal. The skilled author has the power to depict the poignancy of a situation in which even strengths of character may unknowingly contribute to destruction, just as tragedies in "real" life may erupt from the need to do good.

Brahma's creation of the world follows a similar pattern with the added complication that his people create further "lives" of their own. Brahma is the chief "storyteller," whose imagination produces "characters" who, in turn, through the exercise of their desires and imaginations, concoct other "narratives" and other "characters." Brahma's intense thoughts of a king "materialize," let us say, as flesh-and-blood Daśaratha and Daśaratha's unwavering desire for a son "materializes" as Rāma. The intensity of Rāma's own thoughts "completes" itself by attracting all the characteristics of time and space, such as variability and solidity. The impenetrable thought "I am Rāma" reveals mental attachment to the body. The name "Rāma" is fixed to the body and intensifies all the physical characteristics of a body. Further attachment to what's out there, the "external" paraphernalia, generates what we consider to be the "material" world. The universe is born.

Vasiṣṭha emphasizes again and again that "all this [the world as we know it] is mere imagination or thought" (YV III:13, 14). Brahma is a thought form and so are his creations and his creations' creations. Brahma's imagination and thoughts "fire" the existence of others, clothed in matter and form, but he, himself, arises as an idea sprouting out of the breach between Brahman as knower and Brahman as knowable. It is via the imagination that both the story universe and Vasiṣṭha's universe are brought into play.

THE INTERDEPENDENCE OF AUTHOR, READER, AND CHARACTER

Philosophers and authors, such as Martha Nussbaum,[9] David Novitz,[10] and Toni Morrison,[11] have described a topsy-turvy interdependence of imagination that gives elbow room for the development of a three-way alliance between author, reader, and character.

THE RELATIONSHIP BETWEEN AUTHOR AND READER

It is not just the author who is responsible for the development of a story. The author builds a universe and peoples it with credible, tangible characters by the use of her imagination. The reader actively participates in the imaginative world-making activity of the author by willingly stepping into the creative mind of the author. David Novitz writes,

> Authors do not just create fictional worlds and populate them with characters. They also use language in ways which are carefully designed to have special effects: to breed insights, to encourage emotional responses, to highlight certain values and disabuse us of others. To this end metaphors are coined, symbols are invented and strategically deployed, and a wealth of images and figures is devised with the aim of fostering certain associative and emotional responses. Readers, in their turn, try to comprehend the fiction, and this frequently requires them to interpret certain works. They become "caught up in" the fiction, they "identify" with its characters, they laugh with them and weep for them.[12]

The narration is necessarily through the medium of words. The author's inner "picturings" are translated into words and, in the reader, the words are transformed back into rich imagery. From the reader's perspective, the reading of the story is not a sterile repetition of the words, but an invitation for her mind to cross the threshold, the boundaries of skin, and enter the narrative in its full dramatic form. The reader no longer views the novel as representing an illusion but is fully immersed in the author's field of play. She cooperates and participates in the author's vision, and she supplements it, via the workings of her own imagination. As William Carlos Williams notes, the author and reader are "locked in a fraternal embrace."[13]

THE RELATIONSHIP BETWEEN AUTHOR AND CHARACTER

It is often said that characters acquire a life of their own, independently of their creator. They may even end up converting the author to different ideas along the way. The author may not have the finished product in mind when beginning a story. She has the desire to write a particular kind of novel and to convey this storyline to the readers. During her period of research, the author has some notion of the characters, their roles in the narrative, and the evolution of their dramatic lives through the story, but, prior to the writing of the novel, these characters rarely appear as fully fleshed out personalities with all the idiosyncrasies of style and temperament firmly in place. During the process of writing, the author attempts to reach into the character's psyche. If she is successful, the inner "voice" of the character comes to life and takes on a will of its own.

This interplay between author and character is aptly seen in Toni Morrison's exploration of Willa Cather's novel *Sapphira and the Slave Girl*. Morrison illustrates how, in an attempt to represent the efforts of the unstable, white slave owner (Sapphira) to establish herself in the eyes of others, to regain her place in the world, the voices of the African (slave) characters are suppressed at every turn of the story. But "things go awry." Morrison writes,

> As often happens, characters make claims, impose demands of imaginative accountability over and above the author's will to contain them. Just as Rachel's intervention foils Sapphira's plot, so Cather's urgent need to know and understand this Africanist mother and daughter requires her to give them center stage. The child Cather listens to Till's stories, and the slave, silenced in the narrative, has the final words of the epilogue.[14]

The characters go their own way. According to Morrison, Cather attempts to regain control by having Till utter words that affirm the "elevating benevolence" of the institution of slavery. However, Morrison notes that "Till's voluntary genuflection is as ecstatic as it is suspicious" in that it "subverts the entire premise of the novel." The oppression of Till and her daughter, Nancy (the slave girl), and the domination of body, mind, and spirit of one human being by another to the point that no action is possible even by a mother at the impending rape of her daughter stand in stark contrast to Till's words of support of the very institution that created the structures of catastrophe. The reader can only accept such words as the heartbreaking, conciliatory tone of a subjugated and defeated casualty of slavery. For Morrison, the author appears to be controlled by the fictional process as much as she is in charge of it.

THE RELATIONSHIP BETWEEN READER AND CHARACTER

The reader, while fully understanding the fictional nature of the story, is drawn into the experiences and lifestyles of the characters. The skillful author does not just describe a character, but allows the character to gradually reveal herself through the development of the story and in the interactions with the other characters in the story. In *Poetic Justice*, Martha Nussbaum describes the allure of the novel as follows:

> This novel [*Hard Times*] tells a story. In so doing, it gets its readers involved with the characters, caring about their projects, their hopes, and fears, participating in their attempts to unravel the mysteries and perplexities of their lives. The participation of the reader is made explicit at many points of the narration. And it is brought home to readers that the story is in certain ways their own story, showing possibilities for human life and choice that are in certain respects their own to seize, though their concrete circumstances may differ greatly.[15]

Nussbaum's concern is to move away from the notion of human beings as "abstract, undistinguishable units," as "dream and dots" devoid of history and character. She wishes to reveal human beings in all their richness and individuality, arguing that in this literary presentation of the uniquely individual human being lie the seeds of sympathetic identification of the reader with the character. For Nussbaum, the characters in good literature are not two-dimensional, "cardboard" figures, but are fully fleshed out individuals who take on lives of their own. The reader's task is not just to be open to the workings of the author's imagination but also to uncover the voices of the characters, to step into their lives in a manner that understands their hopes, fears, and joys. In so "communicating" with the characters, in appreciating and exploring their development, their freedom and choice to mature or stagnate, the reader may also further understand the message of the author and the importance or otherwise of what is written and not written. According to Nussbaum, the reader realizes that the character's story in many ways is her own story.

It is in such author-reader-character relationships that the evolution of individual lives in Brahma's world begins to look remarkably like the ripening of a story. Brahma is the first storyteller. Not only is Daśaratha created by Brahma and is thus his "character" and Rāma, the son and "character" created by Daśaratha, but Daśaratha is also the reader of Brahma's and Rāma's stories. Rāma is the reader of Daśaratha's and Brahma's stories. As readers, Daśaratha and Rāma "read" and interpret their own *and* other narrative lives in order to communicate with each other and develop their lives in various ways. In addition, as authors, their thoughts are not wholly controlled by Brahma's reign. However, the interactions with other lives, including Brahma's, preclude Daśaratha and Rāma functioning in the world appearance as isolated, autonomous beings. They are not only authors of their own stories but co-authors of each other's stories. The name "Daśaratha" is attached to the body not just by Brahma, but also by Daśaratha, Rāma, and their entire milieu.

To put it in another way, there are particular ties and bonds among the imaginations of Brahma, Daśaratha, and Rāma. The imagination of Brahma creates the original blueprint, Daśaratha. Daśaratha is the character, as well as reader, of Brahma's world, attempting to deal with all the ramifications as best he can. Daśaratha is also simultaneously the author in that he imposes his own imaginative desires into Brahma's storyline (life is wish fulfillment for him too), and thus is responsible for catapulting the narrative in different directions. His "creation" is Rāma. Rāma follows the same pattern of being simultaneously character, reader, and author of his own path. Rāma's imagination takes the "mind-stuff" of Brahma and Daśaratha and constructs his own story. Rāma's world is influenced by Brahma's and Daśaratha's desires and aversions very much in the way that an author's intentions are portrayed in a novel, but simultaneously, Rāma's own needs and wishes shape and propel his life, impacting his creators' creations in unforeseen ways.

Step 2: Imagination and Moral Development

Vasiṣṭha's second step may well be that just as the functioning of the imagination in stories enhances the moral capabilities of the reader, the creative imagination in Vasiṣṭha's world appearance also enables and enriches the development of the ideal moral character. Stories are read for enjoyment and amusement, but they are also viewed as the vehicles by which readers expand their moral knowledge and explore dilemmas, conflicts, and resolutions. Many cultures use stories to impart messages that are considered valuable to the development of a moral being. Characters in stories are used as role models, even if they do not aspire to the standards set by the society. As Nussbaum and others point out, storybook characters reveal different styles of life, disclosing ways to behave as well as ways not to behave. Through such stories, readers develop self-awareness, gain insights into their own characters, and recognize the complications that may arise not just from weaknesses but also from strengths.

Philosophers, such as Martha Nussbaum and David Novitz, have argued that the creative imagination involved in the act of reading advances the pedagogical function in several ways, two of which are as follows. First, the sheer enjoyment of imaginatively engaging with good fiction disrupts the unremitting flow of ingrained thought patterns and encourages an open-minded tolerance that draws the reader into mundane as well as unfamiliar, even bizarre, worlds. It invites the reader's eye to shifting perspectives, to different ways of looking at the world, the reader's mind to different modes of thinking. Second, the creative imagination promotes compassion and empathetic identification with the life of the "other" in such a manner as to enhance the moral personality of the reader, whether she is the reader of a novel or the "reader" of Vasiṣṭha's world appearance. Each of these features will be discussed in turn as it relates to Vasiṣṭha's fiction analogy.

SHIFTING PERSPECTIVES

For Vasiṣṭha, Brahma himself is the cosmic mind, manifesting out of the pure consciousness that is Brahman and unnaturally given form and matter by imaginative activities (YV III:33–35). The world illusion arises out of Brahma's intense and persistent thoughts born out of the imagination, and this illusion is perceived as real by his creations. By obstinately clinging to their own fantasies, Brahma's creations continue to spin the wheel of delusion. The constituents of the mind, according to Vasiṣṭha, are conception, imagination, thought, and memory. It is by their removal that the mind is dissolved (YV V:91). "Conceptualization or [in other words] imagination is productive of error or sorrow," states Vasiṣṭha, "and it can be so easily got rid of by self-knowledge—and when it is got rid of there is great peace. Why does one find it so difficult?" (YV III:111). By equating imagination with the power of conceptualization, Vasiṣṭha emphasizes the destructive power of the mind.

In spite of such derogatory speech against the workings of the imaginative mind, Vasiṣṭha's own teachings to Rāma interweave philosophical discourse with tales of fantasy. His justification for this departure from academically oriented treatises to poetic literature is that melodious words are required to strike and take possession of the heart. Anything else is "thrown away for nothing, like butter poured upon the burnt ashes of an oblation, and has no power to kindle the flame."[16] For Vasiṣṭha, serious words of scholastic erudition may engage the mind in mental gymnastics, but they do not encourage a spiritual transformation unless they also speak to the heart. So, even while berating the work of the imagination as the obstinate fantasy that abandons the inquiry into self-nature and promotes the distorted perception of the world illusion, Vasiṣṭha's methodology in setting the discourses within the framework of stories, the narrative format, his literary style, and the content of the stories themselves are attempts to awaken the deluded ones to different perspectives on life.

There has to be something more to Vasiṣṭha's initial abhorrence of the imagination. As far as he is concerned, ultimate reality is Brahman, pure, undivided, consciousness, and our task in this world is to come to the realization that the world of multiplicity and individuality that we see around us is just illusion. We are Brahman, *tat tvam asi*. The fool, the seeker, and the enlightened sage are used by or use the imagination in obstructive or helpful ways. Vasiṣṭha's fool single-mindedly pursues bodily and worldly pleasures in the belief that these activities lead to or constitute the good life. The seeker is one such as Rāma, who has all the sensory pleasures that a sixteen-year-old prince may desire and is yet deeply dissatisfied. The dreariness and emptiness of the luxurious life is his greatest challenge, and he seeks a way of living in the world without being overwhelmed and conquered by it. The sage is, of course, the enlightened being who has realized Brahman and lives in the world with that knowledge.

It is in the fool that the imagination runs wild. For Vasiṣṭha, with his thesis that there is only Brahman, the fool's problem stems from ascribing reality to the objects of sense experiences. Vasiṣṭha views the very perception of objects as a psychological illness that has to be cured (YV IV:4, 5, 6). In addition, the fool's imagination drives her desires. In the "darkness of her ignorance," she is entranced by the world appearance and her cravings and aversions gather momentum. The fool's pursuit of sensory pleasures (touch, taste, sight, sound, and smell), as well as wealth, honor, and prosperity, serves to further conceal and distort the highest good, the identity with Brahman. "One should not revel in the filth known as sense pleasures as a worm revels in pus," scolds Vasiṣṭha (YV II:4, 5).

For Vasiṣṭha, the fool is in a deluded state of happiness, unaware that the craving for these pleasures is to be treated with great suspicion as it is most prone to divert her from her true path. Immersed in her imaginative activities, she does not see the poisonous nature of these experiences and the ease with which they plunge her deeper and deeper into the sorrows of life (YV VI:1:6) and away from Brahman. According to Vasiṣṭha, the imagination has a strong impact in that life itself is wish fulfillment. Whatever she desires intensely, the fool secures in this life or the next. Her imaginings drive her cycle of birth after birth. She accelerates on her treadmill of pain and suffering.

Whatever remedy Vasiṣṭha has in mind must deflect the fool from indulging further in this sorry state of affairs. As it is the imaginative mind that is responsible for deciding what is enjoyable and what is distasteful, it is through the workings of the mind that the fool begins her inner transformation. Vasiṣṭha, with his mind-creating havoc thesis, wishes to break the mind-sets that are responsible for the fool's dreadful situation. The fool must come to see the workings of the senses as poisonous and turn the light of enquiry inward towards gaining knowledge of her true nature. For Vasiṣṭha, this effortful practice of controlling the mind and the senses is not to be confused with great exertion, which suggests much gritting of teeth and an internal struggle to subjugate the mind in a forceful manner. Instead, it is a gentle and gradual process that promotes a radical shift in the way in which the individual views not just the phenomenal world around her but also herself. The fool is required to change her "angle of vision" by curtailing or redirecting the deluded imagination away from sense pleasures and towards Brahman.

Vasiṣṭha utilizes stories to initiate this transformation in the fool and the seeker. In the Story of the Three Nonexistent Princes Vasiṣṭha remarks explicitly that "what is known as the creation of the world is no more real than this story of the young boy" (YV III:101). In this story, related by a nanny to her young charge, the three princes, two unborn and the other unconceived, live in a nonexistent city. In their travels, they come across three rivers, two dry and the other waterless. Nevertheless, they have refreshing baths and quench their thirst. They reach a huge city still to be constructed, where they discover three palaces of unimaginable beauty, two of which were still unbuilt and the third with no walls. They cook ninety-nine minus one hundred grams of rice and serve the food on pulverized plates to three holy men, two of whom have no body and the third no mouth. And so on.

With such a story, Vasiṣṭha does not simply portray the world as appearance, a rope appearing as a snake, but also as unreality, a logical impossibility that should not even appear. It is not so much that our senses have led us astray in mistaking one object of the world (the rope) for another (the snake), but the perception of the world as solid and real (the rope as rope) is nonsensical to the point of absurdity, as is the notion of a barren woman's son. With strange tales, Vasiṣṭha stretches the boundaries of credibility to the extreme in order to hatch the metaphysical point that the world is illusion. In so doing, he severs the world's hold on Rāma's mind and senses, fracturing deep-rooted ideas of individuality and multiplicity, separation and discord. Who would believe that disembodied sages ate minus-one gram of rice from plates broken to bits? Who would believe that this world is solid and material? Who would believe that the "I" is disconnected from the "thou"? Rāma and the fool are stopped in their well-worn tracks of delusion.

EMPATHETIC IDENTIFICATION AND COMPASSION

Second, the imagination is said to enhance empathetic identification and compassion for the other, thus encouraging moral sensitivities towards the needs of the other. Vasiṣṭha's road to liberation dissolves the I/ thou duality and promotes a compassionate identification with the other. For Vasiṣṭha, "man is non-different from the mind!" (YV II:9). It is the mind that creates the thought of "I," the ego sense that splits asunder the nondifferentiation between "I" and "thou." In the Story of Dāma, Vyāla, and Kaṭa, Vasiṣṭha explains how the ego sense is responsible for the emotional mind-sets that result in evil thoughts and actions. He draws a clear connection between the ability to do one's job effectively and the impact of the senses. With the incessant functioning of the senses and the deluded imagination that considers sense experiences to be the only reality, dualistic notions, such as "I" and "other," arose in the three demons. They began carving up the world into "I," "you," "what I have," "what you have," "what I would like of what you have," "what I would hate," which then interfered with the proper performance of their duties. The demons, once caught in this vicious cycle, became susceptible to pain and suffering, death and destruction.

Rāma, as seeker after liberation, is in a similar predicament. He operates as a human being and cannot step outside of the human perspective. His sense experiences aggravate and promote the deluded imagination in terms of immoderate desires, emotions, ambitions, and hopes. These in turn serve to encourage the biases and prejudices injected by him into his network of beliefs and severely impair his judgments. He is impeded in the completion of his "job" of becoming a liberated sage, the *mahākartā* (the great doer of actions), the *mahābhoktā* (the great enjoyer), and the *mahātyāgī* (the great renunciate). These obstacles can only be eliminated by the dissolution of the ego which requires the control of the mind. Vasiṣṭha recommends practices, such as meditation and yogic control of life breath (*prāṇa*), to assist in the restraint of the mind.

The goal is a complete transformation of the human mind. According to Vasiṣṭha, this is accomplished by habituation. It is by the persistent practice of meditation and the appropriate redirection of the imagination that egotism is quietened (YV III:22, 23). Through right effort comes the settling into one's true nature, Brahman, pure consciousness. Vasiṣṭha uses an analogy of the relative who moves away (YV VIb:66, 67). The bonds of friendship and love are loosened or strengthened by subsequent events. In the twenty-first century, the relationship may be kept alive by telephone calls, e-mails, and visits, but it may also stagnate and be allowed to die through disuse or kept barely alive with birthday cards. In addition, Vasiṣṭha's emphasis is on the *right* effort. If the relative relocates, calling the previous telephone number and writing to the old address will not yield the proper results. If the relative eases the burden of his journey by clearing out the family bank account and stealing the car, it may be appropriate to take measures for the recovery of belongings but not the relative, except to put him in prison.

Similarly, according to Vasiṣṭha, through our imagination, we forge certain attachments to worldly pleasures. These shackles are strengthened by our proximity to them and our continuous interaction with them. Gradually, through persistent effort of redirected imagination and action, the seeker must loosen the ties that create false relationships with the world. Just as by repetitious performance of certain actions, the seeker develops a mental distance between herself and the thieving relative, in this very same manner, by shouldering the burden of certain mental and physical activities, she cultivates a distance between her mind's imaginative activities and worldly pleasures. In persistently exerting this right effort over her deluded imagination and nurturing the creative imagination that influences her towards Brahman, the seeker winds up with her wayward mind under control and the requisite attitude towards herself and her relationship with the world.

How does this restraint of the ego sense relate to empathy and compassion? The restrained mind has great advantages. Vasiṣṭha is adamant that virtues do not leave the body when the ego sense is dissolved but are enhanced (YV V:90). One of the most entrenched dualities is between "I" and "thou." In the seeker with an overactive ego, the virtues, such as compassion, and a fully fleshed discernment of the "other" as "I" cannot be fully functional because the vices that are generated by the "Me and Mine" factor compete for prominence. When the ego sense dissolves, according to Vasiṣṭha, the deluded imagination that feeds such thoughts is cut off at the root. The mind "dies." Personal cravings and aversions disappear. What was once fertile ground for the flourishing of the vices has been cleared away.

For Vasiṣṭha, when this freedom from the "instincts of acquisition and rejection" becomes an integral part of the agent's nature, it allows for the unconstrained, spontaneous emergence of virtuous qualities, such as desirelessness, peace, friendliness, and compassion (YV V:13, VIb:44). In shifting his thinking beyond the dualities of the world, Rāma has come to an understanding of *tat tvam asi*, That thou Art. Thou art Brahman. Of course, Rāma still has desires, but by no longer thinking, "I," "mine," his behavior is not influenced, motivated, or distorted by such appetites as improper anger, fear, lust, and greed. This "mental distancing" from his own needs and desires feeds his ability to see the other as himself.

This is where Vasiṣṭha's emphasis on morality has such resonance with stories and the fiction analogy. Just as the reading of good literary novels transforms the reader's imagination in such a way as to enrich her relationship with the characters and enhance empathetic identification and compassion, in Vasiṣṭha's world, certain practices such as meditation, right action, right feeling, and *prāṇāyāma,* even the telling of stories, encourage the continued workings of the creative imagination that assist in the breakdown of those debilitating mind-sets that are produced by the ego sense and act as barriers to an expansive reaching out to the "other." The disintegration of these entrenched patterns of thought, the notions of "I," "mine" that solidify the ego-sense, generates a change of perception towards the "other." It promotes the empathetic identification with the other.

Thus, we see that just as an active engagement with stories enhances the moral capabilities of the reader, Vasiṣṭha's world appearance also has a similar pedagogical function. In reading the story, the literary imagination comes into play in influencing the reader towards an open and sympathetic mind and promoting empathetic identification with characters far removed from the reader's own milieu. This creative imagination is also central to Vasiṣṭha's world appearance. The journey from fool to seeker to sage is all about transforming the fool's deluded imagination that is entangled with the world appearance into the creative imagination that sees the world as just a story and Brahman as the only reality. Once the barriers between "I" and "thou" are dissolved, the virtues of empathy and compassion are allowed free reign. Just as the reader is not prevented from entering into the lives of the characters occupying a fictional world, as long as the mental constraints such as "I" and "thou" are removed, the physical boundaries of skin, the barriers of flesh and bone, do not prevent Rāma from "stepping" into the *cittākāśa*,[17] the mental space, of the "other" and seeing the other as Brahman, as nondifferent from himself. He has taken the most important step on his path towards the realization of Brahman.

Step 3: Morality Justified

Vasiṣṭha may then conclude that given the special function of the creative imagination, it makes sense for the sage, who knows the world is illusion, to evolve into Vasiṣṭha's ideal moral being. How does this work? The shifting perspectives and the emotions generated by good fiction assist in the identification of reader and character. In the real world too, they encourage the stepping into the shoes of others, in generating concern over what happens to others and the willingness to stick one's neck out for the sake of others. However, it is often argued that empathetic identification alone, the ability to understand the troubles of the characters from their perspective, does not adequately capture the full extent of the responsibilities of the reader. Emotions can play one false and lead the reader down the wrong road. She may be drawn towards one character rather than another simply because she delights in one character more than another or has suffered certain experiences that allow her to place herself more readily in the shoes of one rather than another. Such a stance impairs the impartiality also necessary for accurate moral judgments.[18] How can the reader differentiate between trustworthy and untrustworthy emotions and enhance the ties between reader and character? Martha Nussbaum's solution is that of the judicious spectator.[19] Vasiṣṭha, centuries earlier, emphasizes that the sage is both removed witness and involved participant in the world story.

For Vasiṣṭha, it is the fashioning of this intact and integrated personality of participant and witness that is of profound importance to the development of the sage's ideal moral nature and her embodiment as *mahākartā, mahābhoktā,* and *mahātyāgī*. The sage is the involved participant, the great doer of actions and the great enjoyer, performing "appropriate actions in natural situations" and "enjoying all natural experiences," natural in that these situations and experiences are unaffected by her ego sense, likes, and dislikes. Rāma's questions to Vasiṣṭha express the need to live in a world that is full of pain and death. He has responsibilities to his people and kingdom. "How do you people who are enlightened live in this world?" asks Rāma (YV I:30–31). In addition, the sage also understands the world as illusion and "remains as witness of everything," without being swayed by dualities such as success and failure, pain and pleasure. She is free of the ego sense that generates unbridled emotions and passions. Her senses function on an even keel. She is no longer caught up in her web of thoughts and swayed by the emotions and preferences that seek her own advantage. In "effortlessly and naturally wearing the body," nothing goes against the grain of her desires. Her body may be subject to pleasures and pains, but no notions of seeking happiness or warding off unhappiness arise in her mind. Her heart rests in equanimity (YV VIa:116,117).

It is important to note that this "desireless" state is not indifference to the condition of the world or the elimination of *all* desires. Whether secluded in a cave or ruling a kingdom, Vasiṣṭha's sage lives and acts in the world, but she is no longer troubled, consciously or subconsciously, by conflicting emotions and desires. Vasiṣṭha notes that "the desire that arises in the course of one's natural functions devoid of craving is that of a liberated sage" (YV V:17). Of course, she still has desires, but it is a nonvolitional desire in that she is not beset by her own aversions and cravings and thus views her surroundings with equanimity. Vasiṣṭha speaks of this desire as the desire that existed even before contact with objects began. It is the natural attention given by the sage who is no longer afflicted by the ego sense and thoughts of "I" and "mine" (YV V:17).[20]

Thus, the analogy with fiction allows an explanation for the sage's *sattva* character in a world she knows is illusion. It must be understood that Vasiṣṭha's sage has no mandate to return to the hustle and bustle of city life and earnestly busy herself in the "saving" of other beings. After liberation she may end up as teacher to many seekers, but equally she may choose to stay isolated in a forest, or she may return to her life and duties as a member of a family and community. Whatever she decides, she is still the participant and witness of the lives of the sentient and nonsentient beings that surround her. The nature of the sage is that outwardly she appears very energetic and lively, engaging in righteous conduct, but inwardly she is no longer bound by her own aspirations, needs, and desires. Inwardly she is "swimming in the bliss of the self" (YV VIb:29), ever at equilibrium, her heart and mind at peace (YV V:75).

IV

There are problems associated with this analogy based on fiction. As far as the identity of Vasiṣṭha's world appearance with story is concerned, it may be argued that the stance that there are similarities between an individual's life and the lives of author, reader, and character is ridiculous, particularly in the notion that life is wish fulfillment. If life is indeed the consummation of desires, the critic notes, why are there so many trials and tribulations? If desires are satisfied, everyone should be living happy and contented lives. Vasiṣṭha's neat response is that in the fervor and intensity of the desire, people do not take account of all the ramifications of its actualization.[21] In the Story of Karkaṭī, Vasiṣṭha reveals the unpleasant consequences awaiting the unprepared mind.

Karkaṭī is a terrible demoness who is always hungry. To alleviate her hunger, she hits upon a plan to eat all the people of Jambūdvīpa in a single meal. She performs severe austerities. The Creator God, Brahma, appears before her and grants her wish of becoming Sūcikā, a tiny "living steel pin," a needle, that has the added advantage of being accompanied by cholera (Viṣūcikā). As a cholera-infected needle, she is able to "consume," inflict pain and death, on those who indulge in unhealthy living. Karkaṭī, in the midst of her ambition, fails to discern all the ramifications of her boon. As a needle, she is unable to travel and has to wait for the people to come to her. This puts a limit on the number of people she can consume in a single meal. In addition, cholera also does not live in a wholesome environment. "Sūcikā" is trapped in places of dirt and decay. Rats, fleas, and other vermin are her constant companions. As Vasiṣṭha comments, "How strange, the deluded ones do not have foresight. The selfish person's violent efforts to gain his selfish ends often leads to other results, even as a person is unable to see his face when he runs to the mirror puffing and panting—his own breath mists the mirror" (YV III:70).

This is a plausible view. If the mind is at unrest or in turmoil, there is no end to the fabrications that it can produce unaided by alcohol or drugs. As Vasiṣṭha notes, it is one's own mentality that transforms "sweet things into bitter things and "friends into enemies" (YV III:59, 60).

Even in the duration of just one life, the mind can create havoc. Given the shenanigans of the mind, there is no neutral eye with which to see things and situations exactly as they are. One's own mental imaginings and frustrations influence perceptions of the world and manufacture the difference between heaven and hell. Vasiṣṭha may argue confidently that the notion of life as wish fulfillment is not that far-fetched in that we have the tendency to stubbornly see only what we want to see.

Another objection that can be raised is whether, as Vasiṣṭha argues, egolessness spontaneously promotes virtuous qualities, such as friendliness and compassion. The Story of the Three Demons, Dāma, Vyāla, and Kaṭa, does not have a happy ending in so far as their ego-filled selves are defeated by the gods, and they flee to the netherworlds to escape the wrath of their creator, the demon king Saṃbara. However, Saṃbara, having learned from his mistakes, creates three other demons, Bhīma, Bhāsa, and Dṛḍha, now equipped with "self-knowledge and wisdom" so that they do not succumb to the pitfalls of the ego sense. Vasiṣṭha describes these demons as "devoted to appropriate action in the present, free from all attachment, devoid of the feeling "I did this," intent on doing the work allotted to them by their master, free from desire and from aversion, and endowed with equal vision" (YV IV:34). These demons succeed in defeating the gods, and it is only through the intervention of Lord Viṣṇu himself that they themselves are slain. According to Vasiṣṭha, as soon as their bodies fell, they were enlightened as they were devoid of ego sense. The three demons are described as "endowed with self-knowledge, full of dispassion and sinless" (YV IV:34), even attaining liberation at death, but they are seemingly fighting for the wrong side.

This may not be such a problem in that Saṃbara is not described as an evil despot. In fact, he is much more of a celebrated sorcerer who creates magical cities with beautiful gardens and temples. The jealous gods do feel threatened and terrorized by him. They wage war against the demons at every opportune moment as when Saṃbara is asleep (demons sleep for millennia) or out of the city. Saṃbara then takes revenge and finally ends up being killed by Viṣṇu. However, it is important to note that Vasiṣṭha is adamant that egolessness, the freedom from personal cravings and aversions, results in the spontaneous emergence of all the virtuous qualities. This requires further clarification as the demons possess the egolessness so necessary for liberation and yet are killing machines.

Vasiṣṭha responds with the necessity of childhood training and the presence of the exemplar (YV II:7, 8). He emphasizes the importance of good childhood education in various ways. Rāma, for example, is described as "not yet sixteen years old" (YV I:7, 8, 9). And yet by this age, he had lived in the hermitage of his preceptor and, of his own accord, visited the holy places of pilgrimage (I:3), illustrating the proper care taken in his training. Rāma, in fact, asks, "How is it possible for an ignorant person born in a wicked family and who does not enjoy the company of holy ones to cross this ocean of *saṃsāra?*" (YV VIa:126). Vasiṣṭha's immediate reply is "accidental coincidence." This is not very informative as an example of "accidental coincidence" is given as the fruit of a coconut palm appearing to have been dislodged by a crow that just happened to alight on the tree at that very moment (YV V:9). It just so happened that the bad man became good. However, Vasiṣṭha's claim is that what appears to be inexplicable and put down to fate is "none other than self-effort of a past incarnation" (YV II:4, 5). Good actions in past lives or in the present result in future benefits. Vasiṣṭha also asserts that the very desire to undertake the inquiry into the nature of the self can bring about a change for the better (YV III:102). It must necessarily be an extremely slow process, but Vasiṣṭha is helped by his fool having several lifetimes to perfect this task. A good upbringing improves the chances of producing a seeker rather than a fool.

Vasiṣṭha's second response to the problem of whether egolessness produces the *sattva* character is to introduce the exemplar. The mere following of scriptural instructions, even to the letter, does not guarantee that Rāma acquires the correct mental habits. According to Vasiṣṭha, the "mind is a field" that "is ploughed by right action" and "watered day and night by right feeling" (YV VIb:44). The meaning of such scriptural declarations is exemplified in the manner in which Vasiṣṭha himself acts. Equanimity, understanding, and knowledge, among other things, give the sage the ability to render an accurate reading of the situation and effortlessly respond to it as needed. She is the standard by which appropriate behavior and good character are judged. The seeker has to develop the emotional responses and the deliberative skills of the sage and can do no better than to follow in the footsteps of such a person. The sage is the exemplar whom the seeker emulates. Mirroring the exemplar's behavior augments the habits that create a stable and honorable character.

In Vasiṣṭha's world appearance, the initial gulf between seeker and teacher and the entrenched separation of "I" and "thou" present the opportunities for learning and are used as tools for the teaching of compassionate union with other sentient beings. Without the exemplar-teacher, the seeker may be in danger of being engulfed by her more self-serving character traits and may well end up cultivating expertise in displaying a facade of goodness rather than intrinsic goodness itself.[22]

V

At the end of the day, it seems that what the dream analogy cannot do, the story analogy can. The fiction analogy has many levels. First, the Russian doll-type set-up of the YV exposes the utterly fictional nature of the story world (in which the reader is initially ensnared) and allows her to wonder about the reality of her own world. Second, the character development seen in stories is reflected in Vasiṣṭha's world, in the development from fool to seeker to sage, and reveals to the seeker some of the steps that she has to undertake in her road to liberation. The content of stories breaks the hold of the deluded imagination and brings the creative imagination into play. Third, the workings of the literary imagination mirror the workings of Vasiṣṭha's creative imagination, which, through egolessness, generates the virtues of compassion and empathy. Fourth, the compassionate identification of the reader with the fictional character, in the form of the witness, provides the explanation as to why the enlightened being continues her work, even though she knows that the world appearance and all its occupants are illusion. The sage is both witness to the world appearance and participant in the world appearance. Finally, just as the manifold universe emanates from the one Brahman and then returns to it, the storybook characters originate from the imaginative process of the one author and dissolve in the mind of the one reader.

The dream analogy is predominantly a description of the malady. In likening the world to a dream, Vasiṣṭha unveils the human condition in all its transient pleasures and underlying sorrows. The dreamer is the creator as well as the participant in her dream world, but the dreamer does not know that she is the originator of the dream. She is powerless and hurled around in the dream. This sense of helplessness and the undetectably false impression of objectivity epitomize the predicament of the fool. The world forces itself on the fool just as the dream captures the dreamer. The fiction analogy is the remedy. It details the steps necessary to enhance the humanity of the human condition. The insight of the fiction analogy, its aspect as remedy, is that the heroic transformation of the moral psyche is available in story rather than dream. Authors and readers do become the victims of their own stories as well. They are drawn into their stories as much as the dreamer is pulled into the dream. However, in fiction, at least in good fiction, one has the option of stepping back, of being the impartial witness. The capacity for independent effort gives the elbow room necessary for moral improvement.[23]

And yet it is a mistake to read this chapter as rejecting the dream analogy and adopting the fiction analogy as a sharp division between the two; the dream analogy for the fool and the fiction analogy for the sage. It must be emphasized and accepted that neither analogy is complete in itself. Dream and fiction seep into one another, and this leaves open further avenues of exploration, particularly in the different ways in which dream and fiction mesh together and the impact of such a "seeping" on the journey from fool to seeker to sage. There are no sharp divisions between the fool and the seeker, the seeker and the sage. One gradually moves from being a fool to seeker to sage. One can be the foolish seeker or the seeking fool. The moral consequences of such a gradual shift on the individual may be clarified by a greater understanding of the interactions between dream and story.

The YV is a philosophically ingenious text in that it is self-referential, a feedback loop that begins with story and ends in story. The stories introduce the reader to the realization that her own world may be just "storying" too, that the I/thou distinctions so painstakingly guarded by her ego are as fictional as the "I" of the storybook character. If the illusionism of the YV world is viewed as a story, then each one of us can be seen as a storyteller, who is the author, reader, and the character of the narrative. This turning back and inward into our own lives captures the ego that is nourished by life stories and simultaneously destroyed, allowing us, the fools, and the seekers, to emerge individually as the liberated sage who embodies Brahman in the world. At the end of the day, Brahman is the world, and the world is Brahman. As Vasiṣṭha notes in his concluding teachings to Rāma, "the ordinary life itself is the supreme state."[24]

Notes

1. As the author is unknown, for the sake of convenience I will use the name of her (or his) protagonist, Vasiṣṭha.

2. See Eliot Deutsch, *Advaita Vedānta: A Philosophical Reconstruction* (Honolulu: University of Hawaii Press, 1973), for an elegant explanation of the three levels of being.

3. All quotations are taken from Swami Venkatesananda, *Vasiṣṭha's Yoga* (Albany: State University of New York Press, 1993) unless otherwise stated.

4. Vasiṣṭha's references to the four factors are many and scattered throughout the text. As a preliminary exploration, please see VI.1 and 2.

5. Vasiṣṭha classifies the personalities of human beings as fool, seeker, and enlightened sage, the *jīvanmukta* (III:54), depending on their spiritual depth. The story of Līlā gives an interesting portrayal of this journey.

6. In using the words "story" and "fiction" in this chapter, I will be mainly concerned with short stories and novels rather than theater, film, and opera. Vasiṣṭha is after all a storyteller in this vein. However, make-believe plays a significant role in all of these arts, and they do sit comfortably inside the analogy.

7. Of course wish fulfillment is also a strong factor in dreams. Dreams can be incredibly self-serving and the product of deep-seated cravings. However, the convoluted workings of Vasiṣṭha's imagination, which conjure up an entire kingdom furnished with well-known individuals and familiar events, make this venture into wish fulfillment more compatible with the unfolding of a story than a dream.

8. Another explanation for the resemblance between the two Līlās could be a deep wish of Padma to marry an exact replica of his wife in future lives.

9. Martha Nussbaum: *Poetic Justice: The Literary Imagination and Public Life* (Massachusetts: Beacon Press, 1995).

10. David Novitz, *Knowledge, Fiction and Imagination* (Philadelphia: Temple University Press, 1987).

11. Toni Morrison: *Playing in the Dark: Whiteness and the Literary Imagination* (New York: Vintage Books, 1993).

12. Novitz, 37.

13. William Carlos Williams, *Imaginations* (New York: New Directions Publishing Corporation, 1971), 89.

14. Morrison, *Playing in the Dark*, 28.

15. Nussbaum, 31.

16. Mitra Vihari Lala, trans., *The Yoga-Vāsiṣṭha-Mahārāmāyana of Vālmīki* (Delhi: Indological Book House, 1988), vol. I, 3:84.45–47.

17. Vasiṣṭha utilizes three conceptions of space: *cidākāśa*, the space of pure consciousness; *cittākāśa*, the psychological space of individual minds; and *bhutakaśa*, the physical space. This has interesting implications for the world story, which will be developed at some later date.

18. See, for example, Richard A. Posner, "Against Ethical Criticism," *Philosophy and Literature* 21, no. 1 (1997).

19. Martha Nussbaum, *Poetic Justice: The Literary Imagination and Public Life* (Massachusetts: Beacon Press, 1995).

20. There is still the question as to why the sage is desireless in the morally appropriate way rather than apathetic and indifferent to the world's turmoil. This issue will be dealt with at some later date.

21. It must not be forgotten that Vasiṣṭha is adamant that we are coauthors of our story and the stories of others. This aspect will be explored at a later date.

22. Although rare in the YV, there are seemingly exceptions to this rule. King Janaka, for example, attains liberation solely through his own efforts.

Vasiṣṭha's response is that Janaka met with sages in previous lifetimes. His liberation in this life is the culmination of his efforts through these previous encounters.

23. I am grateful to Arindam Chakrabarti for this interesting depiction of "malady" and "remedy."

24. *Vasiṣṭha's Yoga,* 6.2:175.

11

A Horrid Treehouse or a Charming City?

Yogavāsiṣṭha (*Mokṣopāya*) on Spiritual Culture of the Body

Arindam Chakrabarti

> Just as there is no difference of meaning between "water" and "aqua," the meaning of the word "brahman" is the same as the meaning of the word "body."
>
> —YV VII:210.20

The Field and the Knower of the Field: Do I Find Myself in the World?

If I write a book describing the world as I *found* it, should I include myself in it? Wittgenstein worried about this question (Ludwig Wittgenstein, Tractatus Logico-Philosophicus, ed. Marc A Joseph. Tonawanda: Broadview Press, 2014, 139).[1] He decided that none of us should include himself or herself in the world that he or she finds, because the self, the "I," like the eye of the viewer, stays outside the visual field, stays just outside the limit of the world that is found. But since the world includes all that is there, there should be nothing outside the world. (Wittgenstein evades this threat of inconsistency by defining the world as the totality of facts, not the totality of things.) So, to speak of this self in the same terms as items—facts or objects—in the world would be to produce nonsense. The question comes back to the Upaniṣadic question, now reappearing in some work in brain/consciousness studies: "How can one know the knower, find the finder, see the seer?"

If *Der Welt*—all that is the case—is natural, the self seems, somehow, non-natural or outside the world, like ethical values. Ethics is, in this sense, "transcendental": beyond descriptive words which can depict scientific facts.[2]

"Ātman" is the ancient Sanskrit word for both the self and the body, whatever is referred to as "I." Ātman is not seen, but *ought to be seen*: *ātmā vā're draṣṭavyaḥ* (BU II:5). And the first and last field of physical culture or spiritual cultivation—the subjective body or embodied subject I call "myself" or "me"—is in between the natural world of facts and the transcendental world of consciousness, conscience and morals. Do I work in and with my body, finding it as an object besides other objects, or does my self-aware body (not just my brain, which is not directly self-aware), standing both inside and outside nature, find and transform me? Such questions are not easy to formulate, let alone answer, clearly.

In one important sense, Nature is all that is "found," all that is given to the senses as already happening, as taking *time* to take *place*. Culture, on the other hand, is what we do to use, develop, improve, and add value to nature. To use Rabindranath Tagore's phrase, culture is the "Surplus in Man" (*vide*: his *Religion of Man*). If nature *happens*, culture is the "more" that is *to be done*. Nature is found; culture is made. Nature is studied by the sciences; culture is brought about by ethics, religion, the arts, and technology. If nature corresponds to the ancient Indian *prakṛti*, then culture would correspond to *dharma, kṛṣṭi, śilpa,* and *kalā,*—and as I shall claim at the end of this chapter—*yajña*—to be practiced by living embodied personal and interpersonal consciousness, *puruṣa*.

This self and its body are understood, from at least as early as the Mahābhārata, as the knower-of-the-field and the field. The thirteenth chapter of the *Bhagavad Gītā*, named after this pair of concepts, defines "the field" first as "this body" (where the "this" is to be noted, since, as an indexical "this" cannot be defined except in terms of the "I" and "now," there being no "*idam*" without "*aham*" and "idānīm"). It then goes on to break up the elements of the field into the five material elements—ego-maker, intellect, the Unmanifest energy which evolves into all these, the ten sense organs—and their accessible objects—desire, aversion, pleasure, pain, the collocation (*saṃghāta)*, sentience (*cetanā*), and stability or maintenance (*dhṛti*). The mental and the physical, the inner and the outer, are inseparably intertwined in this list of parts of the body. The last three elements remind us of ancient Indian medicine—*Caraka Saṃhitā*—which uses words like *saṃhanana* (collocation) and *dhāri* (what holds and maintains them all) for the human body.

The concept of the "field" (*kṣetra*) brings back together the two contrasted concepts of nature and culture, happening and making, objects of science and objectives of art. Think of the farmer as the "knower-of-the-field." He grows food-grains in a field, by cultivating the land. With our mundane, intellectual, and soteriological aspirations, we use the body to grow. (The idea of sowing seeds and growing a crop is etymologically packed into one Sanskrit word for the body: *vapu,* just as the idea of the body as a woven textile or text is enshrined in another word for the body: *tanu*). We cultivate ourselves in the process, staying outside and inside nature. The farmers depend on earth, water, minerals, rain, seeds, the atmosphere, and the sun but also have to use their individual and collective knowledge and ingenuity. And we depend on our hands, our legs, our tongue, our reproductive and digestive organs, which are all natural given objects we have *found,* unless one uses a prosthesis or a tool as a hand or foot. But it is we, we claim, who have transformed the field by hard toil and ingenuity into a source of nourishing, cookable, edible, sellable, sharable, offerable, tasty food. Hence the BG says: "This body, O Son of Kunti, is called 'the field,' and one who knows it is called 'the knower of the field' " (BG XII:I).

Of course, here the BG is not alluding to the tradition of physical culture (Haṭha Yoga or body-building) or the arts of cosmetics, which were both rather important *kalās* listed among the sixty-four arts of ancient and medieval India. Immediately following this description, the BG, in this context, goes on to identify the "knowledge" which makes one "knower" of the field, with eighteen inner virtues of the mind or the inner body, such as humility, lack-of-egotism, nonviolence, forgiveness, frankness, and authenticity (BG XIII:8–12).

If we study the subjective body as the field, the distinction and relation between nature and culture would become clearer, unless, of course, the distinction tends, unexpectedly, to melt away altogether. Such merging of nature and culture could, of course, happen with a deeper engagement with the theory of Karma where causality assumes a fundamentally ethical character—you get the environment and body you deserve by your actions. But that is another story.

Even if we start with the concept of Nature as the World which is other than ourselves, "The world," Iris Murdoch remarks, "is not given to us 'on a plate,' it is given to us as a creative task . . . We work, using or failing to use our honesty, our courage, our truthful imagination, at the interpretation of what is present to us, as we. . . . 'make something of it.' We help it to be. We work at the meeting point where we deal with a world which is other than ourselves."[3] This meeting point, I submit, is the body. The "cultural" work of world-making goes on most poignantly and perpetually in our own bodies, at the frontiers of the skin where "I seem to end and the other seems to begin."

One of the reasons why human beings do not just stay content with nature and their own bodies as they find it, and want to cultivate the field, use, fix, and fiddle with nature, and thus indulge in artistic and technological creativity, is that they—with the stir of egotistic desire planted in them by their very nature—find nature, including their own psycho-physical make-up, not good enough as it is found or given. This initial discontent with nature makes them want to make it *better* or make it *different* or make it *new*. This normative urge to *improve, transform,* and *renew* lies at the core of cultural creativity. This tendency to exceed, I believe, is already alluded to by the timeless Hymn to Man (Puruṣa Sūkta) of the Ṛg Veda (maṇḍala X), which announces that the thousand-headed, thousand-eyed, thousand-footed Person fills up all times and all space and then exceeds all this by ten fingers![4]

Thus, in India, China, and Greece were developed rich and diverse traditions of body culture, or gymnastics and martial arts, of exercise and dance, of games and yoga, of ritual attire and festive adornment, a virtue ethic, and an elaborate aesthetic of refinement of the senses. Such renewal, transformation, and improvement is Culture: "*kṛṣṭi*" or "*saṃskāra*." Following Bhartṛhari's (*Vākyapadīya,* Kaṇḍa 1, 144–46) views about the relation between language and refinement, we could assume that before a sound is recognized as a particular word in a language, both the hearing of the listener as well as the pronunciation of the speaker must undergo sophistication and training, just as for sophisticated visual perception of an artistic drawing, both the drawing as well the eyes need to be "cultivated." Listening to Indian classical vocal music, for example, requires *saṃskāra* distilling, training with a view to meeting a standard, of both the voice and the ears. And such training has to be actively received from a tradition-sanctioned source of creative excellence for the result to count as "cultured."

Before we get into the central agenda of this chapter, a close analysis of *Yogavāsiṣṭha*'s (YV) complex attitude towards the nature and culture of the subjective human body, I would like to note just one grammatical-etymological feature of *puruṣakāra* (self-effort), which is a key term of this text. Spiritual and metaphysical wisdom is at the service of *puruṣakāra*. We need to know the nature of mind and its place in nature for us to make self-effort to live well and flourish in this world. Notice how the word combines spirit and matter, consciousness and action, in the parts *puruṣa* and *kāra*. *Kāra* is of course derived from the same root *kṛ* from which *prakṛti* is also derived. In *puruṣakāra,* therefore, *puruṣa* and *prakṛti* come together. By becoming active, the embodied Self or Person gets willingly embroiled in nature. Freedom comes from involvement. And my guess is that at least moral and spiritual "culture" is another name for such engaged emancipation, such creative freedom in happy involvement in the causal mechanics of nature work. Thus, only by doing actions with a particular philosophical and spiritual culture, one should wish to live for a full term of a hundred years, because thus—and in no other way—do actions not cling on to man (*Īśā Upaniṣad* verse 2)[5]. Hence *Mokṣopāya* (MU; the real name of YV, a text of approximately thirty-two-thousand verses coming from eighth-century Kashmir) predicts that in the living liberated person, a perfectly cultured urbanity should spontaneously be manifested: "*parā nāgaratā udeti*" (YV II:18.8). When "refinement"(*saṃskāra*) comes in the intellect, by slowly practicing rational reflection and argumentation, says Vasiṣṭha, then a supreme cultured civility (*nāgaratā*), rich with great virtues, dawns on the character of the person who can intelligently see what lies before and after, cause and effect, like a person walking at night, with a bright lamp.

The Touch of the Hand and Inner Thrill in *Yogavāsiṣṭha*

We have already alluded to the description, in Ṛg Veda, of the thousand-headed, thousand-eyed, thousand-footed Primal Man first arising "in the beginning"—a description that uses the visceral metaphor of it filling up all the earth, and then exceeding it all 'by ten fingers." Why "fingers?" Aristotle and Kant have both found in the structure of the human hand a prefiguring of that rationality which makes man special. In the human body it is the hands which instrumentally and symbolically represent art, craft, and work. Even John Locke talks about the "work of our hands." It is the hand and its ten fingers with which all the crafts of "homo faber" are processed, and of course, the perversion of the hands' purposes converts the writer's grip of the pen, or a musician's plucking of the string, to a killer's grip of the knife or a gunman's pulling of the trigger. The surplus of excellence in Man also runs the risk of surplus evil.

A sudden mention of the thumb and the fingers in the *Utpatti Prakaraṇa* of YV gives the hint that, for a focused "self-cultivator," the tips of the fingers tingle with the same subjectivity which unifies everything in the universe according to nondualistic systems of thought. Here is the text:

> anguṣṭhasy ātha cāṅgulyā vātādyaspars'ane sati/
> jīvatas cetaso rūpam tad rūpam paramātmanaḥ //

> In an alive person there is a form of sentience at the contact
> of the thumb and the tip of a finger, even when there is
> no touch of any wind or anything external. This inner feel
> of living mind, indeed, is the form of that supreme Self.
> (YV III:10.42)

The beginning of any meditative calming down of the mind in a lotus posture, with the open palms on the two knees, is the point where one is often required to find the pulse and feel the *prāṇa* all over the body starting from these joined tips.

Our flexible fingers not only allow us to touch and tell the environment, to caress those whom we love, but also to touch themselves. Only touch and the haptic sensory modality give us a glimpse of that mystery of self-consciousness.

This also explains, for me, why Abhinavagupta opens his gloss on the ninth "Hand" chapter of *Nātyaśāstra* with this following "touchy feely" description of his personal spiritual experience:

> alamkriyante gātrāṇi yat-sparśa vivaśa sthiteh
> sparśa tanmātra vapuṣam saṃstumah parameśvaram/

> We sing the praises of that Supreme Lord, who assumes
> the form of touchable sense-essence when the body
> wears
> the natural ornament of goose-flesh, due to a rapture
> caused by His inner touch felt all over.[6]

It is remarkable that he calls this "natural" hair-raising thrill an ornamentation of the body, since ornaments are the most obvious example of "cultural" adornment!

Five Layers of Embodiment in Upaniṣads

Because it is too well-known, I did not start my reflections on the body with the Upaniṣadic step-by-step analysis of embodiment. We first think of ourselves as this gross body of flesh and blood which is nourished by food. Hence this is called the Food Self—the eater who is eaten up by his own food. Then comes the slightly subtler but still physical breathing self, in relation to which the food-self is a mere outer sheath. The next psychic self is the inner sense-organ lording over other afferent sensations, which uses the breathing body as its outer insulation. The wishing-imagining-choosing mental self, in turn, becomes the outer body of Reason (individuated by the ego), the self which consists of *vijñana* or understanding. In deep sleep even that self appears to be a dispensable body, and the bliss of total ignorance becomes the innermost self. Thus, food, breath, mind, intellect, and bliss become the five successively inner bodies of a human being.

There are two central philosophical messages of this graduated picture. First, there is no sheer body and pure self. Just as "is large" is a vague predicate such that there is no sharp cut-off point where small ends and large begins, "is a body" is also a vague predicate so that there is no sharp point where body ends and soul begins. But just as "X is larger than Y" can be well defined, "X is the body of Y" is a multiply satisfiable schema which can hold clearly between many ordered pairs. This is the relation of embodiment which many successive pairs can exhibit between themselves. The second lesson is that even the vestigial ego self in deep sleep could be thought of as the last causal body for the indescribable pure consciousness which is no one's object and hence no one's body.

Instead of going into this deep metaphysics of the five grades of embodiment, I chose to start with a semiotic close-up on one part of the body which is most closely related to human work and labor: the hands.

The source of classical Indian philosophies of the body is, of course, the Ṛg Veda and the Upaniṣads. A special hymn of the *khila* part (appendix) of the Ṛg Veda describes the body as a "ten-fold machine" which is the "source"(*daśa-yantram, utsam*).

Listing eyes, ears, inner sense, speech, in-breath, out-breath, chest, back, hands, arms, thighs, abdomen, head, body hair, flesh, blood, and bones, it then compares human embodiment with bubbles forming in water. But, within the body, the face is the most important part, commanding its own sacred mantra, which calls the speaker's own mouth the jewel box of the body.

> bhruvau lalāte ca tathā ca karnau hanū kapolau/
> . . . mukha-ratna-kośam

> The two eye-brows, the two sides of the forehead,
> then the ears, the jaws, and the cheeks . . . this jewel-box of the face.

The principle of classification is rather unclear in such ancient passages, and indeed the concept of a faculty, organ, or limb of a body became moot in later systemic Indian thought.

Abhinavagupta (Mālinī Vijaya Vārtika I:530–34) raises serious problems for the standard Sāṃkhya conception of active organs. To go back to our initial example of the motor organ "hands"(*pāṇi-indriya*), its defining function is "getting hold of things" or "grasping"(*grahaṇam*). He analyzes the concept grasping as mine-making: "coming to own what is not one's own" (grahaṇam ca kim ucyeta? svīkāro yadi sammatah/ asvasya svasya karaṇam svīkāra iti bhaṇyate). But then, what is the "ego" in relation to which "own" and "not own" would be decided? Perhaps this *svīkaraṇa* is another name for *ahaṃkāra* function, which is also hinted by the simple Sanskrit name for hand, *"kara,"* the ultimate *doing* instrument, when what is done is own-making. And since any going from one's current place to another place also counts as making what is not one's own (a location) one's own, feet should count as a sort of hands! (Similar criticisms of the Sāṃkhya/ Vedānta concept of *karmendriyas* are found in Jayantabhatta as well.)

What Happens between the Heel and the Head: The Mahābhārata's Meditations on the Body and Senses

In the *Mokṣadharmaparvan* of the 12th book of the Mahābhārata there is a very robust verse which says:

> yad ūrdhvam pāda-talayor avāṅmūrdhnaśca paśyasi/
> etasmin eva kṛtsneyam vartate buddhir antare.

> "All this understanding happens between these limits,
> whatever you see above the bottom of the heels and below

the crown of the head."
(MB XII:285.14)

Thus, all the yoga and spirituality of the Mahābhārata is anchored in the mindfulness towards the minutely noticed body. *The concept of spirituality, of course, is one of the most confused concepts.* It is not accidental that the Sanskrit word *adhyātmika,* which we have adopted as a translation of the English word "spiritual" originally meant "having to do with one's own body." For any fundamental element of the metaphysics of the Upaniṣads, there would be three levels of exposition: the level of the divinities *adhidaivata,* the level of the material external world *adhibhūta,* and finally the level of the analyzed bodily subjectivity: *adhyātma.* In the fourteenth book of the epic, there are many chapters devoted to the representation of the body as a sacrificial scenario with ten priests or with seven priests, and so on. The main moral of all this has been beautifully brought out by Abhinavagupta in his brilliantly original interpretation of a famous verse of the BG: "One who consumes things given by the gods without giving offerings to them first, is a thief." Abhinavagupta interprets that in a novel way. The senses are the gods in our bodies. Indeed Nīlakaṇṭha, the commentator on the Mahābhārata interprets the terms "deva" as sense organs quite often. It is thanks to them that we are able to do any conscious acts. As we see in Old and New Nyāya, the contact between the inner sense and the organ of touch—the skin-mind contact, so to speak—is a necessary condition for any cognition, not just for the perceptual but even for the most abstract thinking or imagining to happen. So, in the name of meditating or withdrawing into a suprasensory world, no one can afford to lose *touch* with their body. If someone does not give the senses their due, such a person is a thief or a fraud. Philosophical thinking, therefore, must start by paying back its debt to the body and its senses, thanks to which any thinking, after all, is possible. To try to be philosophical and spiritual, while ignoring the body and starving the sense organs is a kind of ungrateful act of deception or even theft. From another point of view, this is the denial of any rift between knowledge and action. Abhinavagupta remarks:

jñānam karmaṇā rahitam na bhavati, karma ca kausalopetam
jñāna rahitam na bhavati, ityekam eva vastu jñāna
karmaṇī, . . . tasmat jñanantarvarti karma
aparihāryam . . .

karmendriyaiśca na karoti, avaśyam tarhi manāsā
karoti, pratyūta mūḍhācārah.
Knowledge cannot be without work, and any work, as
long
as it is deliberate and skillful, cannot be without knowledge.

Thus knowledge and work are indistinguishably the same.
Therefore, in the middle of all awareness or
cognition, actions are unavoidable. If they are not done
with motor organs, then surely they are done in the mind,
in imagination, but sometimes a meditator self-deceptively
assumes oneself to be inactive.
(BG III:12, Commentary)

From this analysis, a certain recommendation of authentic life-style follows:

Viṣayayāh indriyair devair eva dattāh, yadi teṣām eva
upabhogāya na dīyante tarhi, stenatvam cauryam syāt,
chhadmacāritvāṭ uktam hi purvameva bhagavatā "mūḍhācārah
sa ucyate iti. Ato'yam vākyārthah: yah sukhopāyam
siddhim apavargam vā prepsati, tena inḋriya kautuka
nivṛttimātra phalatayā eva bhogā yathopanatam
āsevyā iti.

The objects, after all, are given by the deities, i.e.
the sense-organs. If those objects are not offered back
to the (divine) senses for their enjoyment, that would
be a sort of theft, because one would be acting ungratefully
and would be cheating the "gods in the body.

Hence, it has been said by the Lord (Krishna):
"People who restrain their external senses but keep
remembering the objects with their minds are called
'hypocrites' (cheaters). Thus, people seeking ways of
being happy or fulfilled or liberated must spontaneously
enjoy consumable objects as they come their way, since
such natural enjoyment results in satisfying the curiosity
and appetite of the sense-organs."
(BG III:6)

In order to make sense of this original interpretation of the well-known passage from the BG, we must take a quick look at the underlying equation of sense organs and the deities or divinities in the body.

The Gods in the Body: Sense Organs, *Manas*, and the Ego Maker

Vedic piety is said to pervade the life of man, starting at the fertilization of the ovum when he is conceived and ending in cremation. That is why cremation is called the last sacrifice: *antya-iṣṭi*. Incidentally, each of the Sanskrit words for a sacrifice has interesting research potentials. These are: *yaga, iṣṭi, ijyā, makha, satra, adhvara, kratu, havana, yajña,* and so on. The three fires to which a Brahmana is supposed to offer daily oblations are the domestic, the ancestral, and the heavenly. With the first, one sanctifies one's daily food; with the second, one acknowledges one's debts to the forefathers; and with the last one gives away gifts to the divinities. But an act of gift/sacrifice needs an addressee. To which divinity shall we offer our oblations? (kasmai devāya haviṣa vidhema?)—asks the famous Ṛg Veda X.121[7] about the Golden Embryo. Corresponding to the three planes of existence, on earth Fire is the divinity, in the middle region it is Air, and in the heaven it is the Sun. I shall translate *devatā* as divinity because it displays the etymological connection with the Sanskrit root *div*—a polysemic verb meaning both illumination and playing. The word *dyauh*—for the luminous abode of celestials—preserves the first meaning, while the word *dyūta*—for the game of gambling, with epic risks—*a la* Mahābhārata—preserves the second meaning. The word "divinity" also retains the abstraction suffix "ity" echoing the *tā*-ending of *devatā*. With this much philology, let me pass on to the eleven (loosely connected in a family-resemblance way) criteria of deity-hood, features that make a divinity divine.

1. A divinity, primarily, is a tradition-sanctioned target of obligatory or fruit-bearing acts of sacrifice. It has to be community-endorsed, for just as a language cannot be private, a deity cannot be private either. To give to a subjectively invented deity is, to use a Wittgensteinian analogy, like my left hand giving a gift to my right hand, no giving at all. A divinity must be learned about from tradition and then "experienced"

by deepening of revealed word-generated knowledge (*śruti*) through inward contemplation.

2. A divinity must be deathless and ageing-free (*a-mara, nir-jara*) since we take refuge in him or her in order to seek protection from death and the ravages of time.

3. A divinity lords over or controls some sector of reality (*satpati*) usually defined in terms of the worshipper's sensory modalities of grasping reality, the source of all light that is visible, all air that touches us, all earth that is smelt, all water that is tasted, and so on.

4. A divinity must be great, vast, limitless (born of *a-diti*, the unlimited), like the sky (*ākaśa-vat vyāpin, brahman*).

5. A divinity must be a giver of riches, if pleased (*draviṇoda*).

6. A divinity is worship-worthy because we are indebted to him or her for our very embodiment and our continued staying alive (*yajanīya, yakṣa*).

7. A divinity is self-supporting and of discriminating wisdom (*svadhā-van and cikītvan*).

8. They are capable of assuming magically multiple forms, though essentially invisible, since divinities love to conceal themselves in mysteries (*bahurūpa, puru-rūpa, parokṣa, parokṣa-priya*).

9. Full of goodness, bliss, and light, a divinity must be luminous (*śivatama ānandamāya, jyotirmāya*)

10. Every divinity must belong to a locus, a *loka,* and a name, *nāma,* in the space of sacrificial mantra words. This place is usually in the high heavens, but it could be right here on earth, in the corner of one's kitchen, or in one's workplace.

11. Besides lighting, another meaning of the root verb *div* is play, sport (*divyati=krīḍati*). A divinity is a playful, self-exhilarating center of free consciousness.

Given these traditionally identified features of a divinity, let me now state my own conclusion.

A Vedic divinity is a generalized de-personalized sensory power (*indriya-śakti*) taken in the widest possible sense of the word "sense-organ" or any instrument of cognition or action.

This is how I make "sense" out of these many—the more the merrier—deities by offering oblations to whom we can save ourselves from the daily death of egotism. For the Mahābhārata does say that death is spelled with two syllables *mama* (mine), from which the word of ego-offering, *na-mama,* shortened into *nama,* is the only way to save ourselves. The senses in the felt body are naturally divine. They are made mundane and even demonic by individualization and blinkered jealous limitation into smaller egos. Culture is the rediscovery of their divinity, their unlimited vastness by recognizing their ego-free character through the practice of heart sharing in art and poetry, and the practice of unselfishness through moral and spiritual service of others.

Sibajiban Bhattacharya on the Ego's Occupation of the Body

In his pioneering encyclopedic paper on this subject, Professor Sibajiban Bhattacharya made many original contributions to the intriguing issue of the relationship between the body and the ego. He starts by remarking that the "ownership" relation between me and my body is both causal and moral. Trying to unravel the metaphysical meaning of this sense of possession gets us into the mystery of "I and Mine." When the Cārvāka materialist is told: "Surely, the body could not be the self, because it is felt to be "my body," as a possession of the self, the materialist replies: "Not all possessive or genitive cases reflect a distinction. Notice the usage "The City of London," "the head of Rāhu" (when Rāhu is nothing but the head), "the Body of Lenin" (as it is kept now in the Kremlin, this being an example possible only for a modern Russian Cārvāka!). Sibajiban Bhattacharya writes many closely argued pages about this "occupation or possession of the body by the ego-maker."

Here is a controversial passage from those pages:

> The expressions "my knowledge," "my action," "my feeling," may mislead one to think that the ego enters into every mental state in the same way—namely, it is that which *has* or *owns* knowledge, action and feeling . . . [S]till there is a fundamental difference obscured by the grammatical form.

> Although, grammatically, the "knower" and the "doer" have the same form, yet the *empirical subject* is not an *agent* in knowing, as it is in performing a voluntary action. . . . the empirical subject becomes *entangled* in its action, is *responsible* for them; and the ego gets deeply involved in actions, but not in knowledge. Some actions inflate the ego—actions which are considered successes by the doer; others depress it when the subject feels frustrated. . . . [T]he ego enters into actions in a totally different way than in knowing.[8]

K. C. Bhattacharya on Bodily Subjectivity

In his best-known work *Subject as Freedom* K. C. Bhattacharya devotes two consecutive chapters to bodily subjectivity. In each numbered paragraph of these densely argued chapters a new dimension of our ambivalent epistemic relation to the body is unfolded. How do we know our own body? Most obviously, by perception. But what kind of perception? The body cannot be an ordinary object of sense perception because it is, in the first place, the subject or perceiver. My eyes see other things, but they can never see themselves. K. C. Bhattacharya takes the Kaṭha Upaniṣad insight that the senses are cut out to see outside and never see the inner self or even themselves, but he develops much more complex argumentation to prove that not just the proprioceptively felt body but even the externally perceived body is not an ordinary object of perception.

Let us analyze, for example, just the argumentation in paragraph 59 of chapter 3:

"One's own body is only half-perceived, the rest being eked out by imagination." A simple fact, but worth drawing our attention to. I have never seen the center of my own back and the back of my own head. Seeing in a mirror does not count as direct perception. But this is not unique just to my body. Any solid object such as a house, a cup, or an apple is always half-perceived, the other half being remembered or imagined to be there, at the time of seeing the front. In imagining the unseen parts, the perceiver imagines his own body being placed in a different position relative to that solid object. I could go behind the house, turn the cup around in my hand. But we cannot even imagine doing that to our own bodies: my going behind my own body or turning my own body around for me to see, is inconceivable. (It is worth pausing here to reflect, Is this a logical or a physical impossibility?) Cartesians take this rather glibly as a mere physical impossibility. Logically I could go round this body of mine and see it from all sides. But, if I imagine myself as a perceiver to be so independent of my own body that this disembodied myself could go behind my own body or look down at my own crown to take a top view as it were, then it will make no sense to speak of my having a pair of eyes, going behind anything, or having a point of view. A bodiless soul cannot go behind anything or turn its eyes from a certain angle because these goings and turnings presuppose an embodied perceiver and not a bodiless one. Thus, the best I can do to imagine what it would be to look at my own back is to imagine how another embodied perceiver may see my back or the top of my head. So, K. C. Bhattacharya concludes: "In this respect also his own perceived body is uniquely different from other perceived objects and has no place in the objective world that he conceives to be presentable to him as a solipsistic observer."

Note that we have not yet come to the fascinating area of the neither introspective nor external bodily sensations such as a toothache, a dry throat, or simply a bout of acidity which is located like a bodily state, yet unsharably inner like a mental state. Already, lots of tiny but momentous steps have been taken, in this very noninward layer of our perceptual knowledge of the outside of our own bodies. As a compounded whole object of external, say visual, perception, my body cannot be on a par with all those things in the world that I alone can observe or imagine myself to be observing at different times. Part of it is my own view, and part of it is what I imagine to be seen by another perceiver with a different bodily subjectivity. My own perceptual concept of my own body is a hybrid amalgam of both of these views. And KCB then makes the scintillating remark: "The world as a construction out of the views or perspectives of many observers cannot simply be identified with the world constructed out of the views of the same observer in different positions." How on earth, then, does the child ever map her own body—a phenomenal object jointly observed by herself with other perceivers—into the picture of a world as she sees it all by herself? How is such incorporation of the perceiver's in-here-corporeality possible into a world of out-there-objects? KCB has already hinted at a very radical "externalist" solution of this hitherto unnoticed problem. The uniqueness of my body as an object, its "myness" as it were, consists in the necessary involvement of a non-solipsistic multiple-person point of view. I need other observers not so much for the objectivity of a world of physical things, as much as I need them for the egocentric notion of my own body as a unique object of perception!

This really turns the tables on the ordinary notion of the ego as a private solipsist idiosyncrasy, and the world of impersonal objects as intersubjective. Here, the bodily ego is seen to be more intersubjective than the world of impersonal inert objects! I cannot place my own body as a physical object of perception until I actively imagine other bodies as perceivers just like me. Ego is made by the objectification of the one's own body in the imagined eyes/I-s of the others. Independently of Strawson's argument from the generality of P-predicates, this is an anticipation of a Strawsonian conclusion, from an uncannily Kantian phenomenological perspective which is KCB's own. Not only are my own mental contents dependent upon there being other minds grasping the same or similar contents, but my body would not be uniquely mine unless I place it in a nexus of objects that other perceiving bodies perceive the other half of. Right there, I think, there is a new research program for that area of cognitive science which deals with perceptual cooperation at the subpersonal level, a research program which will show the fertility of the elusive Sāṃkhya doctrine of *ahaṃkāra* as the causal source of all the cognitive and motor organs.

K. C. Bhattacharya then goes on to remark:

> The awareness of the body from within is, indeed, sensuous but it can hardly be called sense-perception. It is only not denied to be perception . . . [T]he body is felt as extending from a vague interior to the outer surface that may both be felt and perceived. He also raises new searching questions like the following: "Is the skin that is touched by others from outside and the skin that is felt from inside by the owner of the body the same skin?[9]

But the outer perception of the body stops at the surface, and if it is extended by the imagination of the interior, the interior is still imagined as an external surface. The perceived as well as the imagined (other's) body is always an exterior which may also be felt, but the interior (of one's own felt body) can never be imagined as perceived (can you, for example, ever imagine the surgeon seeing your stomach pain when he takes a good look at your guts or perceiving your pleasure when scanning your amygdala?).

Thus, the felt body cannot be distinguished from the perceived body though the latter is distinguished from the former! Felt body is identical with perceived body, but the perceived body is nonidentical with the felt body. A case of asymmetric identity!

From Phenomenology to Ethics: How Should We Evaluate Our Bodies?

The embodied human is born with debts, says the Śatapatha Brāhmaṇa. To own a body is to owe something to other kinds of bodies and the past which caused this body. We have debts to our ancestors, but for whose procreative and nurturing practices we would not have been here. We have debts to seers and teachers because without them there would not be a language or a tradition in which we could grow up as social beings. We have debts to the environmental gods without whom we or our parents would not have had the food and oxygen which keeps us alive. Hence the first moral duty is to use the body to pay back those debts. Vedic ethics is the ethics of obligatory "giving up and giving back" in the form of daily sacrifice and "giving forward" in the form of learning-teaching and gift-making.

A very early reductive analysis brings down the vital functions of a rational animal's body to two major functions: to breathe (maintain itself) and to talk (to maintain its communicative relationships to other bodies). In the past, when sages had constant mindfulness, the relatively older Kauṣītakī Upaniṣad tells us, they performed *agnihotra* (fire-oblations) inside their bodies. When speaking, they would offer the oblation of Breath to the goddess Speech, and when silent, they would offer the gift of Speech to the deity Breath. Thus they would not spend a single moment without sacrifice. Of course, it is the body which offers the ritual ecology behind this perpetual sacrifice model of life.

Given this inescapable indebtedness of whoever is born at all into a human society, what should be our evaluative attitude towards our own bodies? Should we be disgusted by it, belittle it, ignore it, or should we value it, take care of it, and enjoy it?

As usual, there is no single answer from the Indian philosophers. What then should be our evaluative attitude towards our own bodies which naturally draw us into such egotistical living and yet bear the possibility of such perpetual sacrifice?

The *Yoga Sūtras* almost urge us to cultivate "purity" or cleanness with the hope that we attain the perfection or virtue of "disgust at one's own body" (*śaucāt svāṅgajugupsā* . . .). So the attitude sounds negative. But, even at this level of denigration of the body, the body is regarded as worthy of a lot of care, attention, and never to be ignored. After all, two limbs of Yoga, *āsana,* and *prāṇāyāma* are entirely to be practiced in and through the body. Many of the *saṃyamas* or *dhāraṇās* are focused on different parts of the felt body: in the glottis inside the throat, in the navel, in between the eyebrows, and of course, in the region of the heart.

The *Yogavāsiṣṭha* on the Body

The stereotype of the Indian philosopher as one who is obsessed with Brahman and atman and tells us to ignore the body as false or filthy does not find any corroboration in the text of YV. It is not only the Cārvāka materialists who advise us to enjoy bodily pleasures (even immorally, if necessary!) since we are just conscious bodies with only one chance to live so that self-love is body-love; orthodox Hindu thought explicitly instructs us to take care of the body and respect it as "the primary instrument of dharma" (*ādyam dharma-sādhanam*). Just as we hear so much about how being born in a body is deemed almost a misfortune, and embodiment is looked upon as imprisonment of the soul, we also hear the Mahābhārata praising birth in a human form as "that than which nothing greater can be conceived" (*na manusat śreṣṭha-taram hi kimcit*).

The most dramatic movement from a negative to a positive attitude is illustrated by YV, in the transition from Vairāgya to Sthiti Prakaraṇas. When young Rāma is afflicted by his existential angst and wishes to retire from his princely life of worldly power and pleasures, like a typical spiritual beginner, he shows disgust at the body (*kāya-jugupsā*)..

The primordial image of the body as a kind of tree making up the wilderness of the world dominates these initial anticorporeal reflections. On a more careful reading, the seeds of a critical axiology of the body are contained even in Rāma's initial pessimistic assessment of the body, in the first chapter of YV.

> A convoluted tangle of clammy entrails and veins, tending to turn putrid and fall, this fragile body is nothing but a cause of suffering in this world.
> (YV I:18.1)

Although it is utterly unknowing, the body behaves as if it knows itself and this and that; it is wrapped all around with self-marveling reflexivity (*valitātma-camatkṛtih*). Rationally considered, the body is both beautiful and ugly, and, above all, it is neither an unconscious material being, nor a conscious spiritual being (*na jaḍo nāpi cetanaḥ*).

> Swinging like a pernicious pendulum between the categories
> of inert substance and non-inert conscious substance,
> this indiscriminate intrinsically befuddled body gives us
> nothing but delusions.
> (YV I:18.3)

With a little bit of stimulus, it comes to rejoice, with a little bit again it comes to grief. There is nothing as pitiable, lowly, and abject than this poor body.

The body is like a tree; the arms are its branches; the rows of teeth are like small pillars holding up the upper part of the big fruit which is the head, pierced by the two eyes as if by a pair of beehives. Although it provides living beings with a shady shelter in the journey of life, it is never clear how far it can be trusted and how much it is unreliable. "This body-house is not to my liking at all," complains Rāma, because a "vulture called Egotism has made its nest in this tree, and creepers of conflicting cravings have created a thick net over its roots such that it is extremely hard to cut it off" (YV:I:18:16).

> A burnt-faced disfigured maid called "evil desire" is taking
> care of the baby called "suffering" inside this little house
> where the baby cries even when lying down on a comfortable
> cot of pleasures. "I cannot like this home of which the fierce
> door is a hole called the mouth, guarded by a grimacing little
> monkey called the tongue, showing all its ugly teeth. About to
> get dusty with the powder of old age, muddy with blood and
> fluids, tangled up with veins and nerves, this body-house of
> mine is not to my taste."
> (YV:18.23, 31)

At the beginning of spiritual life, the first existential crisis always is this sickening disgust with one's own confounding confinement inside this half-understood half-felt body. But then, with steady clear reflection other questions start arising: What ought we to do with our bodies? Can I treat my body as of equal value with others' bodies? Do I have special duties towards keeping my own body fit? Finally, the ethical question of whether we have duties towards or rights about our own bodies arises: Do I have the right—or even duty?—to cause pain to my body, such as by asceticism?

After two long chapters full of puzzling narratives proving the entirely subjective mental nature of all objective reality by Sthiti Prakaraṇa, as Vasiṣṭha describes to Rāma the ideal character of living as a liberated person and how he lives blissfully a socially engaged life of the world, the body is praised as a beautiful city where one is lucky to dwell for a period of time. The first verse where this positive shift of attitude is reflected deserves careful analysis:

> Charming is this city-of-the-body, dear Rāma, endowed with
> all excellences. It is enriched by the endless pleasure-play of
> consciousness, and lit up by the Sun of self-illumination.
> (YV IV:23.4)

The windows of the eyes beautifully express the illuminated inside of this city, as well as project the light onto the world outside. The string of celebratory metaphors here keep rippling from one image to the other, from the role of the lotus-like glimpses cast by the eyes, through the smile-flowers that blossom in the garden of the face, to the beautiful lady called "rational reflections on the Self" (*ātmacintā-varāṅganā*) who is roaming around under the trees of the pleasure garden of the mind. The analogy shifts gradually to that of a kingdom, where consciousness (called *jña,* as it is called in the Sāṃkhyakārikā) rules fearless of the enemy state of Ignorance (*ajñana-para-rāṣtra*). Two queens called "Truth" and "Oneness" sit on two sides of this ruling Consciousness as it happily enjoys its city-state, where even the thief called "consumption" (*bhoga*) ceases to be an enemy and becomes a friend, because he is dealt with knowledgeably and mindfully. Reflectively purified and dispassionately witnessed enjoyments and sufferings do not impoverish the body-city, but enrich it. Like people on the roadside watch the drama of men, women, actors, and clowns, Consciousness enjoys the procession of life through this city of the body with the attitude of an onlooker. Just as the eyes of a passer-by fall effortlessly on the mountains, forests, rivers, and ponds, the transaction of ideas and feelings, which goes on in the shop of the heart as memories and desires are brought in and sold out, is looked upon with the delightfully weightless attitude of witness by the spiritually cultured consciousness of the man of "unwavering intelligence" (*dhīra-dhī*, which seems to be a variation of the *Bhagavad Gītā*'s *sthita-prajña*). The key to this transformed attitude towards the same body which was once thought of as a filthy, ugly treehouse and is now looked upon as a beautiful civilized city, is the following insight:

> It is thanks to this body that I can consume enjoyments as well as attain liberation; so like a heavenly city-state, everything stays intact as long as this city stays alive, but when it is lost nothing is lost, for consciousness is independent of it. It is a fully dispensable play-ground for the creative consciousness. Therefore:

> Grasping one hand tightly with the other, grinding teeth against teeth, and as it were propelling one limb with another, one should go forward and get down to the business of winning over the fickle outward greedy sense-organs, curbing the bad ego-maker of selfish identification with an individual body, and taking initiative with the salutary Ego-usage which realizes "I am all this world." (See chapter 33 of Sthiti (YV IV:33), for the distinction between good *ahaṃkāra* and bad *ahaṃkāra*)

Divinification and Purification of Other Bodies: What Is It Like to Breathe Like a Sea-turtle?

In the context, above, of outlining the nature of "sacrifice" as relinquishing of the acquisitive narrowness of the ego, we have spoken of the word of offering, *namaḥ* as meaning "not mine." In the spreading of subjectivity from mine to not-mine—from mama to namaḥ—we have to go through what the Bhāgavatam calls "*jagat-praṇāma*"—the practice of worshipping all external other bodies as the bodies of God.

Others bodies, different kinds of bodies, bodies of nonhumans set up challenges to our egocentric subjectivities. We shrink from them, we are afraid of them, or at best we gawk and gaze at them. But both the Vaiṣṇava and the Tantric spiritual ethos demand that we see divine consciousness especially in the radically other. The incarnations of Viṣṇu facilitate worshipful attitudes towards the entire range. The fish, the amphibian, the half-man half-lion hybrid mammal, and the deviant dwarf all are God's bodies: Hareḥ Śarīraṃ! This is reflected in a beautiful poem describing the waves of the ocean as if they are imitating the rhythm of the deep breathing of the submerged cosmic turtle.

When God became a Turtle, bearing the huge mountain Mandāra spinning on his shell, all that back-scratching made him sleepy, and he heaved heavily, from deep underneath the ocean. Till today, imitating the rhythm of his inhalings and exhalings, the waters of the ocean get withdrawn and again come back up in waves on the shore, relentlessly. May the whiffs of that divine turtle's breath protect you all!

This is an amazing visceral "inscape" of what it is like to have a turtle's body and a shell scratched by rough stony edges of a mountain. And at the same time it brings alive the wave motions of the sea, whereby in imagination you learn to breathe with all turtles and billow back and forth with the sea. This immersion into the interiority of all sorts of bodies is supposed to liberate us from the existential error of regarding only this particular body as mine and every other body to be nonsubjective. One must seek to find the void in the middle of a crowded city, the hole in the heart, the heart as the home of Brahman.

The picture one gets out of looking closely at a Gopuram in South India is of an overcrowded world teeming with life and tapering up towards heaven. In a classic paper on the philosophical significance of the different kinds of bricks used to construct an altar for a Vedic fire ritual Charles Malamoud goes deep into the mystery of this profusion, this filling up of every gap, first through the verb *bhū*—connected both to the word for the Earth, *bhūmi,* and the word for infinite fullness, *bhūman*. To quote Malamoud: "To be is to be like the earth: compact." Abundance, accumulation, satisfying hunger, fulfilling the needs of the people, are thus connected with pūrta, social and civic duties, connected to the act of filling up *pūrti*. But just as one notices in the sacrificial mantras this urgency to fill up the earth, put back together the Primal Prajāpati who fell apart in order to create us, one also notices a countercurrent of keeping some breathing space, some apertures, some elbow room for free movement. In the Brahmana master plan for *agnicayana*, thus, one must place layers of "naturally pierced" bricks, bricks with a hole in them. The body of the *yajña-puruṣa* is symbolized by this porous structure of the altar. The same theme of a hole at the center of the body is picked up by *Chāndogya Upaniṣad* when it describes the body as the city of Brahman, and inside the inner chamber of that the lotus-shaped heart having a cavity, an empty space, *dahara* or *daharākāśa*. In Vedāntic meditation, this sky in the heart becomes identified with the cosmic space filled with light and sound. If the human body is pictured as a city of God, a temple city, in turn, is also pictured as the body of the worshipper: an exuberantly erotic field of surplus desires and their fulfillments, with a luminous stillness and absence in the middle.

I would like to end by recounting my recent amazing experience of the Cidambaram Nātarāja Śiva temple in Tamil Nadu which confirmed this play of fullness and nullity in the body.

About eighty minutes' drive from Pondicherry, stands Cidambaram, a town with a twelve-hundred-year-old famous Śiva temple with four ninety-foot-high, ornately sculpted stone gates marking each of the four cardinal directions. On each of the gates are carved figures displaying hundreds of classical Indian dance postures, ranging from the contemplative to the acrobatic, with a dominant interlude of the erotic and voluptuous. The sculpture galleries on these stone gates are testaments to the best of South Indian culture of the seventh through the eleventh centuries. Beasts, reptiles, birds, fruits, and flowers mingle seamlessly with demigods, semihuman animals, many-handed divinities, demons, and abstract decorative forms in a celebratory riot of bodily differences and disciplines. Clowns and jugglers, peacocks and lions, emaciated ascetics and coquettish courtesans inhabit the same space with gods and goddesses on a thousand pillars which line both sides of the long, dark corridors surrounding the temple.

At the center of this corporeal exuberance is the shrine of dancing Śiva. However, contrary to popular belief, the golden image of Nāṭarāja is not quite the chief deity here. The sanctum sanctorum holds a stunning surprise. The central shrine is literally empty. Śiva is worshipped there in his *ākāśa-liṅgam*—as vacuum. When the oil lamps are lit to illuminate this sheer absence, the meaning of the temple's name suddenly becomes clear: *chit +ambaram,* or literally, "the Space/ Sky (ambaram) of Consciousness (chit)," where all the performing arts starting with dance and theater literally get their inspiration. To live well, one needs to witness the dance of Shiva going on in this empty hall of the heart in the middle of this pulsating, proliferating polity of the body.

The journey, discussed above, from the "horrid house" of Vairāgya Prakaraṇa (*kāya-jugupsā*), Rāma's youthful existentialist "angst" and his "naturalistic" aversion towards this limiting cage of "my body," to the idea of the "Charming city" (*ramyā iyaṃ deha-nagarī*)) of Sthiti Prakaraṇa where the free nonattached thinker celebrates his own embodiment and all its natural ecology thanks to the philosophical culture of Pro-Effort Logico Phenomenological Analysis (Vicāra), is one of the most "applied" examples of using rational reflection and aesthetic culture to reclaim, not so much *the place of mind in nature, but the place of nature in the Mind.* We make our worlds with our "will and ideas" (to recall the title of Schopenhauer's magnum opus); we discover and marvel at what we ourselves make. We are not talking about the addition of our computers and our rockets and airplanes to the mountains and rivers of the earth. The sphere of such psychic and spiritual culture is not just in the fringe of a largely given, intransigent, and unmodifiable nature; its sphere is all-pervasive. Common unalterable nature itself is part of this all-pervasive mind-made karmic Culture-world. The knower of the field is also the maker of the field, in the final analysis. In the section on the nature of deities above, I have delved into the concept of "sacrifice" defined as "offering up one's possessions to one or more devatas" as the root of even that spiritual culture of the subjective body which we have discerned in Vasiṣṭha's celebration of embodiment. The contemplative philosophical analysis through which my body becomes not-mine—Janaka, the philosopher-King in Mahābhārata says, "Even this self-body of mine is not mine, or this entire earth is mine"—and other's body ceases to be other, and "body" and "Brahman" become synonyms is that Cognitive Sacrifice (*jñana-yajña*) which BG and YV both recommend as the purest form of spiritual culture. Such spiritually cultured individuals enjoy their subjective body with the attitude of an entertained onlooker, without feeling trapped by it, simply through nonattached concern and care for others whose subjectivities they assume through identification of the self with all, when all bodies, all of nature, become "my body." Active social concern, skill, and zest for life are perfectly compatible with such a nonegotistic use of "I" because this onlooker attitude is not to be confused with indifference or apathy. Spirituality becomes synonymous with deliberate but spontaneous practice of unselfishness.

Notes

I am grateful to my doctoral advisee Ana Funes for her help with retyping this chapter with the correct diacritical marks.

1. Ludwig Wittgenstein, *Tractatus Logico-Philosophicus,* ed. Marc A Joseph (Tonawanda: Broadview Press, 2014), 139.

2. Ibid., 143.

3. Iris Murdoch, *Metaphysics As A Guide to Morals* (New York: Viking Penguin, 1992), 215.

4. Antonio T. de Nicolás, *Meditations through the Ṛg Veda, Four-Dimensional Man* (York Beach: Nicolas-Hays, Inc., 1976), 225.

5. *The Thirteen Principal Upanishads,* trans. Robert Ernest Hume (Oxford: Oxford University Press, 1995), 362.

6. Parasnath Dwivedi, *Nāṭyaśāstra* (Varanasi: Sampurnananda Sanskrit University, 1955), 379.

7. de Nicolás., 226–27.

8. Sibajiban Bhattacharya, "Body," in *The Encyclopedia of Indian Philosophies* (Delhi: Motilal Banarridass, 1970), 183.

9. Krishnachandra C. Bhattacharya, *The Subject as Freedom* (Bombay: G. R. Malkani, 1930).

III

Engaged Emancipation

12

Embodied Liberation (Jīvanmukti) in the *Yogavāsiṣṭha*

ANDREW FORT

One who stands firm even while doing everyday activity,
Abiding like the empty sky:
he is called liberated while living.
One who does everyday activity having achieved perfect awakening,
In waking (seeming) like one asleep:
he is called liberated while living.
His luminous countenance does not rise in joy or fall in sorrow,
Having attained his proper place:
he is called liberated while living.
One who is awake while seeming asleep,
for him waking does not exist.
Fully awakened without mental impressions:
he is called liberated while living.
Although acting according to passion, hatred, and fear, etc.
One who remains (internally) transparent as the sky:
he is called liberated while living.
One whose nature is not ego-centered,
whose intellect is untainted
While acting or not acting:

he is called liberated while living.
One who comprehends (cosmic) creation and destruction
in the blink of an eye,
He sees the three worlds as his own self:
he is called liberated while living.
One who fears no one and no one fears,
Free from fear, anger, and joy:
he is called liberated while living.
Tranquil amid roiling phenomenal existence,
partless though having parts (limbs),
The one who, though conscious, is without (fluctuating)
mind: he is called liberated while living.
One who is cool while dealing with all things,
Filled with the self while among material objects: he is
called liberated while living.[1]

This passage introduces *jīvanmukti* in the *Yogavāsiṣṭha* (YV),[2] a tenth-century Kaśmiri eclectic mix of myth, poetry, philosophy, and moral exhortation, containing approximately thirty thousand stanzas in six sections (*prakaraṇa*).[3] The reader should thus note that I am not discussing the *Mokṣopāya* or *Laghu Yogavāsiṣṭha* here; Walter Slaje has done important work in distinguishing these respective texts, and future work comparing the precise conceptions of embodied liberation in each is a desideratum.

The YV seems to have played a role in popularizing the notion of liberation while living and to have been important in the development of what I call "Yogic Advaita," also seen in Vidyāraṇya's *Jīvanmuktiviveka* (JMV) and many later Upaniṣads.[4] Briefly, Yogic Advaita holds to Śaṅkara's view that knowledge of the nondual self brings liberation (though the YV is more Gauḍapāda's than Śaṅkara's Advaita), yet adds emphasis to Sāṃkhya concepts[5] and Yoga practices, particularly exerting control of mental states and modifications (and even urging "destroying the mind"). Yogic Advaita also makes an important distinction between *jīvan-* and *videha-* (bodiless) *mukti* and shows much less interest in *prārabdha* (currently manifesting) karma than does mainstream Advaita.

There is no question that the YV has its own unique perspective, however; it contains more Buddhist (particularly *vijñānavāda*) and Purāṇic ideas[6] (but less Upaniṣadic material) than other Yogic Advaita texts such as the JMV or Madhusūdana Sarasvatī's *Gūḍārtha Dīpikā*. These latter texts are closer to Śaṅkara's "mainstream" Brahmanical

Advaita concerns with Vedic statements and ritual, *saṃnyāsa*, the *varṇāśrama-dharma*, and interpreting texts such as the *Yoga Sūtras* and the *Bhagavad Gītā*. Further, as Slaje has pointed out, the Yoga here is more oriented toward cessation of mentation (*nirodha*) than Patañjali's eight-fold discipline (*aṣṭāṅga*).[7] There is a critique of supernormal powers (*siddhis*), *āsanas* and breath control are seen as mere preliminaries, and although *samādhi* (of a certain kind) is endorsed, the term is almost never used when *jīvanmukti* is discussed,[8] and only nondual knowledge is said to bring liberation.[9]

Throughout the text, the liberated sage Vasiṣṭha exhorts his student Rāma (and the reader) to be detached, destroy the ego, lose the mind, know the world to be illusory, and differentiate the transient body from the self. While in the world, one should (generally) do one's duty, follow the sacred texts (*śāstra*), and associate with the wise. According to the YV, liberation while living is possible. Like Śaṅkara, the YV holds that mukti arises from knowledge of the nondual self, not from austerity or right (dharmic) action. The *jīvanmukta* can act in the world or renounce all action with complete detachment. Instead of mainstream Advaita's concern with the body's continuity after liberation due to *prārabdha* karma, the YV (and later the JMV) emphasizes the control of the *jīvanmukta's* mind and destruction of mental impressions, which brings one to a nondual "state" beyond all conscious states.

References to *jīvanmukti* and the *jīvanmukta* appear throughout the text,[10] and as with most topics in the YV, living liberation is not considered systematically. Still, the *Upaśama Prakaraṇa* (chapter on cessation) contains many of the most important passages, and various (largely congruent) themes appear repeatedly. These will be discussed below.

The World and Human Bondage

To begin, we will look at the YV's view of the nature of the world and human bondage in it. As other essay writers will forcefully show, the most common perspective is the Advaitic, particularly Gauḍapāda's *ajātivāda*, view that the world is an illusion, appearing as it does due to ignorance and mind-created delusion; nothing ever arises, and all visible objects are utterly unreal, empty like a rainbow or mirage.[11] While without reality, the manifest world is as if existent; birth and destruction appear but are not real.[12] Perhaps most eloquent is the

Buddhist-sounding (YV V:77.35–37): in this world containing the endless rise and fall of beings, life is like a froth bubble; people arise and scatter perpetually, and the sights of the world vanish in a moment.

Numerous passages detail the characteristics of bondage and those who are bound. First, it is, as Śaṅkara writes, bondage to think the self is a body or otherwise limited. Second, it is bondage to have an uncontrolled mind; such a person is like one drunk or stupid, or like a child, grabbing at everything without knowing its proper application (YV V:77.24–5). Sunk in the muck of everyday enjoyments, those with uncontrolled minds are attracted to useless, sorrow-producing wealth or to beautiful but empty women who lead them to burn in hell.[13]

These attachments bind one to impure *vāsanās* (mental impressions); one now enjoys what one desires, but also suffers from its loss. When addicted to external objects, the presence or absence of desired things gives constantly changing sorrow or joy.[14] Thus, foolish-minded non-*jīvanmuktas* are never at peace;[15] their minds, attached to samsara, buzz with joy and sorrow like flies; the fool is like a worm or a dog, undeserving of liberation.[16]

Knowledge Leads to Liberation

The YV and Advaitins like Śaṅkara concur that the way out of bondage to illusion and sorrow is knowledge (*jñāna*) or right discrimination (*viveka, vicāra*)[17]—specifically knowledge of the self. The defining characteristic of one liberated while living is knowledge (while embodied) of the nondual, unfettered self.[18] The text repeatedly states that those solely intent on *ātma-jñāna* reach liberation while living, and one obtains liberation only by right discrimination; *jīvanmuktas* are termed *ātma-jñānins, tattva-jñas,* and *tattva-vids.*[19] Seeing the self in the not-self or reality in unreality arises from nondiscrimination and is destroyed by discrimination (YV V:86.17). King Janaka is the model of unvarying flawless insight (YV V:12.4–5),[20] but anyone, outcast (*mleccha*) or animal, who attains the highest knowledge is liberated (YV III:18.22). While obtainable only by the few (YV V:74. 56), once obtained *jīvanmukti* is never destroyed (YV III:7.125. 56).[21]

Interestingly, the YV says it is the crucial text which leads to right knowledge and liberation while living. YV III:8.15–6 states that one gains *jīvanmukti* upon hearing this text,[22] and YV III:95.25 asserts that only by studying this "*mahārāmāyaṇa śastra*" does one obtain *jīvanmukti*. YV III [8] continues by claiming that one attains liberation by knowledge alone: *jīvanmukti* is not gained by almsgiving, austerity (*tapas*), or thousands of Vedic performances. YV V:12.17 adds that *jīvanmukti* can't be gained by virtue, guru, sacred text, or associating with the wise, but only by clear discrimination. Further, the highest sage (*sādhu*) is awakened from heaven, future rewards, and the fruits of austerity (*tapas*) or charity (*dāna*); *tapas* and other things destroy suffering only for a short time, but equanimity (*samatā*) brings indestructible happiness (YV VI:101.36–7). While not forbidding performance of dharmic actions, it is clear in these passages that such duties are not the route to *mokṣa*.

The Utter Detachment of the *Jīvanmukta*

The YV, like traditional Advaita, also emphasizes that the living liberated being is detached (*asaṅga, asaṃsakti*) and indifferent (*sama*).[23] *Sama* also suggests being always the same, equable, impartial, and even-minded. The *jīvanmukta* is calm and *sama* in all states of awareness.[24] Amid whatever happens, the liberated sage always remains the same, as motionless water and shifting waves, or still air and gusting wind are the same (YV II:4.1, 5).

Detachment is even more commonly mentioned; entire chapters are devoted to the nature of detachment and behavior of the detached *jīvanmukta* (see YV V:77). Detachment brings the highest end and is the essential cause of crossing samsara.[25] The detached sage is unchanging in joy and despair, thinks "the partless self is all," and has lost all desire and anger.[26] *Jīvanmuktas* wander the world with detached minds whether rulers (like Janaka) or renouncers.[27]

Throughout the YV, the detached *jīvanmukta* is said to be always even-minded and indifferent to the dualities of sorrow and joy, dislikes and (pleasant) desires.[28] He does not give or take praise or blame, joy or grief; he is not ashamed or shameless, elated or sad.[29] The liberated being may laugh or cry on the outside, but truly remains unmoved,[30] desiring neither what most people wish for nor avoiding what people detest.[31] A real sage is to be sorrowless whether god or ruler, failure or worm (YV V:93. 98–99). The YV mentions, but does not emphasize, that the *jīvanmukta* ultimately realizes that there is not even any bondage or liberation. The nondual self can't be bound, and if it's not bound, how can there be release? For one not even considering bondage or liberation, the world is one.[32]

The *Jīvanmukta* and Action in the World

More than any other Advaita text discussing *jīvanmukti,* the YV emphasizes the *jīvanmukti's* detached action in worldly or everyday activity (*vyavahāra*).[33] The text asserts that many men (and gods) abide in samsara while liberated, doing various activities in everyday life with a "cool mind" (YV V:75.25–26). The "inner coolness" (*antaḥśītalatā*) of the *jīvanmukta* is often mentioned and is generally linked to detachment in action and lack of delusion or *vāsanā*.[34] The *jīvanmukta* goes in the world, not abandoning or striving after anything, being in accord with all beings (YV IV:46.26).

Instead of rigorous world renunciation, then, the YV emphasizes that one should do whatever course of action falls to one (YV VIa:56. 3). A *jīvanmukta* performs everyday activities according to his circumstances (*yathā-sthita*) and does whatever is proper to his place without attachment. Internally renounced, the *mukta* acts according to customary or family duties and his own karma.[35] Content with whatever is obtained, the *jīvanmukta* takes whatever comes with equanimity.[36] This peacefulness allows the sage to understand human behavior and the world as they are, without delusion (YV V:18.10). Because of apparent worldliness (and lack of predictable renunciate behavior), the *jīvanmukta* is not recognized as liberated by unliberated folk despite having destroyed all mental impressions and possessing an unmoving mind.[37]

The contrast between external activity (like following customary duties) and inward detachment is a constant theme. We saw earlier that due to internal indifference, the sage is not really joined to any aim and reaps no fruits. That is, the truly detached person never "acts" in the karmic sense (and is certainly never said to do "evil" acts). Outwardly, this being seems active and hoping for good, but inwardly grasps no hope and does not act.[38] While acting and enjoying, the liberated being has abandoned the illusion of being the doer; only fools think "this act will I shun, this act will I choose."[39] The *jīvanmukta* is, in a sense, "sleep-walking"; with a one-pointed "sleep-mind," he is not a doer even while acting. When "asleep while awake," one who does all does nothing (that is, nothing which bears fruit).[40]

The YV clearly takes the position that, according to the highest truth, there is no gain by doing or not doing anything (YV VIb:125.49). Some *jīvanmuktas* have abandoned action and duties, and some haven't. Unlike the more "Brahmanized" JMV, which generally takes a harder line on the importance of *saṃnyāsa*, the YV seems more committed to nonduality than to any conventional ethical or social behavior. This point is made most clearly in YV III:199, which describes the diversity of behavior among detached and liberated beings and begins with the question, "What is the point of abandoning or desiring any action?" The wise know there is nothing to be striven for or abandoned, so, as said above, they do whatever is appropriate to their station. Some with detached minds are kings or householders, and others wander,[41] having abandoned all duties. Some follow actions prescribed in the Veda, adhering to the *agnihotra*, and so on, and those within the four *varṇas* (castes) perform various actions such as meditation and worshipping gods (*devārcana*) (YV III:199.9–12).

On the other hand, some abandon everything and remain beyond all (dharmic) acts eternally. They devote themselves to meditation in empty forests or practice conduct to gain peace, promote virtue, and be loved by the wise and good. Some leave their native places to avoid desire and hatred, and they settle elsewhere. Others wander from place to place—woods, cities, mountains, shores, or caves. Visits to Banaras, Prayāga, Badari, and Mathurā, among other holy cities and mountains, are mentioned with approval (YV III:199.13–24).

Still, the text continues, many sages are settled "in the world," and the cause of liberation is not dwelling in a forest or practicing austerity. In fact, those who are proud of their knowledge and who abandon all action are only half-awakened. The chapter concludes that neither abandoning nor resorting to action is the essential cause of crossing samsara; as stated elsewhere, a detached mind is what brings liberation and nonreturn (YV III 199.28–33).

The Variety of Liberated Beings

The *jīvanmukta* is generally seen as a human being, though there are also a number of references to gods as *jīvanmuktas*.[42] King Janaka is the *jīvanmukta* most cited in the YV. Desireless, cool, and even-minded, Janaka rules and acts without delusion and with flawless insight; he does whatever comes without attachment and knows the self of all beings.[43] *Upaśama* 75 mentions Janaka along with a long list of other humans and gods who are *jīvanmuktas*, acting in the world while detached. This chapter, more than any other in the YV and unlike any other Advaita text when considering *jīvanmukti*, shows the wide variety of beings who are liberated while living. It begins by referring to Janaka, who governs his kingdom while detached, as do Buddha (!) and Manu, who is eternally the form (*ākṛti*) of *jīvanmukti*. Māndhātā also obtained the highest goal, though constantly active in battle.[44] Bali, a renouncer doing good in hell, and Prahlāda, protector of hell, are both detached *jīvanmuktas*. While possessing desire, they act without desire (YV VIb:125.62).[45] Namuci and Vṛtra have inner control and cool minds while fighting; other gods, drinking soma, are detached. Even the sacrificial fire, which eats all, is free while enjoying.

Lord Hari, always free, moves and plays in the sea of duality.[46] Liberated Śiva is joined in body with Gaurī, and Skandha makes war while *mukta*. Sage Nārada, liberated by nature, wanders with cool actions, and the *jīvanmukta* Viśvamitra presides over Vedic sacrifices. Śeṣa bears the earth, Sūrya makes the day, and Yama causes death, all while *jīvanmukta*. Many other *yakṣas, asuras*, and men abide in this realm of rebirth while actually liberated. Acting in everyday life with an inner coolness, they are unmoving like stones.

This passage indicates clearly that dharmic behavior and a liberated mind can be linked. Mental detachment and world renunciation are not identical. Further, as we saw in the previous section, these gods and humans need not reside in any particular place. Some (Bhṛgu, Viśvamitra), having attained the highest knowledge, go to the forest, and some (Janaka) remain as rulers. Some abide in the sky, some in the sphere of the gods, and some (like Bali and Prahlāda) in a cave-like hell. Even some animals are said to be wise, and some gods are foolish. All this indicates that knowledge, not bodily form or location, leads to *jīvanmukti*.

Bodiless Liberation (*Videhamukti*)

The notion that embodiment is not central to defining who is liberated is an important theme in the YV. The point is made explicitly in a number of places: the liberated sage is the same with or without a body, like still water and rolling waves, or gusting wind and motionless air, are the same. With or without form, one does not experience objects or enjoyments; in both conditions, the *jīvanmukta* sees oneness of the self (YV II:4.1–6). A peaceful mind, untouched by joy, sorrow, or their objects, is possible with or without a body.[47]

Upon first reflection, it seems implausible to speak of the irrelevance of the body's presence or absence. However, like Śaṅkara and Vidyāraṇya in the JMV, the YV asserts that one can be "disembodied" while in the body. This notion is put most clearly in YV V:60.2–7 when all-knowing, you are free from life and death in the body. Although embodied, when detached you are *adeha* (not embodied) like the wind in the sky. The body is irrelevant to those at peace and knowing the real. Since you are always one pure consciousness, why should you grasp or reject the body? Echoing Śaṅkara, the YV states that "I am embodied" is a false notion[48] and emphasizes detachment and right knowledge. *Uttaranirvāṇa* (YV VIb 125. 31–2, 38) adds that once liberated, the mind of the embodied *jīvanmukta* is not bound and never again bindable, like a fruit fallen from its stalk. The *jīvanmukta's* essence does not die at (body) death. Thus, one's fundamental identity is not tied to one's body.

Despite this line of reasoning, there are numerous passages distinguishing those liberated in the body (*jīvanmukta*) and those liberated without a body (*a-* or *videha-mukta*). In fact, the "Yogic Advaita" texts introduce the category *"videhamukti,"* not used in scholastic Advaita (though some later scholars refer to *videha-kaivalya*). According to YV V:42.11–3, two types of liberation are possible, with and without a body. The *jīvanmukta* is detached and desireless, while the bodiless *videhamukta* is free from rebirth and does not enter the visible (*dṛśyatā*). *Utpatti 9*, which begins by saying that those who reflect and are solely intent on knowledge of the self reach both forms of *mukti*, later describes *videhamukti* as like motionless wind, not rising or setting, existing or not existing, without I or other.[49] Interestingly, this kind of liberation is here termed nirvaṇa, literally, of course, "extinction."

In this context, it is often implicit or explicit that while *jīvaṇmukti* is truly liberation, *videhamukti* is a little "higher" kind of liberation. YV V:16.14–17 says that complete abandoning of *jñeya* ("thinkable") *vāsanās* leads to cessation and the *videhamukti's* bodiless freedom in all-encompassing Brahman. Merely abandoning *dhyeya* (fit for meditation) *vāsanās* leaves one with a (moving) body, although the body is unafflicted, and one is indifferent and "gone to Brahman-hood." YV V:90.4 says there is extinction of mind (*citta-nāśa*) with form (*sarūpa, jīvanmukti*) and without form *(arūpa,dehamukti).* The latter is the highest: pure, flawless, beyond sattva-bearing good qualities *(guṇa)* and beyond joy and sorrow; nothing at all is seen there (YV V:90.23–27).

Finally, YV V:71. 2–3 asserts that *jīvanmukti* is the mysterious and final "fourth" (*turīya*), but *adehamukti* is beyond the fourth. Only *videhamuktas* reach the distant way of peace, like only birds reach the way of the sky.[50] Thus, although the main stream of the YV suggests that liberation is one, whether in a body or not, nonembodiment here, as elsewhere in the tradition, sometimes seems a higher (non)condition than embodiment.

The Nature of the *Jīvanmukta's* Mind

The nature of the liberated being's mind (*cetas, citta, dhi, manas*)[51] is another oft-discussed aspect of *jīvanmukti* in Yogic Advaita. In many passages of the YV, the mind (the locus of desire and ignorance) is seen as our greatest problem, and its destruction (or at least control), the way to liberation. We shall later see that mental impressions (*vāsanā*) and their presence (or absence) are a particular focus when the mind is discussed. This terminology is largely foreign to the Advaita scholars, though the JMV includes some more systematic reflections on the nature of the mind.

Many passages devalue the mind: the mind pervaded by tamasic dull, ignorant impressions is the cause of birth and is the root and seed of the forest of sorrows (YV V:90. 6–9). The mind is a *vāsanā* mass causing rebirth, and the ignorant (*mūḍha, aprabuddha*) mind is bound and born repeatedly (YV VI:101.28, 31–32). Further, *jīvanmuktas* and those knowing reality (*tattva-jña*) have no minds (or destroyed minds); awakened beings are not "mind-based" (*citta-bhū*). Pure and clear minds are called *sattva*; in such minds, burned by the fire of knowledge, delusion does not sprout again—as burnt seeds sprout no flowers.[52] Other passages point to the *jīvanmukta's* controlled (vs. destroyed) mind: it rests unmoving, with senses controlled and passions gone, without pride, lust, or envy, having doubts burned by knowledge.[53]

Using more traditional Advaitic language, the YV says one should in particular abandon the aspect of the mind called the "I" notion (*ahaṃkāra, ahaṃbhāva*). The attachment to separate "individuality" causes great sorrow. One is a detached and clear-minded *jīvanmukta* when without the "I" in action or rest and when the "me" and "mine" is utterly destroyed.[54] The "I" notion is treated in more detail twice, when it is said that the *jīvanmukta* attains the highest viewpoint. YV IV:33.49–53 describes three types of *ahaṃkāra*: the first (worldly, or *laukika*) imagines the body with hand and foot; this body-based conception must be forsaken as it causes desire and attachment. The second type, linked to *jīvanmukti*, imagines the "I" as a minuscule hair and pure consciousness different from all. The highest liberating conception is of the self as all this ("*ahaṃ sarvam idaṃ viśvam*").

YV V:17.13–20 is roughly similar but adds a fourth kind of "I" notion. The first conception, tied to bondage, sees the "I" and body as made by mother and father; the second, bound for liberation, sees the "I" as finer than a hair and beyond all beings. The third "I" notion is the indestructible self, the essence of world appearance which never experiences sorrow. The fourth "I" concept is held by *śūnyavādins* (adherents of emptiness); to them, the "I" and world are completely empty, like the sky.[55] Each of the latter three are said to shine as *jīvanmukti*.

Both these descriptions hold to an Advaitic understanding: the first concept is dualistic and tied to bondage, the second "almost there" but still contains some separation, and the third recognizes the nondual self. Given that the latter conceptions are "higher," one wonders why the emptiness view is put last; unified fullness should transcend "mere" emptiness.

Mental Impressions (*Vāsanā*) and the *Jīvanmukta*

The existence of latent impressions (*vāsanā*) in the mind, and the need for their destruction, are a particular focus of the YV, and of Yogic Advaita generally. *Vāsanās* are said to be the cause of bondage and their absence the cause of liberation (YV VIb:125.61). As stated above, the mind at root is a mass of mental impressions causing rebirth,[56] and when they are absent, the highest goal is obtained.[57] Attachments are evil (*malina*) vāsanās, and only fools are bound to them. The impure and unreal embodied self (*jīva*) has the form (*ākāra*) of *vāsanās*, and the *jīva* ceases when *vāsanās* cease. Even those devoted to dharma, if not free from impressions, are bound like a bird in a cage. There is no permanent satisfaction even in pleasant *vāsanās*: one bound to impressions enjoys what is desired but also suffers from their loss. *Vāsanās* constantly change to joy or sorrow in the presence or absence of desired objects.[58]

Pure *(śuddha) vāsanās* are free from joy and sorrow and cause no further birth. When fully awakened, one gains no pleasure from objects nor suffers when they are destroyed—so one should try to minimize or remove *vāsanās*.[59] As *mokṣa* is free from *vāsanās*, the *jīvanmukta* is free from the snare of mental impressions; in fact, *vāsanās* destruction is a defining characteristic of one liberated while living (as it is in the JMV). Such absence of *vāsanās* also brings inner coolness.[60]

As mentioned earlier, YV V:16. 9–14 describes two kinds of *vāsanās*, those fit for meditation (*dhyeya*) and those to be known (*jñeya*). The former seems to refer to a more limited set of impressions than the latter. One destroys *dhyeya vāsanās* by acting with a cool intellect (*antaḥśītala-buddhi*) and abandoning the notion of an "I-maker." One devoted to destroying such impressions is a *jīvanmukta* (like King Janaka).[61] The destruction of *jñeya vāsanās* brings indifference, peace, and renunciation of the body, eventuating in attainment of *videhamukti*. The two types of *vāsanās* are unfortunately not described further here, but they do affirm the aforementioned notion that *videhamukti* is a bit "higher" than *jīvanmukti.*

When the *jīvanmukta's vāsanās* (or lack thereof) are discussed, the term *sattva* (sometimes spelled *satva*), untainted wisdom, regularly appears. The *jīvanmukta* is said to possess pure *sattva-vāsanās* which lead to freedom from rebirth. Noble Prahlāda rested 1000 years turned within to his own *sattva-vāsanās*.[62] More commonly, we hear that the *jīvanmukta's* mind is *sattva* when without *vāsanās*. The awakened mind or intellect with clear discrimination is called *sattva*. The *jīvanmukta's "vāsanā"* is not really a *vāsanā,* but pure wisdom (*śuddhasattva*). Worldly *vāsanās* are called mind, but the *jīvanmukta* has gone to the *sattva* realm.[63]

Further, the *sattva*-established mind of the *jīvanmukta* is variously called controlled, abandoned, and destroyed. When the mind is destroyed but with form (*jīvanmukti*), it is explicitly called *sattva*; when one's (destroyed) mind attains formlessness, his pure wisdom, bearing a mass of good qualities (*guṇa*), also disappears.[64] *Sattva* absence, like body absence, is the highest state.

The references above to *sattva,* the *guṇas,* and mental processes generally bring to mind Sāṃkhya/Yoga conceptions. The most interesting passage relevant in this context is YV V:89. 9–21, which looks at why *jīvanmuktas* don't exhibit yogic *siddhis* (supernormal powers) like flying.[65] Following the Advaita view, it is said that knowing the nondual self is different from, and superior to, supernormal powers. Self-knowers are not attached to such powers, unlike the unliberated, who try to master mantras or Yoga. Self-knowers enjoy the self and do not sink into the ignorance of bondage to worldly things (including powers like flying). Knowers could fly if they wanted to, but they are beyond such things, content in the self, doing and desiring nothing.[66]

The *Jīvanmukta's* "State of Consciousness"

A related topic in the YV's Yogic Advaita discussion of *jīvanmukti* is the liberated being's elevated "state of consciousness," particularly when compared to everyday states such as dream and sleep.[67] Even though awake, the *mukta's vāsanās* and *vṛttis* are at rest. Thus, the liberated being is often described as "asleep while awake": detached and desireless, doing all while doing nothing, having perfect equanimity in activity. When acting with a one-pointed "sleep-mind," this being is not a doer and acts without bondage.[68]

The *jīvanmukta's* "state of consciousness" is also frequently discussed in the context of the fourfold *catuṣpād* doctrine (waking, dream, deep sleep, and the unifying "fourth," *turīya*).[69] Waking and dream mislead us into accepting illusory duality.[70] Deep sleep (*suṣupta*) is valued more highly because one then experiences no duality or suffering. In the *vāsanā*-less deep sleep state, the knower has equanimity and coolness within. When detached and possessing the self after "awakening" as a *jīvanmukta*, one sees like one asleep—always fixed on the formless.[71]

Sleep, when *vāsanās* are destroyed, leads to the nondual fourth, *turīya*, which is also *jīvanmukti* (YV III:22.7).[72] Blissful *turīya* is further described as the single object of *jīvanmukti* and of *vāk* (*śruti*), beyond fear, sorrow, and the illusion of samsara, and without the bondage of rebirth or the darkness of egoism.[73] There is even a stage beyond the fourth, called *turīyātīta*, which is a nondual "state" beyond great (and no) bliss. *Turīyātīta*, unsurprisingly, is associated with bodiless (*videha*) liberation.[74]

Jīvanmukti also appears in a seven-stage (*bhūmi*) meditation model linked in the YV with the four-states doctrine.[75] One version (YG VIa:120. 3–9) says *jīvanmukti* begins in the fifth stage (*ānandarūpa* or *śuddha saṃvid*), which is called deep sleep (*suṣupta*) since (like sleep) it is a mass of bliss. *Jīvanmukti* also exists in the sixth ("massed sleep," *suṣupta ghana*) and seventh (equanimous and peaceful *turīya*) stages. The utterly full (*paripraudha*) seventh stage is beyond the fourth (*turīyātīta*), the highest nirvana, ungraspable by mind or words, and not the object of the living (*videhamukti*).

A second version (YV VI:126. 64–71) says the sixth stage, beyond eternally restful "massed sleep," manifests *jīvanmukti*. This stage unites opposites: it is neither I nor not I, being or not being, without duality or oneness, full and empty within and without, like a water-filled pot in the ocean (or an air-filled pot in air). The seventh stage is again called bodiless liberation, which is peaceful and unreachable by words. While these models are not completely congruent (in this and many other respects), they do indicate the high status accorded *jīvanmukti* as well as its "junior" relationship to *videhamukti*.[76]

It is worth mentioning here that when the *jīvanmukta's* elevated state of consciousness is discussed, there is almost never reference to yogic *samādhi*. While, as stated earlier, the YV does not advocate Patañjali's eightfold yoga, a *samādhi* which brings "inner coolness" (*antaḥśītalatā*) is praised and said to bring calmness and a peaceful and actionless mind, whether one is living a worldly life, or in the woods.[77] YV V:56. 20 asserts that this *samādhi*, by which the self is established, is free from sorrow, desire, or fear.

YV V:62 speaks at some length about this "good" (that is, rather Advaitin) *samādhi.* It is the highest cessation, free from all conception (*saṃkalpa*) (YV V:62.4). With an eternally awakened mind (even) while acting in the world, this concentration is always based in the one reality of the self (YV V:62.6). The value of the *samādhi* of *aṣṭhāṅga* yoga then seems to be brought into question: Does one sitting in *padmāsana* with hands joined reach a pure unchanging concentration? (YV V:62.7) Isn't *samādhi* a purifying knowledge of the (nondual) truth, not sitting silently? (YV V:62.8). YV V:62.9 connects this true *samādhi* and the highest insight (*parā prajña*); one is now concentrated, eternally satisfied, and seeing things as they truly are. Verses 10–11 add such *samādhi* is undisturbed, egoless, not following dualities, without doubt, obtaining what is desired, and free from choosing or abandoning anything. When awakened, the ever-yoked mind reaches the uninterrupted concentration of *mahātmas* (YV V:62.12).[78]

Conclusion

Let us now review the main points the YV makes about liberation while living. Like mainstream Advaita, the YV holds that *jīvanmukti* arises from knowledge of the nondual self, not from austerity, powers, or karmic acts. The apparently manifold world with its pleasures and sorrows is an illusion (as bondage itself is ultimately an illusion). More in line with Yogic Advaita is the idea that utter detachment allows the *jīvanmukta* to act freely in the world according to dharma or to renounce the world and all action. Gods and humans are liberated when detached, not due to any form of action—or inaction. Instead, the notion of being an "actor" disappears. Even embodiment itself can be seen as irrelevant to liberation, though there is also a recurrent theme that bodiless liberation is a little "higher" than *jīvanmukti.*

While mainstream Advaita emphasizes the self/body difference, the Yogic Advaita of the YV stresses the cessation of mind and its impressions. The *jīvanmukta's* mind (and especially the individuating "I" notion) must be controlled or destroyed; all mental impressions (*vāsanā*), good or bad, must be removed—ultimately including the highest impression, *sattva.* The mind is fundamentally just a mass of mental impressions causing rebirth. The liberated being also must go beyond the illusions of waking, dreaming, and even undifferentiated deep sleep. The *jīvanmukta* rests in nondual *turīya*, the "state" beyond states of consciousness.

While Śaṅkara's Advaita and the YV emphasize different things, there are no irreconcilable contradictions. The YV spends more time on detached action in the world and the nature of the jīvanmukta's mind (and mental states) than does Śaṅkara. There is also less concern with bodily continuity due to *prārabdha* karma, criticizing other *darśanas* or rejecting dharmic action in the YV. Thus, while still Advaita, the YV is Yogic Advaita.

A Note on Yoga and *Samādhi* in the *Jīvanmuktiviveka*

A comparison of the YV and JMV, probably the two best-known Yogic Advaita texts, is beyond the concerns of this volume. Still, it is worth mentioning here a bit more of Vidyāraṇya's views on yoga and *samādhi.* As said earlier, Vidyāraṇya, quite possibly a "Śaṅkarācārya in Sringeri, feels much more bound to Brāhmanical orthodoxy than does the author of the YV, so he attempts to integrate aspects of the *varṇāśrama-dharma* and *āstika* schools like Yoga, as well as the LYV (in part due to its apparent popularity), into his version of Advaita Vedanta."[79] Despite the tensions among these disparate ideas and schools, Vidyāraṇya's syncretic melange has quite evidently proven compelling. While both texts hold that knowledge of nondual Brahman is the highest goal, leading to living liberation, Vidyāraṇya says much more about, and puts greater value on, Patañjali's eightfold yoga practice (particularly *samādhi),* than does the YV (though the models are not identical, nor does Vidyāraṇya discuss *aṣṭhāṅga* yoga systematically).[80] Yoga is most relevant to *mano-nāśa,* "destroying the mind," a mental therapy which assists and safeguards liberation. Vidyāraṇya claims that yoga and ascetic renunciation (*saṃnyāsa*) together lead to and express the liberating knowledge of Brahman. In the case of yoga specifically, knowledge and yogic practice are linked, for discerning nonduality breeds the cessation of mental activity, and ceasing mental activity by yoga assists seeing nonduality.

Concerning *samādhi* in particular, Vidyāraṇya focuses on superconscious (*asaṃprajñāta*) *samādhi.* For Vidyāraṇya, conscious (*saṃprajñāta*) enstasis seems the peak of yogic practice, demonstrating extraordinary mental discipline but still concerned with control (through one-pointedness). Superconscious enstasis, on the other hand, seems to lead beyond yogic discipline to actual cessation of mental activity, a transformationless and serene absorption in the Self (which is living liberation). Thus we see his syncretic, but finally Advaitic, view: yoga is a foundational element in destroying the mind, which assists and safeguards liberation, but it is not the ultimate aim or achievement.

Notes

1. yathāsthitaṃ idaṃ yasya vyavahāravato 'pi ca
astaṃ gataṃ sthitaṃ vyoma jīvanmuktaḥ sa ucyate

bodhaikaniṣṭhatāṃ yāto jāgraty eva suṣuptavat
ya āste vyavahartaiva jīvanmuktaḥ sa ucyate

nodeti nāstamāyāti sukhe duḥkhe mukhaprabhā
yathā prāptasthiter yasya jīvanmuktaḥ sa ucyate

yo jāgarti suṣupastho yasya jāgranna vidyate
yasya nirvāsano bodhaḥ sa jīvanmukta ucyate

rāgadveṣabhayādīnām anurūpaṃ carannapi
yo 'ntarvyomavad acchasthaḥ sa jīvanmukta ucyate

yasya nāhaṃkṛto bhāvo yasya buddhir na lipyate
kurvato kurvato vāpi sa jīvanmukta ucyate

yasyonmeṣanimeṣārdhād vidaḥ pralayasaṃbhavau
paśyettrilokāḥ svasamaḥ sa jīvanmukta ucyate

yasmānnodvijate loko lokānnodvijate ca yaḥ
harṣāmṛṣabhayonmuktaḥ sa jīvanmukta ucyate

śāntasaṃsārakalanaḥ kalāvānapi niṣkalaḥ
yah sacittopi niścittaḥ sa jīvanmukta ucyate

yaḥ samastārthajāteṣu vyavahāryapi sītalaḥ
padārtheṣvapi pūrṇātmāḥ sa jīvanmukta ucyate.
(YV III:9.4–13)

For references to passages using similar terms. Other good summaries of the nature of *jīvanmukta* appear in YV V:70.1–10 and 77.1–44.

2. *The Yogavāsiṣṭha of Vālmīki*, Vasudeva Laxmana Sharma Pansikar, ed. 2 vols. 3rd edition (Bombay: Nirnaya Sagar Press, 1918. Reprint; Delhi: Motilal Banarsidass, 1984).

3. I abbreviate the *khaṇḍa* names as follows: V=Vairāgya, Up=Upaśama, M=Mumukṣu, P=Pūrvanirvāṇa, U=Utpatti, Ut=Uttaranirvāṇa, S=Sthiti.

4. For more on Yogic Advaita, see part 2 of my *Jīvanmukti in Transformation: Embodied Liberation in Advaita and Neo-Vedanta* (Albany: State University of New York Press, 1998).

5. The *Yogavāsiṣṭha* has many cosmogonic passages which make extensive use of Sāṃkhya categories, but when *jīvanmukti* is considered, the Advaita framework predominates.

6. Readers interested in the Puranic dimension should look at Mackenzie Brown's chapter on Śuka as *jīvanmukta* in the Mahābhārata and the Bhāgavata and Devī-Bhāgavata Purāṇas in Patricia Mummes and Andrew Fort, *Living Liberation in Hindu Thought* (Albany: State University of New York Press, 1996).

7. Walter Slaje, "On Changing Others' Ideas: The Case of Vidyāraṇya and the Yogavāsiṣṭha," *Indo-Iranian Journal* 41 (1998): 112.

8. The only exception of which I know is YV VIb:174.113–14, which states that illusion ceases for the wise due to right knowledge (*saṃyakparijñāna*), and *jīvanmukti*, rising due to the complete impossibility of creation (*sarga*), is here called unending nonconceptual concentration (*nirvikalpa samādhi*).

9. In his article, Slaje claims that *samādhi* (at least of the Pātañjala kind) is "severely criticized by the YV" (113) and contrasts this view with Vidyāraṇya's idea that Patañjali's eight-fold yoga, and particularly *samādhi*, is crucial to the achievement of *jīvanmukti* (see endnote). For the critique of yoga (vs. *jñāna*) generally, see, for example, YV VIb:125.26–29 and YV VIa 13.8–10.

Slaje, taking more from the *Mokṣopāya-ṭīka* than the YV, argues that this *samādhi* is considered incomplete and temporary, as samsara never fully disappears in, and rearises after, *samādhi*. While, as said above, the term is not (with one exception) used in connection with *jīvanmukti*, there are a number of positive references, as Slaje also notes two paragraphs later.

10. The text also mentions many other kinds of sages: *muni, siddha, guru, yogin, sādhu, jñānin*. I will focus on passages where the term *jīvanmukta* is specifically used.

11. One of the distinctive characteristics of the *Yogavāsiṣṭha* is its (often literally) flowery language. Many chapters include luxuriant descriptions of natural phenomena, which are then called illusory and necessary to renounce. Natural metaphors abound: wisdom is said to "blossom like flowers" and "shine like the full moon's beams" in the "forest of awakening" (YV V:18.4–5). The world is ultimately "burnt in the fire of the intellect," and clear minds don't "sprout illusion" like burned seeds don't sprout plants (YV VIa:2.46–9).

The *jīvanmukta* (or his mind) is often termed clear or empty like the cloudless (autumn) sky (YV III:9.8; Up 17.18, 18.25, 53.74, 77.33, 89.19, 56.2). A typical image appears in YV VIb:125.63–65: the *jīvanmukta* sees all characteristics without any difference, like "space" (*akāśa*) in the sky, and knows a brilliant rainbow, like all visible objects, is really only an empty reflection.

12. YV I:3.1–3; YV V:18.28–30; YV VIb:95.17–21; 125.65–68.

13. YV V:18.13–15.

14. The point seems to be, as YV VIb:125.36 says, that the mind is bound and burning whether sad (having body cut up) or happy (sitting on a throne).

15. YV V:17.5, 93.84, 87; YV VIa:120.18–19.

16. YV VIb:95.26, 199.34–35.

17. On *vicāra* and the other "gatekeepers" to liberation, see Slaje's essay.

18. YV III:8.16; YV V:18.30, 34. A common synonym for *jīvanmukta* is *mahātma* ("great self"); both are detached, have a controlled mind, and so on.

19. YV III:9.2; YV IV:46.23–24; YV V:12.15–16, 75.45.

20. A point also made by the texts Mackenzie Brown studies in his chapter in *Living Liberation in Hindu Thought*.

21. As with traditional Advaita, we shall see that the key to liberation lies with neither the body's presence or absence, nor performance of action or nonaction, nor supernatural powers (*siddhi*).

22. In YV VIb:95.16, Vasiṣṭha says he is here teaching among us since he didn't reach Brahmahood. One wishes for further elaboration on this admission.

23. Various forms of the root *śam*, indicating peacefulness, also appear frequently.

24. YV V:53.80, 68.6, 70.23, 86.5, 93.93; YV VIb:125.56.

25. YV V:68.9; YV VIb:199.32.

26. YV V:68.4, 70. 1, 93.90–91.

27. YV V:70.1; YV VIa:101.30; YV VIb:199.9. We shall later consider liberated beings' detachment from supernatural powers (YV V:89) and impure *vāsanās* (YV V:93).

28. YV III:118.18; YV V:12.8–10, 16.18, 68.7, 77.26, etc. Both the JMV and the BG speak of the highest yogin in similar terms.

29. YV V:74.37, 77.12, 32.

30. YV V:18.24; YV VIb:125.37. It is also often said that the *jīvanmukta* smiles while internally detached.

31. YV V:16.19–20, 71.10, 77.43.

32. YV V:18.27–29, 17.8, 77.19–20.

33. There are a few passages which suggest that he does not act at all: the detached man completely abandons all actions and fruits (YV V:68.8), all hopes and undertakings (YV V:74.38), and the self-knower does and desires nothing (YV V:89.17). However, the overwhelming emphasis in the *Yogavāsiṣṭha* is on detachment, not nonaction.

34. YV III:9.13; YV V:16.9, 18.11, 53.82, 70. 22,75. 26, P 56.1; YV VIb:125.35. Inner coolness also rises from investigating the *Yogavāsiṣṭa* (VIb:95.28).

35. YV III:9.4; YV V:18.18–19, 77.10, 93.97.

36. YV III:9.6; YV V:12.2, 17.4, 70.18, 93.93.

37. YV III:22.8, 118.28; YV VIb:125.33. This is much emphasized by Slaje.

38. YV V:18.18–22, 77.9, 27.

39. YV V:77.11, YV VIa:56.5.

40. YV V:70.19–20, 77.8.

41. I translate the root *vi-hṛ*, which appears repeatedly in passages which discuss *jīvanmukti*, as "wander." *Vi-hṛ* suggests both detached roaming in the world and withdrawal or separation from the world. For example, it is said the sage with *jīvanmukti*-mind roams the world following all customs yet indifferent to all, and wanders detached and even-minded while in everyday activity (YV V:18.17–26, 93.92–3; YV VIa:101.30; YV VIb:199.9). Sage Nārada and lord Viśvamitra are said to wander the world as *jīvanmuktas* (YV V:75.22, 86.9).

42. We see the Puranic element of the YV clearly here.

43. YV V:12.1–9, 16.9–13, 75.47; YV VIb:125.59. For more (and for conflicting reports) on Janaka's character, see Mackenzie Brown's article in *Living Liberation in Hindu Thought*.

44. Māndātā's liberation while living is also mentioned in YV VIb:125.60.

45. YV V:42.17 says Prahlāda rested within himself with his own pure *sattva vāsanā* until awoken by a conch.

46. YV VIb:125.51 adds that Viṣṇu, creator and destroyer, is a *jīvanmukta*.

47. YV V:75.50; YV VIa:120.11.

48. YV V:17.13 says the body made by parents is unreal, and YV IV:33.66 states that the highest goal is knowing that the notion of a body-based "I" (ahaṃkāra) is unreal.

49. YV VIb:9.16–21 continues that the *videhamukta* is pervasive, controlling all—as sun, he rules three worlds like the *trimūrti*; as sky, he supports the gods; as earth, he supports animals and plants; as fire and water, he burns and melts; he also becomes light and darkness and makes animals and mind move. Elsewhere (YV VIa:126.71–73), it is said that the peaceful and incomprehensible *videhamukta* is called Śiva, Brahma, or *prakṛti* according to how others imagine the self. These passages are representative of several which suggest that the *jīvan-* or *videha-mukta* is a god or supreme being, rather than an "individual" liberated spirit.

50. YV VIa:126.70–71 makes this same point in a different model: the sixth (of seven) stages is *jīvanmukti*; the seventh stage, called *videhamukti*, is utterly peaceful and unreachable by words.

51. I could find no consistent definitional differentiation among these terms.

52. YV VIa:2. 43,47–49; YV VIa:101.24,27–28; YV V:90.15.

53. YV V:77. 21–22, 86. 12,93.94–95, YV VIa:2.4–5. These *jīvanmuktas* are said to wander detached from joy and sorrow, solely intent on knowing the self, at peace and unaffected by samsara (YV V:68.5–6, 70.1–9; YV VIa:101.30).

54. YV III:9.9, 22.11; YV V:16.20, 18.25. See also YV VIa:112.1–4.

55. This idea is one of several passages apparently influenced by Buddhist ideas in which *jīvanmukti* appears. While Buddhist terms occasionally appear in the *jīvanmukti* context, almost no Buddhist technical language is used. Most common is the word "nirvaṇa," which generally designates the highest goal, often *videhamukti* (YV III:9.25; YV V:3.5–6; YV V:53.75; YV VIa:120.6). The detached but "in the world" *jīvanmukta* might be influenced by the concept of the bodhisattva, but no explicit connection is made.

56. YV VIa:2.43, 101.28.

57. YV VIa:69.37–38.

58. YV V:93.84, 87; YV VIa:120.18–19.

59. YV V:93.85; YV V:120.20.

60. YV I:3.8–9; YV III:22.8; YV VIa:2.45; YV VIa:55.42–45; YV VIa:56.1; YV VIa:101.34. Sleep without *vāsanās* also brings inner coolness and liberation (called *turīya* here). Sleep is said to arise from the *vāsanā*less dream

state, and liberation from *vāsanā*less waking state (YV III:22.4; YV V:70.22, 26; YV VIa:126.64–65).

61. Refer here also to YV VIa:2.44 and YV V:18.3.

62. YV V:42.14–17; YV VIa:101.29.

63. YV III:22.5; YV VIa:2.42–43, 47–49, 101.31.

64. YV V:90.17,21–5; YV VIa:101.30, 33.

65. This topic also appears in the JMV (103, 327), also taken from the LYV.

66. A list of oft-repeated terms describing the *jīvanmukta* follows: eternally satisfied (*nitya-tṛpta*), tranquil self (*praśāntātma*), passions ceased (*vītarāga*), and without *vāsanās*.

67. These ideas are also mentioned in the JMV, but most JMV references to the topics below are borrowed from the YV.

68. YV III:9.5–7, YV V:12.2, 13, 16.19, 22, 60.20, 70.10, 16, 19, 77.8, 86.6, YV VIa:56.6.

69. For more on this doctrine, in the *Yogavāsiṣṭha* and Advaita thought in general, see my book *The Self and Its States* (Delhi: Motilal Banarsidass, 1990).

70. References to dream can be found in YV III:22.1–4 and YV VIb:95.17, 23–24. The theme is that dreams and their objects are unreal and cease with knowledge. Waking is "real" only relative to dreams.

71. YV V:42.15, 70.22, 77.3–4.

72. See also YV V:70.26: when fully established in sleep from repeated yogic practice, this is *turīya*, and Up 71.4: having enjoyed the worldly condition in sleep state, one then goes to the fourth.

73. YV III:118.15; YV V:70.27–33, 71.1.

74. YV III:118.16; YV V:70.32, 71. 5. One passage, in contrast, says one resting in the fourth abides there dead (*kayānta*) or in bodily state (YV V:86.6).

75. For more on this, and connections between the *Yogavāsiṣṭha* and the *Jīvanmuktiviveka*, see J. F. Sprockhoff, "Der Weg zur Erlosung bei Lebzeiten . . . ," *Wiener Zeitschrift fur die Kunde Sud- und Ostasiens* 14 (1970): 137ff.

76. The JMV refers to this passage as well as a third seven-stage model in YV III:118, which says those in the seventh stage are great selves (*mahātma*), great enjoyers (*mahābhāga*), and enjoyers of the self (*ātmarāma*). The latter is a common synonym for *jīvanmukti*; YV III:118.20, for example, states that the enjoyer of the self takes no pleasure in worldly activity like those asleep take no pleasure in beautiful women around them.

77. YV V:56.7, 15, 17.

78. If stretched too far, this *samādhi* can break (YV V:13). More praise of the truly concentrated mind continues in verses 62.21–25, emphasizing its continuous, flawless, and serene nature, focused eternally and solely on the reality of the pervasive self. Again one notes the Advaitin, rather than Pātañjala Yoga, nature of this *samādhi*.

79. See Slaje, IIJ, esp. 115–16.

80. For more on this topic, see my "On Destroying the Mind: The Yogasūtras in Vidyāraṇya's Jīvanmuktiviveka," *Journal of Indian Philosophy* 27 (1999): 377–95.

13

Liberation into Nature

Vasiṣṭha's Embrace of the Great Elements

CHRISTOPHER KEY CHAPPLE

The poetry of the *Yogavāsiṣṭha* (YV) draws deeply from nature imagery. Vālmīki, the author of the *Rāmāyaṇa,* wrote with a great depth of knowledge about the flora and fauna of India. In one set of verses, he describes twenty-five species of trees and plants from mangoes to sandalwood trees.[1] The YV also includes descriptions of India's vast and varied landscape, from the desert of King Lavaṇa's banishment to the listing of India's great mountain ranges. For most of the text, the natural world serves as a backdrop and often as a metaphor for difficulty. However, toward the latter part of the final section of the book, nature becomes the context in which Vasiṣṭha describes his own experience of freedom, an experience that qualified him to become Rāma's teacher.

Nature has been articulated in Indian philosophy through the five great elements (*mahābhūta*): earth, water, fire, air, and space. These are carefully listed in the *Sāṃkhya Kārikā* (SK) and in various philosophical works of literature of the Hindus and Buddhists. They receive prominent mention in the Abhidharma literature of early Buddhism as well as in the later literature of Hindu and Buddhist Tantra. Each of these elements correlates to sensory processes as well as bodily functions. To know the elements, senses, and body constitutes an important foundation for knowledge in Indian thought and literature. This chapter will explore the role of the elements in Vasiṣṭha's spiritual journey, a journey that leads through the world into reverie, and from reverie back into the world.

Nature Literature

Various chapters of this book have employed an interpretive frame for understanding the YV, including Bregman's comparisons with theories of many worlds in contemporary physics, Gansathesan's discussion of feminist values, and Timalsina's analysis of the text in light of the magical realism of Borges. For this chapter, which focuses on the elements of nature, the emerging field of nature literature will serve as a cross-cultural touchstone. The American experience of nature appreciation has deep roots in New England's Transcendentalist movement. In turn, this profound part of the American identity owes a debt to Yoga. Emerson, like Mahatma Gandhi, read the *Bhagavad Gītā* daily, and Thoreau, author of *Walden*, characterized himself as a yogi.

Many Americans today revel in wandering fields and forests, exploring streams and ponds, and especially in Southern California, visiting the beach and hiking in the mountains. The feelings brought forth by these nature encounters engender moments of spiritual connection, affirmed in literature by an array of authors who have repeated the experiment of Walden in a variety of contexts: Terry Tempest Williams in Utah, John Muir in the Sierras, Aldo Leopold in Wisconsin, Mary Austin in Death Valley, Edward Abbey in the desert Southwest, and Annie Dillard in the Blue Ridge Mountains. Each of these writers has helped shape American attitudes of appreciation for nature.

Nature literature values environment and the feelings that one experiences in the wild as important, transformative, and ethically formative. One improves oneself in nature. Emerging from nature, one feels restored and prepared, perhaps, to improve the world. A new field has emerged known as eco-criticism, defined by Mazel as "the study of literature as if the environment mattered."[2] Gatta claims that nature literature evokes "belief in the numinous, regenerative force of the American landscape,"[3] citing Ernest Hemingway, F. Scott Fitzgerald, John Woolman, and even Jonathan Edwards.

India holds a rich classical literature that glorifies the natural world, feminizes nature not for exploitation but for celebration, and prods the individual into productive states of interiority. Emerson and Thoreau read the early translations of some of this material. We now have the benefit of 150 years of additional studies of Indian texts and traditions, as well as a renewed sense of the fragility of nature. Thoreau complained of a locomotive making too much noise, a problem that pales in comparison with the melting of the Arctic sea and the Antarctic ice shelf, not to mention the extinction of countless species and the stunning array of social ills that accompany wasteful contemporary lifestyles. Thoreau anticipated the tenor of these problems and the loneliness and alienation of modern peoples in his now-cherished essays.

The literature that inspired Emerson and Thoreau and indirectly a host of modern nature writers and activists can now be instructive not only on the American stage, but also for India herself as she grapples with postmodernity, postcolonialism, and postsocialism. India faces the challenge of reclaiming her identity of place, of forging a forward-looking culture that recognizes and relies upon its roots.

For more than a dozen years I trained with a teacher from India in Amityville, New York, learning about the interior landscape in relationship to the elements and the senses in the context of classical Yoga. She valued the primacy of the elements, the seasons, the body, and the emotions and used a combination of movement, ethics, and textual study in her remarkable philosophy of education, which was directly inspired by Mahatma Gandhi, Sri Aurobindo, and David Hume. She successfully developed a style of teaching Yoga that drew deeply from her own experience of knowing the body, the senses, and oneself in the context of the American northeast.

D. H. Lawrence, while living in New Mexico, wrote that "Every continent has its own great spirit of place. . . . Different places on the face of the earth have different vital effluence, different vibration, different chemical exhalation, different polarity with different stars: call it what you like."[4] India's vibration, extending from the ancient Vedic tradition to the practice of modern Yoga, emphasizes the human body and breath in relation to a construct of elements and landscapes that hold the key to meaning within the world. From this perception arose an ethic of minimizing harm to oneself and others. Yoga brings a person to a state of inwardness (*pratyāhāra*), an inner understanding of the core of one's being. Yoga, bringing serenity to the body-mind continuum, allows one to feel deep connections with the breath, the senses, and the elements.

The Transcendentalists announced the need to shift from seeking to exploit nature to the cultivation of concern for its preservation.

Perhaps the most-quoted passage that provides support for the emergence of a philosophy of American love for nature can be found in Emerson's essay *Nature*, published in 1836:

> Standing on the bare ground,
> my head bathed by the blithe air,
> and uplifted into infinite space—
> all mean egotism vanishes.
> I become a transparent eye-ball.
> I am nothing. I see all.
> The currents of the Universal Being circulate through me.
> I am part or particle of God.[5]

The Asian traditions such as Yoga that influenced Emerson and Thoreau, like the Quaker traditions of their peers, emphasize interiority and the immanence of God. In this view, the realm of spiritual experience does not reside in outward worship but in states of meditation and contemplation on the natural order. To love nature through Yoga seems like a natural expression born of fecundity as experienced in the Indian subcontinent, with its wealth of flora and fauna, abundant monsoons, and warm climate.

Nature and the Elements in Indian Thought

The earliest of India's texts, the *Ṛg Veda*, composed over thirty-five hundred years ago, celebrates Agni as the god of heat and light, Indra as the deity of the thunderstorm who releases the waters of each year's monsoons, and Soma, the creator of a special herbal elixir. The Vedas also extol Dyaus, the Lord of the heavens (referred to by the Greeks later as Zeus), and Pṛthivī, the goddess of the earth.

The *Atharva Veda*, written a few hundred years later, acknowledges that all works and endeavors rely upon the earth and that medicines arise from the earth. It praises mother earth in various ways, stating that "on her body food is grown everywhere and on her the farmer toils . . . the earth is home to cows, horses and birds . . . sacred are your hills, snowy mountains and deep forests. . . . You are the world for us and we are your children."[6] Without the beneficence of the earth, all would perish.

The Upaniṣads, which were composed starting twenty-eight hundred years ago, praise the body and senses. In particular the

Upaniṣads honor the power of the breath. They redefine the self as beyond name and form and introduce methods of Yoga and meditation. These ideas find distillation in the texts of Yoga and Sāṃkhya around two thousand years ago, which discuss the operations and functions of the elements, the body, and the emotions in regard to transcendental consciousness.

The *Mārkaṇḍeya Purāṇa* (MP) (ca. 400 C.E.) makes correlations between the senses, the elements, and the *cakras*, outlining an ascendant interiority similar to that found in Emerson. Beginning with the earth and increasing in subtlety through water, fire, air, and space, this text suggests that one enter into full understanding of one's thoughts and one's soul, correlating a *cakra* to each of these seven steps. The yogi of the *Mārkaṇḍeya Purāṇa* begins with the *mūla cakra* at the base of the spine and disappears at the seventh stage into supreme bliss.[7] The text states:

> The yogi should contemplate the seven objects,
> starting with the earth.
> He should contemplate the subtle earth;
> when he deems the earth to be
> his soul, he leaves behind its bonds.
> Then he transcends the subtle taste in water,
> the form in fire and the touch in wind.
> As he moves into the subtle form of the mind,
> he leaves behind engagement with the sky and sound.
> He enters with his mind into the mind of all created
> beings in a subtle condition.
> From there he develops religious devotion;
> having traversed all seven
> (earth/smell; water/taste; fire/form; wind/touch,
> space/sound, mind/thought, intellect/devotion),
> he moves to supreme bliss,
> leaving behind all attachment.
> (MP XL:15–23)[8]

The Feminine and Nature

The feminine plays an important role in the conceptualization of the relationship between consciousness and material nature. Referred to in the *Devī Māhātmya* as Good Fortune, the Queen, Intelligence, Nourishment, Patience, and many other qualities, the goddess can be found in all experience. She is also referred to consistently as the gateway to liberation. The YV presents a view that feminizes the natural world, glorifying it as the entry point for transcendental experience. The manifest world provides experience and liberation. Without the story told by the mind and enacted by the body through the senses, there could be no reflection, no suffering, no spiritual journey. In one remarkable tale from the YV, Queen Cūḍālā attains freedom first and then leads her husband to insight, knowledge, and liberation. Most significantly, once the couple have had their fill of both experience and liberation, they return to rule their kingdom justly and in good spirits.

The sage Vasiṣṭha, who saves the story of his own spiritual journey for the very end of his discourse on Nirvāṇa in the YV, watches the goddess (named variously Kālī, Devī, Sarasvatī, Laksmī, and Jayā) as she dances into existence the landscapes of hills and plains, rivers and ponds, the warming rays of the sun, and playful breezes. As he contemplates her munificence, he sees the powers of Kālī in his own body. He ascends chapter by chapter from earth through water, fire, air, into space, and then returns, continuing his work in the world, just as Cūḍālā and her husband returned to rule.

As we examine how the YV describes nature and the elements, we see an unfolding that directly parallels the account given in Sāṃkhya philosophy regarding the progression and unfolding of the fundamental constituents of manifest reality. In Sāṃkhya, these *tattvas* exist in a symbiotic relationship. Consciousness (*puruṣa*) relies upon material reality (*prakṛti*) for experience and liberation, a theme echoed in the *Yoga Sūtra* (YS) as well:

> The Seer only sees; though pure it appears intentional.
> The nature of the Seen is only for the purpose of that (Seer).
> (YS II:20–21)

When the purpose of the Seen or the realm of the manifest (*prakṛti*) has been accomplished, then it disappears, entering into a state of abeyance (*pralaya*). Patañjali's culminating sutra describes this process as

> The return to the origin of the *guṇas*,
> Emptied of their purpose for *puruṣa*,
> Is *kaivalyam*, the steadfastness in own form,
> And the power of higher awareness (*citi-śakti*).
> (YS IV:34)

The *Sāṃkhya Kārikā* (*SK*) employs the metaphor of the dancer to describe the pivotal moment when the purpose of *prakṛti* has been accomplished. The realm of activity goes into abeyance, resulting in liberation:

> Just as a dancer retires from her audience after performing,
> in the same way, *prakṛti* retreats . . . when she has been once
> seen by the seer, she does not appear again.
> (SK 59–61)

The term "embarrassment" has been frequently employed to describe Prakṛti's retreat, an image also found in the story lore of India when Kālī, on a destructive rampage, dances unwittingly onto the body of her supine husband Śiva. When she realizes her mistake, out of deep embarrassment she sticks out her tongue and halts her deadly violence.

These images of the "restraint of the feminine" and the attendant association of manifest reality with the female gender emphasize the renunciation aspects of this tradition. In fact, one of the memorable phrases uttered by Śri Rāmakrishna, wherein he insists that the spiritual seeker give up "women and gold," has been construed as perhaps even misogynist, though this was certainly not his intent. He was emphasizing the need to overcome lust and greed, not denigrating the divine status of women or even necessarily the appropriate use of wealth.

As Menaha Ganesathasan has noted, women play a central role in defining the nature of liberation. In her chapter she states, "She is born, she is active, she hopes, suffers, enjoys, and dies . . . she recognizes that pleasure is also pain . . . [and yet] after liberation . . . goodness . . . is intrinsic to her nature . . . She may have left the world behind, but she has not left behind morality" (this volume, chapter 10). This reflects the liberation story narratives wherein various queens, including Līlā and Cūḍālā, attain spiritual liberation before their husbands.

On two counts, then, Vasiṣṭha liberates the feminine: women achieve the vaunted status of *jīvanmukta*. Nature, rather than being devalued, becomes the object of reverence, providing the experience needed for Vasiṣṭha himself to ascend into *cid-ākāśa*, the enlightened state.

Vasiṣṭha's Liberation: The World within the Rock

In a narrative entitled "The World within the Rock" Vasiṣṭha enters into a darkened cave where he sees Lord Śiva in meditation. A shadow calls his attention to the presence of the goddess. As he gazes upon her, she dances, creating the world, carrying mountains and forests on her shoulders and arms. When she ceases to dance, the world stops and begins to dissolve. Her magical presence intrigues Vasiṣṭha. She tells Vasiṣṭha how she creates the material universe from her body. She inspires him to take up a sequence of concentration exercises (*dhāraṇā*) through which he sees how his own body is connected with the fundamental elements that comprise the world.[9] Contrary to a more Buddhistic approach that would emphasize the putrid nature of decaying flesh, Vasiṣṭha celebrates all that emanates from and remains connected with his body. He enters into an experience of the anthropocosmic, a term used by Eliade from the 1940s through the 1970s "to account for the correspondences between microcosm and macrocosm that appear throughout the history of religions" and more recently used by Tu Wei Ming "to describe the dynamic interconnectedness of Heaven, Earth, and humanity."[10] This episode occurs toward the end of the last book of the YV and indicates his own profession of enlightenment to Rāma. The examples given in other stories are about the experiences of other people. Because this is about Vasiṣṭha's own enlightenment, it merits close consideration.

There is a close relationship between the philosophy of Sāṃkhya and the process through which Vasiṣṭha reaches liberation. According to the *Sāṃkhya Kārikā* and the *Yoga Sūtra*, nature (*prakṛti*) serves two functions, providing experience and liberation.[11] In the story of Vasiṣṭha's realization of liberation through his direct encounter with nature, we find that a goddess starts him on his quest, that he employs the Yoga technique of *dhāraṇā* to enter deep states of interiority, and that his narrative takes the form of a personal confession. He seems delighted, surprised, and even overwhelmed as he discovers that the powers of the elements themselves reside in his own body.

The narrative begins when Kālī shuts down the world through her dance of cosmic dissolution. It then shifts to a reconstruction of the world within the body of Vasiṣṭha himself, celebrated element by element. It concludes (or rather transitions to yet another story) by placing Vasiṣṭha in dialogue with an ascended sage, who gives advice on how to maintain purified consciousness while moving about in the world. The sage tells him:

> The infinite consciousness (*cid-ākāśa*) is I,
> it is the three worlds,
> it is the *puruṣa* (cosmic being)
> and it is you.[12]

This philosophy affirms the validity of the constructed realm and hence forms a foundation for Vasiṣṭha to exhort Rāma to resume his duties.

In order to capture a sense of the rich imagery employed by the author in praise of nature, new translations of portions of successive chapters describing Vasiṣṭha's encounter will follow.[13] In this narrative, Vasiṣṭha undergoes a shift in awareness. He assumes the position of a sovereign king, overseeing the landscape of his domain from a birds-eye view. What begins as rhapsody about the beauties of nature becomes a celebration of the material powers contained within his own body. Vasiṣṭha, as we will see, becomes anthropocosmic.

The Earth

In VII: 89, Vasiṣṭha describes looking down upon the earth. From this vantage point, he sees soil, plants, mountains, and rivers and relates them to his own body:

> 58. Through performing concentration on the earth,
> I dissolved into the form of the earth.
> While still retaining this expanded consciousness,
> I became like a universal ruler (surveying his domain).
> 59. And indeed, through my concentration on the earth,
> I went to the mines at the root of the earth.
> I came to understand my body as the trees,
> the grasses, the mountains, the continents, and more.
> 60. As I took possession of the throne of the earth,
> forests sprouted from my body.
> I became adorned with cities
> as if laced with strings of pearls.
> 61. I was endowed with forests separated by villages.
> The regions of the netherworld were sunk deep in my bowels.
> My arms embraced the mountain ranges
> and my continents were encircled with oceans like bracelets.
> 62. I felt my body covered with grasses like hair,
> as well as tree-tangled mountains,
> held up by the heads of ten elephants
> and the hundreds of heads of the primal serpent Śeṣa.
> 64. The beautiful ridges of the Himalayas and the Vindhyas,
> the clouds high on Mount Meru,

the abundance of the rivers such as the Ganges:
all this evokes a delicate string of pearls.
65. Caves and thickets and marshes
appear to encircle the ocean.
The white salts of the desert
shimmer like a beautiful garment.
66. In ancient times (of the great flood)
the ocean purified all things.
When it receded, the flowery forests
were resplendent with fragrant pollen.
67. Repeatedly, the ground is plowed and turned:
cooled by the winds of the winter,
warmed by the heat of summer
and moistened by the waters of the rainy season.
68. My chest became the expansive plains.
My eyes became pools of lotuses.
My crown was the light and dark clouds.
My body (*mandiram*) contained the ten regions.
72. Filled with floods, deserts, farms, kingdoms, as well
as people,
on named continents of stone with rivers, forests,
and oceans to the end of the horizon,
the Earth is an assemblage of vessels and designs
connected with various adorning marks,
as if flecked with groups of lotuses in a raging river,
or like a pond laced with vines.

Vasiṣṭha describes the planet with great precision and emotion. He sees mountains, forests, deserts, caves, plains, and oceans. He describes the seasons and, like the anthropocosmic sections of the *Bṛhadāraṇyaka Upaniṣad*, makes correlations between his body and the body of the world. He feels vegetation sprout from his body. His arms embrace the mountains. His chest becomes the broad plains, his eyes become lotus pools, and clouds gather around his head. He becomes entranced and absorbed into the beauty of the earth.

The Waters

In the next chapter, Vasiṣṭha explores various forms of water. He again performs *dhāraṇā*, defined by Patañjali as "the binding of the mind to a place" (*deśa-bandhaś-cittasya dhāraṇā*, *Yoga Sūtra* III:1). This practice, when extended, moves one into a state of meditation (*dhyāna*) and ultimately into *samādhi*. Patanjali describes *samādhi* as a state of emptying (*śūnya*) that allows the higher self to shine forth.[14] Vasiṣṭha attains a state of transparency first to earth and then to water, blending and merging with the experience of each:

> VII 90. 9. Just as I experienced the earth-plane
> by earth contemplation (*pṛthivī dhāraṇā*),
> then, just as I saw those many worlds
> held in the form of the earth,
> so also I became water, which was seen
> by me in the same way (as from above).
> 10. By concentration on water, I became water,
> as if this unconscious (substance)
> took on consciousness
> inside the abodes of the oceans with its quiet gurgling.
> 11. [The water] slowly rose up into the veins
> and trunks of creeping vines, grasses, trees,
> tendrils, and groves, as if a caterpillar
> were mounting your limbs.
> 12. That [water] lifts everything like the [rising of sap in]
> the trunk of a tree, cutting patterns like bracelets,
> roiling the water worms gently
> with undulating movements in its hollows.
> 13. Having rested, [the water] formed beautiful lines,
> its full shape taking the form of the leaves and fruits
> of vines, hardwood trees, and palm trees.
> 14. [Water] enters into the hearts [of plants]
> as if through their mouths.
> It lets the roots in the bodies [of plants]
> hold firm during the adversity of the [monsoon] season,
> [growing back] when cut, shaken, eaten, or harvested.
> 15. [Water] takes the form of drops of dew
> asleep in the beds of leaves,
> constant at all times,
> tirelessly gleaming in all directions.
> 16. Along its endless journey,
> [water] takes a home in various lakes and rivers,
> occasionally resting gracefully by a bridge,
> like an old friend.
> 17. Like the consciousness of a simpleton,
> searching out a purpose but lacking support

due to his stupidity,
water swirls up into whirlpools, unaware of its brilliance.
18. By my bad deeds, I was lifted up
to a waterfall at the peak of a huge mountain
and then that self-same swirling whirlpool
was dashed into a hundred rivulets.
19. Having arisen from the woods in the form of mist
into the ocean of the sky,
this indwelling gem stuck
as tear drop jewels in the blue stars.
20. [Water] took rest in the thrones of the clouds,
accompanying Lady Lightning
whose blue sapphire light
illuminated Vasudeva on his Snake Throne.
21. Atoms of water gush forth in tiny drops.
Each holds its essential nature,
like Brahman is found in all souls.
22. Having reached a connection with the highest experience
through the taste buds, my soul was delivered
from the body to the singularity of knowledge.
23. That sweetness is not achieved by me,
nor by my body, nor by anything else.
It is revealed inside, to consciousness.
At that point, ignorance disappears.
24. The bee tastes and takes nectar from various flowers
in all directions across all seasons.
It takes this enjoyable elixir and
passes it along to the next bee.
25. In the connecting joints of the fourteen classes of beings,
water dwells as if it were conscious,
though by its inert nature it has no consciousness.
26. In the form of a rising mist,
[water] ascends on the chariot of the winds,
bestowing joyous fragrance in the channels
of the pure sky.
27. Rāma, by dwelling in that [water concentration]
from the smallest particle
to the ultimate experience of it,
the whole world comes into existence.
28. Through this unconscious thing appearing as if conscious,

through the sameness of myself with this water,
all inner meaning of what is known
and unknowable was revealed to me.
29. I have seen the ascent of hundreds,
thousands, of worlds arising and falling there,
like layers of leaves in a banana tree.
30. Whether a world is beautiful
or a world is ugly,
all of them are consciousness only, like the sky.
Though [they seem] numerous, they are spacious and pure.
31. This knowledge shines forth as the highest purity.
It indeed appears to us as empty.
This vast space, in its expansiveness,
is who you were and who you are.

Vasiṣṭha experiences water in its various forms. Just as he discussed the fragrance of the earth, he mentions the sense of taste in regard to water. In Sāṃkhya, foundational awareness of the earth arises from the power of smelling, and the capacity of tasting is known through and linked with water. He describes dew, drops of rain, the gathering of moisture in clouds, mist, rivers, and waterfalls. Vasiṣṭha talks of how sap rises in plant life. He also discusses how the beauty of water brought him again to a deep appreciation and awareness, stilling his thoughts and revealing vast empty space.

Fire

Fire (*agni, tejas*) finds an important role in the earliest literature of India. The very first hymn of the *Ṛg Veda* offers praise to the god Agni (cognate with the Latin word ignite), and more Vedic hymns address Agni than any other deity. Vasiṣṭha finds fire in a myriad of forms, from the sun and moon and stars to the simple oil lamp. Through light one experiences deep delight and a feeling of safety and security. The correlated sense, seeing, can only function through the presence of light. For Vasiṣṭha, light becomes truly revelatory:

VII 91.1. Then I disappeared into fire
through the brilliant concentration on fire.
I became linked with its various parts such as
the moon, lightning, stars, flames, and so forth.
2. From its essential nature as eternally luminous,

it spreads light like a beloved prince.
It makes all things visible. It makes all things right.
Thieves fail to conceal themselves in its glow.
3. Through its gentle, friendly lamps
it provides thousands of delights.
It allows all purposes to be seen
in every house, like a good prince.
4. It brings good cheer to all the world
through the sparkling rays of the moon and sun.
Through its singular delights it casts light
into the distance, lifting up and pervading
the circumference of the sky.
5. Light destroys the combined qualities
of blindness and affliction.
It possesses the quality of
revealing all truth and awakening.
6. The people proclaim with gusto:
"[Fire] is the axe [that cuts] the tree of darkness.
It provides the foothold for making things exceedingly pure.
It is golden, the ruby among gems."
7. It [energizes] reds, blacks, and whites;
it abides eternally through its gleaming limbs,
like a father gives shape to the bodies
of all his sons.
8. Fire, through its blessings, chooses
to spare the house of children from destruction.
It also protects [the people] from piercing winds
throughout the land.
9. I saw the master [burning] brightly
in the darkest forms of the hell region.
With eyes half open, I saw its active form,
on the surface of the earth and at the crown of existence.
10. I saw [fire] in the abodes of the gods,
where illumined souls are eternally in great splendor,
as well as the light on the ruined huts of the people
and in the recesses covered in great darkness.
11. [I saw] that stainless radiant virgin sky
become smeared with the color of saffron [at sunset],
making way for the illumination of the moon and stars,
as well as the winds that bring night dew.
12. Her grace causes the fields of corn each day

to ripen and grow up out of the darkness.
Her radiance [draws water up] into the clouds
that fill the vast crystal dome [of the sky]
and bring cleansing rains.
13. By her, meaning is bestowed.
Through her, comes illumination.
Like a younger sister, she reveals the highest truth:
there is consciousness only.
14. Her lustre on the lotus pool reflects
the actions of living beings on the earth and below,
just as from consciousness emerges
the wonderment of thought, perception, and form.
15. A necklace of innumerable jeweled stars
is called together from the mist.
Light increases with the days and seasons throughout the year
and froths in fires under the ocean.
16. The moon and sun move briskly
inside the great darkness of the night sky,
just as the one who stands deep in the great universe
is the one eternally moving and imperishable.
17. Fire is the brilliance in gold,
the strength in men,
the crystal gleam in all jewels,
and the flash in lightning storms.
18. It is the splendor in the phases of the face of the moon.
It is the mark of beauty in long eyelashes.
Its undying love flows abundantly.
It glitters in the laughter of friends.
19. Fire is in the love that arises and shines forth
and can be found in the innate allure of the movement
of a face, an arm, an eye,
an eyebrow, a hand, or a lock of hair.
20. Fire shows that these three worlds are as flimsy as straw.
It burns in the slap of one's worst enemies.
It starts the thunderclap
and dwells in the heart of the strong lion.
21. Among excellent, active warriors,
fierce fire can be found in the sound
of their clashing swords, breaking through armor,

and in their harsh, noisy battle cries.
22. It emboldens the gods to fight the Dānava demons
and the demons to resist the gods.
Fire is the force that moves all beings.
It causes plants to sprout upward.
23. Bright-eyed one, I experienced those things
in these coverings of space that make up the world
as if they were shimmering in the desert.
24. I saw the phoenix sun as its streams of light
scattered over all ten points of the horizon.
I saw its limbs flash on chosen mountains,
making them appear as if they were villages
on the face of the earth.
25. The wheel of the sun is filled with treasure
like the desire within a flower's blossom.
Light sits within the universe
like phosphorescence in the darkened sea.
Its continuous line of days unfolds just as fruits ripen on the tree.
26. The face of the moon in the sky
forms a pool of elixir.
Each evening it smiles cheerfully
on the people of the night.
27. (The moon's) power reflects
all lovely good fortune in the world.
His wife, Rohini, (shines) in the night
as the most beloved white lotus flower.
28. To me appeared a gentle trail of stars,
arrayed like nectar flowing through the heavens,
like a web of shining flowers on a vine,
twisted and heaped together.
(The Milky Way!)
[note: commentary suggests *maranda* (nectar) in place of *maśaka* (mosquito).]
29. I saw jewel-like waves in the hands of the oscillating ocean,
as if merchants' hands were tossing them
on their scales to weigh them.
30. I see whirlpools of fish in the water of the ocean,
multitudes of sunbeams on that water,
and in the delicate clouds,
(portents of) lightning igniting a forest fire.

31. I saw the beautiful burning of the sacrificial fire,
its tenacious flames devouring the wood,
spreading throughout all that can be burned,
roaring, strong, and crackling.

Vasiṣṭha explores various metaphors of fire and light, including its ability to dispel ignorance, its ability to provide comfort "like a good prince," its ability to protect and illumine. Like a Buddhist, he proclaims that fires remind us that all things are fleeting. Like a Vedāntin, he hints that just as fire can be found in all manner of things, so also resides the soul.

Air and Wind and Space

When Vasiṣṭha practiced concentration on the wind (*vāyu dhāraṇā*), he proclaimed:

VII: 92.1. Next I came to concentrate
on the operations of the wind,
spreading my thoughts resolutely
to examine the world and satisfy my curiosity.
2. I rose up into the wind [that surrounds] the earth,
playing with the people, the trees,
and the beautiful blooming flowers,
protecting the water lilies.
3. Desiring to bring some relief
to the exhausted bodies of the amorous ones,
I sprinkled down drizzle and mist
with the higher purpose of bringing them joy.
4. I became the teacher of the dancing leaves
of grasses, trees, and tender vines.
I was adorned with the fragrance of flowers
and the splendor of medicinal plants and fruits.
5. At times of quiet and celebration
I fondly caressed the worlds of beautiful women.
At times of calamity (such as earthquakes)
I tossed rocks as if they were feathers.
6. In heaven, I carry the earth's honey and pollen.
I lift up the scent of jasmine that adorns the trees in paradise.
In hell, my gathered fires illuminate the thick fog.

7. In the ocean my undulating movements
can be seen in the pounding of the surf.
In the sky, I move the clouds to hide
and then reveal the mirror of the moon.
8. I support that beneficial vehicle,
the powerful army of stars,
moving perfectly through the three worlds
on their powerful, speedy chariot.
9. Closely resembling how thought
quickly appears and disappears,
the air touches the body though it has no body,
inducing bliss through its movement (spanda)
like the fragrance of sandalwood.
10. [The wind drives] the hard showers of rain and snow.
It brings infirmity to the old.
It makes the young drunken with joy.
For the gentle ones, it brings silence and innocence.
11. Its course lifts up sweetness,
and brings the nectar of happiness to the heavens.
The beloved [winds] of March take away
the fatigue that comes with long love making.
12. Though tired from the incessant
swinging and swaying and undulations of the Ganges,
the wind [in the mountains] does not recognize its own fatigue
and fends off extended exhaustion.

13. Though its caresses, it bends the abundant flowers
and the vines waiting like wives in springtime.
It incessantly shakes and moves the palm fronds.
It dislodges bees from the plants.
14. Having enjoyed pleasures for a long time
under the face of the moon,
the full cloud of sleepiness comes upon the bed.
Exhausted from making love, [the wind] is taken away
to that splendid lotus that throbs in the heart.
15. The wind, like a horse, moves through the sky,
established in and combined with the clouds.
It resembles a dancing elephant
in the throes of sexual desire.[15]

From this expansive moment, Vasiṣṭha roamed into vast space. In words that echo centuries later in Emerson's grand pronouncement quoted above, Vasiṣṭha claims:

> The netherworlds were my feet,
> the earth my abdomen,
> and the heavens my head . . .
> I was spread in all directions
> everywhere at all times
> and I did everything.
> I was the self of all.
> I was all.
> Yet I was pure space.
> I experienced being something and being nothing.
> I experienced universes within every atom
> and universes within the atoms of those universes.
> I myself became all these universes.[16]

In this proclamation, Vasiṣṭha's body expands to encompass the universe. He has attained the pureness of space and hence liberation.

Conclusion

The description of the elements as expressed in the YV anticipates the best passages found in today's nature literature. These passages evoke the experience of what William James called conversion, referred to in the earlier chapter on the *Upaśama Prakaraṇa*. In this narrative, nature speaks to and moves Vasiṣṭha to a place of deep connection. The bliss engendered by Vasiṣṭha's process of immersion in the elements and their correlative senses, one by one, culminates in a universal vision not unlike that experienced by Arjuna in the eleventh chapter of the BG. In the BG, Kṛṣṇa draws all the Mahābhārata warriors into their destruction, like moths to a flame. Vasiṣṭha's epiphany begins as Kālī performs her dance of destruction. This entices him into rarefied states of contemplation that culminate in universal consciousness, an immersion into the *cid-ākāśa*.

Vasiṣṭha's liberation takes place through the very tools of experience. Vasiṣṭha does not retreat from the earth or its smells; he does not disdain water or its tastes; he does not reject light and the forms it reveals; he does not recoil from the various forms of wind. He celebrates each with elation. Each condition becomes a moment for the expansion of consciousness, an important moment in the process of purification. The journey of Vasiṣṭha affirms, piece by piece, the vital importance of the creative powers of the goddess. By contemplating the elements, Vasiṣṭha comes to highest consciousness. By experiencing nature, he experiences liberation.

The poet Mary Oliver has written: "I am sensual in order to be spiritual."[17] The human body, according to Sāṃkhya, is composed of five sense organs (nose, mouth, eyes, skin, ears) and five action organs (anus, genitalia, hands, legs, and voice) that allow one to perceive and operate in the realm of the five elements (earth, water, fire, air, space). Without the senses and the body there could be no engagement of the world. Without engagement, there can be no experience, and without experience, there can be no liberation. Without the story told by the mind and enacted by the body through the senses, there could be no reflection, no suffering, no spiritual journey. Rāma, at the very beginning of the YV, balks at being asked to venture forth from safety to defend the homeland of sages. Vasiṣṭha's advice points out to Rāma that one cannot avoid the unavoidable, but one can engage the world from a place of wisdom. This calls again to mind the poet Mary Oliver, who has written: "There is only one question: how to love this world."[18] Vasiṣṭha, having encountered the goddess, having seen the process of world creation emanate from his own body, having followed a great sage from space back into the world of subject and object, encourages Rāma to take up his duty. Knowing the world gives one power over the world; without the loss of innocence, there can be no knowledge, no liberation.

In one of the great descriptions of unmediated experience, Annie Dillard writes about an unexpected moment during a road trip:

> I am absolutely alone. . . . Before me extends a low hill trembling in yellow brome, and behind the hill, filling the sky, rises an enormous mountain ridge, forested, alive and awesome with brilliant blown lights. I have never seen anything so tremulous and live. Overhead, great strips and chunks of cloud dash to the northwest in a gold rush. At my back the sun is setting—how can I not have noticed before that the sun is setting? . . . Shadows lope along the mountain's rumpled flanks, they elongate like root tips, like lobes of running water, faster and faster. A warm purple pigment pools in each ruck and tuck of the rock;

> it deepens and spreads, boring crevasses, canyons. As the purple vaults and slides, it tricks out the unleafed forest and rumpled rock in gilt, in shape-shifting patches of glow. These gold lights veer and retract, shatter and glide in a series of dazzling splashes, shrinking, leaking, exploding . . . I am more alive than all the world.[19]

For Dillard, this moment contained all meaning in its poignant beauty and silence. This deeply religious encounter gave her a sense of fulfillment, as well as a wistfulness that regrets the inevitable intruding moment when self-consciousness returns and we lose intimacy and wander into thought and distraction.

Like Annie Dillard, Vasiṣṭha writes poetically about the beauties of nature. From nature he learns firsthand of immediacy and evanescence. He also learns intimacy through his successive encounters with the elements and the senses. One truth remains constant through the lessons taught by the great nature writers and by Yoga: once we learn of the ways of nature, we are confined only by our freedom to pay honor to her, to configure and reconfigure our lives as cultivators and agents of renewal. Like Vasiṣṭha and Rāma, we must return.

Notes

1. *Āraṇyakaṇḍa* 14:16–18, as quoted in David Lee, "The Natural History of the Ramayana," in Christopher Key Chapple and Mary Evelyn Tucker, eds., *Hinduism and Ecology: The Intersection of Earth, Sky, and Water* (Cambridge, Massachusetts: Center for the Study of World Religions, Harvard University Press, 2000), 245–68.

2. David Mazel, ed. *A Century of Early Ecocriticism* (Athens: University of Georgia Press, 2001), 1.

3. John Gatta, *Making Nature Sacred: Literature, Religion, and Environment in America from the Puritans to the Present* (Oxford: Oxford University Press, 2004).

4. D. H. Lawrence, *Studies in Classic American Literature* (1923) as quoted in David Mazel, ed., *A Century of Early Ecocriticism* (Athens: University of Georgia Press, 2001), 238.

5. Ralph Waldo Emerson, "Nature" as quoted in Gatta, *Making Nature Sacred.*

6. O.P. Dwivedi and Christopher Key Chapple, translators. *In Praise of Mother Earth: The Pṛthivī Sūkta of the Atharva Veda* (Los Angeles: Marymount Institute Press, 2011), p. 4, 5, 11, 16.

7. *Mārkaṇḍeya Purāṇa*. T. Eden Pargiter, trans. (Reprint Delhi: Indological Book House, 1969), 200.

8. F. Eden Pargiter, *The Mārkaṇḍeya Purāṇa*, translated with notes (Calcutta: The Asiatic Society of Bengal, 1904), 200.

9. This is the title of the story given in the translation by Swami Venkatsananda. This segment is referred to with various chapter titles in Ravi Prakash Arya's editing of Vihari Lal Mitra's 1890s translation, starting with "Description of the Last Night of Death or General Doom" (VII:81) and ending with "Description of the Current Air, as the Universal Spirit" (VII:92).

10. Sam Mickey, "Contributions to Anthropocosmic Environmental Ethics," *Worldviews: Global Religions, Culture, and Ecology* 11, no. 2 (2007).

11. *Sāṃkhya Kārikā* verses 21, 56–62; *Yoga Sūtra* II:20–22.

12. *Vasiṣṭha's Yoga*, 588, VII:96.

13. The translations that follow are by Christopher Key Chapple, with assistance from various students, including Jodi Shaw, Wynanda Jacobi, Viresh Hughes, Benjamin Zenk, Daniel Levine, and Randall Kraus.

14. *Yoga Sūtra* III:1–3.

15. From *Vasiṣṭha's Yoga*, 582, VII:92.

16. *Vasiṣṭha's Yoga*, 582–583, VII:92.

17. Mary Oliver, *Winter Hours* (Boston: Houghton-Mifflin, 1999), 100, as quoted in Gatta, *Making Nature Sacred*, 200.

18. Mary Oliver, "Spring," *New and Selected Poems* (Boston: Beacon Press, 1992).

19. Annie Dillard, *Pilgrim at Tinker Creek* in *Three by Annie Dillard* (New York: HarperPerennial, 1990), chapter 6, 80.

Bibliography

Agrawal, M. M. *The Six Systems of Indian Philosophy*. Chaukhamba Sanskrit Pratishthan, Delhi, 2001.

Aiyar, N. K. Ramasami. *Indian Wisdom, or Readings from Yoga-Vāsiṣṭha*. Second Edition. Adyar, Madras: The Adyar Library and Research Center, 1971. First published, 1896.

Atreya, B. L. *Deification of Man: Its Methods, and Stages according to the Yogavāsiṣṭha*. Second edition. Morabad: Darshana, 1962.

———. *The Essence of Yogavāsiṣṭha*. Morabad: Darshana Yoga-Vāsiṣtha, 1962.

———. *The Philosophy of the Yoga-Vāsiṣṭha*. Adyar: The Theosophical Publishing House, 1936. Second Edition: Mooradabad: Darshana Printers, 1981.

———. "A Probable Date of Composition of Yogavāsiṣṭha." Proceedings and Transactions of the Seventh All-India Oriental Conference, Baroda, December, 1933. Baroda: Oriental Institute (1935): 55–59.

———. *Vāsiṣṭha-darśana: Princess of Wales Saraswati Bhavana Texts*, vol. 64, 1936.

———. *The Vision and the Way of Yoga-Vāsiṣtha*. Chennai: Indian Heritage Trust, 1993.

———. *The Yogavāsiṣṭha and Its Philosophy*. Third Edition, revised and enlarged. Moradabad: Darshana, 1966.

Bhattacharya, Siva Prasad. "The Cardinal Tenets of the Yoga-Vāsiṣṭha and Their Relation to the Trika System of Kāśmīra." *Annals of the Bhandarkar Oriental Research Institute* 33 (Poona, 1951): 130–145.

———. "The Emergence of an Ādhyātma-Śāstra or the Birth of the Yogavāsiṣṭha Rāmāyaṇa." *The Indian Historical Quarterly* 24 (1948): 201–212.

———. "The Siddhas in the Yoga-Vāsiṣṭha Rāmāyaṇa and a Peep into Their Creed." *Indian Culture*. Mahendra Jayanti Volume (Calcutta, 1951): 91–112.

———. "The Yogavāsiṣṭha Rāmāyaṇa: Its Probable Date and Place of Inception." Proceedings and Transactions of the Third All-India Oriental Conference. Madras, 1924. Madras: Law Printing House (1925): 545–553.

Boistard, M.-J. "Les Ambiguités générique du Yogavāsiṣṭa." Edited by Nalini Balbir, 287–324. Genves Littéraires en Inde. Paris, 1994.

Bose, Dhirendra Nath., trans. *The Yoga-Vāsiṣṭha Rāmāyaṇa.* Calcutta: Firma KLM, 1984.

Chakrabarti, Arindam. "A Horrid Tree-House or a Charming City? Yogavāsiṣṭha (Mokṣopāya) on Spiritual Culture of the Body." In *Nature and Culture,* ed. R. Narasimha, S. Menon, to be published by CSS and PHISPC, New Delhi, 2009.

———. "The Concepts of *jñāna, pramā* and *apramā.*" Manuscript.

Chandra, Lokesh, ed. *Sanskrit texts from Kaśmīr* Vol. 8–9. Yoga-Vāsiṣṭha. Śatapiṭaka Series 334, 335. New Delhi: Sharada Rani, 1984.

Chapple, Christopher Key. "The Concept of Will (pauruṣa) in the Yogavāsiṣṭha." Doctoral dissertation, Fordham University, 1980.

———. *Karma and Creativity.* Albany: State University of New York Press, 1986.

———. "The Negative Theology of Yogavāsiṣṭha and Laṅkāvatāra Sūtra." *Journal of Dharma* 6, no. 1 (Bangalore, 1981): 34–45.

———. "The Pauruṣa Paradigm of the Yogavāsiṣṭha." *Journal of Religious Studies* 9, no. 1 (Patiala, 1981): 47–61.

Chenet, François. Psychogenése et cosmogonie selon le Yoga-Vāsiṣṭa. "Le Monde est dans l'ame." Paris: Diffision De Boccard 1998, 748 S. Collége de France. Publications de L'Institut de Civilisation indienne. Série in-8. 67, 1–2.

———. "Vie et mort selon le Yoga-Vāsiṣṭha." *Revue de Histoire des Religions* 201, no. 2 (1984).

Cornford F. M. *Plato's Cosmology: The* Timaeus *of Plato.* Hackett, Cambridge, 1997.

Crick, F. *The Astonishing Hypothesis.* New York: Simon and Schuster, 1994.

Das, Bhagavan. *Mystic Experiences: Tales of Yoga and Vedanta from the Yoga Vāsiṣṭha.* With notes by Annie Besant. Third Edition. Varanasi: The Indian Book Shop, Theosophical Society, 1959. Preface dated 1927. Originally appeared in *The Theosophical Review,* 1899–1910.

Dasgupta, Surendranath. *A History of Indian Philosophy.* Vol. II, 228–272. Delhi: Motilal Banarsidass, 1975. (Originally published at 322 Engaged Emancipation Cambridge, 1932.)

Dawkins, R. *The Blind Watchmaker.* London: Longmans, 1986.

———. *The Selfish Gene.* Oxford: Oxford University Press, 1989.

DeJong, J. W. [Book review of] Peter Thomi, Cūḍālā, Eine Episode aus dem Yogavāsiṣṭha, Wintrach, 1980. *Indo-Iranian Journal* 23, no. 3 (July, 1981): 221–227.

de nicolás, Antonio T. *Meditations through the Ṛg Veda, Four-Dimensional Man.* York Beach: Nicolas-Hays, Inc., 1976.

Divanji, Prahlad, C. "The Date and Place of Origin of the Yogavāsiṣṭha." Proceedings and Transactions of the Seventh All-India Oriental Conference, Baroda, 1933. Baroda: Oriental Institue (1935): 15–30.

———. "Further Light on the Date of the Yogavāsiṣṭha." *Poona Orientalist* 3 (1938): 29–44.

———. "The Text of the Laghu Yogavāsiṣṭha." *New Indian Anitquary* 1, 697–715. Bombay: Karnatak Publishing House, 1938.

———. "Yogavāsiṣṭha on the Means of Proof." *A Volume of Indian and Iranian Studies Presented to Sir. E. Denison Ross*, 102–112. Bombay, 1939.

Fort, Andrew. *Jīvanmukti in Transformation: Embodied Liberation in Advaita and Neo-Vedanta*. Albany: State University of New York Press, 1998.

———. "On Destroying the Mind: The Yogasūtras in Vidyāraṇya's Jīvanmuktiviveka." *Journal of Indian Philosophy* 27 (1999): 377–395.

———. *The Self and Its States*. Delhi: Motilal Banarsidass, 1990.

Gambhirananda, Swami. *Brahma-sūtra-bhāṣya* of Śri Śaṅkarācārya (Transl. English). Calcutta: Advaita Ashrama, 1965.

Gangopadhyaya, M. K. "The Atomic Hypotheses." In *History of Science and Technology in Ancient India*, ed. D. Chattopadhyaya, 2:282–301. Calcutta: Firma KLM, Calcutta, 1991.

Glasenapp, Helmuth von. *Zwei philosophische Rāmāyaṇas*. Wisedbaden: Steiner, 1951. Akademie der Wissenschaften und der Literatur in Mainz. Abhandlungen der gesistes—und sozialwissenschaftlichen Klasse, 1951, no. 6.

Gleick, J. *Chaos: Making a New Science*. New York: Viking Penguin, 1987.

Granoff, Phyliss. "The Yogavāsiṣṭa: The Continuing Search for a Context." *New Horizons of Research in Indology*. Edited by V. N. Jha, 181–2006. Poona: Poona University, 1989.

Hanneder, Jürgen. *Studies on the Mokṣopāya*. Wiesbaden: Harrassowitz, 2006.

———. "Śaiva Tantric material in the Yogavāsiṣṭha." *Weiner Zeitschriff für 323 Bibliography die Kunde Südasiens* 62 (1998): 67–76.

———. "The Yogavāsiṣṭha and Its Kashmirian Recension, the Mokṣopāya. Textual Notes on Their Quality." *Weiner Zeitschriff für die Kunde Südasiens* 44 (2000): 183–210.

———. "Once More to the Long and Short Version of the Yogavāsiṣṭha in Its Relation to Mokṣopāya Review." *Asian Studies* 59.2 (2005): 509–526.

———. "The Mokṣopāya: An Introduction." In *The Mokṣopāya, Yogavāsiṣṭha and Related Texts*. Edited by Jurgen Hanneder, 9–19. Indologica Halensis 7. Aachen: Shaker Verlag, 2005.

———. "The Mokṣopāyasaṁgraha." In *The Mokṣopāya, Yogavāsiṣṭha and Related Texts*. Edited by Jürgen Hanneder, 105–112. Indologica Halensis 7. Aachen: Shaker Verlag, 2005.

Hiriyana, M. *Outlines of Indian Philosophy*. London: George Allen & Unwin, 1952.

Horgan, J. *The End of Science*. Little Brown, London, 1996.

Hulin, Michel. *Sept récits initiatiques tirés du Yoga-Vāsiṣṭha, traduits du Sanskrit avec introduction et notes*. Paris: Berg International, 1987.

———. "Interpenetration des Consciences et Entrelacement des Destinies Selon la Yoga-Vāsiṣṭha." *Eranos Jahrbuch* 57 (1988): 171–200.

Hume, Robert Ernest, trans. *The Thirteen Principal Upanishads*. Oxford: Oxford University Press, 1995. 362.

Jain, Bal Chand. "Berkeley's Subjectivism and the Yogavāsiṣṭha." Doctoral dissertation, University of Saugar, 1966.

Johnson S. *Emergence*. UK: Penguin Books, 2001.

Jyotirmayananda, Swami. *Yogavāsiṣṭha: Part One*. Miami: Yoga Research Foundation, 1977.

Karmarkar, R. D. "Mutual Relation of the Yogavāsiṣṭha, the Laṅkāvatārasūtra and the Gauḍapāda-kārikās." *Annals of the Bhandarkar Oriental Research Institute, Poona* 36 (1955): 298–305.

Lo Turco, Bruno. "Bücherbesprechungen." *Zeitschrift der Deutschen Morgenländischen Gessellschaft*, Band 152- Heft1 (2002).

———. "The Metaphorical Logic of the Mokṣopāya." In *The Mokṣopāya 324 Engaged Emancipation Yogavāsiṣṭha and Related Texts*. Edited by Jürgen Hanneder, 138. Aachen: Shacker Verlag, 2005.

———. "Love and Nature in the Mokṣopāya." *Cracow Indological Studies* 7 (2005): 207–221.

———. "Some Problems Posed by the Yogavāsiṣṭha." *The Mysore Orientalist* 18 (2004): 71–90.

———. "Towards a Chronology of the Yogavāsiṣṭa/Mokṣopāya." *Annali dell'instituto Oriental si Napoli,* 2002. Universitá Degli Studi Di Napoli "L'Orientale," *Annali* 62 (2002): 42–71.

———. "The Story of Līlā: A Paradigm of the World of Shared Experience." Giulani Boccali, Cizzia Pieruccini, ad Jaroslav Vauek, editors. *Pandanus*. Charles University, Prague: Faculty of Arts, Institute of Indian Studies, 2001, 27–43.

———. "Il terzo prakaraya dello Yogavāsiṣṭha (utpatti) e la doctrine Śivaita della vibrazione (spanda)." *Rivista degli Studi Orientali* 76 (2002): 87–120.

———. "Il Mokṣopāya: lo spazio come principio assoluto. Dodici capitol dal Līlopākhyāna. Edizione critica e traduzione annotate." Tesi di didottorato. Universitá degli studu di Roma, "La Sapienza." 1998.

———. "Mokṣopāya III: 25." Raffaela Torella, ed. Le Parole e I marmi. Studi in onore di Raniero Gnoli nel suo 70° compleanno. Roma: Serie Orientale Roma 92, 2001, 513–533.

Mainkar, Trimbak Govind. "The Vāsiṣṭha Rāmāyaṇa: A Critical Study of the Epic of the Vedanta." Doctoral dissertation, University of Bombay, 1962.

———. *The Vāsiṣṭha Rāmāyaṇa: A Study*. Second edition. New Delhi: Meharchand Lachmandas, 1977. First edition published 1955.

McMichael, Douglas. "Idealism in Yoga-Vāsiṣṭha and Yogācāra Buddhism." *Darshana International* 17 (Moradabad, 1977).

Mitra, Vihari-Lala, trans. *The Yoga-Vāsiṣṭha-Mahārāmāyaṇa of Valmiki Translated from the Original Sanskrit*. Vols. 1–4. Varanasi: Bharatiya Publishing House, 1976. First edition, Calcutta, 1891, 1893, 1898, 1899.

Mojtaba'i, Fatahullah. "Muntakhab'i Jug-basasht or Selections from the Yogavāsiṣṭha Attributed to Mir Abu'l-qasim Findirski." Doctoral dissertation, Harvard University, 1977.

Murdoch, Iris. *Metaphysics as A Guide to Morals*. New York: Viking Penguin, 1992.

Narahari, H. G. "The Yogavāsiṣṭha and the Doctrine of Free Will." *Adyar Library Bulletin* 10 (1946): 36–50.

Narasimha, Roddam. "A Metaphysics of Living Systems: The Yoga-Vāsiṣṭha View." *Journal of Bioscience* 27 (2002): 645–50; also (with Sanskrit originals) *Sandhān* 2:155–164.

———. *More Verses for the Brave*. Forthcoming.

———. "Order and Chaos in Fluid Flows." *Curr. Sci.* 56 (1987): 629–645.

———. Review of Wolfram 2002. *Curr. Sci.* 83 (2002): 1271–1273.

———. *Verses for the Brave*. National Inst. Advanced Studies, Bangalore, 2007.

O'Flaherty, Wendy Doniger. *Dreams, Illusion and Other Realities*. Chicago: The University of Chicago Press, 1984. Delhi: Motilal Banarsidass, 1987.

———. "The Dream Narrative and the Indian Doctrine of Illusion." *Daedalus* 111, no. 3 (1982): 93–113.

———. "Hard and Soft Reality: The Indian Myth of the Shared Dream." *Parabola* 7, no. 2 (1982): 55–65. In German as "Der wissenschaftler Beweis mysthischer Ergahrung." *Der Wissenschaftler und das Irrational*, edited by Hans Peter Duerr. Frankfort: Syndicat (1982): 430–456.

———. "Illusion and Reality in the Yogavāsiṣṭha." *Journal of the Royal Society of Arts* 129, no. 5294 (1981): 46–65.

———. "Illusion and Reality in the Yogavāsiṣṭha or The Scientific Proof of Mythical Experience." *Quadrant: Journal of the C.G. Jung Foundation for Analytical Psychology* 14, no. 1 (1981): 46–65.

Pansikar, Vasudeva Laxmana Sharma, ed. *Yogavāsistha, with the Tātparyaprakāśa Commentary*. Delhi: Motilal Banarsidass, 1984. First Edition 1918.

Pathak, Divakar. "Dr. B. L. Atreya's Interpretation of the Yogavasistha." In *The Philosophy of Dr. B. L. Atreya, R. S. Srivastava, Chief Editor*. New Delhi: Oriental Publishers & Distributors, 1977.

Pendse, Shankar Damodar. "Jñāneśvara and Yogavāsiṣṭha." Proceedings and Transactions of the Thirteenth All-India Oriental Conference, Nagpur 1946, vol. 2 (Napur, 1951): 238–243.

Raghavan, V. "The Date of the Yogavāsiṣṭha." *Journal of Oriental Research* 13 (Madras, 1939): 110–128.

———. "The Date of the Yogavāsiṣṭha." *Journal of Oriental Research* 17 (Madras, 1947–48): 228–231.

———. "The Yogavāsistha and the Bhagavadgītā and the Place of Origin of the Yogavāsiṣṭha." *Journal of Oriental Research* 13 (Madras, 1939): 73–85.

———. "The Yogavāsiṣṭha Quotations in the Jīvanmuktiviveka of Vidyāraṇya." *Journal of Andhra Historical Research Society* 12 (1939): 149–156.

Satyavrat. "Un-Pāṇinian Forms in the Yogavāsiṣṭha." *Vishveshvarand Indological Journal* 1 (Hoshiarpur, 1963): 247–266.

———. "Some Anomalies in the Language of the Yogavāsiṣṭha." *Sanskrit and Indological Studies*, Dr. V. Raghavan Felicitation Volume (Dehli, 1975): 325–329.

Shastri, Hari Prasad, trans. *Yogavasistha: The Story of Queen Chudala and Sermons of Holy Vasistha*. London: The Favil Press, 1937. Fifth edition, London, 1975: *The World within the Mind (Yogavasistha): Extracts from the Discourses of the Sage Vasistha to his pupil, Prince Rama, and the Story of the Queen Chudala.*

Slaje, Walter. *Bhāskarakaṇṭhas Moskṣopāya-tikā. Ein Kommentar in der Tradition der kaschmirischen Yogavāsiṣṭha-Überlieferung. Die Fragmente des 3.* (Utpatti-) Prakaraṇa (Materialien für eine kritische Ausgabe des Moksopāya 2) Graz: EWS-Fachverlag, 1995.

———. "The Mokṣopāya Project." *Annals of the Bhandarkar Oriental Research Institute* 77 (1996): 209–221.

———. "The Mokṣopāya Project (II): New Manuscripts and the Present State of Things." ed. M. Ofitsch and Ch. Zinko, 125 Jahre Indogermanistik in Graz (Arbeiten aus der Abteilung 'Vergleichende 327 Sprachwissenschaft' Graz), Graz, 1998, 459–467.

———. "The Mokṣopāya Project (III)." In *The Mokṣopāya Yogavāsiṣṭha and Related Texts.* Edited by Jürgen Hanneder, 37–74. Aachen: Shacker Verlag, 2005.

———. "A Guide to the Philosophical and Religious Terms in The Laghu Yogavāsiṣṭha." *Weiner Zeit Schrift für die Kunde Südasiens* 34 (1990): 147–179.

———. "Sarvasiddhāntasiddhānta: On 'Tolerance' and 'Syncretism' in The Yogavāsiṣṭha." *Weiner Zeitschrift für die Kunde Südasiens* 36 (1992): 307–332.

———. "On Changing Others' Ideas: The Case of Vidyāraṇya and the Yogavāsiṣṭha." *Indo-Iranian Journal* 41 (1998): 112.

———. *Vom Mokṣopāya-Śāstra zum Yogavāsistha-Mahārāmāyaṇa. Philologische Untersuchungen zur Entwicklungs- und Überlieferungsgeschichte eines Indischen Lehrwerks mit Anspruch auf Heilsrelevanz.* Wein: Österreichische Akademie der Wissenschaften. Philos.-hist. Kl. Sitzungsberichte 609. Veröffentlichungen der Kommission für Sprachen und Kulturen Südasiens 27, 1994.

Sprockhoff, J. F. "Der Weg zur Erlösung bei Lebzeiten ihr wesen und ihr Wert, nach dem Jīvanmuktiviveka des Vidyāraṇya" (The Path to Liberation-while-alive, its Nature and significance, in the Jīvanmuktiveka of Vidyāraṇya). *Wiener Zeitschrift fur die Kunde Sud- und Ostasiens* 14 (1970): 137ff.

Stewart, I. *Does God Play Dice*? UK: Penguin Books, 1997.

———. *Life's Other Secret*. UK: Penguin Books, 1998.

Thomi, Peter. *Cūḍālā: Eine Episode aus dem Yogavāsiṣṭha. Nach der längeren und kü rzeren Rezension unter Berücksichtigung von Handschriften aus dem Sanskrit übersetzt.* Wichtrach, Swizerland: Institut für Indolgie, 1980.

———. "The Yogavāsiṣṭha in Its Longer and Shorter Version." *Journal of Indian Philosophy* 2 (1983): 107–116.

"Valimiki." *Return to Shiva: From the Yoga Vāsiṣṭha*. Santa Barbara, California: Concord Grove Press, 1977.

Venkatesananda, Swami. *The Concise Yogavāsiṣṭha*. Albany: State University of New York Press, 1984.

———. *The Supreme Yoga*. Elgin, Cape Province, South Africa: Chiltern Yoga Trust; Shivanandanagar, UP: The Divine Life Society, 1995.

———. *Vasiṣṭha's Yoga*. Albany: State University of New York Press, 1993.

Wittgenstein, Ludwig. *Tractatus Logico-Philosophicus*. Edited by Marc A. Joseph. Tonawanda: Broadview Press, 2014.

Wolfram, S. *A New Kind of Science*. Champagne IL: Wolfram Media, 2002.

Contributors

Garth Bregman is the Head of Discretionary Portfolio Management at Insinger de Beaufort in Amsterdam.

Arindam Chakrabarti is Professor of Philosophy at the University of Hawaii.

Christopher Key Chapple is Doshi Professor of Indic and Comparative Theology at Loyola Marymount University in Los Angeles.

Andrew Fort is Professor of Religion at Texas Christian University in Fort Worth.

Menaha Ganesathasan teaches at the University of Hawaii, Hilo.

Pranati Ghosal is a research scholar at the Indira Gandhi National Centre for the Arts, Varanasi.

Bruno Lo Turco is a faculty member and researcher in Oriental Studies at La Sapienza University of Rome.

Matthew MacKenzie is Associate Professor of Philosophy at Colorado State University in Fort Collins.

Roddam Narasimha is Professor and Chair, Engineering Mechanics Unit, at the Jawaharlal Nehru Centre for Advanced Scientific Research, Bangalore.

Sthaneshwar Timalsina is Professor of Religious Studies, California State University, San Diego.

Index